A SURVEY OF THE VATICAN ARCHIVES
AND OF ITS MEDIEVAL HOLDINGS

Leonard E. Boyle, O.P.

This guide is a rich introduction to one of the world's most remarkable historical resources. While concentrating on material surviving from the Middle Ages, it is also useful to those researching other periods.

A brief sketch of the history and formation of the Archivio Segreto Vaticana opens the volume. Included are many useful suggestions for contemporary users, including procedures to be followed for gaining access to the Archives, bibliographical aids both for students in the early stages of archival and diplomatic studies and for more experienced scholars, and an additional compendium of guides, inventories and calendars.

The rest of the book is divided into two parts. The first is a summary guide to the holdings of the Archives. The schematic form allows for historical treatments both of the Archives as a whole and of the various collections. It begins with that most puzzling of labyrinths, the index room, through the confusion of which it succeeds in laying down a thin but strongly spun thread. As a result, prospective researchers will save themselves considerable time, and will approach the task of using the indices with far less puzzlement and perplexity.

Next comes a discussion of the original archives as they were established in the seventeenth century, followed by descriptions of the complete holdings of the ASV organized by departments. The largest, and one of the most important of these, is the section devoted to cameral materials. Here we have a lucid summary, including a brief historical sketch, of a confusing mass of material—not merely the traditional *fondo camerale*, but also of other cameral sources found elsewhere in the Archives, easily overlooked by the unwary or the unwarned. All of this is supplemented by cross-references to the relevant indices and to secondary articles and books.

Part II returns to some of the more important collections described summarily in the earlier sections. All of these are medieval; all have been examined closely by the author. The result is not only a valuable discussion of those parts of the Archives of primary importance to medievalists, but as well the revelation of a personal adventure, a kind of travelogue full of advice and anxious warnings, and not a few entertainments along the way. The entire section is carefully and logically arranged and easily consulted by the future user of the Archives. And again, each part is related at every step to the relevant bibliography, catalogues and indices.

Perhaps the most valuable contributions are the several excellent critical evaluations of some of the standard publications of ASV materials, the size and nature of which have often suggested that the Archives which they purport to summarize need no longer be consulted. Boyle's warnings about their shortcomings not only go far to correct this impression, but will also help readers use these publications more intelligently.

This second edition is updated with cross-references to *Vatican Archives*, by Francis X. Blouin et al. (1998), and to the recent publications found there which supplement the original text of the *Survey*.

SUBSIDIA MEDIAEVALIA 1

A Survey
of the Vatican Archives
and of its
Medieval Holdings

Leonard E. Boyle, O.P.

Revised edition

Pontifical Institute of Mediaeval Studies
Toronto

LIBRARY OF CONGRESS CATALOGUING DATA [REVISED]

Boyle, Leonard Eugene, 1923-1999
    A survey of the Vatican archives and of its medieval holdings.
    Revised edition.

(Subsidia mediaevalia, ISSN 0316-0769 ; 1)
Includes bibliographic references and index
ISBN 0-88844-417-6

1. Archivio vaticano.   2. Catholic Church – History – Sources –
Bibliography.   3. Church history – Middle Ages, 600-1500 –
Sources – Bibliography.   4. Manuscripts, Medieval – Vatican
City.   I. Pontifical Institute of Mediaeval Studies.   II. Title.
III. Series: Subsidia mediaevalia (Pontifical Institute of Mediaeval
Studies) ; 1

CD1586 2001   016.282′09

CONTENTS

Preface to the Original Edition

This *Survey* aims at providing a general introduction to the Vatican Archives as a whole and to its medieval holdings in particular. It has grown out of a seminar in Diplomatics in Toronto over the past eight years [1964-1972], and, more proximately, out of a report prepared a short while ago for a forthcoming symposium on "Sources of Medieval Irish History" (hence most of the documents cited to illustrate the various holdings are related to Ireland or to the British Isles in general).

While I hope that this work may prove of use to those from English-speaking countries who propose to work in the Vatican Archives, I also have had in mind those students who may wish to know something about the Archives and its holdings at a distance, as part, that is, of a general historical culture, or of a course in general Diplomatics. For this reason there is first a brief history of papal archives and of the growth of the present Archives (Introduction); then a survey of the original 17th-century Archives and of its present-day holdings (Part One); finally a short discussion of a few of the best-known medieval holdings (Part Two). Where possible I have attempted to show how the present deposits reflect the development and workings of the medieval papal curia. The bibliography and index are designed to introduce beginners in papal diplomatics to some of the more common bibliographic tools.

My best thanks to John Arnold, John Coughlan, Frank Mantello, Heather Phillips, Daniel Williman, Professor Michael Sheehan and, above all, Professor Norman Zacour, for their ready help, valuable criticisms and friendly encouragement.

–L.E.B.

PREFACE TO THE SECOND (REVISED) EDITION

Leonard E. Boyle, OP, never found the time to update his *Survey of the Vatican Archives* (first published in 1972), which is why it remained out of print for so long. However, with the publication of

> Francis X. Blouin, Jr., et al., *Vatican Archives: An Inventory and Guide to Historical Documents of the Holy See* (New York and Oxford: Oxford University Press, 1998)

(a project with which Fr. Boyle collaborated) such an update has been made. At the same time, Fr. Boyle's *Survey* still remains extremely useful for scholars of the Middle Ages.

    We have reprinted the original edition (with minor corrections and additions privately noted by Fr. Boyle) but included in the margins are cross-references to the sections of Blouin, et al. where further information can be found. Used together, we think that the wishes of Fr. Boyle for a "revised" edition have been met.

Ron B. Thomson
Pontifical Institute of Mediaeval Studies
Toronto
July 2001

ABBREVIATIONS

*	[Part I: pp. 27-99]–Holdings or subdivisions which are discussed at some length in Part II.
*	[Bibliography: pp. 173-221]–Supplemental entries in the Addenda (pp. 221*-221**)
*	[Index: pp. 222-250]–Entries referring to the Bibliography (pp. 173-221)

AA	*Archivum Arcis*
AHP	*Archivum historiae pontificiae*
ASV	Archivio Segreto Vaticano
BAPI	*Bolletino dell'Archivio paleografico italiano*
BAV	*Bibliografia dell'Archivio Vaticano*
BEFAR	*Bibliothèque des Écoles Françaises d'Athènes et de Rome*
BIHBR	*Bulletin de l'Institut historique Belge de Rome*
BISIAM	*Bullettino dell'Istituto Storico italiano per il Medio Evo e Archivio Muratoriano*
Blouin	Francis X. Blouin, Jr., et al., *Vatican Archives: An Inventory and Guide to Historical Documents of the Holy See* (New York and Oxford, 1998)
CPL	*Calendar of Papal Letters*
Coll.	*Collectoriae* volumes of the *Fondo Camerale*
CPP	*Calendar of Papal Petitions*
de Loye	J. de Loye, *Les archives de la Chambre apostolique au XIVᵉ siècle* (Paris, 1899)
Fink	K.A. Fink, *Das Vatikanische Archiv* (Rome, 1951²)
Gasparolo-Lonigo	G. Gasparolo, "Costituzione dell'Archivio Vaticano, e suo primo indice," *Studi e Documenti* 8 (1887), 3-64.
Giusti, *Studi*	M. Giusti, *Studi sui registri di bolle papali* (Vatican City, 1968)

Guérard   L. Guérard, *Petite introduction aux Inventaires des Archives du Vatican* (Rome-Paris, 1901)

HVD   L.-E. Halkin and D. van Derveeghde, *Les sources de l'histoire de la Belgique aux Archives et à la Bibliothèque Vaticanes* (Brussels-Rome, 1951)

IE   *Introitus et Exitus* volumes of the *Fondo Camerale*

Katterbach EI   B. Katterbach, "Archivio Vaticano," in *Enciclopedia Italiana*, IV (1929), pp. 88-90.

Kehr (1900)   P.F. Kehr, "Papsturkunden in Rom," in *Nachrichten der kgl. Gesellschaft der Wissenschaften zu Göttingen*, Philol.-hist. Klasse, 1900, pp. 111-197, 360-434.

Kehr (1903)   P.F. Kehr, "Nachträge zu den römischen Berichten," in *Nachrichten der kgl. Gesellschaft der Wissenschaften zu Göttingen*, Philol.-hist. Klasse, 1903, pp. 507-532

Macfarlane   L. Macfarlane, "The Vatican Archives," *Archives* 4 (1959), 23-44, 84-101.

MAH   *Mélanges d'archéologie et d'histoire*

MGH   *Monumenta Germaniae Historica*

MiöG   *Mitteilungen des Instituts für österreichische Geschichtsforschung*

OS   *Obligationes et Solutiones* volumes of the *Fondo Camerale*

QFIAB   *Quellen und Forschungen aus italienischen Archiven und Bibliotheken*

RA   *Registra Avenionensia*

RHE   *Revue d'histoire ecclésiastique*

RHM   *Römische historische Mitteilungen*

RL   *Registra Lateranensia*

RQ   *Römische Quartalschrift für christliche Altertumskunde und für Kirchengeschichte*

RS   *Registra Supplicationum*

RV   *Registra Vaticana*

RVA   *Registra Avenionensia* volumes now found among *Registra Vaticana* volumes

Sussidi I, II, III   *Sussidi per la consultazione dell'Archivio Vaticano* (1926, 1931, 1947)

ZSSRGKA   *Zeitschrift der Savigny-Stiftung für Rechtsgeschichte, kanonistische Abteilung*

INTRODUCTION

(i)

From apostolic times the Popes conserved letters, acts of martyrs and other important documents in a *Scrinium* or *Chartarium*. This repository functioned both as archives and library, and usually followed the Popes about from residence to residence. By 649 at least it had a permanent home in the Lateran palace in Rome; but some time before the 11th century it was moved from there to the slope of the Palatine Hill near the Arch of Titus in the Roman Forum.[1]

Very little that is original survives from the papal archives or from the products of the papal chancery before the end of that century, mainly because the Popes were very slow to change over from the traditional if uncertain papyrus to the more durable parchment. A certain amount of original papal material is extant from the period immediately after the introduction of parchment (c. 1020), but before the pontificate of Innocent III (1198-1216) there appears not to have been a consistent archival policy. Innocent was the first to regularize papal records, and the first series of registers of copies of outgoing letters begins with his pontificate.

It is difficult, however, to judge just how extensive the archives were before or during Innocent's pontificate, for they suffered great losses, apparently, during the thirteenth and subsequent centuries. To some extent this was due to the mobility of the medieval Popes, especially from Innocent IV onwards. In 1245 he took a part of the archives with him to the Council of Lyons; after the Council this part remained for a time in the custody of the monastery of Cluny. At the beginning of the 14th century

---

[1] See in general J. B. Pitra, *Analecta Novissima* I (Rome 1885), pp. 152-161; and, for the early history of the Papal Archives, P. Künzle, 'Del cosidetto "Titulus Archivorum" di Papa Damaso', in *Rivista di Storia della Chiesa in Italia* 7 (1953) 1-26; K. Silva-Tarouca, 'Die Quellen der Briefsammlungen Papst Leos des Grossen', in *Papsttum und Kaisertum*; *Paul Kehr zum 65 Geburtstag* (Munich 1926), pp. 23-47; *Pontificum Romanorum diplomata papyracea quae supersunt in tabulariis Hispaniae, Italiae, Germaniae* (Rome, 1929).

Benedict XI (1303-1304) placed the archives in Perugia, whence they were moved for safe-keeping to Assisi by Clement V (1305-1314). In Clement's pontificate, indeed, a section of the archives (eight volumes of registers of Boniface VIII, one of Benedict XI, ten of Clement himself—probably Clement's "working" archives) was located at Carpentras, and after his death was retrieved only with difficulty. As for the volumes at Assisi, they remained there until 1339, when Benedict XII had them transported to Avignon.[2]

At the end of the Schism, the current papal archives were transferred by boat and wagon from Geneva to Rome during the years 1419-1422, and were first lodged by Martin V in S. Maria sopra Minerva, then in 1428 in his new family palace (Colonna) at the foot of the Quirinal Hill. In the pontificate of Eugene IV part of the curial and cameral registers was moved from Rome to Florence for the Council (1435), then to Bologna (1437) and Ferrara (1438) and back again to Florence in 1440, where an inventory was taken, finally returning to Rome in 1443.

It is not clear whether the material transferred by Martin V after the Council of Constance included items from the Avignon archives, but some at least of the Avignon archives had been moved from Avignon to Rome by the time of the Florence inventory of 1440; indeed it is likely that the core of the papal archives (parchment registers of letters — the present "Vatican" registers — and cameral records) had reached Rome from Avignon before Martin's death in 1431.[3] Other material, however, remained at Avignon for centuries; and although various Popes recalled small sections of the archives from time to time (e.g. Pius V in 1566, when some 158 volumes, mostly from the Library, were taken from Avignon to Rome),[4] some 500 archival volumes, including the great series of paper registers of letters (353 vv.) now known as the "Avignon" registers, did not leave Avignon for Rome until 1783.

[2] Pitra, *loc. cit.* See also H. Denifle, 'Die päpstlichen Registerbände des 13. Jahrhunderts und das Inventar derselben vom Jahr 1339', in *Archiv für Litteratur- und Kirchengeschichte* 2 (1886) 1-105.

[3] F. Ehrle, 'Die Uebertragung des letzten Restes des päpstlichen Archivs von Avignon nach Rom', in *Historisches Jahrbuch* 11 (1890) 727-729; F. M. Bååth, 'L'inventaire de la Chambre Apostolique de 1440', in *Miscellanea Archivistica Angelo Mercati* (Studi e Testi 165, Vatican City 1952), pp. 135-157; A. M. Corbo, 'Martino V, Eugenio IV e la ricostituzione dell'archivio papale dopo Costanza', in *Rassegna degli Archivi di Stato* 28 (1968) 36-66.

[4] A. Maier, 'Der Handschriftentransport von Avignon nach Rom im Jahr 1566', in *Mélanges E. Tisserant* VII (Studi e Testi 237, Vatican City 1964), pp. 9-27, nn. 1, 32, 33, 74. In 1583 two registers of Gregory XI were sent from Avignon to Gregory XIII (Pitra, p. 157).

After Nicholas V (1447-1455) had founded the Vatican Library, a distinction began to be drawn between literary and documentary material, especially under Sixtus IV (1471-1484). Sixtus provided the Library with its own quarters and gave it its first administrative structure. Here he also established a *Bibliotheca secreta* in which general archival documents were to be preserved in walnut-wood chests; the more precious documents, however, particularly those containing privileges of the Church, records of claims, etc., were placed in Castel S. Angelo (formerly the tomb of the Emperor Hadrian), a short distance away from the Vatican on the near bank of the Tiber. It was also this same Pope who founded the archives of the Roman Curia, when setting up a College of Notaries in 1483.[5]

Under the energetic Julius II (1503-1513) an attempt was made to put the archives of the apostolic Camera in order. Since parts of the archival material were outside the Camera itself in the Wardrobe and in the College of Secretaries, and some of it was in the hands of nephews and heirs of previous popes, Julius ordered (18.8.1507) the sequestration of all public and private writings belonging to the Camera.[6]

In spite of the efforts of Sixtus IV, Julius II and other popes, it was only in the wake of the Council of Trent that the idea took shape of establishing a central Archives of the Church. The Council had shown interest in archival areas by prescribing that all parish priests should keep registers of baptisms and marriages.[7] Towards the end of the Council Pius IV announced that a central Archives would be set up in the Vatican palace; and later ordered (15.5.1565) that all likely places (e.g. Anagni, Viterbo, Perugia) were to be searched for volumes and documents which should be in these Archives.[8] It was left to his successor to further this plan. In May 1566 Pius V sent to Avignon for some of the papal material still remaining there;[9] a month later (6.6.1566) he extended to the Church at large the decree of Charles Borromeo in the provincial synod of Milan in 1565[10] that archives should be instituted in every church and inventories compiled of

---

[5] See L. Pastor, *The History of the Popes*, II, ed. I. Antrobus (London 1891), pp. 207-214; IV (London 1894), pp. 433-458.

[6] G. Ramacciotti, *Gli Archivi della Reverenda Camera Apostolica* (Rome 1961), pp. 1-14.

[7] *Enchiridion Archivorum Ecclesiasticorum*, ed. S. Duca and P. Simeon (Vatican City 1966), p. 1.

[8] *Ibid.*, pp. 329-330.

[9] *Ibid.*, pp. 5-6.

[10] *Ibid.*, pp. 2-5.

existing holdings. On 19 August 1568 he added his own weight to Pius IV's brief of 1565, decreeing *motu proprio* that a search should be made at Anagni and in all private or other archives in the papal states for registers of letters and other papal documents, and further, that inventories were to be made of all books, registers and documents in the Vatican, Castel S. Angelo and Avignon.[11]

More than thirty years, however, were to pass before Pius IV's plan for a central archives came to full maturity. Then in 1610 Paul V (1605-1621) built the main part of the present archives, continuing a resolve he had shown from the earliest days of his pontificate, when he demanded (25.1.1606) the return within six days to the Library or the Camera or Castel S. Angelo of all archival material pertaining to the Papacy or to the Camera.[12]

The first transfer of documents to the new archives took place in December 1611, and the first custodian was appointed some six months later.[13] The nucleus of the archives was made up of material from Sixtus IV's *Bibliotheca secreta* (yielding, among other things, 279 volumes of parchment registers from John VIII to Sixtus IV — the bulk, that is, of the present Vatican Registers series);[14] from Castel S. Angelo (e.g., a great mass of "Secretariate of State" documents was moved from there to the Archives on 13 May 1614); and from the Apostolic Camera. This last source provided great quantities of material. The first transfer from the Camera to the Archives consisted of some 170 volumes, mostly copies and *rubricellae* of registers of Gregory VII, Innocent III, etc. This was followed on 30 Jan. 1612 by another similar deposit of 103 volumes from John XXII to Sixtus IV. Towards the end of the same year (4.11.1612) 1388 volumes of *Introitus et Exitus*

---

[11] Archivio Segreto Vaticano, *Arm.* LII, f. 172.

[12] *Enchiridion Archivorum*, pp. 31-37. For the legislation of Popes between Pius V and Paul V, see *ibid.*, pp. 8-31.

[13] For what follows see G. Gasparolo, 'Costituzione dell'Archivio Vaticano, e suo primo indice, sotto il pontificato di Paolo V. Manoscritto inedito di Michele Lonigo', in *Studi e Documenti di Storia e Diritto* 8 (1887) 3-64. M. Lonigo da Este (1572-1649), whose account of the arrival of the first holdings in the Archives is printed by Gasparolo at pp. 34-62, was a custodian of the Archives under Paul V. Lonigo's MS. account, which Gasparolo discovered in the library of Giancarlo Rossi, is now in the Vatican Library as MS. Vat. lat. 10247. The MS. contains 373 pages, of which the first 53 were published by Gasparolo. Pages 54-76 are blank, while the unpublished pages 77-373 contain an "Index librorum omnium novi archivii Vaticani a sanctissimo domino nostro Paulo V erecti", with a description of each *Armarium*.

[14] Originally there were 258 volumes, but some were divided during binding, giving a total of 279 eventually: Lonigo, pp. 4-5; Gasparolo, p. 36.

from Martin V to Leo X were placed "in armariis" in the new Archives, and other cameral material followed on 15 May 1613. Finally, volumes of *Collectoriae*, quittances and taxes were transferred from the Camera on 20 December 1614. Like all the other deposits, this cameral material was placed in great cupboards (*Armaria*), some 80 in all, and particularly, as we shall note later, in *Arm.* XXIX-XXXIV and LXV-LXXIV.[15]

Under Urban VIII, who in 1625 set up an Archivio del Sacro Collegio to house consistorial materials (see below, Part One, JI), what may be termed the "original" Vatican Archives was almost completed by the addition, in 1630, of volumes of "secret" (*Diversorum*) letters from the Apostolic Secretariate (Sixtus IV-Pius V) which were added to the Vatican Registers series. These were accompanied by books, registers, and *Minutae brevium* (Alexander VI — Pius V) from the Secretariate of Briefs, by 16th-century Nunciature records and other material from the Wardrobe, and by volumes on the Council of Trent from Castel S. Angelo. With the transfer of many Secretariate of State volumes by Alexander VIII about 1656,[16] the first phase (1611-1656) of the "original" Vatican Archives (*Arm.* I-LXXX) comes to a close.

After this there were no more notable additions to the Archives for almost a century and a quarter, until, that is, the remainder of the Avignon Archives (chiefly the "Avignon" registers) reached Rome in 1783, and the so-called "Diplomatic Archives" were transferred from Castel S. Angelo (*Archivum Arcis*) in 1798.

Great losses, however, were sustained by the Archives in the Napoleonic period. A year, indeed, after the *Archivum Arcis* had been moved hastily to the Vatican Archives through fear of a French occupation of Rome, it was taken to Paris at the order of Napoleon. Other holdings made a similar journey in 1800, 1810, 1811 and 1813. Altogether some 200,435 items travelled to Paris in some 3239 chests. Many items perished on the way (e.g., when a boat foundered on the Lago di Garda); many others disappeared in France (e.g., about a third of the "Lateran" Registers) or, like a part of the Archives of the Inquisition, were deliberately destroyed by the Papal Commissioners who supervised the return of the Archives to the Vatican from Paris after the Congress of Vienna.[17]

---

[15] Lonigo ed. Gasparolo, art. cit., pp. 44-56, 60-62 (transfers from Camera); 57-60 (from Castel S. Angelo).

[16] Gasparolo, art. cit., pp. 31-33.

[17] See G. Marini, 'Memorie storiche dell'occupazione e restituzione degli Archivi

Since those stormy days the most notable event in the life of the Archives was the decision of Leo XIII in 1879 to open the Archives in general to qualified students.[18] New accessions came quickly in the years that followed, and have continued to the present day. In 1892 the Fondo Borghese was given to the Archives, and the Archives of the Datary (chiefly the chancery registers now known as the"Lateran Registers"and the Registers of Supplications) were moved there from the Lateran Palace; in 1902 the Barberini Archives, containing masses of Secretariate of State material, found a home in the Vatican Library next door to the Archives; in 1906-1908 the fine series of Lateran Briefs reached the Archives, being joined in 1907 by the Archives of the College of Cardinals and of the Consistorial Congregation, by registers from the Secretariate of Briefs (1908), by the Fondo Santini (1909) and by holdings from the Secretariate of Letters to Princes (1914). Since then the principal accessions include cameral volumes from the Archivio di Stato di Roma (1918-1919), in exchange for the Archives of the Congregation of Buon Governo, the Chigi Archives (1923), the Archives of the Congregations of the Council (1926) and of Rites (1927), Fondo Fini (1929), the Casa Borghese (1932) and Buoncompagni (1949) Archives, the Archives of the Secretariate of Latin Letters (1937) and of some Nunciatures and Legations (1951).[19]

---

della Santa Sede', printed in *Regestum Clementis Papae V*, I (Rome 1885), pp. ccxxviii-cccxxv; R. Ritzler, 'Die Verschleppung der päpstlichen Archiv nach Paris unter Napoleon I. und deren Rückführung nach Rom in den Jahren 1815 bis 1817', in *Römische historische Mitteilungen* 6-7 (Graz-Cologne 1964) 144-190.

[18] On 20 June 1879 the historian J. Hergenröther was appointed "Cardinal-Archivist of the Holy Roman Church", but the Archives as such did not open to students until 1 January 1881. On 18 August 1883 Pope Leo addressed his famous letter on historical studies to Cardinals Pitra, De Luca and Hergenröther (*Leonis XIII P. M. Acta*, III, Rome 1884, pp. 259-276). The rules of the Archives were first published on 1 May 1884 (see E. Soderini, *Il Pontificato di Leone XIII*, I, Milan 1932, pp. 294-296). There are interesting reflections on the opening of the Archives in the address of Pius XII to the 10th International Congress of Historical Sciences, 7 September 1955 (see *Acta Apostolicae Sedis* 47 (1955) 672-682).

[19] See K. A. Fink, *Das Vatikanische Archiv* (Rome 1951²) for most of these dates; others are supplied from Mercati's pencilled notes in the Archives copy of Fink. For the Nunciatures and Legations received in 1951, see *L'Attività della S. Sede nel 1951* (Vatican City 1952), p. 378; and for further volumes (111 vv. containing 232 processes) from the Congregation of Rites in 1952, see *L'Attività della S. Sede nel 1952* (Vatican City 1953), p. 260. This unofficial year-book, *L'Attività*, in the section *Archivio Segreto Vaticano*, provides useful information on accessions, and on publications containing documents from the Archives, e.g. *Nunziaturberichte*, and volumes from the various Roman Institutes noted above. — It may be noted here that summaries and inventories of the ecclesiastical archives of Italy (capitular, parochial, etc.) are available in the Archives, the result of a census begun by Cardinal G. Mercati, brother of Angelo Mercati, in 1942 (see *Acta Apostolicae Sedis* 34 (1942) 384-389). According to a letter of the Congregation of the Council of 30 December 1952

(ii)

The official title of the Vatican Archives is *Archivio Segreto Vaticano* (commonly contracted, as in this *Survey*, to ASV). The adjective *segreto* owes its immediate presence in the title to the fact that the ASV is the successor of the *Bibliotheca secreta* of Sixtus IV. Essentially, however, it conveys the information that the ASV, like the original *Bibliotheca*, is a private establishment that is not of its nature open to public consultation.

Admission is therefore strictly controlled. In any given year the number of researchers does not go much beyond 500; in 1968, for example, 525 persons were granted permission to work in the Archives, and these (328 foreigners, 197 Italians) represented some 35 nations.[20] Generally a letter from one's University or other academic institution, or from someone of academic standing, is necessary before an application will be considered.[21] When permission is granted, it takes the form of an admission-card (*tessera*) which has to be surrendered in exchange for a numbered locker-key on each visit to the ASV; this carries a photograph of passport size of the researcher, his signature, and the stamp of the Archives. The duration of the *tessera* is from mid-September of one year to mid-July of the following; like the Vatican Library, the ASV is closed from mid-July to mid-September each year. During the open period the working hours are from 8.15 a.m. to 1.30 p.m. (13.30); there is no access later in the afternoon or evening. To reach the Archives one enters Vatican City by the Porta di S. Anna on the Via di Porta Angelica, and then proceeds straight to the Cortile del Belvedere. The entrance to the Archives is in the far right-hand corner as one enters the Cortile; it is (since 1965) separate from that to the Library, which is in the immediate right-hand angle.

[These opening times may change.]

The Library, of course, is a distinct entity from that of the Archives, but permission to work in the ASV entitles one in fact to the use of the open shelves (with some 16,000 volumes) of the

(*ibid.*, 45 (1953) 101-102), students, on a reasonable demand, may have material from these archives deposited for consultation in the ASV: see G. Battelli, 'Epistula circa il prestito del materiale conservato negli archivi ecclesiastici in Italia', in *Monitor ecclesiasticus* 78 (1953) 205-208.

[20] See *L'Attività della S. Sede nel 1968* (Vatican City 1969), p. 1438.

[21] "Per esservi ammessi occurre la permissione del Sommo Pontefice, che l'interessato deve chiedergli con domanda scritta accompagnata dalla commendatizia di un istituto scientifico o di un personaggio autorevole, il quale stia mallevadore per lui a riguardo de l'Archivio... Domanda e commendatizia si presentano al Prefetto": *Regolamento dell'Archivio Vaticano* (Rome 1927), art. 8.

great Sala Leonina of the Library, for the Sala was set up specifically by Leo XIII in 1892 as the reference library of the Archives.[22] It should be noted, however, that one is not free to move books from the Sala to the Archives without special permission, and that for the use of the Library in its own right (and in particular of its MSS collections) a special *tessera* is required.

Since the Archivio Segreto Vaticano was opened to general consultation in 1881, thousands of scholars have made their way to it. Before that, however, selected scholars already had had access to its sources: Rainaldi, for example, had used it extensively for his continuation (1648-1677) of the *Annales Ecclesiastici* of Baronius, and Pallavicino for his *Istoria del Concilio di Trento* (1656-1657).[23] Moreover, from 1815 onwards countries such as Austria, Denmark, England, Hungary, Russia and Sweden were given permission to have copies made of sources relative to their history (hence, for England, the "Marini Transcripts" in the British Museum).[24] The interest aroused all over Europe by these researches was heightened most of all, perhaps, by the labours of the Vatican Archivist Augustin Theiner.[25] Between 1832 and 1872 he published some 29 volumes of ASV material, including the fine *Vetera monumenta Hibernorum et Scotorum* (1864) which had been undertaken at the request of Cardinal Cullen of Dublin when he was rector of the Irish College in Rome.[26] Understandably, there was a great influx of scholars when at

---

[22] "Ottenuto il permesso pontificio, lo studioso... può frequentare la sala di studio ed avere accesso alla Sala Leonina di consultazione della biblioteca": *ibid.*, art. 82. For the Sala Leonina see M. Ugolini, *La nuova Biblioteca Leonina nel Vaticano* (Rome 1893), and, in general, G. Battelli, 'Mezzi bibliografici d'informazione e di studio presso d'Archivio Vaticano', in *Rassegna degli Archivi di Stato* 22 (1962) 25-32.
[23] See G. Battelli, 'Le ricerche storiche nell'Archivio Vaticano', in *Relazioni del X Congresso internazionale di Scienze Storiche, Roma 1955*, I (Florence 1955), pp. 448-477.
[24] British Museum, London, MSS Add. 15351-15398, with indexes in MSS Add. 15399-15401. These chancery, cameral, Datary and Secretariate of State transcripts ("Monumenta Britannica ex autographis Romanorum pontificum regestris ceterisque documentis deprompta") were deposited in the British Museum in 1829. For these and other transcripts, and for later microfilm deposits, in London, Edinburgh and Dublin, see L. Macfarlane, 'The Vatican Archives', in *Archives* 4 (1959) 99-100. — With respect to microfilms, it may be useful to note here that, since 1959, the ASV possesses its own photographic service, and that, with the Vatican Library photographic service, it does not require payment in advance. On juridical problems connected with photographic copying of archival material, see G. Battelli, 'Aspetti giuridici ed esigenze scientifiche nella fotografia dei fondi archivistici', in *Archiva Ecclesiae* 3-4 (1960-1961) 58-61.
[25] For Theiner (1804-1874) see H. Jedin in *Lexikon für Theologie und Kirche*[2], X, 15-16; H. Rumpler in *New Catholic Encyclopedia* (New York 1967), XIV, 9. He became Archivist in 1850 and Prefect in 1855.
[26] See Theiner's preface. Cullen was rector from 1832-1850.

last a limited public access to the Archives was permitted in 1881. Publication of source-material began almost at once, and since then portions of nearly every ASV holding (*fondo*) have been edited or cited in books and periodicals of most European countries.

It is no injustice to the staff of the Archives (see e.g., Denifle, Hoberg, Katterbach, Mercati, *Rationes Decimarum Italiae*, etc., in the General Bibliography below) to say that most of the work done over the past ninety years to make ASV material available in print, is due to the enterprise of foreign schools already existing in Rome in 1881 or founded afterwards.[27] Shortly before 1881, indeed, the prolific École française de Rome (founded in 1873) had begun the calendaring of papal letters from Gregory IX onwards; the first fascicule (Innocent IV, by É. Berger) was published in 1884, and the project has now reached almost to the end of the Avignon Papacy (see pp. 123-127). As well, many articles based on ASV material have appeared in the *Mélanges d'archéologie et d'histoire* (1881—) of the École, which also has recently initiated the *Acta Nuntiaturae Gallicae* (1961—) in conjunction with the Gregorian University, Rome. To the Oesterreichische Historische Institut, founded in 1883, we owe articles on ASV material in the *Mitteilungen des Instituts f. österreichische Geschichtsforschung* (1880 —), the many writings of e.g. Tangl, von Ottenthal, Santifaller and Hageneder, and the recent beginnings of a critical edition of the registers of Innocent III (1198-1216). In 1888 the Preussische (later Deutsche) Historische Institut and the Historische Institut der Görresgesellschaft were founded in Rome. From the former come the *Nunziaturberichte aus Deutschland* (1892—), the annual volume *Quellen und Forschungen aus italienischen Archiven und Bibliotheken* (1898—), the *Repertorium Germanicum* (1916—), and many works using ASV materials in the *Bibliothek des Deutschen Historischen Instituts in Rom* (1905—; Fink's *Das Vatikanische Archiv* is n. 20 in the series; see also Göller, Haller, Herde, von Hofmann, Schillmann, in

[27] The best general account in English of these Institutes and Schools is still that of P. M. Baumgarten, 'Institutes, Roman Historical', in *The Catholic Encyclopedia* III (1910), pp. 61-65 (there is not, unfortunately, a corresponding article in the *New Catholic Encyclopedia*, 1967); see also E. Strong, 'Istituti stranieri a Roma. Cenni storici', in *Annales Institutorum* I (1929) 15-60. — Berger of the École française certainly was working in the Archives before 1881 (see G. Battelli, *art. cit.*, in n. 23 above; and the introduction to *Tables des Registres de Clément V publiés par les Bénédictins* (Paris 1948-1957), p. vi). Pastor, who died in 1928, began working in the Archives in 1879: see his preface to the last volume of the *Geschichte der Päpste*, XVI (Freiburg im Breisgau 1933).

Bibliography). From the Görresgesellschaft, which is specifically dedicated to the publication of ecclesiastical sources, there have appeared the many volumes of the *Quellen und Forschungen aus dem Gebiet der Geschichte* (1892 —), the great *Vatikanische Quellen zur Geschichte der päpstlichen Hof- und Finanzverwaltung 1316-1378* (see Part Two, V), and the periodical *Römische Quartalschrift für christliche Altertumskunde und für Kirchengeschichte* (1887 —; see Ehses, Göller, Kraus, etc. in Bibl.). A Belgian Historical Institute also was set up in Rome in 1904, and this has sponsored the splendid *Analecta Vaticano-Belgica* (1906 —), the *Nonciature de Flandre* (1924 —), volumes on ASV material in the *Bibliothèque de l'Institut historique Belge de Rome* (e.g. Halkin), and articles in the *Bulletin de l'Institut historique Belge de Rome* (1919 —; see Belgium, Berlière, Halkin, Jadin, etc. in Bibliography).[28]

If these great Institutes and Schools have contributed most to a fundamental understanding of the medieval, renaissance and post-reformation Papacy through the publication of ASV materials, other foreign centres in Rome have not been slow to exploit the Archives in relation to the history of their own countries: the Hungarian Academy (1882) in the *Monumenta Vaticana historiam Regni Hungarici illustrantia* (1885—); the *Monumenta Vaticana res gestas Bohemicas illustrantia* (1903 —) of the Centre which was re-established as the Czech Academy in 1920; the *Monumenta Poloniae Vaticana* (1913 —) of the Polish Library (1886; later the Polish Historical Institute); the *Anthologica Annua* (1953 —) of the Instituto Español de Estudios eclesiásticos. Nor must one forget the work done by private persons, e.g. Eubel, Ritzler and Sefrin in the *Hierarchia Catholica*; Rius Serra in his *Rationes decimarum Hispaniae*; the *Pontificia Hibernica* of M. P. Sheehy; the volumes on papal taxation by W. E. Lunt; Mrs A. I. (Cameron) Dunlop on Scottish supplications and taxation; the patient work of Caspar Wirz in the six volumes of *Regesten zur Schweizergeschichte aus den päpstlichen Archiven*, and of Professor and Mrs C. R. Cheney in *The Letters of Innocent III concerning England and Wales*. As well, there are the publications sponsored by learned bodies in many countries, e.g. the *Nunziature* volumes (Venezia, Savoia, etc.)

---

[28] On individual Institutes see, A. Cauchie, 'De la création d'une école belge à Rome', in *Congrès de la Fédération archéologique et historique de Belgique. Compte rendu des travaux du dixième congrès tenu à Tournai du 5 au 8 août 1895* (Tournai 1896), pp. 739-802; W. Goldinger, 'Oesterreich und die Eröffnung des Vatikanische Archivs', in *Archivalische Zeitschrift* 47 (1951) 23-52; W. Holtzmann, 'Das Deutsche historische Institut in Rom', in *Arbeitsgemeinschaft für Forschung des Landes Nordrhein-Westfalen* 46 (1955) 7-43; R. Fawtier, 'Un grand achèvement de l'École Française de Rome', in *Mélanges d'archéologie et d'histoire* 71 (1960) I-XIII.

published by the Istituto storico italiano per l'età moderna e contemporanea in the *Fonti per la storia d'Italia*; the Danish *Acta Pontificum Danica* (1904 —); the Swedish *Acta Pontificum Suecia* (1936 —); the Swiss *Acta Pontificum Helvetica* (1891), the British and Irish *Calendar of Papal Letters* (1893 —).[29]

Unfortunately there has been little or no liaison between these various Institutes, Schools and individual scholars, with the result that the same ground has been covered time and again, and that there has been much wastage of effort. A case in point is the important and homogeneous series of Registers of Supplications (7365 vv., 1342-1899). The series as a whole, and the medieval part in particular, merits a collaborative effort at a systematic calendar, volume by volume, item by item. Instead, the student is now faced with an array of "national" excerpts or calendars in publications all over Europe, e.g., British Isles, 1342-1419 (1896); Bohemia, 1342 (1903); Belgium, 1342 — (1906); Hungary, 1342 — (1916); Livonia and Estonia, 1342-1378 (1925); Scotland, 1418-1428 (1934); Holland, 1342-1366 (1937) — not to speak of the mass of medieval supplications used in the *Repertorium Germanicum* (1916 —), or published in general collections of documents for Denmark, Franconia, Friesland, Sweden, Switzerland, the diocese of Constance, etc.[30] This proliferation means that often one and the same supplication, because it touches on two or more countries or areas, has been edited or calendared several times over. Attempts, of course, have been made to coordinate the projects of the various schools, as when a "Commission pour la coordination des recherches aux Archives Vaticanes" was set up in the late 1920s, but without any appreciable success.[31]

At all events the dedicated activity of the many scholars who individually or through national institutes have explored the

---

[29] For useful lists of the publications of these schools, institutes and scholars, relative to sources of the history of the medieval papacy, see L. Santifaller, *Neuere Editionen mittelalterlicher Königs- und Papsturkunden* (Vienna 1958), pp. 40-56; R. C. van Caenegem and F. L. Ganshof, *Kurze Quellenkunde des westeuropäischen Mittelalters* (Göttingen 1964), pp. 208-213. A. M. Stickler, *Historia iuris canonici latini. Institutiones Academicae* I, *Historia Fontium* (Turin 1950), pp. 306-318, also gives lists of published material from Leo I onwards. There is also in Stickler (c. 3: 'De collectionibus Actorum Curiae Romanae': pp. 318-358) a fine survey, with historical notes, of inedited as well as of printed records of all curial departments.

[30] The beginnings of an 'Italian' edition of supplications will be found in T. Gasparrini Leporace, *Le Suppliche di Clemente VI* (Regesta Chartarum Italiae, 32, Rome 1948), but no other volume has appeared since.

[31] *Bulletin of the International Committee of Historical Sciences* 2 (1929-1930) 469-479.

resources of the ASV since 1881, has indeed produced a rich
crop of books, monographs and articles in most European and
in many other countries. But this in itself creates further difficulties. For until recently there was no record available of just
what had been published from the various holdings of the ASV
over the past three generations. And given the variety of publications and countries in which ASV materials have been edited
or extensively used, it was often very hard indeed for a beginner
to find out whether his "discoveries" had ever been worked upon
if not published. One student I know was so excited by the
contents of some documents relative to the Fifth Lateran Council
which were on display during the "Concili Ecumenici" exhibition
in 1964, that he began, after reasonable enquiries, to transcribe
the documents for publication, only to find by chance some
months later that they had been edited in full some seventy
years earlier by Hergenröther, and are tucked away in an appendix to his edition of Hefele's *Konziliengeschichte*.[32]

So vast, and at times so inaccessible, has been the output of
scholars who have exploited the ASV holdings, that proposals
were made some forty years ago to prepare a bibliography of the
Archives. In 1931 the International Commitee of Historical
Sciences set up a permanent commission for this purpose;
the main work was to be done by the individual historical Institutes in Rome, each of which would look after the publications of
its own country. So far as I can make out, only the Belgian Institute took the matter up in any effective way.[33]

Present-day students, however, are fortunate in having to hand
the excellent *Bibliografia dell'Archivio Vaticano* which the ASV
and its Scuola di Paleografia e Diplomatica began publishing
in 1962. This bibliography, of which four volumes have appeared
to date, proposes to note any book or article which in any way
has used the ASV holdings since 1881. In each volume the
fondi of the Archives are listed alphabetically (e.g. *Archivum Arcis*
to *Tribunale della Sacra Romana Rota* in vol. I), bibliographical
information being then provided for individual volumes within
each *fondo* and, wherever possible, for folios within volumes.

---

[32] C. J. von Hefele, *Konziliengeschichte*, ed. J. Hergenröther, VIII (Freiburg-im-
Breisgau 1887), pp. 810-832: Appendix A-F (from *AA. Arm.* I-XVIII, nn. 3014,
3015, 3016, 3017).

[33] See plans and reports in *Bulletin of the International Committee of Historical Sciences*
4 (1932) 347, 356; 5 (1933) 819; 8 (1936) 191; and P. Fedele, 'La Commission pour
la Bibliographie des Archives du Vatican', *ibid.* 11 (1939) 224-235. An early attempt at a bibliography (to 1909) is in G. Melampo and V. Ranuzzi, *Saggio bibliografico dei lavori eseguiti nell'Archivio Vaticano* (Rome 1909).

Thus if one is interested in a letter in Reg. Vat. 81, f. 279r, a careful glance at the *Bibliografia* (all volumes, of course) should help to establish whether the letter in question has been published before or has ever been studied. It goes without saying that it will be many years before the *Bibliografia* exhausts all possible publications since 1881 in which ASV material is used or printed (e.g. Pastor's *Geschichte der Päpste* and Hefele-Hergenröther, *Konziliengeschichte*, have not been covered to date), not to speak of the many pre-1881 publications (Theiner's volumes, for example), but it is hoped that by the time the present phase of the work is completed a reasonably exhaustive bibliographical instrument will have been placed in the hands of students.[34]

In bibliographical as well as archival difficulties, of course, one can always call on the small and unflaggingly courteous staff of the Archives. English-speaking beginners, moreover, often feel more at ease when they know that they may turn for advice in their own language to the Vice-Prefect, Msgr Hermann Hoberg, to the Administrative Secretary, Dr Sergio Damiani, and, needless to say, to Fr Charles Burns. However, some previous knowledge of the workings of papal departments in the Middle Ages and modern times will go a long way towards a minimum wastage of one's own time and that of the staff. If, for example, one is looking for the record of the appointment of some bishop or abbot, it is important to know which ASV holdings should be tried first, and which should be left to the last or omitted altogether. Much time also will be frittered away if one is not thoroughly familiar with chancery and other formulae, and with the usual lay-out of papal letters, briefs, supplications, account-books and other products of curia departments.

In effect, a knowledge of papal diplomatics, and an easy familiarity with material in print from papal and cognate sources (e.g. formulary books, chancery rules, collections of papal letters), are essential before one addresses oneself to research in the Vatican Archives (or, for that matter, *mutatis mutandis*, to research in any other archives). At the end of this *Survey* there is a general bibliography of books and articles which publish or discuss

---

[34] See G.Battelli, 'La Bibliografia dell'Archivio Vaticano', in *Rivista di Storia della Chiesa in Italia* 14 (1960) 135-137. Current bibliographies also will be found in the *Revue d'histoire ecclésiastique* (Louvain, 1900 —), chiefly in bibliographical sections I.2Ba ("Bibliographie des sources; Sources d'archives et Sources littéraires"), I.3 ("Paléographie; Chronologie; Diplomatique"), II.2 ("Sources d'archives et Critique diplomatique"). The more recent annual *Archivum Historiae Pontificiae* (Gregorian University, Rome, 1963 —) devotes many pages each year to a superb survey of publications of ASV materials and of the history of the Papacy in general.

material (chiefly medieval) from the ASV. However, it may be useful at this point to list briefly some of the more important introductions to the study of archival materials and of papal diplomatics. The standard work is Harry Bresslau's *Handbuch der Urkundenlehre für Deutschland und Italien*, I² (Leipzig 1912), II.1 (1912), II.2 (1931), especially I, pp. 149-161 (all volumes have now been reprinted, Cologne-Graz 1958; and there is a *Register* of the whole work by H. Schulze, Berlin 1960); but other useful introductions are in A. Giry, *Manuel de Diplomatique* (Paris 1884; reprinted 1925), A. de Boüard, *Manuel de Diplomatique française et pontificale*, 2 vv. (Paris 1929, 1948), G. Tessier, *La diplomatique*, (*Que sais-je?* n. 536, Paris 1952), and his article 'Diplomatique' in *L'histoire et ses méthodes*, ed. Ch. Samaran (*Encyclopédie de la Pléiade*, XI, Paris, 1961), pp. 633-676 (see also the fine survey of R. H. Bautier, 'Les Archives', in the same volume, pp. 1120-1126).

Good treatments of papal diplomatics as such, or of specific points, are to be found in R. L. Poole, *Lectures on the Papal Chancery down to the time of Innocent III* (Cambridge, 1915: essential; and the only general survey of its kind in English); L. Santifaller, *Die Abkürzungen in den ältesten Papsturkunden* (Weimar 1939); R. Foerster, *Urkundenlehre* (Bern 1951: a useful collection of texts); H. Fichtenau, *Arenga. Spätantike und Mittelalter im Spiegel von Urkundenformeln* (Graz 1957); P. Rabikauskas, *Die römische Kuriale in der päpstlichen Kanzlei* (Rome 1958), *Diplomatica pontificia* (Rome 1968²); M. P. Sheehy, *Pontificia Hibernica* I (Dublin 1962; introduction); K. A. Fink, 'Urkundenwesen, päpstlicher', in *Lexikon für Theologie und Kirche²* X (1965) 560-563; C. R. Cheney, *The Study of the Mediaeval Papal Chancery* (Glasgow 1966); M. Giusti, *Studi sui registri di bolle papali* (Vatican City 1968). Helpful samples of the handwriting and of the diplomatic formulas of medieval papal departments will be found in G. Battelli, *Acta Pontificum* (Exempla Scripturarum III², Vatican City 1965), in B. Katterbach, *Specimina supplicationum ex registris vaticanis* (Rome 1927), in B. Katterbach and C. Silva-Tarouca, *Epistolae et Instrumenta Saeculi XIII* (Exempla Scripturarum II, Vatican City 1930), in the facsimiles accompanying F. Bock's *Einführung in das Registerwesen des Avignonesischen Papsttums* (Rome 1941), and in the superb but now unobtainable *Specimina Palaeographica ex Vaticani tabularii Romanorum Pontificum registris selecta* (Rome 1888) of Denifle and Palmieri.[35]

---

[35] All of these works are repeated under fuller titles in the general bibliography at the end of this *Survey*.

But however well-prepared, a beginner may feel bewildered during his first days in the Archives. For one thing, the ASV does not possess an overall and comprehensive inventory of its holdings. For another, the order of the Archives, and in particular of its medieval sections, is not at once apparent. The blame however, should not be placed squarely on the shoulders of archivists of the past. Apart altogether from the sheer mass of material, they were faced with holdings which had been put together without too much discrimination long before the ASV was set up in 1611. In the long run it is the Popes of the Middle Ages and Renaissance who are responsible for much of the seeming disorder. From pontificate to pontificate there were changes of operational procedures in the various curial departments, and these often led to improvisation, to duplication and on occasion to general confusion where records were concerned. Up until the 14th century the three main departments of the Curia were the Chancery, the Camera and the Consistory; by and large the products of these offices are to be found recorded in the Vatican Registers. Between the beginning of the 14th century and the Council of Trent, however, new bureaus were developed or refashioned such as the Datary, Sacred Penitentiary, Rota, Secretariate and Signatura; their records occur in one or other, and sometimes several, of the various sets of registers of the period: Vatican and Avignon Registers, Registers of Supplications, Lateran and Cameral registers, registers of Briefs. To add to an already complex situation, the various Congregations, Secretariates and Tribunals founded in the 16th and 17th centuries developed their own systems of registration of business.

In the three and a half centuries that have passed since the records of many of these departments were put together from deposits in the Bibliotheca Secreta, the Camera, Castel S. Angelo and the Wardrobe, to form the Archivio Segreto Vaticano, many archivists and assistant-archivists (e.g. Felice Contelori, G.B. Confalonieri, P. D. De Pretis, G. Garampi, G. Marini, M. Marini, A. Theiner, J. Hergenröther, H.-S. Denifle) worked with varying success to provide indexes or to rearrange holdings. That the present order in its main outline does not take too long to understand is largely due to the indefatigable archivist Angelo Mercati (1870-1955).[36] For more than forty years this fine scholar and Prefect of the Archives (1925-1955) explored *fondi*, compiled

---

[36] See L. Santifaller in *Lexikon für Theologie und Kirche*[2], VII, 304; K. A. Fink in *New Catholic Encyclopedia*, IX, 668-669.

indexes, drew up inventories; and where inventories or indexes already existed, he added invaluable notes (generally in pencil in a neat, minute hand) in order to keep track of migrations from one holding to another or to make good lacunae and correct inaccuracies. If his labours were ably seconded by assistants such as Msgr P. Guidi, Professor P. Sella and Fr M.-H. Laurent, his greatest spur, in all likelihood, was the brilliant work done on the Registers of Supplications by the Franciscan Bruno Katterbach (1883-1931), whose untimely death was an incalculable loss to the Archives and to its School of Palaeography and Diplomatics.[37] Mercati's schema of the Archives, published in 1933,[38] forms the basis of the two most useful Guides to the ASV: K. A. Fink's *Das Vatikanische Archiv. Einführung in die Bestände und ihre Erforschung* (Rome 1951²), and Leslie Macfarlane's 'The Vatican Archives: with special reference to sources for British medieval history', in *Archives* 4 (1959) n. 21, pp. 29-44, n. 22, pp. 84-101. Either of these works (but preferably both) should be studied carefully before a student embarks upon work in the Archives. The interleaved ASV copy of Fink (with handwritten notes of Mercati and others) should also be consulted for changes, corrections and additions.

Of course, given the history and the complexity of the ASV holdings, it is inevitable that no scheme — even that of Mercati — will prove satisfactory on every count. One has only to look at Fink's outline (pp. 20-24) of the many schemata proposed or used in practice by various authors (e.g. Kehr, Wirz, Baumgarten, François, Katterbach) to understand just how different from one another the approaches to the ASV holdings can be. What is important, however, from a student's point of view, is that every schema should at least make him aware of the character and range of any given holding, and of the correct title under which a volume from any holding may be ordered and cited.

The present general outline of ASV holdings does not aim at much more than this. And since the *Survey* concentrates on the medieval holdings, the notes for the medieval *fondi* are fuller than those for the post-Tridentine period. There is, of course, a further reason for the incompleteness of information about modern holdings. While the author has had to look at one time or another

---

[37] See G. Battelli in *Enciclopedia Cattolica*, VII, 661; O. Schäfer in *Lexikon für Theologie und Kirche²*, VI, 93.

[38] 'Schema della disposizione dei fondi nell'Archivio Vaticano', in *Bulletin of the International Committee of Historical Sciences* 5 (1933) 909-912.

into most of the medieval *fondi*, his direct acquaintance with modern sections of the Archives is limited to a few holdings such as the Fondo Albani and the *Registra Brevium*, and to odd volumes from other collections. However, it was thought better to provide an overall view of the Archives rather than to ignore everything after about 1570 (end of the Council of Trent; end of the Vatican Registers). This at least allows one to see how the Archives developed from its original holdings (Part One, B, below) of 1611-c.1656 to its present-day strength[39].

As we have seen above, the original ASV consisted of material transferred from the Bibliotheca secreta, the Camera, Castel S. Angelo (Archivum Arcis) and the Wardrobe. Of the 80 *Armaria* (*Arm.* I-LXXX) designed to house this material, the last six appear never to have been used. Of the remaining 74 *Armaria* (*Arm.* I-LXXIV), all are still in use today, but some are never cited as such. Thus *Arm.* I-XXVIII, which contain the Vatican Registers, are not used as "call-numbers", since the Vatican Registers are ordered and cited simply as *Reg. Vat.* (or RV) and volume (e.g. RV 201). Likewise, *Arm.* LVII and LXV-LXXIV are never cited as such, since the cameral material contained in them is now known simply as *Fondo Camerale* and is ordered and cited by collection (*Introitus et Exitus* or IE; *Obligationes et Solutiones* or OS; *Collectoriae* or *Coll.*). All other collections in *Arm.* I-LXXIV (with the possible exception of *Arm.* LXII-LXIII, which often are cited together as *Concilio* or *Concilium Tridentinum*) continue to be ordered and cited by the *Armarium* number.

In the present schema of the ASV all the *Armaria* of the original ASV are listed one after another (I-LXXIV) in section B. Although this allows one at a glance to see the extent of the original ASV holdings, all of the *Armaria* are not described under B. Thus the description of *Armaria* which contain cameral material (*Arm.* XXIX-XXXIV, XXXVI-XXXVII) is placed in a fuller context under Cameral Holdings (C), while that of the *Armaria* of Briefs (*Arm.* XXXVIII-XLV) is held over until the discussion of the Apostolic Secretariate (G. I) and the Secretariate of Briefs (G. II).

---

[39] Until recently the modern part of the Archives was not open to consultation beyond the year 1846. Since 1 January 1967, however, the whole pontificate of Pius IX (16 June 1846-7 February 1878) has been opened to students: see *L'Attività della S. Sede nel 1967* (Vatican City 1968), p. 1505. This step had been promised by Pius XII in the address of 1955 noted above in n. 18.

[extended (in 1974) to 1922]

Accessions to the original ASV, and later additions, are listed as chronologically as possible. After the title of each holding the accession date (where ascertainable) is recorded in brackets, thus : *Bullarium Generale* (ASV 1783); in the case of Secretariates and Congregations the date of foundation is also placed within the brackets, thus: Archivio della Congregazione Concistoriale (1588; ASV 1907). Unless otherwise stated, the title given to a holding, or to a section of a holding, is that by which it normally is cited in publications and ordered in the Archives, e.g., Secretariate of Briefs: a. *Registra Brevium*. For each holding, and for each sub-division within it, one or two useful books or articles are listed, generally by a short title (full titles will be found in the General Bibliography at the end of the *Survey*). Holdings or sub-divisions which will be discussed at some length in Part Two are marked with an asterisk, and bibliographical references are reduced to a minimum. In the case of holdings which do not receive special treatment in Part Two, a few lines of description are given, and, where possible, some examples of their use by scholars.

PART ONE

THE HOLDINGS
OF THE VATICAN ARCHIVES

A. GUIDES, INVENTORIES AND CALENDARS

a. Printed

The following, in chronological order, are general guides to or monographs on all or some of the holdings of the Archivio Segreto Vaticano. All are not of equal value. Since some of the more important will be referred to often when the holdings themselves are being described, they are accompanied here by *sigla* in bold type, thus : **Kehr (1900)**, **Kehr (1903)**, **Sussidi I**, **Sussidi II**, **Sussidi III**, **Katterbach EI**, **Fink**, **Macfarlane**, **BAV**, **Giusti**. For the sake of completeness, all of the authors listed under the present heading are repeated in the General Bibliography at the end of this *Survey*.

M. Lonigo, "Index Archivii Vaticani" (c. 1620), edited from Vatican Library, MS. Vat. lat. 10247, pp.1-53, by G. Gasparolo in *Studi e Documenti di Storia e Diritto* 8 (1887) 3-64, at pp. 34-62 (see Gasparolo, below).

G. Marini, *Memorie istoriche degli Archivi della Santa Sede*, ed. A. Mai (Rome 1823).

M. Marini, "Memorie storiche dell'occupazione e restituzione degli Archivi della Santa Sede" (c. 1820), printed in *Regestum Clementis Papae V*, I (Rome 1885), pp. ccxxviii-cccxxv.

G. Moroni, *Dizionario di erudizione storico-ecclesiastica*, II (Venice 1840), pp. 277-288: 'Archivi della Santa Sede'.

H. Laemmer, *Monumenta Vaticana historiam ecclesiasticam saeculi XVI illustrantia* (Freiburg-im-Breisgau 1861), pp. 431-453.

M. Gachard, *Les Archives du Vatican* (Brussels 1874), especially pp. 113-128 for the inventory of the holdings removed to Paris in 1810.

G. Gasparolo, 'Costituzione dell'Archivio Vaticano, e suo primo indice, sotto il pontificato di Paolo V. Manoscritto inedito di Michele Lonigo', in *Studi e Documenti di Storia e Diritto* 8 (1887) 3-64 = **Gasparolo-Lonigo**.

C. H. Haskins, 'The Vatican Archives', in *American Historical Review* 2 (1896-1897) 40-58.

J. de Loye, *Les archives de la Chambre apostolique au XIVe siècle* (Paris 1899) = **de Loye**.

P. F. Kehr, 'Papsturkunden in Rom', in *Nachrichten der königl. Gesellschaft der Wissenschaften zu Göttingen, philologisch-historische Klasse* (Göttingen 1900), pp. 111-197 ('Erster Bericht'), 360-434 ('Zweiter

Bericht') = **Kehr** (1900); 'Nachträge zu den Römischen Berichten', *ibid.*, 1903, pp. 505-591 = **Kehr** (1903).

L. Guérard, *Petite introduction aux Inventaires des Archives du Vatican* (Rome-Paris 1901) = **Guérard**.

U. Berlière, 'Aux Archives Vaticanes', in *Revue Bénédictine* 20 (1903) 132-173; and the various works of Berlière listed in the Bibliography below under *Belgium* (2, 3, 5).

G. Melampo and V. Ranuzzi, *Saggio bibliografico dei lavori eseguiti nell'Archivio Vaticano* (Rome 1909).

C. R. Fish, *Guide to the Materials for American History in Roman and Other Italian Archives* (Washington, D. C. 1911), pp. 20-100.

G. Brom, *Guide aux Archives du Vatican* (Rome 1911²).

P. M. Baumgarten, 'Vatican Archives', in *The Catholic Encyclopedia* XV (Washington 1912), pp. 286-290.

H. Bresslau, *Handbuch der Urkundenlehre*, I (Leipzig 1912²), pp. 149-161.

E. Audard, 'L'histoire religieuse de la Révolution française aux Archives Vaticanes', in *Revue d'histoire de l'Église de France* 4 (1913) 516-535, 625-639.

Sussidi per la consultazione dell'Archivio Vaticano, I (Studi e Testi 45, Rome 1926): pp. 1-48: Schedario Garampi; 49-144: Registri Vaticani; 145-190: Registri Lateranensi; 191-202: Rationes Camerae; 202-222: Inventario del Fondo Concistoriale = **Sussidi I**. (For **Sussidi** II and III see Katterbach, *Referendarii*, and Mercati, *Il Bullarium*, below).

B. Katterbach, 'Archivio Vaticano', in *Enciclopedia Italiana* ("Treccani"), IV (Rome 1929), pp. 88-90 = **Katterbach EI**.

B. Katterbach, *Referendarii utriusque Signaturae a Martino V ad Clementem XI, et Praelati Signaturae supplicationum a Martino V ad Leonem XIII* (*Sussidi per la consultazione dell'Archivio Vaticano*, II: Studi e Testi 55, Rome 1931) = **Sussidi II**.

B. Katterbach, *Inventario dei Registri delle Suppliche* (*Inventari dell'Archivio Segreto Vaticano*, I, Vatican City 1932).

M. François, 'Les sources de l'histoire religieuse de la France au Vatican', in *Revue d'histoire de l'Église de France* 19 (1933) 305-346.

A. Mercati, 'Schema della disposizione dei fondi nell'Archivio Vaticano', in *Bulletin of the International Committee of Historical Sciences* 5 (1933) 909-912.

A. Mercati, 'Cité du Vatican' in Société des Nations, Institut international de coopération intellectuelle, Paris: *Guide international des Archives, Europe* (*Bibliothèque des Annales Institutorum*, IV, Paris-Rome 1934), pp. 326-341.

A. I. Cameron, 'Vatican Archives, 1073-1560', in *An Introductory ¡Survey to the Sources and Literature of Scots Law* (Stair Society, I, Edinburgh 1936), pp. 274-281.

J. W. Thompson, 'The Papal Registers', ¡in *Church Quarterly Review* 127 (1938) 37-75.

P. Fedele, 'La Commission pour la Bibliographie des Archives du Vatican', in *Bulletin of the International Committee of Historical Sciences* 11 (1939) 224-235.

V. Meysztowicz, *Repertorium bibliographicum pro rebus Polonicis Archivi Secreti Vaticani* (Studja teologiczne XI, Rome 1943).

E. MacFhinn, 'Scríbhinni í gCartlainn an Vatican: Tuarascbháil', in *Analecta Hibernica* 16 (1946) 1-280: a description in Gaelic of materials, mainly post-Reformation, in the ASV relative to the history of Ireland.

A. Mercati, 'La Biblioteca Apostolica e l'Archivio Segreto Vaticano', in *Vaticano*, ed. G. Fallani and M. Escobar (Florence 1946), pp. 489-493.

C. Moran, 'Les Archives du Saint-Siège, importantes sources de l'histoire politico-religieuse du Canada', in *Culture* (Ottawa) 7 (1946) 151-176.

A. Mercati, *Il Bullarium generale dell'Archivio Segreto Vaticano e Supplementi al registro dell'Antipapa Niccolò V. — Dall'Archivio dei SS. Gregorio e Siro di Bologna* (*Sussidi per la consultazione dell'Archivio Vaticano*, III: Studi e Testi 134, Vatican City 1947) = **Sussidi III.**

G. Battelli, 'Archivi ecclesiastici — Speciali provvidenze della Santa Sede per la conservazione degli archivi ecclesiastici', in *Enciclopedia Cattolica*, I (Rome 1948), col. 1832.

K. A. Fink, *Das Vatikanische Archiv. Einführung in die Bestände und ihre Erforschung* (Bibliothek des Deutschen Historischen Instituts in Rom, XX, Rome 1951²) = **Fink.**

L.-E. Halkin and D. van Derveeghde, *Les sources de l'histoire de la Belgique aux Archives et à la Bibliothèque Vaticanes. État des collections et répertoire bibliographique* (Bibliothèque de l'Institut historique Belge de Rome, III, Brussels-Rome 1951) = **HVD.**

G. de Bertier, 'L'histoire religieuse de la Restauration (1814-1830) aux Archives du Vatican', in *Revue d'histoire de l'Église de France* 38 (1952) 77-89.

D. E. R. Watt, 'Sources for Scottish history of the fourteenth century in the archives of the Vatican', in *Scottish Historical Review* 32 (1953) 101-122.

P. Bonenfant, 'Rapport au Comité Directeur de l'Institut historique Belge de Rome sur les publications à faire pour les XVe siècle', in *Bulletin de l'Institut historique Belge de Rome* 28 (1953) 357-366.

G. Battelli, 'Archivio Vaticano', in *Enciclopedia Cattolica*, XII (1955), cols. 1131-1134.

G. Battelli, 'Le ricerche storiche nell'Archivio Vaticano', in *Relazioni del X Congresso internazionale di Scienze Storiche, Roma 1955*, I (Florence 1955), pp. 448-477.

N. Summers, 'Vatican City', in D. H. Thomas and L. M. Case, *Guide to the Diplomatic Archives of Western Europe* (Philadelphia 1959), pp. 290-300.

L. Macfarlane, 'The Vatican Archives: with special reference to sources for British medieval history', in *Archives* (Journal of the British Records Association) 4 (1959) 29-44, 84-101 = **Macfarlane.**

A. Ramacciotti, *Gli Archivi della Reverenda Camera Apostolica, con inventario analitico-descrittivo dei registri camerali conservati nell'Archivio di Stato di Roma nel Fondo Camerale Primo* (Rome, Reverenda Camera Apostolica, 1961). At pp. 269-275 there is an alphabetical index of 166 *fondi* of the Vatican Archives, followed (pp. 276-298) by a similar index of 701 *fondi* of the Archivio di Stato di Roma.

H. L. Hoffmann, *De Archivo Secreto Vaticano qua centrali* (Rome 1962). *Bibliografia dell'Archivio Vaticano* (Vatican City 1962): Four volumes to date, especially I, 69-73; II, 53; III, 47-48; IV, 49-50 (guides, inventories, etc.) = **BAV**.

V. Ilardi, 'Fifteenth-Century Diplomatic Documents in Western European Archives and Libraries (1450-1494)', in *Studies in the Renaissance* 9 (1962) 64-112, at pp. 87-94 (now reprinted in Italian in *Rassegna degli Archivi di Stato* 28 (1968) 349-403, at pp. 375-381).

L. W. Daly, 'Early alphabetical indices in the Vatican Archives', in *Traditio* 19 (1963) 483-485.

F. J. Weber, 'The Secret Vatican Archives', in *American Archivist* 27 (1964) 63-66.

H. Hoberg, 'Vatikanische Archiv', in *Lexikon für Theologie und Kirche*[2], XII (1964), cols. 635-636.

R. Ritzler, 'Die Verschleppung der päpstlichen Archiv nach Paris unter Napoleon I. und deren Rückführung nach Rom in den Jahren 1815 bis 1817', in *Römische historische Mitteilungen* 6-7 (Graz-Cologne 1964) 144-190.

G. Mollat, 'Registres pontificaux', in *Dictionnaire de droit canonique*, VII (1965), cols. 536-538.

S. Duca and P. Simeon, *Enchiridion Archivorum Ecclesiasticorum* (Pubblicazioni della Pontificia Commissione per gli archivi ecclesiastici d'Italia, II, Vatican City 1966).

K. A. Fink, 'Vatican Archives', in *New Catholic Encyclopedia*, XIV (New York 1967), pp. 551-555.

L.-E. Halkin, *Les Archives des Nonciatures* (Bibliothèque de l'Institut historique belge de Rome, XIV, Brussels-Rome 1968).

M. Giusti, *Studi sui registri di Bolle Papali* (Collectanea Archivi Vaticani 1, Vatican City 1968) = **Giusti, Studi**.

I. B. Cowan, 'The Vatican Archives. A report on pre-reformation Scottish material', in *Scottish Historical Review* 48 (1969) 227-242.

L. M. Ambrosini, *The Secret Archives of the Vatican* (Boston 1970).

L. Pásztor, *Guida delle fonti per la storia dell'America Latina negli archivi della Santa Sede e negli archivi ecclesiastici d'Italia* (Collectanea Archivi Vaticani 2, Vatican City 1971). This splendid work, which in fact contains (pp. 1-301) a most complete guide to the Vatican Archives, unfortunately reached me while the present *Survey* was in page-proof.

b. Manuscript

1. *Ancient Indici*   2. *Modern Indici*

In the Index or Catalogue Room of the Vatican Archives there are many manuscript inventories, calendars, summaries, etc. of ASV holdings. Made at various periods (the work of indexing, cataloguing, etc. is still in progress), they are labelled with the general name *Indici*, and vary greatly in quality and legibility. Altogether they now (May 1970) total nearly 800 volumes, and may be divided for present purposes into *Ancient* (681 volumes compiled for the most part during the first three hundred years of the life of the ASV and put together as a series in 1901) and *Modern* (volumes compiled after 1901 and numbered from n. 1001).

What follows is a partial list of these Ancient and Modern *Indici*; later on each *Indice* will be noted in its proper place, in relation, that is, to the holding of which it is an index, inventory or calendar. In Part Two certain *Indici* will be discussed at some length; in the present summary list these are marked with an asterisk.

On the *Indici* in general or in particular see Guérard; *Sussidi* I, especially pp. 1-48 and footnotes; Fink 26-30; BAV I, 353-360, II, 384-393, III, 415-427, IV, 357-368; for *Indici* 320-430 see Giusti, *Studi*, pp. 104-106, 112-119.

1. *Ancient Indici*.

30-47: Calendars of *Brevia secreta* of the Secretariate of Briefs (see G. II).

56-57: Index of *Archivum Arcis* by G. B. Confalonieri, 1628 (see also Indici 1001-1012, 1074).

133: "Inventarium Archivi secreti Vaticani": an inventory of the *Armaria* (*Arm.* I-LXXIV), volume by volume, of the original ASV, begun in the pontificate of Benedict XIII (1724-1730) by Petrus Doninus de Pretis (ob. 1741). For some of the *Armaria*, e.g. XXIX-XXXIX, this is the only inventory, and frequent references will be given to it when dealing with the original ASV holdings. Migrations, and additions made after the inventory was compiled, are noted in later hands.

134: An inventory of the *Nunziature* by the same de Pretis.
136: An inventory of the *Miscellaneorum Armarium*, I-XV (see H.II).
137: An inventory of *Arm.* XXXVII (*Informationes camerales*).

138: An inventory of *Arm.* XXXVI (*Informationes camerales*).

145-147: Inventory of the Avignon Archives, 1594.

157: Calendar of *Fondo Garampi*, nn. 1-271 (for nn. 272-300 see Indice 1068).

158-167: Garampi's alphabetical index (A-Z) of all miscellaneous collections, e.g. the *Miscellaneorum Armarium*. There is a list of his *sigla* in 158 (see p. 71).

168-184: Garampi's "Indice cronologico dell'Archivio Segreto Vaticano", 1550-1721.

195A: Inventory (ff. 47-62) of the *Brevia Lateranensia* (below, pp. 52-53).

196-239: Now in Vatican Library.

240-289: These 50 volumes were once in *Arm.* L-LI of original ASV, and contain various *rubricellae*, etc. of Vatican Registers from John VIII to Sixtus V (872-1590); see Gasparolo-Lonigo, pp. 44-48; *Sussidi* I, pp. 52-54. Some of these volumes are of great importance: thus Indice 254 was compiled for the Camera about 1270, and consists of brief extracts, with incipits, from letters of surviving as well as now lost registers of Innocent III: see A. Haidacher, 'Beiträge zur Kenntnis der verlorenen Registerbände Innozenz III.', in *Römische historische Mitteilungen* 4 (1960-1961) 36-62; E. Pásztor, 'Ricostruzione parziale di un registro pontificio deperdito del sec. XIII', in *Mélanges E. Tisserant* V (Vatican City 1964), pp. 199-207.

290-316: Inventories and partial calendars of volumes (mainly minutes of Briefs, 1478-1636) in *Arm.* XL-XLIII of original ASV.

317-319: Chronological index of *Fondo Veneto*, 1226-1795.

320-430: *Rubricellae* and summaries of Lateran Registers, 1389-1799:

*320: Fair copy (1618) of Ranaldi's *Summarium* (MS. Vat. lat. 6952) of letters of Boniface IX (1389-1404). For Indici 320-324A see Part Two, III, pp. 135-145.

*321: Another copy, by F. Contelori, of Ranaldi's *Summarium.*

*322: Summary by G. B. Confalonieri, 1618, of letters of Gregory XII (1407-1408).

*323: Summary by the same of letters of Alexander V (1409-1410).

*324: Fair copy (1618) of Ranaldi's *Summarium* (MS. Vat. lat. 6952) of letters of Innocent VII (1404-1406) and John XXIII (1410-1415).

*324A: Summary by Confalonieri of volumes of John XXIII.

325-327: Summary of letters of Calixtus III (1455-1458) and

others. Used by the *Calendar of Papal Letters* XI (1921), pp. VII-VIII, etc.

328-329: Pius II (1458-1464). Used by the *Calendar* XII (1933), pp. xx, etc.

330-331: Paul II (1464-1471). Used by the *Calendar, ibid.*

332-335: Sixtus IV (1471-1484). Used by the *Calendar*, XIII, pp. 865-915.

336-338: Innocent VIII (1484-1492).

339-343: Alexander VI (1492-1503).

344: Pius III (1503), Julius II (1503-1513).

345-348: Julius II.

349: Julius II (pp. 1-374), Pius III (pp. 375-378).

350-354: Leo X (1513-1521).

355: Leo X (pp. 6-136), Adrian VI (pp. 137-231).

356: Adrian VI (1522-1523).

357-365: Clement VII (1523-1534).

366-370: Paul III (1534-1549).

372: Julius III (1550-1555), Paul IV (1555-1559).

373: Paul IV, Pius IV (1559-1565).

374: Pius IV.

375-430: Others from Gregory XIII to Pius VI, 1572-1799.

431-436: Summaries of Registers of Supplications.

437-444: Garampi's notes towards an *Orbis Christianus*.

445-556: These volumes, together with Indici 670-681, form the great *Schedario Garampi*, an incomplete series of 124 volumes into which G. Garampi (1725-1792), when Prefect of the Archives (1751-1772), pasted about a million and a half index-slips that he and his assistants had compiled from the holdings of the ASV. (On Garampi see C. Traselli in *Enciclopedia Italiana* V, pp. 1931-1933; J. Wodka in *Lexikon für Theologie und Kirche*[2] IV, col. 515). Garampi, of course, used his own set of *sigla*, and this sometimes makes for difficulties; most of these *sigla*, however, have been unravelled by Msgr Mercati in *Sussidi* I, pp. 1-48 (the copy to consult is that in the ASV, with Mercati's pencilled corrections and changes). This vast — and invaluable — undertaking of Garampi is divided as follows:

[Mercati: the principal author is P. Guidi. (M. Dykmans)]

445-474: *Benefici*, with the benefices in alphabetical order.

475-511: *Vescovi*: in chronological order, diocese by diocese; and within each diocese the bishops are listed alphabetically.

512-534: *Miscellanea* I: arranged by diocese, alphabetically. See 670.

535-537: *Abbati*: alphabetically by diocese and monastery.

538-549: *Cronologico*: chronological indexes from 1630-1808.
550: *Papi*: in alphabetical order.
551: *Cardinali*: in alphabetical order.
552-554: *Officiali*: curial officials (*Abbreviatores... Scriptores...*).
554-556: *Chiese*: Roman churches, in alphabetical order.

*557-641: Calendar of Avignon Registers made by P. de Montroy at Avignon, 1718-1732. Alphabetical, diocese by diocese. See Part Two: *Avignon Registers* (pp. 127-131).
*642-669: Calendar of Avignon Registers made by J. de Martin at Avignon, 1711. Each volume is calendared in turn, pontificate by pontificate, item by item. See Part Two.
670-681: *Miscellanea* II of Garampi's *Schedario: Abbas-Zupilium*.

2. *Modern Indici.*

*1001-1012: Calendar (1910-1927) by V. Nardoni, etc., of the archives of Castel S. Angelo (*Archivum Arcis* or *AA*.). See below, *Diplomatic Holdings* (pp. 57-60).
1013-1035: Calendars of Secretariate of State (SS.) holdings:

1013-1014: SS. *Cardinali.*
1015-1016: *Vescovi.*
1017-1018: *Principi.*
1019-1021: *Particolari.*
1022: *Soldati.*
1023: Legations of Avignon, Bologna, Ferrara, Romagna, Urbino, Ubaldini.
1024: Nunciatures of Florence, Genoa, Corsica, Malta, Naples, Savoy, Venice (and its *Archivio*).
1025: Nunciatures of France, Portugal, Spain.
1026: Flanders, Paci, *Nunz. diverse*, Avvisi, *Memoriali-Biglietti*, *Emigrazione rivoluzione francese*, Salviati, Benincasa.
1027: Nunciatures of Germany, Cologne.
1028: Nunciature of Switzerland.
1029: *Misc. Arm.* I-XV: inventory (1029.1); index (1029.2).
1030: *Misc. Arm.* IV-V ("Bandi"): inventory.
1031: *Interni*, 1814-1833.
1032: *Esteri*, 1814-1850.
1033: *Interni, Esteri*, 1816-1822.
1034: *Rubricellae*, 1816-1860; *Protocolli*, 1816-1851.
1035: *Rubricellae*, 1816-1860: alphabetical index.

1036: Inventory of *Fondo Camerale: Obligationes et Solutiones, Introitus et Exitus, Collectoriae, Obligationes Particulares*, cameral parts of Avignon Registers.

1037: Vatican Registers, vv. 1454-1684 (Paul III, 1534-1549): alphabetical list of dioceses, with volume and folio reference, e.g. Armachan. (RV 1486, 50).
1038: Vatican Registers, vv. 1724-1782 (Julius III, 1550-1555): alphabetical list of dioceses, as in 1037.
1039: Inventory of Lateran Registers 1-1127 (1389-1503).
1040: Inventory of Lateran Registers 1128-2467 (1503-1892).
1041: Inventory of Lateran Briefs 1-883 (1490-1807).
1042: Index by diocese of *Minutae brevium* (1523-1599).
1043: Index by diocese of *Libri Annatarum* (1421-1797).
1044: Index by diocese of *Resignationes* (1457-1594).
1045: Index of Consistorial processes (1563-1906).
1046: Inventory of Datary processes (1622-1900).
1047: Index of processes of Congregation of Rites (1588-1920).
1048: Inventory of *Secretariatus Camerae* (1470-1796).
1049: *Fondo Bolognetti.*
1050: *Fondo Carpegna.*
1051: *Fondo Confalonieri.*
1052: *Fondo Borghese, Salviati.*
1053: *Fondo Finy.*
1054: *Fondo Girolamini.*
1055: Archives of Nunciature of Vienna.
1056: Chronological table of *Instrumenta Miscellanea.*
1057: Index of dioceses in *Manualia* of Rota (1461-1800).
1058: Archives of *Scrittore Segreto* (1734-1906).
1059: *Piante e Carte Geografiche.*
1060: *Fondo Ronconi.*
1061: Registers of *Abbreviatori di Curia* (1735-1906).
1062: Consistory Bulls of Benedict XIV.
1063: Congregation of *S. Palazzo Apostolico.*
1064: Archives of Protonotaries Apostolic.
1065: *Memoriali* (Supplications) (1636-1796).
1066: *Fondo Santini.*
1067: *Carte Farnesiane.*
1068: *Fondo Garampi* (vv. 272-300; for 1-271 see Indice 157).
1069: Inventory of *Epistolae ad Principes* (1560-1914).
1070: Archives of Nunciature of Lucerne.
1071: SS. England, Bavaria; *Cardinali, Vescovi, Principi, Particolari* (supplementing Indici 1013-1022).
1072: *Positiones* of Rota (1620-1660).
1073: *Diaria* of Rota (1560-1870).
1074: Concordance (1965) of Indici 56-57 (1628) and 1001-1012 (1910-1927) of *Archivum Arcis*: see pp. 58-60.
1075: *Archivio Della Valle-Del Bufalo.*

1076: Congregation of *Buon Governo*.
1077: *Fondo Gesuiti*.
1078: Visitations of Roman Hospitals.
1079: *Bandi sciolti*.
1080: *Fondo Cibo*.
1081-1086: Archives of Nunciatures:

> 1081: the Hague (L'Aja).
> 1082: Cologne (Colonia).
> 1083: Brussels (Bruxelles).
> 1084: Florence (Firenze).
> 1085: Naples (Napoli).
> 1086: Paris (Parigi).

1087: *Missioni*.
1088: *Carte Pasolini-Zanelli*.
1089: *SS. Esteri* (1851-1913).
1090: Archives of Nunciature of Madrid (1847-1876).
1091: *Fondo Pio*.
1092: *Positiones* of Rota (1627-1870).
1093: Archives of S. Silvestro, Nonantola (802-1780).

B. ORIGINAL ARCHIVIO SEGRETO VATICANO

(1611-c. 1656)

After the ASV had been set up in 1611, the eighty specially-constructed *Armaria* gradually were filled during the pontificates of Paul V, Urban VIII and Alexander VII with material from the *Bibliotheca secreta* in the Vatican Library, from the Camera, from Castel S. Angelo (*Archivum Arcis*), the Wardrobe, the Secretariate of State and the Secretariate of Briefs. The chief deposit was the great series of parchment ("Vatican") registers from the *Bibliotheca*, occupying over a third of the cupboard space (*Arm.* I-XXVIII). The remaining *Armaria*, only *Arm.* XXIX-LXXIV of which appear to have been used, became the repositories of other Chancery material from the *Bibliotheca*, and of exchequer records, copies of chancery registers, *rubricellae*, from the Camera; of briefs from the Secretariate of Briefs; of nunciature material from the Wardrobe; of Secretariate of State documents from Castel S. Angelo and the Secretariate itself; and of records of the Council of Trent from Castel S. Angelo. In general see Gasparolo-Lonigo, pp. 3-64; Kehr (1900) 366-379; Fink 30-34; HVD 21-29; Macfarlane 33-36; BAV I.119; II.100; IV.100-101.

The following list of the original *Armaria* does not describe in full those *Armaria* whose contents are more usefully considered under later headings, e.g. Cameral Holdings, Secretariates.

a. CHANCERY MATERIAL (ASV 1612-1614)

Arm. I-XXVIII: **Registra Vaticana*: 2042 vv. (872-1605),   3.2.6.8
cited as Reg. Vat. or RV, and volume. Origin is Chancery, Camera, Secretaries and Apostolic Secretariate, but provenance is, for the most part, *Bibliotheca secreta*. General inventory in *Sussidi* I, pp. 49-113. Indexes to vv. 1454-1684 in Indice 1037, and to vv. 1724-1782 in Indice 1038.

See Gasparolo-Lonigo 36-39; Kehr (1900) 366-368; Fink 34-37; HVD 178-194; M. Giusti, 'I Registri Vaticani e le loro provenienze originarie', in *Miscellanea A. Mercati* (Vatican City 1952), pp. 382-459, now reprinted in Giusti, *Studi*, pp. 1-79, with new material on provenance at pp. 129-148; BAV I.537-706, II.534-633, III.598-790, IV.559-670. For remarks on these registers see Part Two, pp. 103-113.

b. CAMERAL MATERIAL (ASV 1611-1614)

- *Arm.* XXIX, XXX: *Diversa Cameralia*: see Cameral Holdings, C. II, pp. 43-44.

3.2.3.8

- *Arm.* XXXI: Cameral copies, etc. of chancery registers. 85 vv. (John VIII-Clement VIII, 872-1605). Origin and provenance: Camera, 1611. Cited as *Arm..* XXXI and volume.

See Indice 133, 143r-146v; Kehr (1900) 367; Fink 31; BAV I.119-120, II.100-103, III.129-131, IV.101-104.

For vv. 5-10 see D. Mansilla, *La documentación pontificia hasta Innocenzo III* (Rome 1955). The famous formulary of Marinus of Eboli, Vice-Chancellor of Innocent IV, is v. 72: see F. Schillmann, *Die Formularsammlung des Marinus von Eboli* (Rome 1929); P. Herde, *Marinus von Eboli Super revocatoriis et De confirmationibus* (Tübingen 1964). There are *bullae de diversis* of Martin V in v. 44; letters of Boniface VIII in vv. 46-48, of Eugene IV, etc. in vv. 47-54.

3.2.3.9

[see also the articles by Mansilla noted in the supplement to the Bibliography, p. 221**]

- *Arm.* XXXII: Copies, probably cameral in the main, of papal letters (13th-16th c.). 62 vv. Provenance: Camera, 1611. Cited as *Arm.* XXXII and v.

See Indice 133, 147r-149v; Gasparolo-Lonigo 44-48; Kehr (1900) 368; Fink 31; BAV I.121-123, II.103, III.131, IV.104-105.

These copies cover letters of Innocent IV (v. 1), Boniface VIII (v. 2), and of various Popes to Spain (vv. 3-4), Portugal (v. 5) and other countries (e.g. v. 12: subsidies for the Holy Land). Usually the volumes are indexed. A register of dispensations of the Sacred Penitentiary, *sede vacante* 1521-1522, is in v. 61.

- *Arm.* XXXIII: *Quindennia*: see Cameral Holdings, C.IIc.
- *Arm.* XXXIV: *Instrumenta cameralia*: see C.IId.

3.2.3.12

- *Arm.* XXXV: Copies of registers, volumes of privileges (esp. vv. 3-12) of the Holy See (12th-16th c.). 152 vv. Origin: possibly cameral; provenance: *Bibliotheca secreta* 1612. Cited as *Arm.* XXXV and v., or *Acta privilegiorum*.

See Indice 133, 159r-165r; Gasparolo-Lonigo 36-38; Kehr (1900) 369; *Sussidi* I, p. 39, n. 3; Fink 31; BAV I.127-131, II.108-113, III.134-138, IV.108-112.

The famous *Liber censuum* of Cencius Camerarius is v. 18. In v. 147 there is a summary of the process against the Templars in England and Ireland in 1310; whence printed by K. Schottmüller, *Der Untergang des Templer-Ordens* (Berlin 1887), II.1, pp. 75-102.

- *Arm.* XXXVI-XXXVII: *Informationes camerales*: see C.IIe,f.

c. MATERIAL FROM THE SECRETARIATES (ASV 1623-1644)

- *Arm.* XXXVIII: Original briefs: see Secretariates, G.IIa.
- *Arm.* XXXIX: *Registra brevium*: see G.Ia.
- *Arm.* XL.-XLIII: *Minutae brevium*: see G.Ib.
- *Arm.* XLIV-XLV: *Brevia ad principes*: see G.Ic.

d. SECRETARIATE OF STATE MATERIAL (ASV 1614, 1656)

- *Arm.* XLVI: Copies of papal letters to Dukes of Ferrara. 62 vv., cited by *Arm.* and volume. See Kehr (1900) 374-375; BAV II.158, III.180, IV.155.   3.2.14.10

- *Arm.* XLVII: Barrofaldi collection of documents concerning Ferrara. 30 vv. Now in Vatican Library as MSS. Vat. Lat. 12576-12605.   3.2.14.11

- *Arm.* XLVIII: Mainly copies of material concerning Ferrara, Modena, etc. 54 vv. See BAV IV.156-157.   3.2.14.12

- *Arm.* XLIX: Material relative to various Italian cities. 52 vv. See Kehr (1900) 376; BAV II.159, IV.157.   3.2.14.13

e. CAMERAL RUBRICELLAE (ASV 1612)

- *Arm.* L, LI: Important series of *rubricellae* of papal registers from John VIII to Sixtus V (872-1590). 77 vv., of which 50 are now among the Indici volumes as Indici 240-289. Provenance: Camera, 1612. See Gasparolo-Lonigo 48; *Sussidi* I, 52-54.   3.2.3.15

f. CHANCERY AND VARIA (ASV 1612)

- *Arm.* LII: 65 vv. of *signaturae*, judgements, audiences, visitations, of Commissioners-general of Holy See. *Signaturae*, 1552-1562, are in vv. 1-16, 40, 41; vv. 17-22 contain reports of Cardinal Santori, 1566-1602.   7.3.2

See Indice 133, 224r-226r; *Sussidi* I, 42, n. 2; Fink 32-33; BAV I.165-167; II.159-160, III.180-181, IV.157-158; L. Pásztor, 'Contributo di un fondo miscellaneo all'archivistica e alla storia: Arm. LII dell'Archivio Segreto Vaticano', in *Annali della Scuola speciale per Archivisti e Bibliotecari dell'Università di Roma* 6 (1966) 1-31.

- *Arm.* LIII: Formularies of Chancery and Datary, c. 1200-1500. 79 vv.   7.3.3

See Indice 133, 228r-230v; P. M. Baumgarten, *Von der apostolischen Kanzlei* (Cologne 1908); W. von Hofmann, *Forschungen zur Geschichte der kurialen Behörden* (Rome 1914); BAV I.167-168, II.160-162, III.181-182, IV.158-160.

- *Arm.* LIV : 35 vv. (originally 48), containing (vv. 1-13) a *Thesaurus historicus* (c. 1750) of Cornelius Margarini, as well as volumes on the Great Schism ('Libri de Schismate') and   7.3.4

Martin Luther. Inventory of *Thesaurus* on file-cards (15 bound vv.) in ASV Index Room. Provenance: Castel S. Angelo.

See Kehr (1903) 377; M. Seidlmayer, *Die spanischen Libri di Schismate des Vatikanischen Archivs* (Münster 1940); Fink 33; BAV I.168-170, II. 162-165, III.182-184, IV.160-161.

- *Arm.* LV, LVI: Empty. See BAV III.184, IV.161.

- *Arm.* LVII: Mixed cameral material now in Fondo Camerale (see Cameral Holdings, B.IIf). Present Reg. Vat. 244 A-N belonged here : 13 vv. of minutes of papal letters, 1342-1378.

- *Arm.* LVIII, LIX: Empty.

g. SECRETARIATE OF STATE (ASV 1614, 1630, 1656)

3.2.14.14   - *Arm.* LX: 52 vv. (originally 31) pertaining to dukedom of Urbino. Mostly copies. Came to ASV probably from Castel S. Angelo in 1614. Cited by *Arm.* and v.

See Kehr (1900) 379; F. Bock, 'Mittelalterliche Kaiserurkunden im alten Urbinater Archiv', in *Quellen und Forschungen* 27 (1936-1937) 252-263; Fink 33; BAV I.170-171, II.165-166, III.184-185, IV.161-162.

3.2.14.15   - *Arm.* LXI: 64 vv., mostly copies, pertaining to dukedoms of Parma and Piacenza. Probably from Castel S. Angelo in 1614. See Fink 33; BAV I.171.

3.2.14.16   - *Arm.* LXII, LXIII: Documents relative to the Council of Trent, 1537-1588. In all 154 vv., some of which (vv. 45-48, 85-86) are now in the Vatican Library. Provenance: Castel S. Angelo, 1630 (Pitra, *Anecdota* I, p. 157). Cited as *Arm.* LXII-LXIII and volume; but often cited simply as *Concilio*, or as *Concilium Tridentinum* (thus BAV). The *Armaria* were much used by the Görresgesellschaft for its monumental *Concilium Tridentinum* (14 vv., Freiburg-im-Breisgau 1901-1938). See BAV I.283-289, II.166, 275-284, III.294-297, IV.278-282.

3.2.14.17   - *Arm.* LXIV: Nunciature reports of 16th century. 34 vv. See below, H.I.

h. RATIONES CAMERAE (ASV 1611-1614)

- *Arm.* LXV-LXXIV: Volumes from the Camera, 1611-1614, chiefly of *Introitus et Exitus, Obligationes et Solutiones, Collectoriae.* Now in Fondo Camerale: C.I.

See Gasparolo-Lonigo 48-50, 55-56; *Sussidi* I, 193-201 (for a concordance between the old *Rationes Camerae* and the present arrangement); BAV III.186.

C. CAMERAL HOLDINGS (ASV 1611-1614; 1918-1919)

From at least 599 there existed an *Arcarius* for the administration of papal finances, and from about 700 a *Sacellarius* to take care of expenses. Together with the *Vestiarius* and the *Maiordomus* these had offices in the Lateran Palace. The name *Camerarius* first occurs in 1105, and very soon this functionary began to absorb these earlier offices. By the middle of the twelfth century there appears to have been an independent office of the *Camera*, complete with staff under the *Camerarius*. But it was only with the great reorganization effected by Cardinal Cencio Savelli ("Cencius Camerarius") at the end of that century, that the Camera became fully a department in its own right, parallel to that of the Chancery, and with its own clerks, notaries and scriptors. The tasks of the *Camerarius* were judicial as well as fiscal, but for the most part juridical processes of the Camera rested with the *Auditor Camerae*, who is first mentioned in 1234. During the Avignon Papacy the Camera was given the status of a full Tribunal (*Audientia Auditoris Camerae*) for the judging of financial cases and, on occasion, of certain civil suits. On 8 September 1380, Urban VI extended its competence further to all *causae* touching the rights and interests of the Camera. Its scope was further increased by Innocent VIII in 1481, and (after a brief period of suppression under Paul IV) by Pius IV in 1562.

Apart from the *Camerarius*, the chief officer of the Camera from the 13th century onwards was the Treasurer, whose duties included the collection of revenue and the custody of the Treasury. The *Camerarius* (Camerlengo) often was a Cardinal, but the office as such did not become cardinalitial until the 15th century, by which time there also was a permanent assistant — *Vice-Camerarius* — in the Camera.

As shall be noted at length in Part Two, the business of the Camera was vast, and its interests ranged all over Europe in the Middle Ages. It goes without saying that its organization and its surviving records are of great importance for social and economic history: see, for example, A. Gottlob, *Aus der Camera apostolica des 15. Jahrhunderts* (Innsbruck 1889); W. E. Lunt, *Papal Revenues in the Middle Ages*, 2 vv. (New York 1934); G. Felici, *La reverenda Camera apostolica. Studio storico-giuridico* (Rome 1940); Y. Renouard,

'Intérêt et importance des Archives Vaticanes pour l'histoire économique du Moyen Age, spécialement du XIVᵉ siècle', in *Miscellanea Archivistica A. Mercati* (Vatican City 1952), pp. 21-41; John E. Weakland, 'Administrative and Fiscal Centralization under Pope John XXII, 1316-1334', in *Catholic Historical Review* 54 (1968) 39-54, 285-310.

The Cameral Holdings of the ASV came for the most part from the Camera in 1611-1614; in 1918-1919 some further medieval volumes came from the Archivio di Stato di Roma (where there are still some important late-medieval and other cameral deposits). The holdings fall into four main classes: obligations incurred by bishops and abbots, and their payment (*Obligationes et Solutiones*); records of monies paid to Collectors (*Collectoriae*); income and expenditure of the Camera (*Introitus et Exitus*); other cameral material. Of the many scholarly works which have used these holdings the best-known is that dedicated to the editing of the records of income and expenditure of the Avignon Papacy: the *Vatikanische Quellen zur Geschichte der päpstlichen Hof- und Finanzverwaltung, 1316-1378*, of the Görresgesellschaft, seven volumes of which have appeared to date, e.g. I: *Die Einnahmen der apostolischen Kammer unter Johann XXII.*, ed. E. Göller (Paderborn, Verlag Schöningh, 1910); II: *Die Ausgaben der apostolischen Kammer unter Johann XXII., nebst den Jahresbilanzen von 1316-1375*, ed. K. H. Schäfer (1911). These and other volumes of the *Vatikanische Quellen* will be discussed below in Part Two (p. 160 ff.).

For England (and, in passing, for Ireland) abundant use has been made of these holdings, and many documents edited, by W. E. Lunt, *Financial Relations of the Papacy with England to 1327* (Cambridge, Mass., 1939); *Financial Relations of the Papacy with England 1327-1534* (*ibid.* 1962); *Accounts rendered by Papal Collectors in England 1317-1378* (Philadelphia 1968). Nearly a hundred years ago, W. Maziere Brady, *The Episcopal Succession in England, Scotland and Ireland, A.D. 1400-1875*, 3 vv. (Rome 1875), made extensive use of cameral holdings, e.g. in v. I, pp. 288-323 (Ireland), he drew on 23 vv. of *Obligationes*, (1489-1789), 16 vv. of *Quittantia* (1396-1484), 14 vv. of *Formatari* (1425-1480). Of course these volumes were in the Archivio di Stato di Roma in Brady's day, as, indeed, were the volumes of *Annatae* of which M. A. Costello made great use in his *De Annatis Hiberniae* I (Dundalk 1909), and in the various posthumous publications noted below. Many of these Archivio di Stato volumes were handed over to the ASV in 1918-1919 (see p. 45, below).

I. Fondo Camerale
(ASV 1611-1614, *Arm.* LVII, LXV-LXXIV)

3.2.3.28

See Indice 1036 (inventory); Gasparolo-Lonigo 48-50, 55-56; J. de Loye, *Les archives de la Chambre apostolique au XIVe siècle* (Paris 1899); Kehr (1900) 379-380; *Sussidi* I, pp. 193-201 (for a concordance of the *Rationes Camerae* as they were in *Arm.* LVII, LXV-LXXIV of the original ASV with the present order of the Fondo); Fink 45-48; BAV I.174, III. 190, IV.168.

The three parts of the Fondo are cited by the titles given below or by *sigla*.

a. *Obligationes et Solutiones* (OS).   91 vv.   1295-1555.   3.2.4.44

Indice 1036; de Loye 1-118; Fink 51; HVD 128-133; H. Hoberg, *Taxae pro servitiis communibus ex libris obligationum ab anno 1295 usque ad annum 1455 confectis* (Studi e Testi 144, Vatican City 1949); BAV I.269-281, II.257-271, III.277-290, IV.260-276. See Part Two, Cameral Registers, pp. 157-164.

b. *Collectoriae* (Coll.).   504 vv.   1274-1447.   3.2.3.22

Indice 1036; de Loye 119-179; Fink 50-51; HVD 72-74; Lunt, *Accounts*; Y. Renouard, *Les relations des Papes d'Avignon et des compagnies commerciales et bancaires de 1316 à 1378* (Paris 1941); BAV I.175-207, II.186-203, III.206-213, IV.168-188. See Part Two, pp. 165-168.

c. *Introitus et Exitus* (IE).   565 vv.   1279-1524.   3.2.3.3

Indice 1036; de Loye 180-250; Fink 49; HVD 89-93; *Vatikanische Quellen zur Geschichte der päpstlichen Hof- und Finanzverwaltung 1316-1378* (Paderborn 1910 —); BAV I.229-269; II.229-256; III.242-275, IV.215-259. See Part Two, pp. 168-172.

II. Cameral Armaria of Original Vatican Archives
(1611-1614)

Over and above *Arm.* LVII, LXV-LXXIV, which now form the Fondo Camerale, there are other *Armaria* of the original ASV that contain cameral material. Unlike the *Armaria* that form the Fondo, they are usually cited by *Arm.* and volume, although (as in BAV) *Arm.* XXIX-XXX can be cited as *Diversa Cameralia, Arm.* XXXIV as *Instrumenta Cameralia*, etc.

a. *Arm.* XXIX: *Diversa Cameralia*.   161 vv.   1389-1555.   3.2.3.6

Indice 133, 130r-136v; E. von Ottenthal, 'Römische Berichte IV: Bemerkungen über päpstliche Cameralregister des 15. Jahrhunderts', in *Mitteilungen des Instituts für österreichische Geschichtsforschung* (MIöG) 6

[note especially the chono-

logical
index by
P. Sella]

(1885) 615-626; U. Berlière, *Inventaire analytique des Diversa Cameralia des Archives Vaticanes au point de vue des anciens diocèses de Cambrai, Liège, Thérouanne et Tournai* (Rome-Namur 1906); A. Clergeac, *La curie et les bénéfices consistoriaux* (Paris 1911); A. I. Cameron, *The Apostolic Camera and Scottish benefices, 1418-1488* (Edinburgh 1934), pp. 310-341; Fink 51; HVD 81-83; BAV I.207-227, II.203-229, III.213-240, IV.118-215. (HVD and BAV take *Arm.* XXIX and XXX together).

Diversa Cameralia is a very elastic term. This *Armarium* — and *Arm.* XXX — contains cameral correspondence, quittances of bishops, copies of prorogations, etc. On occasion the information can be unexpectedly detailed, e.g. *Arm.* XXIX, 8 ("Diversa cameralia Martini V"), f. 182r: Richard (Belmer), bishop-elect of Achonry in Ireland was consecrated by Thomas (Polton), bishop of Chichester, in the church of St James (at Porta di S. Maria del Popolo), Rome, on 14 June 1424, by mandate of Martin V. Vols. 1-74 cover 1389-1525.

3.2.3.7

b. *Arm.* XXX: *Diversa Cameralia.* 90 vv. 1550-1578.

Indice 133, 137r-141v. Other references as above for XXIX.

3.2.3.10
3.2.7.26

c. *Arm.* XXXIII: *Quindennia*, etc. 90 vv. 1419-1766.

Indice 133, 151r-154v; Fink 54; BAV I.123-125, II.104-105, III.131, IV.105-106. According to Katterbach EI 88 there are also 299 vv. of *Quindennia* for 1690-1869.

Ostensibly registers of *Quindennia* (taxes paid every 15 years on benefices annexed to religious corporations), the volumes in fact also contain records of other taxes, tenths, quittances of census (there are census returns in 33A for 1291, and in vv. 34-90 for 1464-1766). Vol. 2 covers *Quindennia* from Martin V to Julius III; v. 4 covers the same period, giving returns from countries such as Poland, Hungary, Portugal and Spain. In v. 26 there is a copy made c. 1612 (the year it reached the ASV) of the *De officio Collectoris in Anglia* of Pietro Griffi (c. 1500); an edition of this treatise (but from MS. Ottob. lat. 2948 of the Vatican Library) is about to be published by Michele Monaco.

3.2.3.11

d. *Arm.* XXXIV: *Instrumenta Cameralia.* 57 vv. 1313-1826.

Indice 133, 155r-157r; Fink 31; BAV I.125-127, II.105-108, III.132-134, IV.106-108.

Although some volumes do indeed contain *instrumenta* (thus vv. 3 and 8: *Instrumenta Imolensia*, 1376-1431), the contents of the *Armarium* are quite varied: v. 1 (1327-1474) records payments, procurations, libel actions; v. 2 (1313-1343) contains various *instrumenta*, etc. concerning those involved with the anti-pope

Nicholas V (1328-1330), as well as much information (ff. 115v-117v) on Benedict XII and the consequences of the Beatific Vision controversy (see Th. Kaeppeli, *Le procès contre Thomas Waleys O.P.*, Rome 1936, where, however, no use is made of this volume); v. 8 contains safe-conducts, remissions of annates, delays in payment (1424-1431). It may be noted that vv. 1-3 run from 1313-1400; vv. 4-51 from 1400-1585; vv. 52-57 from 1697-1826.

e. *Arm.* XXXVI: *Informationes Camerales.*   50 vv.   1335-1700.   3.2.3.13

Indice 133, 167r-168r, but more specifically Indice 138; Kehr (1900) 373-374; *Sussidi* I, p. 40, n. 4; Fink 31; BAV I.131, II.113-116, III.138-139, IV. 112-113.

Mainly (vv. 10-25) *informationes* of F. de Rubeis, fiscal advocate of the Holy See, 1644-1673.

f. *Arm.* XXXVII: *Informationes Camerales.*   43 vv. c.1500-1700.   3.2.3.14

Indice 133, 168r-169r, but more specifically Indice 137; Kehr (1900) 374; *Sussidi* I, p. 25, n. 2; Fink 32; BAV I.131, II.116-119, III.139-140, IV.113-114.

Largely (vv. 1-27) *informationes* of G. Contelori, Commissioner-general, c. 1650.

III. Fondo dell'Archivio di Stato (ASV 1918-1919)   3.2.3.29

The following holdings were given to the ASV in 1918-1919 by the Archivio di Stato di Roma in exchange for parts of the Archivio del Buon Governo. They had been taken over from the Camera in 1870 by the Archivio di Stato, where, in fact, there are still many cameral holdings (see p. 48).

Indice 41 at desk of ASV; E. Göller, 'Die neuen Bestände der Camera Apostolica im päpstlichen Geheimarchiv', in *Römische Quartalschrift* 10 (1922) 38-53; A. Lodolini, *L'Archivio di Stato di Roma. Epitome d'una guida degli archivi dell'amministrazione dello Stato Pontificio* (Rome 1960), pp. 134-135.

These Archivio di Stato holdings are cited by the titles given here:

a. *Obligationes communes.*   31 vv.   1408-1798.   3.2.3.43

Indice 1036; Brady, *Episcopal Succession*, I, pp. 288-323, etc.; BAV I. 269, II.256-257, III.275-277, IV.259-260. Vols. 1-18 cover 1408-1550.

b. *Obligationes particulares.*   9 vv.   1419-1507.   3.2.3.45

Indice 1036; BAV I.281, II.271-2, III.290-291.

3.2.3.54   **c.** *Servitia minuta.*   3 vv.   1416-1455.
BAV II.273, III.292-293.

3.2.3.2   **d.** *Annatae.*   136 vv.   1413-1797.

Indice 1043 (alphabetical inventory by diocese); F. Baix, *La Chambre Apostolique et les Libri Annatarum de Martin V* (Rome 1947); Fink 55; BAV I.174, II.168-186, III.190-206, IV.168.

Annates were taxes levied by the Holy See on minor reserved benefices. They were first introduced by John XXII, but were not enforced in some countries (e.g. Ireland) until after 1400. Benefices not exceeding 27 gold marks (about six English marks sterling) were regarded as poor and therefore exempt. Boniface IX (1389-1404) ordered that an appointee to a benefice should pay as tax half of the revenue of the first year before his letters of appointment were handed over; the Council of Pisa (1409), on the other hand, ruled that the tax need not be paid until a reasonable time had passed after canonical possession of the benefice. In letters of provision (as in the volumes of Lateran Registers in Trinity College, Dublin, described in Part Two, p. 145) the annate tax is noted between the date of provision and the date of the expedition of the letters.

Of the present collection of *Annatae*, vv. 1-45 cover 1413-1500, and vv. 46-82 the years 1500-1570. One example of their use by scholars may be given here. Between 1870 and 1906 Fr. Michael A. Costello, O.P. transcribed all the medieval entries for Ireland from the *Libri Annatarum* (then in the Archivio di Stato di Roma). He died as the first volume was in the press (see the memoir in M. A. Costello, *De Annatis Hiberniae*, I: *Ulster*, Dundalk 1909, pp. xxx-xxxi), and his notes for further volumes have been printed by various editors (see *Ireland* in the general bibliography) in the *Archivium Hibernicum* from 1913 onwards (but without, apparently, checking Costello's transcripts against the originals, and without giving the present ASV numeration). For his work Costello used not only the *Libri Annatarum* but also the *Libri Quietantiarum* (which are still in the Archvio di Stato di Roma: see below, IV), and what he calls *Libri Diversorum*. The latter, in fact, are now part of the ASV *Annatae*, with the result that e.g. Costello's "*Diversorum Martini V (1425-1427)*" is now *Annat.* 2 in the ASV.

3.2.3.3   **e.** *Annatae et Quindennia.*   19 vv.   1742-1797.
Katterbach EI (who gives 88 vv. from 1742-1850); Fink 55.

f. *Taxae.*   38 vv.   1426-1815.   3.2.3.55
BAV II.273-274, III.293.

g. *Libri Computorum.*   10 vv.   1527-1679.   3.2.3.35

h. *Bullarum Distributiones.*   14 vv.   1478-1560.   3.2.3.18
BAV III.206.

These are monthly records of payments for expedition of bulls.

i. *Registra Bullarum.*   4 vv.   1643-1679.   3.2.3.19
BAV II.272-273.

j. *Relaxationes Bullarum.*   6 vv.   1691-1798.   3.2.3.20

k. *Formatarum Libri.*   14 vv.   1425-1524.   3.2.3.30

L. Schmitz, 'Die *Libri Formatarum* Camerae Apostolicae', in *Römische Quartalschrift* 8 (1894) 451-472; G. Pellicia, *La preparazione ed ammissione dei chierici ai santi ordini nella Roma del sec. XVI* (Rome 1946); Fink 55; BAV I.227-229, II.229, III.240-242.

These *Formatari* volumes contain lists of ordinations of bishops, priests, etc., and of *litterae dimissoriales* and payments for dispensations. They have been used for England, Ireland and Scotland by Brady, *Episcopal Succession*, who describes them in I, pp. XXVII-XXVIII.

l. *Rubricellae.*   38 vv.   1342-1549.   3.2.3.50

BAV III.292.

Brief rubrics of selected letters of interest to the Camera, beginning from Clement VI. In v. 1 only a few folios are devoted to letters running from Clement VI to Paul III (1342-1549); the series proper begins in 1, f. 113r, with Martin V.

m. *Resignationes et Consensus.*   A: 295 vv.   1457-1594.   *Resignationes:*
                                   B: 249 vv.   1528-1869.   3.2.3.49

BAV II.273, III.291-292 (*Resignationes*); III.213 (*Consensus*). Indice 1056.   *Consensus:* 3.2.7.12

These volumes contain conditions for resignations of benefices as well as notarial instruments presented at the curia to certify that benefices really were vacant: see v. 1, 1r: "Hic incipit liber in quo notuntur resignationes seu cessiones quorumcumque beneficiorum ecclesiasticorum factae in camera apostolica...". The early volumes of series A run as follows: 1: 1457-1470; 2: 1482-1484; 3: 1484-1488; 4: 1488-1491; 5: 1491-1492; 6: 1492-1496; 7: 1496-1499; 8: 1499-1502. In Indice 1056 (ff. 236-256) there is a good index of dioceses occurring in series A, with volume and folio references, for example, Casselen. (1501-1504): Res. 9, 114; Dublinen. (1517-1520): Res. 25, 211; Glendelacen. (1484-1488): Res. 3, 195.

3.2.3.51
3.2.7.12

| n. Rubricellae. | A. Resignationum | 13 vv. | 1523-1555. |
| | B. Consensuum | 2 vv. | 1548-1591. |

IV. CAMERAL HOLDINGS OF THE ARCHIVIO DI STATO DI ROMA

A. Lodolini, *L'archivio di Stato in Roma e l'archivio del Regno d'Italia* (Rome 1932). Fink 55-59. A. Lodolini, *L'archivio di Stato di Roma. Epitome d'una guida degli Archivi dell'amministrazione centrale dello Stato Pontificio* (Roma 1960) ; G. Ramacciotti, *Gli archivi della Reverenda Camera Apostolica con inventario analitico-descrittivo dei registri camerali conservati nell'Archivio di Stato di Roma nel Fondo Camerale Primo* (Reverenda Camera Apostolica, Rome 1961) ; L. Sandri, 'Note sui registri delle "Rationes decimarum" dell'Archivio di Stato di Roma', in *Mélanges E. Tisserant* V (Studi e Testi 235, Vatican City 1964) pp. 339-359.

Not all of the cameral material in the Archivio di Stato di Roma (where it has been since the Archivio was founded in 1871) was handed over to the ASV in 1918-1919. There are thus large Cameral holdings today in the Archivio di Stato, in Part One of the *Archivio Camerale*. By and large these holdings have to do with Italy in general and the Papal States in particular, but it may be of value to list here (following Ramacciotti, pp. 69-71 rather than Lodolini, 1960, pp. 68-71) the main medieval holdings, one of which (X: *Libri Quietantiarum*) was used extensively by Brady, *Episcopal Succession*, and Costello, *De Annatis*. The Archivio serial numbers are from Ramacciotti.

Archivio di Stato di Roma. Archivio Camerale. Parte Prima.

		vols.	ser. no.	span
III.	*Decreti*	78	289-366	1508-1850
IV.	*Diversa negotia*	348	367-714	1467-1839
VI.	*Mandata cameralia*	63	824-896	1418-1802
VIII.	*Mandati di providendo*	11	1088-1098	1517-1654
IX.	*Gratiarum expectativarum*	13	1099-1111	1485-1536
X.	*Libri Quietantiarum*	31	1112-1142	1396-1511
XI.	*Collectoriae: Computa**	544	1143-1232	1387-1713
XII.	*Depositoria della Crociata*	5	1233-1237	1453-1490
XIII.	*Decimae* (mostly Roman)	48	1238-1282	1501-1718
XXVII.	*Conti annuali**	266	1752-2017	1413-1743
XXVIII.	*Collectoriae*	185	2018-2202	1479-1795

* Section XI consists of 544 envelopes. The Collectors' accounts mostly refer to Italy, but there is also material relative to Portugal (1532-1686), Spain (1416-1670), Albania, and Dalmatia (1432-1462). Section XXVII contains many *Introitus et Exitus* volumes, e.g. nn. 1752, 1753, for the years 1428-1429. (See Ramacciotti, pp. 128-129, 237-246, for both these sections, and for fairly detailed accounts of all sections of this *Fondo*).

After the Great Schism (1378-1415), no attempt was made to recover the papal archives from Avignon until shortly before the death of Martin V in 1431, by which date, probably, the present "Vatican" Registers and the main cameral records had reached Rome. Although small sections of the remainder were returned to Rome under Pius V and Gregory XIII (see above, pp. 9-10), it was only in 1783, some six years before the invasion of the Avignon Papal States by the French revolutionaries, that the whole of the Avignon archives was reunited in Rome. Of the 500 volumes then brought from Avignon to Rome (see G. Marini, *Memorie istoriche*, p. 26), the largest section by far was occupied by the great series of paper registers of papal letters and cameral material that we know today as the "Avignon" Registers. Since these registers will be discussed at length in Part Two, a brief note will suffice here.

*_Registra Avenionensia_ (Reg. Aven., Reg. Av., RA) 353 vv.   3.2.6.6
1316-1418.

Indici 557-641 (Alphabetical index, diocese by diocese, made at Avignon in 1718-1732 by Pierre de Montroy); Indici 642-669 (calendar of registers, excepting those of Gregory XI, volume by volume, made at Avignon by Joseph de Martin in 1711); F. Bock, *Einführung in das Registerwesen des Avignonesischen Papsttums*, with an album of 39 plates (Rome 1941, being the whole of v. XXXI, 1941, of *Quellen und Forschungen aus italienischen Archiven und Bibliotheken*); Fink 37-39; HVD 144-163; BAV I.430-480, II.485-499, II.491-532, IV.418-499; 'Prospetto dei Registri Avignonesi' in M. Giusti, *Studi*, pp. 149-151. Cameral materials occur in at least 121 vv. of RA and are inventoried in Indice 1036 (*Fondo Camerale*). Some of these RA volumes are noted below in Part Two (p. 156).

E. ARCHIVES OF THE DATARIA APOSTOLICA
(ASV 1892)

Traces of the office of *Datarius* are found in the pontificate of Martin V (1417-1431). Its origin is due to the distinction introduced at the beginning of the Great Schism between the *signatura* on papal letters and the actual dating of the letter, the fixing of which was entrusted to a specific person. Under Sixtus IV (1471-1484) the duties of this *Datarius* were expanded, and by the end of the 15th century he is found as the head of a special office (*Dataria*) for the preparation and dating of grants of favour, especially of non-consistorial benefices reserved to the Holy See, and of certain dispensations. During the 17th century the *Dataria* usually was presided over by a Cardinal with the title of *Pro-Datarius*. See L. Célier, *Les dataires du XVe siècle et les origines de la Daterie apostolique* (Paris 1910); W. von Hofmann, *Forschungen zur Geschichte der kurialen Behörden* (Rome 1914), I, pp. 80-88, II, pp. 98-104; Fink 66-74; Macfarlane 37-40; BAV IV. 289-290.

The Datary Archives were first set up as such by Clement X on 11 Jan. 1671 (*Enchiridion Archivorum*, pp. 58-63), and later were housed in the Lateran Palace. It was only in 1892 that they were transferred to the ASV. A part of these archives (e.g. the early volumes of registers of supplications) belongs to the period when the Datary was developing out of the chancery. Other parts belong to the period (c. 1450-1500) after the establishment of the Datary as such, when it had full powers to handle all graces which did not fall within the competence of the Penitentiary (matters of conscience) or of that of the Rota (matters under dispute). As a result of the vast amount of business with which the Datary eventually had to deal (supplications, collations to benefices, dispensations, pensions, alms, saleable offices, informative processes relative to episcopal appointments, validation of graces, exchanges of benefices, etc.), new sets of registers were introduced over and above the old registers of supplications. And, as the volume of business grew, more expeditious forms of letters of grace also were devised, and were registered in *Registra brevium*.

One of the great Datary deposits, however, really belongs to the Chancery in origin, and is only Datary, so to speak, by provenance. This is the series of registers known as the "Lateran"

Registers (RL). Although the letters registered in RL were sent out *per cancellariam*, the registers were in the charge of the Datary, and as such were housed in the *Archivum Bullarum* of the Datary in the Cortile of Sixtus V in the Vatican (hence Garampi's *siglum* AB — *Archivum Bullarum* — in his *Schedario* to denote the registers we now call RL). On the return of the depleted RL series to Rome from Paris in 1817, it was housed in the Datary Archives in the Lateran Palace, whence it reached the ASV in 1892.

This consistent connection with the Datary often gives rise to the impression that the RL are Datary in origin as well, but they are in fact products of the Chancery, where they took over from the Avignon (and from the Vatican) registers the recording of outgoing common letters of grace. Strictly speaking, therefore, the RL should be considered under the heading "Chancery registers", but since they reached the ASV from the Datary, and in fact have always been the preserve of the Datary, it seems more appropriate that they should be listed here. They will be considered in more detail in Part Two.

a. **Registra Supplicationum* (RS; Reg. Suppl.)   7365 vv. 1342-1899.   3.2.7.68

    B. Katterbach, *Inventario dei Registri delle Suppliche* (Vatican City 1932); Fink 42-45; HVD 171-178; BAV I.505-537, II.524-534, III.565-598, IV.540-559.
    Calendar of entries in the Papal Registers relating to Great Britain and Ireland: Petitions to the Pope, I (1342-1419), ed. W. H. Bliss (London 1896); B. Katterbach, *Specimina supplicationum ex registris vaticanis* (Rome 1927); F. Bartoloni, 'Suppliche pontificie dei secoli XIII e XIV', in *Bullettino dell'Istituto Storico Italiano per il medio evo* 67 (1955) 1-187. For further bibliography and a discussion of these registers see, pp. 149-153.

b. **Registra Lateranensia* (RL; Reg. Lat.)   2467 vv. 1389-1892.   3.2.6.7

    Inventories in *Sussidi* I, 145-190; Indici 1039 (RL 1-1127: 1389-1503), 1040 (RL 1128-2467: 1503-1892). Calendars in Indici 320-436 (see Part Two).
    Fink 43-45; HVD 165-171; BAV I.480-505, II.499-523, III.532-564, IV.499-539; M. Giusti, 'Note sui registri Lateranensi', in *Mélanges E. Tisserant* V (Studi e Testi 234, Vatican City 1964), pp. 229-249, now in Giusti, *Studi*, pp. 98-119 (followed at pp. 152-159 by a 'Prospetto dei registri Lateranensi'). British Isles entries in vv. 1-840 (1389-1492) are calendared in *Calendar of entries in the Papal Registers..., Papal Letters*, vv. IV-XIV, ed. W. H. Bliss, J. A. Twemlow (London 1902-1960). For further bibliography, discussion of these registers and notes on the volumes of RL in Trinity College, Dublin, see pp. 132-148.

3.2.7.5   **c.** *Brevia Lateranensia.*   883 vv.   1490-1807.

Inventories: Indice 195A, ff. 47-62 (still useful); Indice 1041 (modern, by M.-H. Laurent O. P.). See Fink 69-70; HVD 63; BAV I.173-174, II, 167, III.187-188, IV.165-166; and K. A. Fink, 'Untersuchungen über die päpstlichen Breven des 15. Jahrhunderts', in *Römische Quartalschrift* 43 (1935) 55-86, 'Zu den Brevia Lateranensia des Vatikanischen Archivs', in *Quellen und Forschungen* 32 (1942) 260-266; A. Petrucci, 'Note di diplomatica pontificia', in *Archivio della Società Romana di Storia Patria* 89 (1966) 47-85. In addition to the 883 vv., there are some 2000 packets (-1908).

The term "Brief", although used in the Middle Ages for various types of documents, is generally restricted today to a special kind of papal document which came into use at the end of the 14th century (the oldest known original Brief dates in fact from 17 October 1390). The Brief was distinct from the *Bulla* in as much as in its internal and external characteristics it lacked the solemnity of the Bull; its most distinctive element was that of the corroboration "sub anulo piscatoris" in the dating clause immediately after the place of issue. In the 17th century the practice of closing the Brief and sealing it with wax was dropped in favour of an open document.

Originally the Brief was a form of "littera secreta", that is, a letter of political or administrative import written by a papal secretary (see the volumes of Briefs in *Arm.* XXXIX-XLV listed below in G.I., and discussed by Fink above in his RQ article); and this "political" Brief became the basis of official diplomatic correspondence when Innocent VIII established the Apostolic Secretariate in 1484, and, indeed, of the later *Brevia ad Principes*. But side-by-side with the development of the "political" Brief, steady use began to be made of the Brief for any and every form of concession. This Brief "of grace and favour" soon became the basis of much of the correspondence of the Datary, and, more specifically, of the Secretariate of Briefs set up by Alexander VI in 1502 to handle non-diplomatic correspondence.

In the Datary special registers of Briefs (the *Lateranensia*) began to be kept from 1490, while those of minutes of Briefs "in forma gratiosa" came into being about 1523. The early volumes of the *Brevia Lateranensia* are valuable in that they include the original supplication as well as the text of the outgoing Brief; but from 1520 onwards the registers cease to record the contents of supplications, simply noting the fact that an original signed petition reached the Datary for despatch. A good illustration of the fuller form of registration comes from one of several Irish entries in the early volumes, in this case in *Brevia Lateranensia* I, f. 317r:

> Priorissa et conventus b. m. de Grayn, ordinis sancti augustini, Dublinensis diocesis, (Priory of Our Lady, Graney, Co. Kildare), petunt dari adiunctum iudicibus eis suspectis in causa, si in evidentem habent signaturam. Concessum est quod detur adiunctus et in aliis prout de iure, in praesentia domini nostri pape. A. Card. Alerien. Et per breve Decano ecclesiae Corkagiensis.
>
> Decano Corkagiensi. Dilecto filio salutem. Mittimus tibi supplicationem praesentibus introclusam manu dilecti filii nostri A. Cardinalis Alerien. in praesentia nostra signatam. Volumusque et tibi committimus ac mandamus ut una cum iudicibus in causa deputatis ad illius executionem vocatis vocandis procedas iuxta eius signaturam. Datum Romae die ultima Augusti 1490 anno 6⁰.

d. *Minutae brevium in forma gratiosa.*   465 bundles. 1523-1599.   3.2.7.35

Inventory by diocese and item in Indice 1042. See Fink 70; BAV I. 410-411, II.452-453, III.463-464, IV.386.

The 465 bundles contain in all 30059 items, 460 bundles containing dated minutes (29770), and the remaining 5 forming an appendix of undated minutes (289 items). Since Indice 1042 lists items for any given diocese and not the bundle in which the item occurs, the *minutae* are ordered by item number, though in fact one will then receive the whole bundle to which the requested item belongs. Thus, if one orders *Minutae brevium* 24308 (mandate of 11 July 1586 to bishops of Derry and Down with respect to a petition of Edward, bishop of Ardagh), 24309 (petition in respect of tithes due to fabric of metropolitan church of Armagh, 11 July 1586, the archbishop being in prison), 24310 (Armagh), 24311 (Clogher), what will arrive from the stacks is bundle 394, covering nn. 24226-24365 (July 1586).

Each *minuta* is invariably a long, badly written and often much-corrected strip of paper, generally folded in eight. The date of the expedition of the Brief corresponding is on the dorse of the minute, and the volume and folio in which the Brief has been registered are also noted, e.g. on the dorse of 24308: *anno 2⁰, vol. 5, 152.* Bearing in mind the losses in registers that various curial departments have suffered over the years, it is therefore unwise to confine one's researches to the *Brevia Lateranensia* and to omit the *Minutae* as redundant. As it happens, Indice 1042, with its alphabetical list of dioceses, makes initial research in the *Minutae* not too onerous, e.g. *Achaden*: 13979, 14549, 17662, 28814, ... *Ardachen*: 13979, 20099, 24186, 24308, 23409, 24310...; and although the *Minutae* are on occasion rather difficult to decipher, one can always catch the drift of the supplication and of the ensuing grace.

3.2.7.64   **e.** *Processus Datariae.*   258 vv.   1622-1900.

Indice 1046 (*Index diocesium*); Katterbach EI 89 (who gives 340 vv. from 1564-1868); Fink 70-71; BAV I.429-430, II.483-485, III.486-491, IV.417-418. See also L. Jadin, 'Procès d'information pour la nomination des évêques et abbés des Pays-Bas, de Liège et de Franche-Comté, d'après les archives de la Daterie, 1631-1775', in *Bulletin de l'Institut historique Belge de Rome* 11 (1931) 347-389: R. Ritzler, 'Procesos informativos de los obispos de España y sus dominios en el Archivo Vaticano', in *Anthologica Annua* 4 (1956) 465-498; C. Giblin, 'The *Processus Datariae* and the appointment of Irish bishops in the 17th century', in *Father Luke Wadding Commemorative Volume* (Killiney-Dublin 1957), pp. 508-616.

Note that the *Processus Datariae* are not to be confused with the *Processus Consistoriales* (see below, p. 83). The Datary processes are the originals of informative processes held in the Roman curia in the post-Tridentine period. The Consistorial processes are simply copies of these, though they also contain records of informative processes held outside of the Roman curia.

3.2.3.53   **f.** *Secretariatus Camerae (Sec. Cam.).*   222 vv.   1470-1796.

Indice 1048 (inventory); Fink 52-53 (as *Secretaria Camerae*); M. Giusti, 'I registri Vaticani e la loro continuazione', in *La Bibliofilia* 60 (1958) 130-140, now reprinted in Giusti, *Studi*, pp. 83-96; BAV II.523-524, III.564-565, IV.530-540.

This series (vv. 1-64 of which run from 1470-1563) is often considered as Cameral, and indeed came to the ASV from the Camera. However, if one excludes vv. 68 and 75-77 (registers of *bullae* of the Camera) and the volumes of *Diversorum* from the Apostolic Secretariate given below, the contents of the *Secretariatus Camerae* prove to be by and large Datary in character. The first seven volumes, for example, are totally taken up with expectative graces, the preserve of the Datary: 1: Sixtus IV (1480-1484); 2: Innocent VIII (1487); 3: Innocent VIII (1489); 4: Alexander VI (1495); 5: Alexander VI (1495); 6: Alexander VI (1496); 7: Julius II (1505). Much information of importance is to be found in the Datary, not to speak of the other parts of the series: confirmation of bulls of previous popes; bulls of provision; grants of expectative benefices; exchanges of benefices; changes in expectative graces; validation of graces; confirmation of local ordinances. An example of this last is in *Sec. Cam.* 1, ff. 351v-352v, where, on 12 September 1473, a decree is confirmed at the request of the king of England whereby abbot William of Jervaulx is given power to correct and punish the clergy of the collegiate church of Middleham, Yorkshire. The few volumes I have examined carry useful indexes, with folio references, but at times only a name is given, not the diocese.

The series also contains volumes of *Diversorum* of the Apostolic Secretariate from Gregory XIII to Clement X (1572-1676: vv. 65, 74, 78-83, 108-112, 115-124, 146-149, 154-156, 163, 166). When the Apostolic Secretariate was suppressed in 1678 these volumes passed to the Camera; their predecessors—*Diversorum* volumes from 1487-1570 — entered the ASV in 1630, and now form part of the RV series. 3.2.10.3

g. *Expeditiones.*   64 vv. 1620-1799.   3.2.7.20

There is a rough inventory in Indice 45 (*Dataria*) at ASV desk. See Fink 71-72. Besides these 64 vv. there are three bundles (1878-1896). Some 48 vv. were lost during the transportation of the Archives to Paris under Napoleon I. In general the series contains summaries of *Bullae* and *Brevia* from RL, *Brevia Lateranensia*, etc.

h. *Officiorum vacabilium.*   c. 160 vv. 1522-1809.   3.2.7.58

Inventory in Indice 45 (ASV desk). Material relative to saleable offices of the curia.

i. *Abbreviatores de curia.*   38 vv. 1735-1906.   3.2.1.2.
                                                                        3.2.1.3
Indice 1061 (inventory); Katterbach EI 88; Fink 72-73; BAV   3.2.1.4
III.112-113, IV.97-98.

For the office of Abbreviator in the Middle Ages see Bresslau, *Handbuch*, I, 274-275. As officials of the Chancery (and later of the Datary and the Secretariate), the abbreviators drew up minutes of letters, prepared supplications, etc. This series of personal registers (minutes of *Bullae* and *Motus proprii*) is valuable for the modern period. Unfortunately there is no similar series for earlier ages.

j. *Archivio dello Scrittore Segreto* (ASV 1912)   45 vv. 1734-1906.   3.2.7.1

Indice 1058 ((inventory) Fink 73-74. These archives contain notes, etc. of various *Scrittori segreti* towards bulls (visitations, suppression of bishoprics, canonizations, etc.) to be sent out "per viam secretam".

k. *Per obitum.*   275 vv. 1587-1899.   3.2.7.61

Provisions to benefices, whether capitular or parochial, vacant by the death of the incumbent. Irish entries have been calendared by A. Donnelly, 'The "Per obitum" volumes in the Archivio Vaticano', in *Archivium Hibernicum* 1 (1912) 23-38.

3.2.7.29	l. *Mandati di pagamento.*	48 vv.	16th-19th c.
3.2.7.83	m. *Supplicationes originales.*	c. 1000 nn.	1814-1898.
	BAV III.314-315.		

Datary Miscellanea

The following holdings are not usually mentioned in guides to the ASV (e.g. in Fink). The present selection, taken from Msgr Guidi's inventory of the *Dataria* archives (Indice 45 at ASV desk), suggests that much work remains to be done on modern Datary material. In January 1968 (see *L'Attività della S. Sede nel 1968*, Vatican City 1969, p. 1438) the Datary deposited material relative to the period 1800-1938 in the ASV: 346 bundles of *Positiones* on benefices, 1800-1908, and of provisions, 1908-1938; as well as 180 vv. of Registers, Protocols, *Per obitum* and "Notabilia".

3.2.7.26	n. *Quindennia.*	7 vv.	1701-1853.
	o. *Acta Datariae.*	14 vv.	18th c.
3.2.7.59	p. *Pensiones.*	21 vv.	1576-1854.
3.2.7.25	q. *Provisiones.*	46 vv.	1771-1908.
3.2.7.76	r. *Resignationes.*	53 vv.	1709-1800.
3.2.7.19	s. *Elemosinarum.*	36 vv.	1810-1821.
3.2.7.33	t. *Matrimonia* A.	74 vv.	1804-1898.
3.2.7.34	B.	87 vv.	1808-1897.
	u. *De diversis.*	27 vv.	1671-1809.
	v. *Attestationes episcoporum.*	97 vv.	1800-1897.
3.2.7.87	w. *Decreta circa vacabilia.*	93 vv.	1630-1895.
3.2.7.7	x. *Broliardus Supplicationum.*	34 vv.	1689-1898.

F. DIPLOMATIC HOLDINGS
(ARCHIVIO DIPLOMATICO)

I. INSTRUMENTA MISCELLANEA (ASV 1789). 7809 nn. 819-1903   7.4.17

Indice 1056 (chronological). In the Index Room there is also a calendar on file-cards bound in 32 vv., as well as a chronological calendar in 40 vv. See Kehr (1900) 115-123; Kehr (1903) 507-517; U. Berlière, 'Inventaire des "Instrumenta Miscellanea" des Archives Vaticanes au point de vue de nos anciens diocèses', in *Bulletin de l'Institut historique Belge de Rome* 4 (1924) 5-162, 7 (1927) 117-138; P. Lefèvre (continuing Berlière), *ibid.*, 9 (1929) 323-340; A. Mercati, 'Dagli Instrumenta Miscellanea dell'Archivio Segreto Vaticano', in *Quellen und Forschungen* 27 (1936-1937) 135-177, 'Le pergamene di Melfi all'Archivio Segreto Vaticano', in *Miscellanea G. Mercati* V (Rome 1946) 263-323; Fink 148-149; HVD 88-89; R. J. Dodd, 'Vatican Archives: *Instrumenta Miscellanea*', in *Archivium Hibernicum* 19 (1956) 135-140; BAV I.360-409, II.393-451, III.427-463, IV.370-385.

Originally located in Castel S. Angelo and there used by Garampi for his *Schedario* (citing them simply as *Instr.*), the *Instrumenta Miscellanea* which Garampi knew (4106) have since been increased from various sources to 7809. This fine collection of original *instrumenta* is to a large extent cameral in origin and covers a wide range of subjects: inquests; *bullae, instrumenta* and accounts of collectors; *obligationes* and *solutiones* of bishops and abbots, etc. Fr. Dodd has calendared those relating to Ireland, some of which have been edited in full by Theiner, *Vetera Monumenta Hibernorum et Scotorum*, e.g. pp. 510-534: pontificate of Leo X. Many *Instrumenta* of 1316-1334 have been calendared by G. Mollat in *Jean XXII. Lettres communes* (Paris 1904-1947), at nn. 5465-5496, 8357-8376, 10245-10269, 12242-12287, 14330-14389, 16170-16204, 18137-18172, 20337-20403, 23137-23178, 26446-26476, 29686-29714, 42381-42429, 46222-46269, 50713-50764, 54806-54840, 58212-58219, 61261-61295, 63893-63917, 64228-64234. See also *Exempla Scripturarum* II, *passim*.

The collection of *Instrumenta Miscellanea* is very easy to use because of the excellent indexes and calendars. It is cited as *Instr. Misc.* or IM, and is ordered and quoted by number, e.g. IM 516, *Instr. Misc.* 2003.

7.1

II. Archivum Arcis (AA.) or Archivio di Castel S. Angelo (ASV 1798)

Indici 56-57 (1628); Indici 1001-1012 (1910-1927, etc.); Kehr (1900) 115; Fink 146-148; D. Mansilla, *La documentación española del Archivo del Castel S. Angelo, 395-1498* (Rome 1959); BAV: *general*: I.74-75, II. 53-54, III.48, IV.49-50; *AA. Arm. I-XVIII*: I.75-107, II.54-82, III.48-70, IV.51-93; *AA.A-M*: B: II.82; C: I.107-116, II.82-88, III.70-100, IV. 93-97; D: I.116, II.88-91, III.110-111, IV.97; E: I.116, II.91-91, III. 111-112, IV.97; F: II.92, III.112.

From the 13th century it was the custom of the papacy to collect and keep together all records of papal privileges, deeds to lands and the like. Sixtus IV (1571-1484) was responsible for placing these records in Castel S. Angelo for safe keeping, where they remained until 1798. Then on the day after the arrest of Pius VI by the French, they were transferred with great haste to the Vatican Archives. As it happened, however, they were among the very first holdings to be shipped to Paris in 1799 when the transfer of the ASV was begun at Napoleon's order. They were returned, more or less intact, to Rome in 1817.

The central sections of the *Archivum Arcis* (AA.) contain some of the oldest documents of royal and imperial relations with the Papacy: royal letters and privileges, diplomata of Emperors — including 78 royal diplomata with golden *Bullae* from Frederick II to Napoleon I (see P. Sella, *Le Bolle d'oro dell' Archivio Vaticano*, Vatican City 1934). But other sections are also of great interest, and in fact cover wide areas of history, e.g. acts of homage to popes (n. 465 — or *Arm*. II.c.IV, 29 —: an authentic transcript of 1339 of the homage of King John to Innocent III on 7 October 1213); authentications of councils by bishops (n. 1290 — or *Arm*. IX.c.VIII, 4: confirmation of the acts of 2 Lyons in 1274 by bishops of England, Ireland, Scotland, with fragments of seals pending); lists of bishops (3458 — or *Arm*. XII.c.III, 90 —: a list of bishops nominated in England, Ireland, Scotland, from Alexander VI to Clement VIII). Items for 1316-1334 are in Mollat, *Jean XXII. Lettres communes*, at nn. 5497-5511, 8377-8388, 10270-10279, 12288-12296, 14390-14409, 16205-16224, 18188-18196, 23179-23399, 26477-26492, 29715-29728, 42430-42497, 46270-46320, 50765-50815, 54841-54863, 58233-58252, 61296-61322, 63918-63933.

The vast and very rich collection of the *Archivum Arcis* is housed in a series of *Armaria*, which in turn are divided into upper cupboards (*Armaria superiora*) and lower cupboards

(*Armaria inferiora*). The upper cupboards are set off by letters of the alphabet, and are therefore cited by letter and the serial number of the *Armarium* in question, thus: AA. *Arm.* C. 79 (a letter of Edward III c. 1330 to John XXII. The letter, written in French, bears the autograph signature of Edward; it is reproduced in C. Johnson and H. Jenkinson, *English Courthand*, Oxford 1915, II, plate XXIIb). The lower cupboards, on the other hand, run from I to XVIII, and the volumes are numbered in series from 1-6722; hence an item from a lower cupboard is cited by AA. *Arm.* I-XVIII and the serial number of the item, thus: AA. *Arm.* I-XVIII, 4071 (a letter of John XXII to Edward II of England about Irish *gravamina*). These serial numbers for *Arm.* I-XVIII (and the volume numbers in *Arm.* C-F) are to be found in the calendar (Indici 1001-1012) which in a good, clear hand Dott. Vicenzo Nardoni began in 1910, and others were to continue (but in typescript) after his death on 2 February 1927 (by which time he had completed *Arm.* C-F and nn. 1-5719 of *Arm.* I-XVIII).

The pre-Nardoni connotation for the *Armaria* was by *Arm.*, *capsula* (c.) and item or folio number; and this is the connotation used by G. B. Confalonieri (1628) in Indici 56-57, where all of *Armaria* and I-XVIII are covered in reasonable detail. An excellent typed concordance (1965) of the Nardoni and Confalonieri Indici will be found in Indice 1074. Since many writers in the past (and consequently the *Bibliografia dell'Archivio Vaticano*) use the old Confalonieri connotation, it is often more helpful to cite (or at least to note for one's own purposes) the AA. holdings by both Nardoni and Confalonieri numbers, particularly in respect of AA. *Arm.* I-XVIII, thus: AA. *Arm.* I-XVIII, 2463 (*Arm.* XI. c. I, n. 92) — an intriguing "Progetto per introdurre il S. Uffizio in Hibernia" of the end of the 16th century.

It must be noted, however, that although the Nardoni Indici cover only C-F of the *Armaria superiora* (A-M), it is only rarely that the Confalonieri Indici have to be consulted for the remaining *Armaria* A-B, G-M. This is because there is very little now in those *Armaria* omitted by Nardoni. Most of *Arm.* A. is now in the Vatican Library or has been transferred to other *Armaria*; *Arm.* B. now contains only some 96 vv. of expense-accounts of the pontificate of Sixtus IV; the contents of *Arm.* G. are now for the most part in the last *Armaria* of I-XVIII; *Arm.* H. and *Arm.* I. carry only two volumes each of printed matter; *Arm.* K. has some copies of bulls of 1606; *Arm.* L. possesses a few printed pieces; *Arm.* M. once had some 16 vv. of "Informationes civiles" but is now empty. In effect, the student will find all he requires in the Nardoni Indici (1001-1012), so it may be useful for beginners to have the following breakdown of those Indici:

Ind. 1001 pp.	1-118: *Arm.* C: 199 items.				
	119-138: Corrections and additions.				
	139-238: *Alphabetical index* to C.				
	239-334: *Arm.* D: 231 items.				
	341-407: E: 194 items.				
	407-410: F: 5 items.				
	411-466: *Alphabetical index* to D, E, F.				
	467-501: *Chronological index* (1123-1862) to C, D, E, F.				
1002	1- 68: nn.	1-164	*Arm.* I		
	68-239:	165-836	II		
1003	1-120:	837-1304	III		
	123-180: *Alphabetical Index*:			nn.	1-1304
	183-210: *Chronological Index*:	(962-1803)			
1004	1- 88:	1305-1516	IV		
	89-181:	1517-1729	V		
	181:	1730	VI		
	182-228:	1731-1859	VII		
	228-303:	1860-2038	VIII		
	304-376: *Alphabetical Index*:				1305-2038
	377-413: *Chronological Index*:	(1044-1791)			
1005	1-129:	2039-2268	IX		
	134-172:	2269-2371	X		
	174-215: *Alphabetical Index*:				2039-2371
	218-230: *Chronological Index*:	(600-1802)			
1006	1-410:	2372-3326	XI		
	412-499: *Alphabetical Index*:				2372-3326
	501-550: *Chronological Index*:	(1162-1823)			
1007	1- 91:	3327-3572	XII		
	91-280:	3573-3935	XIII		
	281-335: *Alphabetical Index*:				3327-3935
	338-359: *Chronological Index*:	(945-1769)			
1008	1-304:	3936-4566	XIV		
	305-352: *Alphabetical Index*:				3936-4566
	354-378: *Chronological Index*:	(998-1776)			
1009	1-340:	4567-5248	XV		
	342-376: *Chronological Index*:	(567-1796)			
	377-400: *Alphabetical Index*:				4567-5248
1010	1-200:	5249-5719A	XV		
	205-232: *Chronological Index*:	(1188-1744)			
	233-373: *Alphabetical Index*:				5249-5719A
1011	1- 46:	5720-5933	XV		
	46-185:	5934-6377	XVI		
	186-246: *Chronological Index*:	(876-1789)			
	247-331: *Alphabetical Index*:				5720-6377
1012	1- 27:	6378-6427	XVI		
	27- 60:	6428-6494	XVII		
	60- 81:	6495-6517	XVIII		
	82-152:	6518-6722	varia		
	153-174: *Chronological Index*:	(805-1808)			
	175-281: *Alphabetical Index*:				6378-6722

III. Archivio della Cancellaria della Nunziatura Veneta
(ASV 1835)

4.100.1
4.100.2

Indice 1024, 209-215 ; 317-319 (chronological index, 1226-1795) ; Kehr (1900) 123-124; Kehr (1903) 519-520; P. Cenci, 'L'Archivio della cancellaria della nunziatura Veneta', in *Miscellanea F. Ehrle* V (Studi e Testi 41, Rome 1924), pp. 273-330; Fink 149-150; BAV I.342-353, II. 382-384, III.380-415, IV.348-357.

This collection — which is cited as ACNV or as *Fondo Veneto* — comes from 31 monasteries suppressed at one time or another in the Veneto region, and it reached the ASV with the archives of the Venice Nunciature. It contains some 16892 items. Facsimiles of ACNV 8290, 8830, 9058, 9131, 9325, 9326, 9468, 9469, 9710, 9815, 10009, are to be found in *Exempla Scripturarum* II: *Epistolae et Instrumenta saeculi XIII* (Vatican City 1930). For a recent example of the use of ACNV holdings, see R. Brentano, *Two Churches. England and Italy in the Thirteenth Century* (Princeton 1968), pp. 80, 171, etc.

In the Index Room of the ASV there is a chronological calendar (9th-18th century) on cards which have been bound together to form 62 vv. With them there are 3 vv. of a similar calendar for the *Fondo Toscano* (a collection of documents from monasteries suppressed in Tuscany).

G. THE SECRETARIATES

Just as the need of popes for more frequent, prompt and expeditious forms and channels of correspondence gave rise in the late 14th century to the "Brief" form of letter (see pp. 52-53) and in the early 15th century to new curial departments such as the Datary, so also the growing demands of secret and political correspondence were met in the time of Martin V by the formation of the *Camera secreta*. Although most of the secret letters continued to be registered for some time afterwards in the parchment or "Vatican" registers, the bulk of the political correspondence, for which the new "Brief" form was preferred, was confided to registers of Briefs. Later the Apostolic Secretariate was set up on 31 December 1484 by Innocent VIII for diplomatic correspondence in Latin, taking over the larger part of the functions of the *Camera secreta*. The new department was composed of 24 secretaries, the chief of whom was the *Secretarius Domesticus*. From Alexander VI (1492-1503) until the time the Secretariate ceased to be of major importance towards the end of the 16th century, the Domestic Secretary was directly responsible to the Cardinal-nephew (Cesare Borgia in Alexander's pontificate). In the press of business in the 16th century, and especially after the introduction of vernacular correspondence into the curia, new Secretariates (the Secretariate of Briefs, the Secretariate of State, the Secretariate of Letters to Princes) developed out of or grew up alongside the Apostolic Secretariate. By 1570 it was largely effete, but it lingered on, shorn of most of its functions, until it was abolished in 1678.

On the origin and development of the Secretariates in general, see P. Richard, 'Origine et développement de la Secrétairerie de l'État apostolique, 1417-1823', in *Revue d'histoire ecclésiastique* 11 (1910) 56-72, 505-529, 728-754; A. Kraus, 'Secretarius und Sekretariat. Der Ursprung der Institution des Staatssekretariats und ihr Einfluss auf die Entwicklung moderner Regierungsformen in Europa', in *Römische Quartalschrift* 55 (1960) 43-84; L. Pásztor, 'L'histoire de la curie romaine, problème d'histoire de l'Église', in *Revue d'histoire ecclésiastique* 64 (1969) 353-366, esp. pp. 356-357, where there is a rich bibliography.

I. THE APOSTOLIC SECRETARIATE (1484; ASV 1630)

3.2.10

Parts of the archives of the Apostolic Secretariate (including registers of political briefs from the old *Camera secreta* of Martin V) reached the ASV in 1630, where, together with material from the Secretariate of Briefs, they were housed in *Arm.* XXXIX, XL-XLIII, XLIV-XLV, of the original ASV; further additions were made between then and the suppression of the Secretariate in 1678. Other parts of the Secretariate archives — *Diversorum* volumes from 1484-1572 — were, however, merged with the parchment or "Vatican" registers, from which, in fact, they had largely taken over the role of registration of secret letters after 1484. When the Secretariate was abolished, the later *Diversorum* volumes (1572-1676) passed not to the ASV but to the Camera, and are in fact now in the ASV as part of the *Secretariatus Camerae* series which has already been noted above (E.f) under the heading "Datary Archives" (pp. 54-55).

Since political letters in Latin, which had formerly been the preserve of the *Camera secreta* established by Martin V, were the main concern of the Apostolic Secretariate, the Brief, sealed by the Ring of the Fisherman, also continued as the basic epistolary form used by the Secretariate.

a. *Arm.* XXXIX: *Registra Brevium.* 69 vv. 1417-1565.

7.3.1

Indice 133, 176r-178v (inventory); HVD 23; BAV I.132-140, II.119-129, III.140, IV.115-126. The Registra are cited by *Arm.* and volume, e.g. *Arm.* XXXIX, 39.

See K. A. Fink, 'Die ältesten Breven und Brevenregister', in *Quellen und Forschungen* 25 (1933-1934) 292-307 (using vv. 4-7A), 'Die politische Korrespondenz Martins V. nach den Brevenregistern', *ibid.*, 26 (1935-1936) 172-244 (using vv. 6, 7A); G. Lang, *Studien zu Brevenregistern und Brevenkonzepten des XV. Jahrhunderts* (Rome 1938); Ch.-M. de Witte, 'Notes sur les plus anciens registres de brefs', in *Bulletin de l'Institut historique Belge de Rome* 31 (1958) 153-168; G. Gualdo, 'Il "Liber brevium de curia anni septimi". Contributo allo studio del Breve Pontificio', in *Mélanges E. Tisserant* IV (Vatican City 1964), pp. 301-345 (*Arm.* XXXIX, 12).

The series is not as rich now for the 15th century as it was once (vv. 4, 5, 7A, for example, are 17th century transcripts of registers now lost), but other 15th century collections of Briefs will be found in the Vatican Library, MS. Chigi D.VII.101 (129 briefs of Martin V) and MS. Ottob. lat. 3014 (185 Briefs of 15th c.). Some volumes in *Arm.* XXXIX (e.g. 7A: 17th c. transcripts of Briefs of Martin V and Eugene IV) carry minutes or summaries of the Briefs in the margins. Unfortunately, the Briefs

Vol. 1 of the series actually relates to the pontificate of Innocent III (1198-1216) [I. B. Cohen]

are not dated in many volumes (e.g. 4: Briefs of Martin V, with much material relative to the Hundred Years War).

b. *Arm.* XL-XLIII: *Minutae Brevium* (ASV 1630).

3.2.10.1   - *Arm.* XL   57 vv.   1478-1588.

Indice 133, 180r-182r; BAV I.140-149, II.129-137, III.149-157, IV. 126-132.

3.2.10.1   - *Arm.* XLI   72 vv.   1536-1554.

Indice 133, 183r-185r; BAV I.149-157, II.137-143, III.157-166, IV.132-138.

3.2.11.4   - *Arm.* XLII   63 vv.   1555-1629.

Indice 133, 187r-191v; BAV I.157-160, II.143-147, III.166-172, IV.138-143.

3.2.11.4   - *Arm.* XLIII   32 vv.   1630-1656.

Indice 133, 192r-194r; BAV I.160, II.147-148, II.172, IV.143.

These volumes in *Arm.* XL-XLIII contain corrected drafts of Briefs, and are not at all easy to use. In *Arm.* XL, 1, for example, the minutes are pasted on to the pages, and indeed sometimes on top of one another. The vv. in each *Armarium* are cited by *Arm.* and number. In Indici 290-316 there are old but still useful indexes.

Arm. XL and XLI belong to the high period of the Apostolic Secretariate (1484-c.1570), while *Arm.* XLII and XLIII are really Secretariate of Briefs in origin, belonging to the years when that Secretariate, after a complete reorganization in 1560, had taken over some of the functions of the Apostolic Secretariate. It was, in fact, through the Secretariate of Briefs that the present volumes of *Minutae* reached the ASV in 1630. J. M. Rigg, *Calendar of State papers, Rome*: II (London 1926), has used *Arm.* XLII, 34. See also HVD 23-25.

3.2.10.2   **c.** *Arm.* XLIV-XLV: *Brevia ad Principes et alios viros* (ASV 1630).

- *Arm.* XLIV   59 vv. 1513-c.1621.

Indice 133, 196r-198v; BAV I.160-164, II.148-153, III.172-178, IV.143-152.

- *Arm.* XLV   43 vv. c.1623-1730.

Indice 133, 200r-201v; BAV I.164, II.153-158, III.178-180, IV. 152-155.

When Leo X (1513-1521) introduced the office of *Secretarius Maior* (or *Intimus*) for the administration of state business and for vernacular letters to Nuncios in various parts of Europe (see H: Secretariate of State), the old Latin political Briefs of *Arm.* XXXIX were relegated to a second place in diplomatic correspondence, being employed only on very special occasions. The drafting of these occasional *Brevia ad Principes et alios viros* still remained the duty of the Domestic Secretary of the Apostolic Secretariate, but to ensure the highest quality of Latin document Leo X divided the office between two of the greatest Latinists of the period, Pietro Bembo and Jacopo Saldato (see e.g. *P. Bembi Epistularum Leonis X scriptarum Libri XVI*, Venice 1547).

A part of these Brevia reached the ASV through the Secretariate of Briefs in 1630; the remainder (Urban VIII-Benedict XIII) in the time of Benedict XIV (so Indice 133, 202r). There is much English, Irish and Scottish material in *Arm.* XLIV, esp. in vv. 22-24, 28: see Rigg, *Calendar of State Papers, Rome:* II (London 1926); F. Jones in *Archivium Hibernicum* 17 (1953) 51-68, who uses XLIV, 45. See also HVD 25-27.

II. THE SECRETARIATE OF BRIEFS (1502, 1560; ASV 1630, 1968)   3.2.11

Following the establishment of the Apostolic Secretariate for secret and political correspondence in 1484, a new and distinct department, the Secretariate of Briefs, was created by Alexander VI in 1502 for letters of non-diplomatic and spiritual content. When this was reorganized in 1560, it also took over most of the work of preparing political Briefs and *Brevia ad Principes* from the Apostolic Secretariate, together with, in all likelihood, that Secretariate's collection of *Minutae* and *Brevia*. In 1630, as we have seen, those registers of *Brevia, Minutae* and *Brevia ad Principes* went to the ASV and were housed in *Arm.* XXXIX-XLV.

The archives of the Secretariate of Briefs as such, however, falls into two sections: that originating in the first period of the Secretariate's existence (1502-1560), and that belonging to the reorganized *Secretaria Brevium*. Items dating from the first period were lodged, together with additions after 1560, in the ASV in 1630 and placed in *Arm.* XXXVIII. The archives of the new *Secretaria Brevium*, however, did not find a home in the ASV until 1968; for although these archives were officially given to the ASV in 1908, when the Secretariate of Briefs was suppressed, the archives were then housed in the Secretariate of State and had to be consulted there. (See *L'Attività della S. Sede nel 1968*, Vatican City 1969, p. 1438, where it is noted that the transfer of the archives of the Secretariate of Briefs from the Secretariate of State was completed in May 1968, and that the series of volumes includes everything up to 1908).

3.2.11.3   **a.** *Original Secretariate of Briefs* (1502; ASV 1630).

- *Arm.* XXXVIII: Original Briefs, cited as *Arm.* and volume:
1. *Cartella A* on lower shelf: 3 vv.   1508-1734.
   One-volume calendar (311 items) on file-cards in Index Room.
2. *Arm.* XXXVIII proper: 27 vv.   1513-1721.

Indice 133, 174r-175r; Fink 32; BAV I.132, II.119, III.140, IV.114-115.

b. *Secretariate of Briefs* (1560, ASV 1968)   7754 vv.   1561-1908.

Indice n. 45 (Guidi) at ASV desk; Fink 76-78. Note that section 1 below is cited as *Sec. Brev.* simply, but that sections 2-6 are cited as *Sec. Brev.* and title of particular section.

3.2.11.23   1. *Secretaria Brevium* (*Sec. Brev.*)   6219 vv.   1561-1908

Indici 30-47, 317, 399, etc.; HVD 207-208; BAV I.706-713, II.635-667, III.791-808, IV.671-709 (*Sec. Brev.*); II.667, III.808, IV.709 (*Indici*). It should be noted that the *Indici* provide short but useful and accurate calendars, and that the volumes are cited simply as *Sec. Brev.* and not as *Brevia secreta*. Briefs, in fact, form only a part of this great series, there being also volumes of *Diversorum* (1566 —), *Matrimoniorum* (1566 —), *Cedulae. consistoriales* (1561 —) and *Bullarum'* (1572 —), the latter in fact being a continuation of the *litterae secretae* of the now suppressed "Vatican" Registers (see Giusti, *Studi*, pp. 93-94, for a list of these 290 vv. of *Bullae*).

3.2.11.13   2. *Indulgentiae ad tempus*   578 vv.   1625-1908.

BAV I.713-714, III.808-809.

3.2.11.14	3. *Indulgentiae perpetuae*	276 vv.	1572-1908.
3.2.11.15	4. *Indulta personalia*	220 vv.	1824-1908.
3.2.11.1	5. *Altaria ad tempus*	90 vv.	1771-1908.
3.2.11.2	6. *Altaria perpetua*	210 vv.	1579-1908.

III. THE SECRETARIATE OF STATE

Since the Secretariate of State developed within the Apostolic Secretariate out of the office of *Secretarius Maior* instituted by Leo X (1513-1521) for vernacular diplomatic correspondence, it would be logical to speak of it here, immediately after the Secretariate of Briefs. However, the ASV holdings from the Secretariate of State are so vast and complicated that it is more convenient to consider them on their own below (H) under the special heading "Secretariate of State".

IV. THE SECRETARIATE OF EPISTOLAE AD PRINCIPES ET OPTIMATES   3.2.12
(1560; ASV 1908)

Epistolae ad Principes   380 vv.   1560-1914.

Indice 1069 (inventory); Richard in *Revue d'histoire ecclésiastique* 11 (1910) 525-529; Fink 79; HVD 84; A. Serafini, 'Le origini della pontificia Segretaria di Stato', in *Apollinaris* 25 (1952) 165-139 (for vv. 1-164); BAV I.174, II.297, III.315-318, IV.290-301.

This Secretariate was founded in the pontificate of Paul IV (1559-1565). Its *Epistolae* differ from the *Brevia ad Principes et alios viros* (*Arm.* XLIV-XLV) instituted by Leo X in the Apostolic Secretariate, in that their style is less pompous than that of the *Brevia*, and that, unlike Briefs in general, they were not sealed with the Ring of the Fisherman. They did not, however, replace the *Brevia ad Principes*, but rather ran parallel to them. In effect, the *Epistolae* were used for routine letters in Latin, while the *Brevia* were reserved for special occasions.

*
* *

By 1560-1570 these three new Secretariates (of Briefs, of State, of Letters) had taken over so much of the work of Innocent VIII's Apostolic Secretariate that its competence in the remaining hundred years of its life seems to have been limited for the most part to casual work on *Litterae secretae* and the like which were then registered in the *Diversorum* volumes mentioned above (pp. 54, 63). According as the load on the established Secretariates increased, some other Secretariates came into existence after 1570. It will be sufficient to mention them here briefly, before going on to consider the Secretariate of State:

V. SECRETARIATE (AUDIENTIA) OF CONTRADICTED LETTERS
(c.1570)

Registra Contradictarum   198 vv.   1575-1799.   3.2.7.67

Inventory in Indice 45 at ASV desk; Fink 80.

This department came into existence in the pontificate of Innocent III (1198-1216), but unfortunately there is no extant series of registers for the Middle Ages such as that which begins here in the late 16th century. The *Audientia litterarum contradictarum* was competent for a variety of letters, but mainly for letters of ordinary justice, which were no longer to be read out aloud to the pope and were granted without his specific assent by the officials of the Chancery. In the *audientia*, the initial proceedings took place before the *Auditor litterarum contradictarum*. After this the original letter was read in a public hearing and then handed over for sealing. This public reading exposed the letter to the "contradiction" of the defendants or their procurators. If someone entered a protest against letters thus published in the *audientia*, new negotiations had to take place before the Auditor.

See G. Barraclough, 'Audientia litterarum contradictarum', in *Dictionnaire de droit canonique* I (1935) 1387-1399; P. Herde, *Beiträge zum Kanzlei- und Urkundenwesen im dreizehnten Jahrhundert* (Kallmünz 1961), pp. 164-170; 'Papal Formularies for Letters of Justice', in *Proceedings of the Second International Congress of Medieval Canon Law* (Rome-New Haven 1965), pp. 321-346; *Audientia litterarum contradictarum. Untersuchungen über die päpstliche Delegationsgerichtsbarkeit vom 13. bis zum beginn des 16. Jahrhunderts*, 2 vv. (Tübingen 1970); J. Sayers, 'Canterbury Proctors at the Court of the *Audientia Litterarum Contradictarum*', in *Traditio* 22 (1966) 311-345.

VI. SECRETARIATE OF MEMORIALI OR SUPPLICATIONS (ASV 1905)

Indice 1065; Fink 80.

3.2.16.2	a. *Memoriali*		292 vv.	1636-1796.
3.2.16.1	b. *Segretaria dei Memoriali*	i.	260 bundles	19th c.
		ii.	59 bundles	1814-1897.

VII. SECRETARIATE OF LITTERAE LATINAE (ASV 1937)

3.2.13.1   *Litterae Latinae*   240 vv.   1823-1914.

Fink 79-80. Note that the series is distinct from the *Brevia ad Principes* (*Arm.* XLIV and XLV) and the *Epistolae ad Principes* (G.IV).

H. THE SECRETARIATE OF STATE
(1513, 1560; ASV 1614-1656, etc.)

In 1513 Pope Leo X instituted a *Secretarius Maior* in the Apostolic Secretariate to take care of political correspondence and correspondence with Nuncios (the first permanent Nunciature —
that of Vienna — dates from this period: see pp. 75-78). His
great innovation was that the correspondence entrusted to the
Secretarius Maior was to be in the vernacular rather than in the
customary Latin. The modern era of the Papal curia begins
with this first introduction of the vernacular.

The Apostolic Secretariate continued, of course, to use Latin
for general political correspondence, as did the *Secretarius Domesticus* for Briefs to Princes, but as the volume of political and
diplomatic letters in the vernacular increased over the years,
the post of *Secretarius Maior* began to overshadow the Apostolic
Secretariate and the post of *Secretarius Domesticus*, and came to
be regarded as a distinctive office. Under Paul III (1534-1549)
the office gained much in importance; under Pius IV (1559-1565)
and his cardinal-nephew, St. Charles Borromeo (who is often,
if erroneously, called the first Secretary of State), the *Secretarius
Maior* became the *Secretarius Intimus* and absorbed the office of
Secretarius Domesticus. The Secretariate of State proper dates from
this period.

Like the Apostolic Secretariate and the *Secretarius Domesticus*
from the pontificate of Alexander VI until their eclipse between
1560 and 1570, the *Secretarius Maior (Intimus)* was from the beginning directly responsible to the cardinal-nephew. And although
Gregory XIII (1572-1585) made a determined effort to reduce
the status of the cardinal-nephew, the practice of considering the
Secretariate of State as the preserve of the family of the reigning
pope continued until Innocent XII (constitution of 1692) finally
freed the Secretariate of State from the influence of cardinal-
nephews. After this, the *Secretarius Intimus* (or, as he came to be
called from about 1580, the *Secretarius Status*) now became the
head of the Secretariate of State.

The dominant position enjoyed by cardinal-nephews and
papal families in Secretariate of State affairs for almost two centuries accounts to some extent for the presence of so many

Secretariate of State records in the archives of certain Roman families (see H.IV, below: Archives of cardinal-nephews and of former papal families). Some material from the Secretariate of State was moved from Castel S. Angelo, the Wardrobe and the Secretariate itself to the original ASV between 1614 and 1656; but the greater part of the present ASV holdings have come in the past 150 years from Nunciatures and Legations, and through the acquisition of the archives of former papal families.

See in general: P. Richard, 'Origine et développement de la Secrétairerie de l'État apostolique, 1417-1823', in *Revue d'histoire ecclésiastique* 11 (1910) 56-72, 505-529, 728-754; A. Kraus, 'Secretarius und Sekretariat. Der Ursprung der Institution des Staatssekretariats und ihre Einfluss auf die Entwicklung moderner Regierungsformen in Europa', in *Römische Quartalschrift*, 55 (1960) 43-84; L. Pásztor, 'L'histoire de la curie romaine, problème d'histoire de l'Église', in *Revue d'histoire ecclésiastique* 64 (1969), 353-366; BAV I.716-829, II.667-759, III.809-906, IV.710-832.

I. HOLDINGS OF ORIGINAL ASV: *Arm.* LXIV (ASV 1635)

3.2.14.17   *Arm.* LXIV   34 vv. c.1520-1630.

Fink 34; BAV I.171, II.166, III.185-186, IV.162-165. The contents are cited as *Arm.* LXIV and volume.

Arm. XLVI-XLIX and LX-LXI of the original ASV (see pp. 39, 40) contain material in one way or another connected with early Secretariate of State business. Possibly their contents were formed from documents transferred from Castel S. Angelo in 1614 (Gasparolo-Lonigo, p. 30) and 1630 (Pitra, *Anecdota* I, p. 157), and from the Secretariate of State itself in 1656 (Pitra, p. 158). The only *Arm.*, however, of the original ASV which undoubtedly belongs to the early Secretariate as such is *Arm.* LXIV. This contains 34 vv. of Nunciature reports relative to various European countries which reached the ASV from the Wardrobe in 1635 (Gasparolo-Lonigo, p. 30). Volumes 1-27 concern Germany; volumes 29-34 deal with Poland, Portugal, Spain, France and Savoy; v. 28 is entitled *Anglia, Hibernia et Scotia*, and was used by J. M. Rigg for the *Calendar of State Papers, Rome*, II. *Arm.* LXIV, 17 is sometimes cited as *Acta Wormacensia*.

II. SECRETARIATE OF STATE MISCELLANY
(*Miscellaneorum Armarium*)

Indice 1029 (inventory and alphabetical index), Indice 1030 (inventory of sections IV-V); Kehr (1900) 380-390; Katterbach EI 89; Fink 97-99; HVD 95-98; BAV I.411-428, II.453-479, III.464-485, IV.386-417.

The *Miscellaneorum Armarium* is divided I-XV and is cited as *Misc. Arm.*, section and volume (e.g. *Misc. Arm.* I.16). Apart from Indici 1029 and 1030, there are for the *Misc. Arm.* in general two volumes of file-cards in the ASV Index Room ("Schedario Melampo"); while for *Misc. Arm.* IV-V (which are often cited simply as *Bolle e Bandi* or *Bandi*) there is a calendar in 36 volumes of file-cards. There is also an old, summary inventory in Indice 136.

The *Misc. Arm.* originally contained about 2500 volumes (16th-18th c.), but there are now only about 1488. Many of the original volumes are missing or have been transferred to the Vatican Library or some other department. Volumes which are extant but are no longer in the *Misc. Arm.* are noted in *Sussidi* I, 46-48 (1926), but Mercati's own copy of the *Sussidi* should be consulted further, since many of the items listed as missing in 1926 have since been located or identified.

In Indici 158-167 there is a useful and clearly-written index (A-Z) which Garampi compiled of all ASV miscellaneous collections (but chiefly of the present *Misc. Arm.*). With the help of the *sigla* given in Indice 158, or with the aid of the key to Garampi's *sigla* in *Sussidi* I, the references to *Misc. Arm.* (e.g. those under *Hibernia* in Indice 163, pp. 59-60) are not too difficult to track down. Garampi's *Indice cronologico dell'Archivio Segreto* (1550-1721) in Indici 168-184, also uses *Misc. Arm.*, as does his *Indice cronologico* (1630-1808) in Indici 538-549.

In general the contents of *Misc. Arm.* may be described as political, but in fact there are non-political items also, as the following brief summary will indicate:

Misc. Arm.

I   Originally consisted of 226 vv., being mostly Nunciature and Secretariate of State correspondence relative to various countries, c. 1500-1700. Volumes 15-17 are of prime importance for the history of the British Isles. Thus v. 16 contains a considerable amount of material for 1647-1649, e.g. appeals from Queen Henrietta Maria for help for her husband Charles (25r-31v); a report of 12 December 1647 on the state of Ireland (33r-41v).

7.2.2   II Originally 182 vv., dealing with various countries, of *Politicorum varia*. Indice 110 is still useful.

7.2.3   III Originally 307 vv. of *Politicorum varia*, 144 of which are now in the Vatican Library. For vv. 31-47 see Indice 218.

7.2.4   IV-V 376 vv. of *Bandi*, most of which have been published in *Registri di Bandi, editti, notificazioni e provvedimenti relativi alla Città di Roma e allo Stato pontificio*, 5 vv. (Comune di Roma, Rome 1920-1934). This great collection of public notices, posters, etc. is often cited simply as *Bandi* instead of *Misc. Arm.* IV-V. Moreover, vv. 203-258 — "Collectio Ottoboniana" — are sometimes cited as *Bandi verdi* because of their green binding: see Indici 150, 151.

7.2.5   VI Originally 174 vv. of notes on the history of Roman churches by 17th century antiquarians. They are now for the most part in the Vatican Library.

7.2.6   VII Originally 139 vv. (now about 110) of visitations of various parts of the papal states, Roman colleges and churches. They are mostly records of the S. Congregation of Visitation in the time of Alexander VII (1655-1667).

7.2.7   VIII Originally 102 vv. (now 68) of records of the *Congregatio Status Regularium* in the pontificate of Alexander VII, etc.

7.2.8   IX About 100 vv. from the *Congregatio Immunitatis*, 1633 — c. 1750.

7.2.9   X Originally 203 vv., now about 60, of material from the Holy Office, the Congregation of Rites and the Congregation of the Council.

7.2.10   XI Originally 274 vv., now about 50, concerning Conclaves, 1447-c.1780.

7.2.11   XII Originally 222 vv. of diaries, etc., now mostly in the Vatican Library, and of Consistorial records, now for the most part in *Fondo Concistoriale*.

7.2.12   XIII Originally 158 vv. of diaries (beginning 1405), records of ceremonies, etc., including the great diaries of P. de Grassis; mostly in Vatican Library now. See F. Combaluzier, 'Sacres épiscopaux à Rome de 1565 à 1662. Analyse intégrale du Ms. "Miscellanea XIII, 33" des Archives Vaticanes', in *Sacris Erudiri* 18 (1967-1968) 120-305.

7.2.13   XIV Originally 5 vv.; now empty.

7.2.14   XV About 215 vv. Besides records of conclaves, etc., there are reports of journeys and legations of various cardinals, e.g. that of Pole in England in 1553 (v. 26).

III. SECRETARIATE OF STATE: GENERAL CORRESPONDENCE

Indice 134; Indici 1013-1022, Indice 1071 (covering those parts of Indice 134 not included in Indici 1013-1022); Fink 94-97.

Distinctions between the following divisions are not watertight:

a. *Lettere di Cardinali* (*SS. Card.*)   209 vv.   1523-1803.   3.2.14.71

Indice 134, 173r-177v; Indici 1013-1014, 1071; BAV I.718-721, II. 674-676, III.810-812, IV.716.

b. *Lettere di Vescovi* (*SS. Vescovi*)   533 vv.   1500-1791.   3.2.14.75

Indice 134, 178r-186v; Indici 1015-1016, 1071; HVD 232-234; BAV I.832-839, II.755-759, III.902-906, IV.829-832.

c. *Lettere di Principi* (*SS. Principi*)   291 vv.   1515-1815.   3.2.14.73

Indice 134, 187r-194v; Indici 1017-1018, 1071; HVD 141-144; BAV I.783-796, II.725-731, III.874-882, IV.785-797.

d. *Lettere di Particolari* (*SS. Particolari*)   421 vv.   1518-1809.   3.2.14.72

Indice 134, 195r-201v; Indici 1019-1021, 1071; HVD 139-140; BAV I.772-778; II.715-722, III.864-869, IV.775-776.

e. *Lettere di Soldati* (*SS. Soldati*)   88 vv.   1572-1755.   3.2.14.74

Indice 134, 203r-205v; Indice 1022; BAV I.801, II.736, II.885.

IV. ARCHIVES OF CARDINAL-NEPHEWS
AND OF FORMER PAPAL FAMILIES

a. *Carte Farnesiane* (ASV c.1890)   21 vv.   1475-1580.   7.5.34.1

Indice 1067; S. Ehses, 'Die Carte Farnesiane des Vatikanischen Archivs', in *Römische Quartalschrift* 28 (1914) 41-47; HVD 67-68; BAV I. 282, II.274, III.293, IV.276.

The *Carte* contain material from the pontificate of Paul III (Alessandro Farnese, 1534-1549), some of which is important for the early stages of the Council of Trent. Quantities of documents relative to Paul's pontificate are also to be found in Farnese holdings at Parma and Naples: see G. Drei, *Gli archivi Farnesiani, loro formazione e vicende* (Parma 1930), *L'Archivio di Stato di Parma: Indice generale storico descrittivo ed analitico* (Bibliothèque des Annales Institutorum VI, Rome-Paris 1941).

7.5.13.1 **b.** *Fondo Borghese* (ASV 1891) c. 2000 vv. 1485-1621.

Indice 193 ("Indice dell'Archivio Borghese donato all'Archivio Vaticano dall'Istituto storico Prussiano"); Fink 100-101; HVD 43-60; BAV I.307-321, II.312-350, III.321-349, IV.303-328.

This great collection of Secretariate of State material covers the pontificates of Clement VIII (Ippolito Aldobrandini, 1592-1605) and Paul V (Camillo Borghese, 1605-1621), and is divided into four series. It should be noted that in series I, nn. 1-199 precede 1592 (e.g. n. 114 contains a copy of letters of Gregory VII); and that in nn. 880, 888, 890 (second series), there are items from 1485-1512. The collection has been used extensively for local post-Tridentine history, e.g., A. Pasture, 'Archives du Vatican: Inventaire du fonds Borghèse au point de vue de l'histoire des Pays-Bas', in *Bulletin de la commission royale d'histoire* (Brussels 1910), pp. 1-217; J. Hagan, 'Some papers relative to the Nine Years War', in *Archivium Hibernicum* 2 (1913) 274-320, etc.; and D. Conway, 'Guide to Documents of Irish and British interest in Fondo Borghese', *ibid.*, 23 (1960) 1-147 (series I), 24 (1961) 31-102 (series II-IV).

7.5.3.1 **c.** *Fondo Barberini* (Vatican Library 1902) 3250 vv. 1300-1650.

These 3250 vv. form part (nn. 6559-9808) of the Barberini collection of manuscripts in the Vatican Library and are cited by the serial number of that collection, e.g. MS. Barb. lat. 6559. An inventory of the 3250 vv. is likewise to be found in the general MS. catalogue of the Barberini MSS in the Index Room of the Sala dei Manoscritti at nn. 363-375 ("Carteggi diplomatici"); n. 370 of this catalogue covers the British Isles.

Basically the Fondo Barberini consists of Secretariate of State material from the pontificate of Urban VIII (Maffeo Barberini, 1623-1644), but it is far from being confined to these dates. See A. Pasture, 'Inventaire de la bibliothèque Barberini à la bibliothèque Vaticane au point de vue de l'histoire des Pays-Bas', in *Bulletin de l'Institut historique Belge de Rome* 3 (1924) 43-157; C. Giblin, 'Vatican Library: MSS Barberini latini', in *Archivium Hibernicum* 18 (1955) 67-144; HVD 30-42.

7.5.23.1 **d.** *Fondo Chigi* (Vatican Library 1923) 3916 vv. c.1600-1700.

Indici 186, 189-190 of Sala dei Manoscritti; Fink 102; HVD 68-72. These volumes contain much Secretariate of State material from the pontificate of Alexander VII (Fabio Chigi, 1655-1667).

e. *Fondo Albani* (ASV 1751)   265 vv. c.1700-1721   7.5.25.1

Indici 143-144 of ASV; *Sussidi* I, p. 23, n. 2; Fink 125; BAV I, 298-304, II.308-311, III.318-320, IV.301-302.

This Fondo (formerly called *Bibliotheca Albani* and *Miscellanea Clementis XI*) contains materials towards a history of the pontificate of Clement XI (Gianfranco Albani, 1700-1721), put together at his order. While not, strictly speaking, a Secretariate of State collection, there is enough cognate material in it to justify its inclusion here. In Indice 143, 27r-41v, there are six volumes noted as containing information relative to the British Isles. See C. Giblin, 'Miscellaneous Papers', in *Archivium Hibernicum* 16 (1951) 66-73, and 'Material relative to Ireland in the Albani Collection', in *Irish Ecclesiastical Record*, 5th series, 102 (1964) 389-396.

V. NUNCIATURES AND LEGATIONS

From the earliest times popes were represented in councils and other important affairs by legates. Generally these legates were chosen from the Roman clergy, or, at a later date, from Italian bishops directly dependent on the papacy. These "legations" took on greater importance when, from the 11th century onwards, they were entrusted to Cardinals ("de latere"). In special cases, or for minor matters, bishops were delegated and were known not as *legati* but as *nuntii*. In the 14th century *nuntii* became more common than *legati*, and in the 16th century permanent nunciatures were established in many kingdoms, republics and independent principalities. The first permanent nunciature was set up by Leo X at Vienna in 1513 (it was re-established in 1591); Lucerne dates from 1579, Cologne from 1582, Brussels from 1597, and these were followed early in the 17th century by nunciatures at Paris, Madrid, Lisbon, etc. See P. Richard, 'Origines des nonciatures permanentes: la représentation pontificale au xve siècle, 1450-1513', in *Revue d'histoire ecclésiastique* 7 (1906) 52-70, 317-338. Lists of all nunciatures and nuncios from the beginnings of the nunciature system until the present day are to be found in three invaluable volumes: H. Biaudet, *Les nonciatures apostoliques permanentes jusqu'en 1648* (Helsinki 1910), L. Karttunen, *Les nonciatures apostoliques permanentes de 1650 à 1800* (Geneva 1912), G. de Marchi, *Le nunziature apostoliche dal 1800 al 1956* (Rome 1957).

Early nuncios had powers similar to those exercised by *legati de latere*, but the Council of Trent (session 24, c. 20) placed restrictions on these powers, especially in relation to local bishops.

After Gregory XIII had strengthened the system of papal diplomacy in 1584, giving it an organic structure and a set of clear-cut regulations, nuncios were chiefly concerned with preserving relations between various states or missionary areas and the papacy. They also acted as supervisors in behalf of the Congregation of the Council, thus promoting the reforms of the Council of Trent. Further they represented the pope in certain circumstances, handled current political affairs, and exercised judicial authority with respect to appeals of an ordinary nature.

Naturally, the existence of nunciatures occasioned a flow of correspondence between the Secretariate of State and the various nuncios. Hence the nunciature holdings of the ASV fall into two classes: *Nunziature e Legazioni*, or holdings from the Secretariate of State itself; *Archivio delle Nunziature*, or holdings which have reached the ASV from the nunciatures.

3.2.14.106   **a. Nunziature e Legazioni,** being the Secretariate of State side of correspondence to and from the nuncios (who were expected to write at least once a week). Note that each nunciature or legation is cited *either* as *SS.* and place or name (e.g. *SS. Colonia; SS. Bologna*) as the BAV does, *or* as *Nunz.* and place (e.g. *Nunz. Colonia; Nunz. Bologna*), as Halkin (1968) and others do.

Indice 134; Indici 1024-1028, 1071; Katterbach EI 89; Fink 82-92; HVD 99-128; L.-E. Halkin, 'Les Archives des Nonciatures'. Rapport au Comité Directeur de l'Institut historique Belge de Rome', in *Bulletin de l'Institut historique Belge de Rome* 33 (1961) 649-700, now published in an enlarged form as *Les Archives des Nonciatures* (Brussels-Rome 1968); BAV I.117.

	Nunziatura di	*vv.*	*dates*	*Indice and ff.*		*BAV*
3.2.14.88	Baviera	49	1786-1808	1071,	3-5	II. 673, III.810.
3.2.14.89	Colonia	339	1575-1797	1027,	117-157	I.721-727, II.676-680, III.818-818, IV.716-725.
3.2.14.90	Corsica	11	1655-1801	1024,	33-34	III.818-819.
3.2.14.91	Fiandra	207	1552-1800	1026,	5-27	I.728-736, II.680-683, III.820-828, IV.726-738.
3.2.14.92	Firenze	271	1532-1809	1024,	1-25	I.736-737, II.683-685, III.828-829, IV.738-740.
3.2.14.93	Francia	727	1517-1826	1025,	1-70	I.737-750, II.685-699, III.829-846, IV.740-758.
3.2.14.94	Genova	21	1463-1808	1024,	31-32	III.846-847.
3.2.14.95	Germania	787	1515-1809	1027,	1-113	I.750-757, II.699-706, III.847-854, IV.758-767.
3.2.14.96	Inghilterra	32	1555-1856	1071,	1-2	I.757-758, II.706, III.854, IV.767.
3.2.14.62	Malta (Inq. di)	186	1432-1797	1024,	39-55	I.758-768, III.854, IV.767-770.
3.2.14.97	Napoli	646	1191-1808	1024,	61-120	I.768, II.707-714, III.855-862, IV.770-772.
3.2.14.107	Paci	71	1628-1716	1026,	33-39	I.768-771, II.714, III.862, IV.772.

Nunziatura di	vv.	dates	Indice and ff.		BAV	
Polonia	396	1541-1810	134,		I.778-781, II.722-724, III.869-871, IV.776-784.	3.2.14.98
Polonia-Russia	30	1793-1806	134,			3.2.14.99
Portogallo	245	1535-1851	1025,	77-98	I.781-783, II.724-725, III.871-874, IV.784.	3.2.14.100
Savoia	349	1560-1803	1024,	125-155	I.796-801, II.731-736, III.883-885, IV.797-804.	3.2.14.101
Spagna	491	1524-1808	1025,	103-105	I.801-816, II.736-749, III.886-897, IV.804-823.	3.2.14.102
Svizzera	327	1532-1815	1028.		I.816-818, II.749-752, III.897, IV.823-825.	3.2.14.103
Venezia	420	1524-1807	1024,	161-204	I.818-823, II.752-755, III.892-902, IV.825-829.	3.2.14.105
Nunz. diverse	308	1462-1807	1026,	45-81	I.771, II.714, III.862-864, IV.772-775.	3.2.14.105
(Legazione di)						
Avignone	381	1231-1792	1023,	1-36	I.716, II.668, III.809, IV.710.	3.2.14.65
Bologna	395	1450-1796	1023,	41-72	I.716, II.674, III.810, IV.712.	3.2.14.66
Ferrara	408	1597-1797	1023,	77-105	I.727, II.680, III.819, IV.725.	3.2.14.67
Romagna	197	1524-1797	1023,	110-124	III.882, IV.797.	
Urbino	223	1624-1798	1023,	130-143	II.752, III.898.	3.2.14.69
Ubaldini (Arch.)	49	1187-1752	1023,	148-151		7.5.78.1

Note that the *Nunziature diverse* (cited as *SS. Nunz. diverse*) contain material relative to most of the nunciatures given above (and to *Nimega*), as well as sets of Istruzioni, Lettere varie, Relazioni. Note also that the *Archivio Ubaldini* (cited as *SS. Arch. Ubaldini*), while strictly speaking a family archives, is a source for the Urbino legation.

b. Archivio delle Nunziature, being the local archives of each nunciature, including the nunciature side of correspondence between the Secretariate of State and the nuncios. These holdings are cited *either* as *Archivio della Nunziatura di...*, as the BAV does (hence *SS. Colonia* for the Nunciature of Cologne, but *Archivio della Nunziatura di Colonia* for the Cologne archives), *or*, as Halkin and others do, as *Arch. Nunz.* and place (hence *Nunz. Colonia* for the Nunciature, but *Arch. Nunz. Colonia* for the archives).

The archives of the Venice nunciature (see also p. 61, above: *Cancellaria della Nunziatura Veneta*) came to the ASV in 1835, those of Vienna in 1921, the remainder in 1927-1928, etc. See Indici 1081-1086; Fink 92-94; HVD 18-19; Halkin, *Les Archives des Nonciatures* (Brussels-Rome 1968), BAV I. 117.

	Archivio della Nunz. di	vv.	dates	Indice	BAV
4.9.1	Bruxelles	75	1835-1904	1081	III.118-119
4.20.1	Colonia	318	1500-1796	1081	II.93-94, III.119, IV.98-99.
4.96.1	Firenze	425	1590-1859	1084	II.94-95
4.70.1	L'Aja (The Hague)	20	1802-1846	1081	I.95
4.79.1	Lisbona	427	1580-1910		III.119
4.92.1	Lucerna	451	1606-1873	1070	II.95, II.120, IV.99
4.90.1	Madrid	484	1623-1912	1090	II.95-96, II.120, IV.99-100
4.8.1	Monaco di Baviera	241	1818-1907		III.120
4.69.1	Napoli	410	1818-1860	1085	III.121
4.37.1	Parigi	82	1819-1850	1086	II.96, III.121-122
4.84.1	Torino	220	18th-19th		
4.78.1	Varsavia	189	1658-1795		I.117, II.96, III.122, IV.100
4.100.3	Venezia	90	1226-1795	1024, f. 209	II.97
4.6.1	Vienna	555	1607-1860	1055	I.118, II.98-100, III.123-125.

VI. Modern Secretariate of State Holdings

All these holdings are cited as SS. and title. In general see L. Pásztor, 'Per la storia della Segretaria di Stato nell'Ottocento. La riforma del 1816', in *Mélanges E. Tisserant* V (Vatican City 1964), pp. 200-250, 'La Segretaria di Stato di Pio IX durante il triennio 1848-1850', in *Annali della Fondazione Italiana per la storia amministrativa* 3 (1966) 308-365.

3.2.14.19	a. *Avvisi*: 159 vv. Indice 1026, 87-128; BAV I.716, II.668-673, III.809, IV.711.
3.2.14.116 & 117	b. *Biglietti, Dispacci e Lettere*: 103 nn., 1800-1824.
3.2.14.31	c. *Brevi apostolici*: about 3300 items (including 2197 registers) which reached the ASV in 1968 (*L'Attività della S. Sede nel 1968*, p. 1438).
	d. *Buste separate*: BAV IV. 713-716.
3.2.14.118	e. *Coadiutorie, Commende*, etc.: 58 vv., 1775-1830.
	f. *Commissione di Vigilanza*: 50 bundles relative to police of Papal States (19th c.).
3.2.14.49	g. *Emigrati rivoluzione francese*: 53 vv., 1792-1802. Indice 1026; A. Theiner, *Documents inédits relatifs aux affaires religieuses de la France, 1790-1800* (Paris 1858); BAV I.727, IV.725.
3.2.14.30 & 52	h. *Epoca Napoleonica*: E. Audard, 'L'histoire religieuse de la Révolution française aux Archives Vaticanes', in *Revue d'histoire de l'Église de France* 4 (1913) 516-535, 625-639; J. Leflon and A. Latreille, 'Répertoire des fonds napoléoniens aux Archives Vaticanes', in *Revue historique* 203 (1950) 59-63; BAV I.727.

i. *Fondo Moderno* (1814-1886): Cited as *SS.*, title, year, fascicule, thus: *SS. Int.* 1816, f. 9. Fink 105-113: BAV I.829-830, II.759, III.906, IV.832. 3.2.14.98

i. *Interni*	1005 fasc.	1814-1833	Indice 1031	3.2.14.63
ii. *Esteri*	666 fasc.	1814-1850	Indice 1032	3.2.14.56
iii. *Int.-Est.*		1816-1822	Indice 1033	3.2.14.64
iv. *Esteri*	850 fasc.	1851-1913	Indice 1089	3.2.14.57

j. *Memoriali e Biglietti*: 316 vv. Indice 1026; BAV III.855. 3.2.14.79

k. *Rubricellae*: 1816-1860. Indici 1034, 1035. 3.2.14.120

l. *Protocolli*: 1816-1851. Indice 1034; BAV III.882. 3.2.14.115

m. *Spogli Sala*: BAV III.897.

J. ARCHIVES OF THE CONSISTORY (1625; ASV 1907)

The College of Cardinals goes back in origin to the 11th century, and by the 12th and 13th centuries it occupied the central position in the papal curia: see J. B. Sägmüller, *Die Thätigkeit und Stellung der Cardinäle bis Bonifaz VIII.* (Freiburg im Breisgau 1896); H.-W. Klewitz, 'Die Entstehung des Kardinalskollegiums', in *Zeitschrift der Savigny-Stiftung für Rechtsgeschichte, kan. Abt.* 25 (1936) 115-221; S. Kuttner, 'Cardinalis. The History of a Canonical Concept', in *Traditio* 3 (1945) 129-214; C. G. Fürst, *Cardinalis. Prolegomena zu einer Rechtsgeschichte des römischen Kardinalskollegiums* (Munich 1967); G. Alberigo, *Cardinalato e Collegialità* (Florence 1969). When called together by the Pope, the cardinals formed with him a *Consistorium* or deliberative assembly that was the principal consultative body upon which the Pope depended, and was, in fact, the supreme tribunal of the church. By a constitution of 27 October 1340 (M. Tangl, *Die päpstlichen Kanzleiordnungen von 1200-1500*, Innsbruck 1894, pp. 118-124), the role of the Consistory was defined by Benedict XII as "querelae denuntiatio, accusatio et aliae iurgantium causae". The Consistory had its own court and its own advocates for important cases; less important cases were delegated by mandate to local judges, generally three. Among other things, the Consistory also concerned itself with provisions to benefices that were vacant by the death of bishops in, or on the way to or from, the Roman curia.

In spite of efforts of Leo X (1513-1521) and Paul III (1546), it was only in the pontificate of Urban VIII that a special Archives of the College of Cardinals was formed. A commission instituted by Urban decided on 18 August 1625 that all consistorial acts, *libri propositionum*, informative processes, and all other documents relating to the College, were to be placed in special archives in the Vatican. These archives were officially constituted by Urban on 15 December 1625, when he ordered that all acts, processes, decrees, and any documents in any way pertaining to the College, were to be put together from all curial departments and deposited in the *Archivum sacri collegii cardinalium* (see *Enchiridion archivorum ecclesiasticorum*, Vatican City 1966, pp. 47-58).

During the transfer of the Vatican Archives to Paris under Napoleon, the *Archivum sacri collegii* suffered much damage and lost its unity. On the return of the Archives to Rome in 1817, the *Archivum* was first housed in the courtyard of S. Damaso in the Vatican. In 1907 it was placed in the ASV, and together with the *Archivio del Sostituto* (ASV 1906) went to form the *Fondo Concistoriale* and the *Materiale Concistoriale*. As a result, the collection which today goes by the name *Archivio del Collegio dei Cardinali* (see p. 83) bears little relation to the original *Archivum sacri collegii* (see R. Ritzler, 'Per la storia dell'Archivio del Sacro Collegio', in *Mélanges E. Tisserant* V [Vatican City 1964], pp. 300-338).

In the following schema (which attempts to put Ritzler's conclusions into practice) the ASV holdings from the original *Archivum sacri collegii* are kept together as far as possible under the heading *Fondo (Archivio) Concistoriale*. It should be noted, moreover, that the holdings of this *Fondo Concistoriale* are not to be confused with the archives of the *Congregatio Consistorialis* (pp. 86-87), a Congregation that was set up in 1588 to prepare material for meetings of the Consistory proper.

All the following sections are cited as *Fondo Concistoriale* (or simply *Concistoriale*) and title of section, e.g. *Fondo Concistoriale, Acta Miscellanea* 5.

I. FONDO (ARCHIVIO) CONCISTORIALE   3.1.3.19

a. *Acta Camerarii*   61 vv.   1489-1866.   3.1.3.1

Sussidi I, 204-206 (list of volumes); R. Ritzler, 'Die archivalischen Quellen der *Hierarchia Catholica*', in *Miscellanea Archivistica A. Mercati* (Vatican City 1952), pp. 61-64, 'Per la storia dell'Archivio del Sacro Collegio', in *Mélanges E. Tisserant V* (Vatican City 1964), at pp. 320-321; BAV I.323-328, II.351-359, III.351-361, IV.330-336.

The *Acta*, which belonged originally to the *Archivum sacri collegii* set up by Urban VIII in 1625, contain official notes of questions treated in secret, public or semi-public meetings of the Consistory, and in "general" or "particular" assemblies. Volumes 1-48 run from 1489-1600, and vv. 49-61 from 1800-1866. Each volume possesses good though not exhaustive alphabetical indexes. Thus, although the index at ff. 1-21 of *Acta* I (the title of which is "Liber provisionum ecclesiarum et monasteriorum consistorialium inceptus die prima ianuarii MCCCCLXXXIX") reveals at a glance that there are the following Irish items, *Achaden.*, ff. 2, 39, *Aladen.*, f. 86, *Corkagen.*, ff. 9, 73, 76, etc., there are in fact many more Irish entries in the volume than the index would suggest. Brady (*Episcopal Succession*, Rome 1876) has made good use for the British Isles of this series (which in his day was in the Cortile di S. Damaso of the Vatican), and of Consistorial Acts in the Barberini (81 vv.: 1492-1565) and Corsini (15 vv.: 1498-1673) libraries (see his list of sources in v. II, pp. 251-256). However, a comparison of *Acta Camerarii* I with Brady gives the impression that further research into the *Acta* (at least on the part of British and Irish scholars) might not be a waste of time. Thus, to take one example, he has omitted the provision (f. 110v: 21.8.1500) of Franciscus Ioannis to Glendalough, vacant by death of bishop Ivo (hence, possibly, a confused entry in the *Handbook of British Chronology*, London 1961², p. 338, where it is stated that John O.F.M. was provided to Glendalough on 21 August 1495 on the death of Ivo, and that Francis (of Corduba) was "prov. 1500").

3.1.3.6   **b.** *Acta Vicecancellarii*   18 vv.   1492-1632.

    Sussidi I, 206-207; Ritzler, 'Per la storia', p. 321; BAV I.333, II.362, III.365-368, IV.339-341. The *Acta* belonged originally to *Archivum S. Collegii.*

3.1.3.4   **c.** *Acta Miscellanea*   100 vv.   1409-1809.

    Sussidi I, 207-213 (list); HVD 76-77; Ritzler, 'Per la storia', p. 321; BAV I.329-333, II.360-362, II.361-365, IV.336-339.

The *Acta* principally are extracts from, or copies of, *Acta Camerarii* and *Acta Vicecancellarii*, but there are also some minutes of consistorial acts. Volumes 1-12 cover 1406-1572. Apart from information on provisions, the *Acta Misc.* sometimes serve as a diary of the curia. Thus *Acta Misc.* I (1409-1434) is valuable for papal itineraries, lists of cardinals, etc. (e.g. f. 28v: John XXIII leaves Bologna on 31 March 1411 and arrives in Rome on Friday, 11 April). This and other volumes have been used effectively by Brady, *Episcopal Succession*; D. S. Chambers, *Cardinal Bainbridge at the Court of Rome, 1509-1514* (Oxford 1965), uses vv. 6, 54, 70. The *Acta* belonged originally to the *Archivum S. Collegii.*

3.1.3.16   **d.** *Consistoria* (*Archivio del Sostituto*)   230 vv.   1498-1896.

    Ritzler, 'Per la storia', pp. 321-322; L. Pásztor, 'Il Sostituto del Concistoro e il suo archivio', in *Archivum Historiae Pontificiae* 5 (1967) 355-372.

These volumes, which originally belonged to the Archivio del Sostituto del Concistoro and reached the ASV c. 1904, contain propositions, allocutions, decrees of the Consistorial Congregation and of the Congregation *De Propaganda Fide*. They were used for the first time by Ritzler and Sefrin in v. V of the *Hierarchia Catholica* (Padua 1952). The first general study of the holding is that of L. Pásztor, from whom I take the following summary:

1. *Libretti del Papa*	76 vv.	1740-1896.	3.1.3.16
2. *Atti*: a. *Copie*	12	1498-1644.	⎰ 3.1.3.16
		1517-1628.	⎱ 3.1.3.3
		1657-1668.	
b. *Serie regolare*	219	1644-1892.	3.1.3.16

3. *Varia* (correspondence; bulls; briefs, etc.).

e. *Cedularum et Rotulorum*   66 vv.   1504-1879.   3.1.3.13

Fink 64; Ritzler, 'Per la storia', p. 322. The series, which was once part of the *Archivum S. Collegii*, is mainly made up of registers of distribution of payments to Cardinals, and of the expenses of the Sacred College.

f. *Processus consistoriales*   299 vv.   1563-1906.   3.1.3.29

Indice 1045 (inventory); Fink 62-63; R. Ritzler, 'Die bischöflichen Informativprozesse in den "Processus Consistoriales" im Archiv des Kardinalskollegs bis 1907', in *Römische historische Mitteilungen* 2 (1957-1958) 204-220; BAV I.334-337, II.363-372, III.368-377, IV.341-342.

Basically this series contains *original records* of all informative processes conducted *outside* the Roman curia with respect to the provision of bishops. But it also contains *copies* of all informative processes conducted *within* the curia itself (the original records of which are to be found in the *Processus Datariae*, above, p. 54). When Urban set up the *Archivum S. Collegii* in 1625, he ordered that such copies of Datary processes should be made for and lodged in the *Archivum*.

II. Archivio del Collegio dei Cardinali

a. *Conclavi*   c. 160 vv.   1458-1846.   1.5

Katterbach EI 88; Fink 66.

b. *Spogli*   c. 250 vv.   16th-19th c.   7.10

Fink 66. The collection contains bequests, etc., of some 95 curial cardinals.

K. ARCHIVES OF CONGREGATIONS

In the 16th century special commissions (*Congregationes*) of Cardinals were set up to handle certain administrative affairs, thus lessening the load on the Apostolic Chancery. The first commission of a permanent character was that of the Holy Office or Sacred Congregation of the Inquisition (1542). This was followed by the Congregation of the Council (1564) and Congregations such as that of the Index of Prohibited Books (1571). In 1587 Sixtus V reorganized the existing Congregations and introduced some new ones, e.g. the Consistorial Congregation, bringing the number up to 15. Other popes later added to this number, notably Gregory XV when he instituted the Congregation *De Propaganda Fide* in 1622; but substantially the form given to the Congregations by Sixtus V remained intact until 1908, when Pius X suppressed some and refurbished others. Recently, in the wake of the reforms of the Second Vatican Council, some of the Congregations have been re-named (e.g. the Holy Office which, since 1965, bears the title *S. Congregatio pro doctrina fidei*) or have had their scope re-defined (see the Apostolic Constitution, *De Romana Curia*, of Paul VI of 15 August 1967: *Acta Apostolicae Sedis* 60 [1967] 885-928).

It may be useful here to note that much material relative to areas proper to the Congregations will be found among Secretariate of State holdings in the ASV. This is because the Secretariate acted as an intermediary between the Pope and the Congregations, and between the Congregations and the Nunciatures. Diplomatic agents, for example, rarely communicated directly with the Congregations, but rather with the Secretariate, which acted as a sort of clearing-house. And it was the Secretariate of State and not the relevant Congregation that transmitted to the Nunciatures the various decisions taken in Consistory, any nominations to benefices, resolutions of cases of conscience, dispensations, graces and favours, etc. In general see N. del Re, *La curia romana: lineamenti storico-giuridici* (Rome 1952²). A good survey of the history and character of the Congregations, and of literature treating of them, is in A. M. Stickler, *Historia iuris canonici latini: Institutiones academicae* I (Turin 1950), pp. 318-337.

I. Archives of Extant Congregations

a. *Sacra Congregatio Romanae et Universalis Inquisitionis* (1542).

The roots of this Congregation of the "Holy Office" are to be found in the repressive measures against heretics adopted by the Church at the end of the 12th and the beginning of the 13th century. Innocent III (1198-1216) set up an inquisitory tribunal at Viterbo and Orvieto, and later popes delegated judges elsewhere to exercise inquisitorial jurisdiction (see, e.g., F. Bock, 'Studien zum politischen Inquisitionsprozess Johanns XXII', in *Quellen und Forschungen* 26 [1935-1936] 20-112, 27 [1936-1937] 108-134). These various tribunals and judges-delegate were never knit together, however, to form a permanent, organized papal institution or department. It was only with Paul III (bull of 21 July 1542) that a permanent Roman Congregation and Tribunal of Inquisition was set up, with powers to defend and to maintain the integrity of the faith, and to examine and proscribe errors and false teaching. See A. Mercati, *Il Sommario del processo di Giordano Bruno, con appendice sull'eresia e l'Inquisizione a Modena nel secolo XVI* (Studi e Testi 101, Vatican City 1942); del Re, *La curia romana*, pp. 39-47; Stickler, *Historia*, pp. 329-347.

The Archives of the Holy Office are not in the ASV, but are in the Palazzo del S. Uffizio, Piazza S. Offizio 11, Rome. They are not open to consultation. Some parts of the Archives were lost during the transfer of the papal archives to Paris in the Napoleonic era, and a part of the *Processus* series was deliberately destroyed by the papal commissioners before the return of the papal archives to Rome in 1817. The present Archives of the Holy Office, so far as is known, contain about 7000 volumes. Some 54 volumes, probably from among those dispersed in or on the way to Paris, have been in Trinity College, Dublin, since 1854, together with volumes of the Lateran Registers (see Part Two: *Lateran Registers*). These volumes at Dublin have been noted by C. Corvisieri, 'Compendio dei processi del Santo Uffizio di Roma da Paolo III a Paolo IV', in *Archivio della Società Romana di Storia Patria* 3 (1879) 261-290, 449-471, at pp. 264-265 and footnotes; and the volumes are listed in T. K. Abbott, *Catalogue of Manuscripts in the Library of Trinity College, Dublin* (Dublin-London 1900), pp. 243-284:

i. *Catalogue*, nn. 1224-1242: 19 vv. of sentences, 1564-1659.
ii. *Catalogue*, nn. 1243-1277: 35 vv. of proceedings of Inquisition Courts in Italy, 1570-1660. The larger part of this

group of volumes concerns processes between 1625 and 1660 at Ancona, Civitavecchia, Faenza, Genoa, Malta, Mantua, Naples, Perugia, Pisa, Rome, Siena, Spoleto and Velletri.

Microfilm copies of these volumes in Trinity College were presented to the ASV on 20 May 1953 (see *L'Attività della S. Sede nel 1953*, Vatican City 1954, p. 334).

3.1.2　**b.** *Sacra Congregatio Concilii Tridentini* (1564, 1588; ASV 1926).

Stickler, *Historia* 320-322; del Re 65-74; Fink 119-120; HVD 78-79. A corpus of the decisions of the Congregation from 1718-1908 is in the 167 vv. of the *Thesaurus Resolutionum S. Congregationis Concilii* (Urbino-Rome 1739-1908).

Instituted by Pius IV in 1564 with the title of "Sacred Congregation of the Cardinal Interpreters of the Council of Trent", it was designed to watch over the interpretation and practical observance of the decrees of the Council of Trent. Later, Sixtus V entrusted to it the revision of acts of provincial councils, and the control of *ad limina* visits, reports of dioceses, decrees of local synods, etc. Today the Congregation is known as *Sacra Congregatio pro Clericis* (see the Constitution *De romana curia*, 1967, nn. 65-70), and has retained competence over many matters which were the objects of the reforms of the Council of Trent, particularly in respect of the diocesan clergy.

Since 1926 most of the old archives have been transferred to the ASV. At present these holdings are cited as *Congregazione del Concilio* (followed by title of section):

3.1.2.5　　i. *Libri decretorum,* 1573-1914: BAV I.289, III.300, IV.286.
3.1.2.6　　ii. *Libri litterarum,* 1564-1903: BAV III.301-303.
3.1.2.7　　iii. *Libri visitationum,* 1590-1880: BAV III.303.
3.1.2.19　　iv. *Relationes diocesium,* 1590-1908: c. 400 vv.: HVD 199-204; BAV I.290, II.284-290, III.303-310, IV.287-288.
3.1.2.2　　v. *Synodus provinciales,* 1590-1908: c. 100 vv.: BAV III.310.
3.1.2.23　　vi. *Visitationes apostolicae,* 1562-1803: c. 105 vv.: BAV I.291, II.290.

3.1.3　**c.** *Sacra Congregatio Consistorialis* (1588; ASV 1907).

The Consistorial Congregation was instituted by Sixtus V in 1588. Its chief function was to prepare, and to discuss in a preliminary way, certain matters which would later be debated and decided upon in the Consistory, e.g. the erection or division of dioceses, provisions to those dioceses and abbacies which were the province of the Consistory (see J. above: *Archives of the Consistory*).

When Pius X suppressed the Congregation of Bishops and Regulars in 1908, the competence which that Congregation had exercised in respect of bishops in general was handed over to the Consistorial Congregation; consequently, in the recent reform of the Roman curia the name has been changed from Consistorial Congregation to *Sacra Congregatio pro Episcopis* (Constitution *De romana curia*, 1967, nn. 46-53).

In general see Stickler, *Historia*, 331-332; Fink 61-65; and in particular, T. Vanyo, 'Das Archiv der Konsistorialkongregation', in *Festschrift Leo Santifaller* I (Mitteilungen des österreichischen Staatsarchiv, Vienna 1950), pp. 151-179.

i. *Acta Congregationis Consistorialis*   c. 368 vv.   1584-1908.   3.1.3.2

Katterbach EI 88; *Sussidi* I, 213-214; HVD 15-16; Ritzler, 'Per la storia', 322; Vanyo; BAV I.291-294, II.290, III.310-311, IV.287-288.

These *Acta*, which originally were in the *Archivum S. Collegii* (see pp. 80-81), proceed year by year, and, within each year, by session. They are incomplete for the early years of the Congregation.

ii. *Congregationes Consistoriales*	20 vv.	1674-1852.	
iii. *Positiones*	17 vv.	1765-1839.	
iv. *Positiones Congreg. Em. Cap. Ordinum*	77 vv.	1656-1867.	3.1.3.26
v. *Praeconia et Propositiones*	36 vv.	1658-1907.	3.1.3.27
vi. *Iuramenta et Professiones*	24 vv.	1654-1904.	3.1.3.20

d. *S. Congregatio pro Sacris Ritibus et Caeremoniis* (1588; ASV 1927).   { 3.1.22
         { 3.1.27

Processus, Positiones, Decreta   4255 vv.   1588-1920.   3.1.27.1

Indice 1047 (inventory of *Processus* volumes); Stickler, *Historia* 334-336; del Re, *La curia*, 81-91; Fink 120-121; BAV I.294-297; II.294-295; III.311-313, IV.288-289.

This Congregation was set up in 1588 for liturgical discipline and the examination of all proposals for beatification and canonization. See P. Burchi, *Catalogus Processuum Beatificationis et Canonizationis qui in tabulariis et bibliothecis Urbis asservantur* (Rome 1965).

e. *S. Congregatio de Propaganda Fide* (1622).   3.1.6

Stickler, *Historia*, 323-328 (excellent bibliography and list of printed sources); B. Millett, 'The Archives of the Congregation *de Propaganda Fide*', in *Proceedings of the Irish Catholic Historical Committee 1956* (Dublin 1956), pp. 20-27; N. Kowalsky, *Inventario dell'Archivio storico della S. Congregazione "de Propaganda Fide"* (Les Cahiers de la Nouvelle Revue de science missionaire 17, Schöneck/Beckenried, Switzerland, 1961);

G. Metzler, 'Indici dell'Archivio storico della S. C. De Propaganda Fide', in *Euntes Docete* 21 (1968) 109-130.

The Archives of this Congregation in Palazzo della Propaganda, Piazza di Spagna, Rome, though not pertaining in any way to the ASV, are included here for the sake of completeness, and because they form the richest source in Rome for the religious history of the British Isles and other "missionary countries" from 1622 to the middle of the 19th century.

f. Other extant Congregations whose archives are in the ASV are

3.1.21   i. *Congregatio pro negotiis ecclesiasticis extraordinariis* (1814): Fink 113-115; L. Pásztor, 'La Congregazione degli Affari Ecclesiastici Straordinari tra il 1814 e il 1850', in *Archivum Historiae Pontificiae* 6 (1968) 191-318; BAV III.297-300, IV.282-284.

3.1.5   ii. *Congregatio de disciplina Sacramentorum* (1908; ASV 1938, but not ordinarily open to consultation).

II. Archives of Extinct Congregations

3.1.15   **a.** *S. Congregatio... Episcoporum et Regularium...* (1601; ASV 1886).

The Congregation *super consultationibus Episcoporum et aliorum Praelatorum* was founded by Pius V in 1572, and that *pro consultationibus Regularium* by Sixtus V in 1588. In 1601 the two were united by Clement VIII as *Congregatio negotiis et consultationibus Episcoporum et Regularium praeposita.* This arrangement continued for some three centuries, although subsidiary Congregations for Regulars were introduced from time to time (e.g. the *S. Congregatio super Statu Regularium* [1652-1698] for Italian regular clergy; this later became the *S.C. super Disciplina Regulari* [1695-1908], to which was added the *S. C. super Statu Regularium* in 1847). An index to ASV holdings of these subsidiary Congregations is in Indice 113 at ASV desk. In 1908, however, the two sections — Bishops and Regulars — were separated once more, bishops being placed under the Consistorial Congregation, and Regulars being given their own special *Congregatio de Religiosis* (presently called *C. pro Religiosis et Institutis Saecularibus:* Constitution *De curia romana*, 1967, nn. 71-74).

The powers of the original as well as of the joint Congregations were vast, extending to any and every aspect of the discipline of Religious Orders and the conduct of dioceses. Altogether there are over 7000 vv. from the archives of the Congregation in the ASV, running from 1573-1908. A handwritten inventory (indice 111) is kept at the ASV desk. See Katterbach EI 89; Stickler, *Historia*, 332-334; del Re, *La curia*, 131-135; Fink 117-118.

I owe the following summary of the ASV holdings to the kindness of Fr. Charles Burns of the staff of the ASV:

i. *Registra Episcoporum*	344 vv. 1573-1908	BAV III.314	3.1.15.25
ii. *Registra Regularium*	307 vv. 1599-1908	BAV I.297,	3.1.15.27
	II.296, IV.289		
iii. *Registra Monialium*	240 vv. 1646-1908	BAV II.296	3.1.15.26
iv. *Positiones Episcoporum*	c. 2200 vv. 1573-1908	BAV III.313	3.1.15.18
v. *Positiones Regularium*	c. 2000 vv. 1626-1908	BAV III.314	3.1.15.18,
vi. *Positiones Monialium*	c. 1500 vv. 1626-1908	BAV II.295	20, 21
vii. *Archivum Secretum*	c. 160 vv. 1727-1908		3.1.15.19
viii. *Rubricellae* (Ind. 116)	c. 250 vv. 1590-1908		3.1.15.32
ix. *Protocolli*	89 vv. 1839-1908		3.1.15.24

b. *S. Congregatio super Consultatione* (1585), or *Sacra Consulta.*   5.1.38

Causae criminales   c.   50 vv. 1585-1870   5.1.38.1

Fink 116-117; del Re, *La curia*, 168-170; A. Lodolini, *L'Archivio di Stato di Roma* (Rome 1960), pp. 112-116 (for the period 1814-1870). The full title was *Congregatio super consultatione negotiorum Status ecclesiastici.*

c. *S. Congregatio super negotiis Avenionis* (1692).   5.1.44

F. Benoît, 'Les archives de la Sacrée-Congrégation d'Avignon au Vatican', in *Mélanges de l'académie de Vaucluse* 23 (1923) 1-28; del Re, *La curia*, 187-189; Fink 118; BAV I.289. There are some 224 vv. for 1693-1790.

d. *Other extinct Congregations:*

   i. *Lauretana* (1698: for the administration of Loreto): c. 580   3.1.14.1
   vv. 1698-1910.

   ii. *Economica* (administration of Papal States): 150 vv., 1746-   5.1.72.1
   1900. BAV I.294, II.297, II.314.

   iii. *dei Confini*: c. 150 vv. 18-19c. BAV II.294.   5.1.53

   iv. *dell'Immunità della Chiesa*: BAV IV.288.   3.1.13

   v. *Visitationis Apostolicae*: (ASV 1943) 157 nn., 16-19 c.: BAV II.   3.1.41.1
   297.

L. ARCHIVES OF TRIBUNALS

Of the tribunals set up in the papal curia in the Middle Ages
— the *Rota* and the Penitentiary (13th century), the tribunals
of the Apostolic Camera and of the Auditor of the Camera (13th-
14th c.), and the *Signatura* (15th c.) — three still exist today:
the *Rota* and the *Signatura* for cases in the external forum;
the *Poenitentiaria* for those in the internal forum (see the Constitution *De curia romana*, 1967, nn. 104-113).

3.3.2

I. Sacra Romana Rota (ASV 1927)

The *Rota* (probably so called from the circular hall in which
the Tribunal used to meet) began as an extension of the Chancery.
Its chief officials were the Chancellor (later the Vice-Chancellor),
the Auditor of contradicted cases and the chaplains. These
chaplains (*Auditores causarum camerae domini papae*) had the duty
of preparing cases for presentation. Given power by Innocent
III (1198-1216) to pass sentence (see *Decretales Gregorii IX*, 2.1,
29), they became a permanent tribunal under Gregory X (1271-
1276). In 1332 (Constitution *Ratio iuris*) the tribunal was reorganized by John XXII, who also allotted the Auditores a
permanent residence. The number of the Auditores was set
at 12 by Sixtus IV (1471-1484).

The high point of the *Rota* was in the 15th and 16th centuries,
but its position was considerably diminished by the foundation of
the Congregations in the second half of the 16th century. It
died a natural death in 1870, only to be resurrected by Pius X
in his reform of the curia in 1908.

See F. E. Schneider, *Die römische Rota*, I (Paderborn 1914); E. Cerchiari, *Capellani Papae et Apostolicae Sedis Auditores causarum sacri palatii
apostolici seu Sacra romana Rota, ab origine ad diem usque 20 Septembris 1870:
Relatio historica-iuridica*, 4 vv. (Rome 1919-1921), especially v. III, pp.
viii-xxxv (archives); F. E. Schneider, 'Ueber den Ursprung und die
Bedeutung des Namens Rota als Bezeichnung für den obersten päpstlichen Gerichtshof', in *Römische Quartalschrift* 41 (1933) 29-43; A. M.
Stickler, *Historia iuris canonici latini* I (Turin 1950), pp. 338-344; C.
Lefebvre, 'Rote romaine', in *Dictionnaire de droit canonique*, VII (1960-
1961) 742-771; E. A. Fus, 'Rota, Roman', in *New Catholic Encyclopedia*
(New York 1967), XII, pp. 683-685; BAV I.839-840, II.790, IV.670.

The competence of the *Rota* extended, whether in cases of
first instance or of appeal, over a vast area, to the exception of
criminal cases and the like. Primarily it was concerned with
cases of beneficial law, but it also judged cases involving exemption, jurisdiction, betrothal, filiation, legitimation, patronage,
religious profession, nullity of matrimony, divorce, etc. Many
of the *Decisiones* of the *Rota* were put together from 1336 onwards,
the earliest collection being that of the Englishman Thomas
Fastolf (printed in *Decisiones Novae, Antiquae et Antiquiores*, Lyons
1555). For these collections and the various editions of them,
see A. Fliniaux, 'Contribution à l'histoire des sources de droit
canonique. Les anciennes collections des *Decisiones Rotae*', in
Revue historique de droit français et étranger, 4th series, 4 (1925) 61-
93, 382-410.

The *Rota* holdings of the Vatican Archives come to some 9000
vv. They begin with the pontificate of Martin V (1417-1431)
and continue, with some gaps, until 1870. During the First
Roman Republic (1799-1814) the archives of the *Rota* suffered
considerable losses, and these losses were increased during
the Second Republic (1849), when the *Rota* was the headquarters
of the Civil Guard. A part of the modern *Rota* archives (some
1000 vv., 1800-1870) is in the Archivio di Stato di Roma: see
A. Lodolini, *L'Archivio di Stato di Roma* (Rome 1960), pp. 110-
112. The following is a list of the main ASV holdings:

a. *Manualia*   1043 vv.   1461-1800.   3.3.29

Kehr (1900) 396-397; Kehr (1903) 532 (with important items from
John XXII and Martin V); N. Hilling, 'Die römische Rota und das
Bistum Hildesheim am Ausgang des Mittelalters (1464-1513)', in *Reformationsgeschichtliche Studien und Texte* 6 (1908) 6-27; Fink 122-124; H. Hoberg, 'Die Protokollbücher der Rotanotare von 1464-1517', in *Zeitschrift
der Savigny-Stiftung für Rechtsgeschichte, kan. Abt.* 39 (1953) 177-277, 'Die
"Admissiones" des Archivs der Rota', in *Archivalische Zeitschrift* 50-51
(1955) 391-408 (on *Rota* personnel, 1417-1681); D. S. Chambers, *Cardinal
Bainbridge in the Court of Rome, 1509-1514* (Oxford 1965), using *Man.*
27, 87, 92; BAV I.840, II.634, III.790, IV.670.

This section, *Manualia Actuum et Citationum*, is the earliest
extant part of the *Rota* archives. There is a useful inventory
in Indice 1057. The only volume that the present writer has
looked at (*Man.* 1) goes from 1461-1474, and is a fat volume of
896 folios. There are cases in it from all over Europe with respect to prebends, deaneries, chaplaincies, the census, fruits
of benefices, dowries, goods, marriage, with interesting asides
on free days and feasts in the *Rota*, and notices of deaths, etc. of

personnel; there are a number of protracted beneficial cases from Scotland (e.g. Glasgow, ff. 67r, 269v, 273r, 500r, 520v, 528v, 538v).

3.3.2.5   **b.** *Diaria*   187 vv.   1566-1870.

Indice 1073; BAV I.839-840, II.633-634, III.790-791, IV.670-671. Some excerpts from the *Diaria* are in Cerchiari, v. 3.

i. vv.	1-157	*Diaria privata*: 1566-1870.
ii. vv.	158-184A	*Diaria Camerariorum*: 1688-1870.
iii. vv.	185-187	*Diaria Decanorum*: 1590-1861.

3.3.2.15	**c.** *Positiones*	268 vv.	1620-1660.
3.3.2.3	**d.** *Commissiones*	42 vv.	1480-1790.
3.3.2.16	**e.** *Processus*	1063 nn.	1580-1800.
3.3.2.10	**f.** *Miscellanea*	28 vv.	1395-1889.
& 11			

3.3.1

II. Sacra Poenitentiaria

By the end of the 12th century there is mention of a cardinal whose duty it was to absolve from censures which the pope had reserved to himself; by the time of Honorius III (1216-1227), this cardinal is being designated as "Penitentiary". He was virtually the head of a department, and was assisted by chaplains or "minor" penitentiaries, as well as by *correctores, scriptores, grossatores* and *distributores* for the expedition of letters of absolution or dispensation; to these Benedict XII added in 1338 an expert in Canon Law. This structure endured until 1569, when the Sacred Apostolic Penitentiary of modern times was established by Pius V. See E. Göller, *Die päpstliche Pönitentiarie von ihrem Ursprung bis zu ihrer Umgestaltung unter Pius V.* (Bibliothek des kgl. Preussischen Historischen Instituts in Rom, III-IV, VII-VIII, Rome 1907, 1911: 2 vv., each of two parts, with separate pagination for each of the four parts).

The archives of the Sacred Penitentiary are in the Sacra Penitenziaria Apostolica, Via della Conciliazione 34, Rome, and are not open to consultation. According to Göller, 'Das alte Archiv der päpstlichen Pönitentiarie', in *Kirchengeschichtliche Festgabe Anton de Waal (Römische Quartalschrift*, Supplementheft 20, Rome 1913), pp. 1-19, there are some 139 volumes in the archives of the Penitentiary for the years 1409 (Alexander V) to 1565 (Pius IV). This probably represents no more than a portion of what once existed for the medieval period; and it is unknown how many volumes of medieval material were among the 4256 volumes (3488 vv. of supplications, 134 vv. of *expéditiones*, 634 vv. of marriage cases) which were taken to Paris in 1810 and are now lost (see M. Gachard, *Les archives du Vatican*, Brussels 1874, p. 119). However, as Göller has pointed out, we are not entirely destitute of medieval sources. For the period 1200-1500 there are some useful formulary books: Göller, *Die päpstliche Pönitentiarie*, I, 1, pp. 65-74, notes some 15 MSS of formularies, while H. C. Lea, *A Formulary of the Papal Penitentiary in the Thirteenth Century* (Philadelphia 1892), has published a formulary book by Cardinal Giacomo Tommasini Caetani, 1295-1300 (but which Lea took to be by Cardinal Thomas of Capua, c. 1216).

III. SIGNATURA IUSTITIAE   3.3.5

What was meant by a *signatura* was a supplication sheet on which popes, from Boniface VIII onwards, wrote "fiat" when granting a petition. Hence the fixing of the pope's signature gave the name *signatura* to the successful supplication sheet itself. The task of preparing petitions for the papal signature was committed to reporters known as *Referendarii*, the first mention of whom occurs in the pontificate of Boniface VIII: see K. A. Fink, 'Zur Geschichte des päpstlichen Referendariats', in *Analecta Sacra Tarraconensia* 10 (1934) 75-100. It also was the duty of the *Referendarii* to give the pope precise information on the supplications presented and to help the pope prepare grants, concessions and replies in cases involving benefices. Hence, taken collectively, the *Referendarii* became known as the *Signatura*. In the pontificate of Eugene IV (1431-1447) a permanent office of *Signatura* was created, and the *Referendarii* were allowed to sign certain petitions (using, however, "concessum" in place of the papal "fiat"). This *Signatura gratiae et commissionum* was divided by Julius II (1503-1513) into two sections or dicasteries: a *Signatura gratiae* and a *Signatura iustitiae*, the latter becoming a full tribunal. (See B. Katterbach, *Referendarii utriusque Signaturae a Martino V ad Clementem XI, et Praelati Signaturae supplicationum a Martino V ad Leonem XIII*, Studi e Testi 55, Vatican City 1931, esp. pp. VII-XXXVIII).

The *Signatura gratiae* was turned into a Congregation by Sixtus V in 1588, but it lost its importance in the 17th century, when the Datary began to take over the granting of all graces and favours. It appears not to have kept special registers; what records there are will be found in the Registers of Supplications. The *Signatura iustitiae,* on the other hand, continued until 1870, and later was reconstituted by Pius X in 1908. Many of its *Decisiones* are in print (see the list of editions in Stickler, *Historia iuris canonici latini,* I, p. 345), and there is a collection of some 766 volumes of registers from 1614-1870 in the Archivio di Stato di Roma (Lodolini, *L'Archivio di Stato di Roma,* p. 116). The Vatican Archives possesses 148 volumes from 1679-1700 (Katterbach EI 89; Fink 124).

In general see Katterbach EI 88-89; Fink 124-125; HVD passim.

1. *Archivio*   *Beni* (ASV 1933): 163 nn. (1359-1916), and 126   7.5.9.1
parchment documents (1297-1393), relative to
Beni family of Gubbio. BAV I.116.

2.   *Borghese* (ASV 1932): 8690 nn. Indice 1052;   7.5.15.1
BAV II.93, III.113-118.

3.   *Buoncompagni* (ASV 1949): 418 nn. BAV II.92-93.   7.5.14.1

4.   *Colonna*: 105 nn., 1707-1855.

5.   *della Basilica di S. Lorenzo in Damaso* (ASV 1948):   7.8.2.1
1241 nn. from 1436-1880.

6.   *Della Valle-Del Bufalo* (ASV 1947): 227 nn., 1462-   7.5.31.1
1881, with respect to extinct Della Valle family.
Indice 1052; BAV I.116, III.125-126.

7.   *Girolamini* (ASV 1945): see *Fondo*.

8.   *Patrizi-Montoro* (ASV 1946): BAV I.118.   7.5.55.1

9.   *Pio IX*: a. *Corrispondenza con Sovrani e Particolari*   7.5.59.1
(Austria, Baden, ... Wurtemburg); b. *Oggetti vari*:
2187 nn. BAV. I.118, III.126-128.

10.   *del Vicariato*: In 1933 this rich deposit of parochial   7.4.5.1
registers (1570-), etc. of the diocese of Rome was
placed in charge of the ASV and was housed in
St. Peter's in the Braccio di Carlo Magno. In
1964, however, it was transferred to the new Vicariate Archives at St. John Lateran (Via dell'Am-
ba Aradam, to the right of the entrance to the
Lateran University): see *L'Attività della S. Sede
nel 1964* (Vatican City, 1965, pp. 696-697).

11. *Arciconfraternità del SS. Crocifisso in S. Marcello* (ASV 1926):   7.6.4.1
BAV I.118-119.

12.   *del Gonfalone*: c. 1500 bundles. BAV III.128.   7.6.2.1

13.   *della Pietà dei Carcerati*: 260 vv. BAV III.128.   7.6.1.1

14. *Bandi Sciolti*: Mainly printed notices of 16th-19th centuries   7.4.13
relative to the Papal States, though bulls of earlier
periods are often cited or rehearsed. Often known
as "Bolle e Bandi, Serie III". 80 nn., ranging
from 1425-1904. Indice 1079; BAV I.172.

7.5.6.1	15. *Bullae Benedicti XIII*: 2 nn., 1724-1730. BAV III.188, IV.166.	
7.5.7.1	16. *Bullae Consistoriales Benedicti XIV*: 29 nn., 1740-1758. Indice 1062; BAV II.167-168, IV.166.	
7.4.14	17. *Bullarium Generale* (ASV 1783): A collection of 219 original bulls from 13th-15th c. formed by B. Katterbach (*ob.* 29.12.1931) from two large bound volumes in the Archives: v. 1: nn. 1-111: Alexander III-Clement VI; v. 2: nn. 1-108: Innocent VI-Martin V. A calendar of these bulls is in A. Mercati, *Il "Bullarium generale" dell'Archivio Segreto Vaticano* (Studi e Testi 134, Vatican City 1947), pp. 1-76. See Fink 150-151; BAV I.174, II.168, III.188-189, IV.166-168.	
7.5.17.1	18. *Carte*	*Canosa*: BAV I.281, II.273.
7.5.34.1	19.	*Farnesiane*: see above, H.IVa (Secretariate of State).
7.5.35.1	20.	*Favoriti-Casoni* : 9 vv., 1661-1689.
7.5.44.1	21.	*Kanzler*: 71 vv. (19th c.) of General Kanzler (*ob.* 1888) of papal army. BAV I.282.
7.5.46.1	22.	*Macchi*: 22 bundles (19th c.) of Cardinal Macchi (*ob.* 1860).
7.5.58.1	23.	*Pistolesi*: BAV III.293-294.
7.5.76.1	24.	*Theiner*: BAV I.282, II.275, IV.277-278.
2.1.8.1	25. *Collegio Protonotari* (ASV 1931): 90 nn., 1600-1903, mainly concerning administration and members of the college of Protonotaries.	
7.5.16.1	26. *Collezione Brancadori*: 20 vv. of collections of L. Brancadori (*ob.* 1859) relative to Papal States in 18th-19th c., and to 1831-1849 in particular. BAV I.282.	
7.5.73.2	27.	*Spada*: 418 nn. of papers of G. Spada (1796-1867) with reference to Roman Republic of 1849. BAV I.282, III.348.
5.1.17.1	28. *Commissariato delle Armi*: 984 nn. relative to papal army, 1643-1749.	
3.2.14.37	29.	*straordinario delle quattro legazioni*: 279 nn., being in the main documents of the Inspectorate General of the legations of Bologna, Ferrara, Forlì, Ravenna, 1832-1847.
7.7.3.1	30. *Fondo Agostiniani*: 187 nn., 1287-1762. BAV I.298, IV.301.	
7.5.25.1	31.	*Albani*: see H.IVe, above (Secretariate of State).
7.7.28.1	32.	*Basiliani*: Kehr (1900) 391; Kehr (1903) 521-522; BAV I.305, II.311, III.320, IV.302.
7.5.11.1	33.	*Benincasa* (ASV 1928): 34 nn., mainly 17th c., of Benincasa family of Ancona. Indice 1026.

34.   *Bolognetti* (ASV after 1810): 346 nn., mainly 17th-18th c., relative to French and Italian churches. Indice 1049; BAV I.306, II.311, III.320, IV.302.   7.5.13.1

35.   *Borghese*: see p. 74 above. To be distinguished from the *Archivio* or *Casa Borghese* of M.2, above.   7.5.15.2

36.   *Carinci*: 91 nn. 1420-1909.   7.5.19.1

37.   *Carpegna*: 237 nn. of Card. Gaspero Carpegna, with Datary and other material, acquired by the Holy See in 1753. Indice 1050; BAV I.321, II.350, III.349, IV.328.   7.5.20.1

38.   *Castellani*: BAV I.322, III.350.   7.5.21.1

39.   *Celestini*: 343 nn., 1267-1762. Two-volume calendar on file-cards. BAV I.323, II.329.   7.7.14.2

40.   *Certosini*: 27 nn.   7.7.13.2

41.   *Confalonieri*: 89 vv., 1550-1636, of G. Confalonieri, prefect of archives of Castel S. Angelo (*ob.* 1648). Vols. 84-85 concern *De auxiliis* Congregation. Indice 1051; BAV I.337, II.372, IV.342.   7.5.28.1

42.   *Cybo* (ASV 1927): 26 nn, of papers of Card. Camillo Cybo (*ob.* 1743),, mainly relative to the business of the Congregation of Bishops and Regulars. Indice 1080; BAV I.337.   7.5.24.1

43.   *Domenicani*: 466 nn., 1207-1765, and 12 large bundles of papers, 1405-1809. BAV I.337, II.372, III.377, IV.343.   7.7.19.2

44.   *Finy* (ASV 1925): 36 vv. of Francesco Finy (*ob.* 1743), mainly relative to pontificate of Benedict XIII (1724-1730). Indice 1053; BAV I.338, II. 374.   7.5.38.1

45.   *Francescani*: 8 nn. BAV II.374.   7.7.20.1

46.   *Garampi*: 300 vv. of original documents or of those copied by G. Garampi (1725-1792); vv. 134-138 are known as "Adversariorum". Indici 157 (nn. 1-271), 1068 (nn. 272-300). Kehr (1900) 392-394: Kehr (1903) 522-555; Fink 135-136; BAV I.338, II.374-376, III.377-379, IV.344.   7.5.39.4

47.   *Gesuiti*: 59 nn., 1545-1807. Indice 1077. BAV II.376, III.379.   7.7.22.1

48.   *Girolamini*: 66 nn., 1422-1803; 191 nn., 19th-20th c. Indice 1054.   7.7.21.1

49.   *Mencacci* (ASV 1935): 7 vv. of letters etc. of P. Mencacci (1827-1897), especially relating to last years of Papal States. BAV I.339.   7.5.49.1

7.5.54.1	50.	*Pasolini-Zanelli* (ASV 1931): 23 nn. relative to family of Leo XII (1823-1829) ; Indice 1088.
7.5.57.1	51.	*Pio*: 292 vv., 16th-19th c., containing Secretariate of State material, and reports of conclaves of 16th and 17th century. Belonged to Card. Pio Carlo di Savoia, and acquired by Benedict XIV in 1753. Indice 1091; BAV I.340, II.376-381, III.379, IV.345-348.
7.5.59.3	52.	*Pio IX*: 39 nn. of private correspondence, family papers, etc., covering 1725-1878. Cf. *Archivio Pio IX*, above, n. 9.
7.5.62.1	53.	*Ronconi*: 23 nn., 17th-18th c., of Filippo Ronconi, prefect of the ASV (*ob.* 1751). Indice 1060. BAV II.381.
7.5.66.2	54.	*Salviati*: 81 nn. Indice 1052.
7.5.26.1	55.	*S. Coleta*: 22 nn., 1442-1632.
7.8.12.1	56.	*S. Trifone*: 8 nn., 957-1188. BAV II.381.
7.5.68.1	57.	*Santini* (ASV 1909): 252 nn., mostly of Datary material ("Notariorum matriculae"), from 15th to 18th century, which belonged to Giuseppe Santini, an official of the Datary. See J. Lesellier, 'Notaires et archives de la curie romaine', in *Mélanges d'archéologie et d'histoire* 50 (1933) 250-275; Indice 1066; BAV I.341, II.381. Some entries relative to England from a lost register of Eugene IV are printed from this *Fondo* by J. A. Twemlow in *Calendar of Papal Letters*, XIII, pp. XIV-XVI.
7.7.31.1	58.	*Scolopi*: 94 nn., 1614-1672.
4.100.7	59.	*Toscano*: BAV III.380. See F.III: p. 61.
	60.	*Veneto*: see F.III above: *Cancellaria della Nunziatura Veneta.*.
7.5.15.3	61. *Instrumenta Burghesiana*: 178 nn. relative to Borghese family, 1322-1721. One-volume calendar of file-cards. BAV IV.368-370.
7.4.16	62.	*Melfiensia*: 53 nn., 1102-1694.
7.4.18	63.	*Pactensia*: 3 nn., 1171-1447.
7.8.10.1	64.	*Perusina*: 232 nn., 1214-1774. BAV I.409, III.463, IV.385.
7.8.4.1	65.	*Tudertina*: 29 nn., 1051-1511. Kehr (1900) 124; BAV I.409-410, II.451-452, IV.385-386.
7.4.19	66. *Miscellanea Diplomatica*: 108 nn., 1077-1906. BAV IV.417.
3.1.6.25	67. *Missioni*: Indice 1087. BAV II.480, III.485-486; H. Hoberg, 'Der Fonds Missioni des Vatikanisches Archivs', in *Euntes Docete* 21 (1968) 97-107.

68. *Monastero dei SS. Gregorio e Siro di Bologna* (ASV 1886):   7.8.3.1
    186 nn., including four original briefs addressed
    to Eugene IV. Indice 155; *Sussidi* 3, 76-91;
    BAV I. 428-429, II.480-482, III.486.
69.   *di S. Silvestro di Nonantola*: 426 nn., 802-1474.   7.8.11.1
    Indice 1093. BAV II.482, IV.417.
70.   *SS. Domenico e Sisto*: 870 nn.   7.8.18.1
71. *Ospizio di S. Galla* (ASV 1936): BAV II.482.   7.8.7.1
72.   *di S. Marta*: 235 nn. BAV II.483.   7.8.15.1
73. *Piante e Carte Geografiche*: Indice 1059. BAV II.483.   7.4.21
74. *S. Palazzi Apostolici*: ca. 4000 nn., 17th-19th c.   2.2.23
75. *Tribunale del Governo di Roma*: 236 nn., 19th c.   5.1.166.2
76. *Uditore Santissimo* (ASV 1931).   2.2.1

PART TWO

NOTES ON SELECTED
MEDIEVAL HOLDINGS OF THE ASV

[Addenda to p. 113]

Calendar of entries in Papal Registers relating to Great Britain and Ireland:
Calendar of Papal Letters...

XV: 1484-1492 (M.J. Haren [Dublin, 1978])
      Innocent VIII   RL 841-924, 929   1-519
                                      TCD 1223.5   519-523

XVI: 1492-1498 (A.P. Fuller [Dublin, 1986])
      Alexander VI   (1492-1493)   RL 924-1026, 2463 1-623
                                        TCD 1223.6   622-624

XVII: [not yet published]

XVIII: 1503-1513 (M. Haren [Dublin, 1989])
      Pius III   (1503)   RL 1127   1-8
                                    RL 1141   323
      Julius II   (1503-1513)   RV 885-990   8-187
                                      RL 1129-1208   187-602

The existence of registers of papal letters as early as the 4th century is generally admitted by scholars, but the evidence is very slight. There are, however, definite traces of the use of registers in the pontificate of Leo I (440-461)[1]; and there is no doubt that some of the extant letters of Gregory the Great (590-604) come from registers of his time, for in the 9th century there still existed in the archives of the Lateran some 14 rolls of his letters, each containing a year of his pontificate.[2] Remarks of writers and canonists of the period testify to the presence of other papal registers in the 7th and 8th centuries. For the 9th century, apart from fragments of the letters of Leo IV, John VIII and Stephen V that have been transmitted through canonical collections,[3] the most important evidence of registers is provided by a copy of 314 letters from the last six years of John VIII (872-882). This was written at Montecassino in the late 11th century, and is now in the Vatican Archives as RV I. Like the lost registers of Gregory the Great, each roll of which began from September, John's letters are divided by indiction,[4] but in all likelihood they do not represent complete registers for each year of his pontificate.[5]

The first extant original register is that of Gregory VII (1073-1085), now RV 2 of the Vatican Archives (there is a later copy in RV 3). It contains 381 letters, and is divided into books according to pontifical years. Besides these letters, there are

---

[1] C. Silva-Tarouca, 'Nuovi studi sulle antiche lettere dei Papi,' in *Gregorianum* 12 (1931) 3-56, 349-425, 547-598.

[2] *Gregorii I Registrum Epistolarum*, ed. P. Ewald and L. M. Hartmann, 2 vv. (*Monumenta Germaniae Historica, Epistolae* I, II, Berlin 1887-1899); E. Posner, 'Das Register Gregors I.', in *Neues Archiv* 41 (1922) 243-315.

[3] See A. M. Stickler, *Historia iuris canonici latini: Institutiones Academicae* I (Turin 1950), pp. 144-165, etc. For Stephen V (885-891) see *Fragmenta Registri Stephani V papae*, ed. E. Caspar (*Monumenta Germaniae Historica, Epistolae* VII, Berlin 1928, pp. 334-353).

[4] For chronological terms such as these see C. R. Cheney, *Handbook of Dates for Students of English History*[2] (London 1961); and for general diplomatic terminology, K. Klauser and O. Meyer, *Clavis Mediaevalis. Kleines Wörterbuch der Mittelalterforschung* (Wiesbanden 1962).

[5] H. Steinacker, 'Das Register Papst Johanns VIII.,' in *Homenatge a Antonio Rubió i Lluch: Miscellanea d'Estudis literaris, històrics i lingüistics* (Barcelona 1936), I, pp. 479-505; D. Lohrmann, *Das Register Papst Johannes VIII.* (Tübingen 1968).

also *notitiae* in this register relative to councils and other events (e.g. Gregory's election) of the period, as well as the famous text known as the *Dictatus Papae*.[6] For Gregory's immediate successors, however, there are only references and extracts, although there is a 13th-century copy at Montecassino of a fragment (38 letters, mostly of May 1130) of a register of the antipope Anacletus II (1130-1138). There were, apparently, many 12th-century registers (including, possibly, four volumes of registers of Alexander III) still in existence in the time of Honorius III (1216-1227), but they have long since disappeared.[7]

It is with the pontificate of Innocent III (1198-1216) that the registers of papal letters in the ASV properly begin. For the 13th century there is a single series of registers, the *Registra Vaticana* (here abbreviated to RV), and this continues to the last half of the 16th century. In addition to RV the 14th century has the so-called *Registra Avenionensia* (here denoted simply as RA) in 359 volumes (1317-1415), as well as the *Registra Supplicationum* (RS : 7365 volumes, 1342-1899). A third letter-series begins in

---

[6] *Gregorii VII Registrum. Das Register Gregors VII.*, ed. E. Caspar (*Monumenta Germaniae Historica, Epistolae Selectae* II, Berlin 1920); F. Bock, "Annotationes zum Register Gregors VII.,' in *Studi Gregoriani* I (Rome 1947), pp. 281-306; L. Santifaller, *Quellen und Forschungen zum Urkunden- und Kanzleiwesen Papst Gregors VII*, I: *Urkunden* (Studi e Testi 190, Vatican City 1957); A. Murray, 'Pope Gregory VII and his letters,' in *Traditio* 22 (1966) 149-202. For possible registers of Urban II (1088-1099) see J. Ramackers, 'Zwei unbekannte Briefe Urbans II. Zugleich ein Beitrag zum Problem der Register dieses Papstes', in *Quellen und Forschungen* 26 (1935-1936) 268-276.

[7] See J. B. Pitra, *Analecta Novissima* I (Rome 1885), pp. 146-148, etc. For fragments of registers of Alexander III (1159-1181), see S. Löwenfeld, *Epistolae pontificum Romanorum ineditae* (Leipzig 1885), pp. 149-209. — For the period up to 1198, the standard general collection of papal letters, whether from registers or other sources, is P. Jaffé, *Regesta pontificum Romanorum a condita Ecclesia ad annum p. Chr. n. 1198* (Berlin 1851), in the second edition by S. Löwenfeld, P. Ewald and F. Kaltenbrunner, 2 vv. (Leipzig 1885-1888, reprinted Graz 1956; usually cited as Jaffé-Löwenfeld or J.-L.). This has to be supplemented to some extent by J. von Pflugk-Harttung, *Acta pontificum Romanorum inedita*, 3 vv. (Tübingen-Stuttgart 1880-1888; reprinted Graz 1958), but most of all by the *Papsturkunden* series of P. F. Kehr and others. In 1896 Kehr (1860-1944) had the idea of collecting, editing or describing all papal documents prior to 1198 wherever they were to be found. He himself began with Italy, publishing his findings in a celebrated series of *Papsturkunden* papers in the *Nachrichten* of the Academy of Science at Göttingen from 1896-1924. On the basis of these researches in Italian archives, Kehr inaugurated the *Regesta Pontificum Romanorum* with his *Italia Pontificia* volumes (10 in all, 1906-1966). Under his direction, others began similar work in the libraries and archives of Germany, France, Spain, Portugal and England, but thus far only the reports of researches (*Papsturkunden*) in these countries have appeared and not the *Regesta* volumes, with the exception of Germany. On Kehr's work see his own address, 'Ueber die Sammlung und Herausgabe der älteren Papsturkunden bis Innocenz III. (1198)', in *Sitzungsberichte der preussischen Akademie der Wissenschaften*, Phil.-hist. Kl. 10 (Berlin 1934) 83-92. For an evaluation of Kehr see W. Holtzmann (one of Kehr's closest collaborators) in *Deutsches Archiv* 8 (1950) 26-58.

1389 with the *Registra Lateranensia* (RL) and continues until 1897 (2467 volumes). To these must be added the various secretarial registers of bulls and briefs, for example, 222 volumes of the *Secretariatus Camerae*, 1470-1796 (above, pp. 54-55), 883 volumes of *Brevia Lateranensia* (pp. 52-53), and 380 volumes of *Epistolae ad Principes* (p. 67).

Because of this great array of registers we now possess a formidable wealth of letters from 1198 onwards. Some idea of this wealth may be gained from the fact that the RV volumes for the pontificate of Clement VI (1342-1352) contain some 86,651 items, and that there are altogether some 250,000 papal letters for the period 1198-1417. However, it must be remembered that the extant registers do not contain all the letters, not to speak of all the transactions, of the various popes. For although Stephen of Tournai asserts late in the 12th century that the custom of the Roman church is "that when it sends an important business letter to anyone, it keeps a copy itself, and that all these copies are placed in a book called a register",[8] this was not universally true, at least in the 13th century. Large numbers of original letters still survive, many of which are not in fact to be found in extant registers of the period. An international scheme for a *censimento* (census) of all original letters was inaugurated in 1953, and results so far obtained suggest that the number of letters actually registered is comparatively small compared to the overall production of the medieval papal chancery.[9] Further, copies of papal letters are often to be found in cartularies, chronicles and indeed, with respect to earlier pontificates, in the papal registers themselves,[10] and many of these copies, too, find no echo in the extant registers.

[8] Quoted in H. Bresslau, *Handbuch der Urkundenlehre* I[2] (Leipzig 1913), p. 121, n. 2.
[9] F. Bartoloni, 'Per un censimento dei documenti pontifici da Innocenzo III a Martino V (escluso),' in *Atti del Convegno di studi delle fonti del medio evo europeo in occasione del settantesimo della fondazione dell'Istituto storico italiano, Roma, 14-18 aprile 1953*, II: *Comunicazioni* (Rome 1957), pp. 3-22, with 9 plates and 6 tables. This paper is also to be found in *Relazioni, Comunicazioni ed Atti, Convegno internazionale...* Rome 1953, II, pp. 7-40; and in a separate booklet, *Per un'Censimento...* (Rome 1955). For a notice of Bartoloni and a list of his writings see R. Morghen and A. Pratesi in *Bullettino dell'"Archivio paleografico italiano,"* n. s. 2-3 (1956-1957): *Numero speciale in memoria di Franco Bartoloni*, I, 7-15. See also L. Santifaller, 'Der "Censimento" der spätmittelalterlichen Papsturkunden,' in *Mitteilungen des Instituts für österreichische Geschichtsforschung* 62 (1964) 122-134. The most notable result of Bartoloni's scheme has been the work of A. Largiadèr: *Die Papsturkunden des Staatsarchiv Zürich von Innozenz III. bis Martin V.* (Zürich 1963), *Die Papsturkunden der Schweiz von Innozenz III. bis Martin V., ohne Zürich. Ein Beitrag zum Censimentum Helveticum*, I: *von Innozenz III. bis Benedikt XI., 1198 bis 1304* (Zürich 1968).
[10] For examples of pre-1198 letters in papal registers of 1198-1550, see P. Kehr, 'Ältere Papsturkunden in der päpstlichen Registern von Innozenz III. bis Paul

[For original letters in the National Archives in Paris, see B. Barbiche in the addendum to the Bibliography, p. 221*.]

Hence, strictly speaking, the series of registers in the ASV do not exhaust all the possibilities. For researches outside the ASV, a useful instrument is now available to students in the *Schedario Baumgarten*, an anastatic reproduction of which is now in progress under the editorship of Giulio Battelli: *Schedario Baumgarten. Descrizione diplomatica di Bolle e Brevi originali da Innocenzo III a Pio IX*: I: *Innocenzo III-Innocenzo IV, 1198-1254* (Vatican City 1965); II: *Alessandro IV — Benedetto XI, 1254-1304* (1966). This great personal index of 8643 file-cards (4799 of which are covered by volumes I and II) was made by P. M. Baumgarten (1860-1948) during many years of researches in archives and libraries all over Europe, and was donated to the Vatican School of Palaeography and Diplomatics in 1922. Its prime value is that it records a large part of original papal letters existing in deposits other than the ASV, including, for example, those in the Archivio di Stato of Naples destroyed in the Second World War.[11]

[This exaggerates the completeness of this valuable index (C.R. Cheney)]

Within the Vatican Archives the *Registra Vaticana* constitute the most important and ancient series of registers of medieval papal letters. And although many losses were sustained in the 13th and succeeding centuries, this great series of parchment registers still contains 2042 volumes.[12] The volumes are ordered according to pontificates, and within each pontificate in chronological groups. The series proper begins at RV 4 (RV 1 is a copy of the register of John VIII; RV 2 is generally accepted as an original register of Gregory VII; RV 3 is a later copy of RV 2), with the pontificate of Innocent III; it ends with the pontificate

III.,' in *Nachrichten der k. Gesellschaft der Wissenschaft zu Göttingen, philologisch-historische Klasse*, 1902, pp. 393-558.

[11] See G. Gualdo, 'Lo "Schedario Baumgarten" e gli studi di diplomatica pontificia,' in *Rivista di Storia della Chiesa in Italia* 20 (1966) 71-81, and the critical review of the *Schedario* by P. Rabikauskas in *Archivum Historiae Pontificiae* 4 (1966) 347-375. There are some examples of the use of the *Schedario* in E. Pásztor, 'Per la storia dei registri pontifici nel duecento,' *ibid.*, 6 (1968) 71-112, at pp. 72-82. For Baumgarten see H. Jedin in *Lexikon für Theologie und Kirche,*[2] III. 69.

[12] For lost registers of the 13th century see H. Denifle, 'Die päpstlichen Registerbände des 13. Jahrhunderts und das Inventar derselben vom J. 1339.' in *Archiv für Litteratur- und Kirchengeschichte* 2 (1886) 1-105; and the article of E. Pásztor cited in the last note. Many registers of the 14th and other centuries are also missing, for reasons suggested elsewhere in the present work. On a rare occasion a "lost" register may come to light and be offered for sale, as in the case of a parchment register (RV) of the 9th year of Innocent VI from the Phillipps collection which was sold recently by Sotheby of London to the Italian Government. See the sale catalogue, *Bibliotheca Phillippica: New Series; Medieval Manuscripts, Part III, 28 November 1967*, p. 50, where among 42 MSS of the 7th to the 17th century, this "Register of letters of Pope Innocent VI for the year 1361 (Phillipps n. 4760)" was lot 98, and was sold for $6240.

of Pius V (1572), but three additional volumes containing mixed material bring the series up to 1605. An excellent chronological survey of the whole series will be found in *Sussidi* I (1926), pp. 49-125, where the year or part of year covered by each volume is also indicated.

As the RV series exists at present it reflects the arrangement of the early 17th century when, on the formation of the ASV, groups of registers were thrown together without any account being taken of the department in which they originated.[13] From 1198 until the beginning of the Great Schism (1378) the series is reasonably homogeneous, the registers as a whole having the Chancery or the Camera as their origin. Hence volumes 4-290 contain *Litterae communes* from the Chancery, *Litterae secretae* from the Camera, and *Litterae de curia* from both departments, although it must be remembered that the RV volumes of *Litterae communes* for the Avignon period, 1305-1378, are not primarily Chancery registers of common letters, but are rather official copies on parchment of the original Chancery registers of common letters which today form the series known as *Registra Avenionensia* (RA). During the Schism (1378-1415), and particularly after 1389 when Boniface IX began to register common letters in the paper series now called the *Registra Lateranensia*, the RV series loses its contact with the Chancery and is largely Camera in origin from then on, but many *Diversorum* volumes from the Apostolic Secretariate for the years 1484-1572 were merged with the series in 1630. To further complicate the story, there are some RV volumes (e.g. RV 214-218, 242-244, 251, 262, 272-281, 288-290, 300-309, 321-322) in the present arrangement which really belong to the paper *Registra Avenionensia* series, while there are some others (e.g. RV 318, 357-358) which have the characteristics of *Registra Lateranensia*.[14]

---

[13] The standard study of the "Vatican Registers" (RV) is M. Giusti, 'I registri vaticani e le loro provenienze,' in *Miscellanea A. Mercati* (Studi e Testi 165, Vatican City 1952), pp. 383-459, now reprinted in Giusti, *Studi sui registri di bolle papali* (Vatican City 1968), pp. 1-79. In the same *Studi*, pp. 129-132, 133-148, Msgr Giusti provides an overall view of the RV series according to origin (Chancery, Camera, Secretaries, Apostolic Secretariate).

[14] Not every RV volume is a register properly so-called: RV 30, 30A, 33-36, are 14th-century volumes which contain political and private letters of Clement IV from 1261-1268, and possibly were copied from an original register of secret letters; RV 244 A-N (13 volumes) contain minutes of Letters of Clement VI, Urban V and Gregory XI; RV 62 is a collection of letters relating to the Tartars; RV 6, of course, is famous, and has been the object of much discussion: see the critical edition by F. Kempf, *Regestum super negotio Romani Imperii Innocentii III* (Rome 1947), and the same author's *Die Register Innocenz' III: Eine paläographisch-diplomatische Untersuchung* (Rome 1945).

[Potthast
compiled
his *Regista*
without ac-
cess to the
Vatican
registers
from 1216
to 1304
(C.R.
Cheney)]

Calendars of most of the RV series up to about 1378, and transcriptions or critical editions of some, have been published by
schools or by various individual scholars, and the work is still
in progress.[15] For RV volumes up to 1304 there is the general
calendar of A. Potthast, *Regesta pontificum Romanorum inde ab A. post
Christum natum MCXCVIII ad annum MCCCIV* (2 vv., Berlin
1874-1875); and for the beginning of the series, there are editions
in the *Monumenta Germaniae Historica* of the registers of John VIII
(ed. E. Caspar in *Epistolae karolini aevi* V, Berlin 1928, pp. 1-272)
and Gregory VII (ed. E. Caspar, in *Epistolae Selectae* II, Berlin
1920-1923), and editions of the registers of Innocent III (first
full edition in Migne, *Patrologia Latina*, vv. 214-216; new edition
by O. Hageneder and A. Haidacher, *Die Register Innocenz' III.*,
Graz-Cologne 1964-),[16] and Honorius III (E. Pressutti, *Regesta
Honorii papae III*, Rome 1888-1895). For RV from the pontificate
of Gregory IX (1227-1241) to the end of the lAvignon Papacy
(and for the *Registra Avenionensia* from 1316-1378), there are the
fine calendars, pontificate by pontificate,[17] of the École française
de Rome, a summary list of which is given below, pp. 125-127.
The period from the Great Schism to the Council of Trent and
the end of the Vatican Registers is quite neglected by comparison,
apart from the *Repertorium Germanicum* (1378-1447)[18] and Hergenröther's edition of the registers of the first three years of the pontificate of Leo X (1513-1521).[19]

So far as the British Isles are concerned, the most useful volume
of original texts from the Vatican Registers and other sources

---

[15] See the lists in L. Santifaller, *Neuere Editionen mittelalterlicher Königs- und Papsturkunden: Eine Übersicht* (Weimar 1958); R. C. van Caenegem and F. L. Ganshof,
Kurze Quellenkunde des westeuropäischen Mittelalters (Wiesbaden 1964), pp. 210-212.
[16] See the present writer's review in *Speculum* 42 (1967) 153-162. A very useful
selection of the letters of 13th-century popes is in *Monumenta Germaniae Historica,
Epistolae saeculi XIII. e regestis Pontificum Romanorum selectae*, ed. G. H. Pertz and C.
Rodenberg, 3 vv. (Berlin 1883-1894).
[17] A notable exception is the pontificate of Clement V. Clement's registers were
published by the Benedictines of Monte Cassino, *Regestum Clementis papae V*, 8 vv.
(Rome 1885-1892), but the École française later published *Tables des registres de
Clément V* (Paris 1957). See also T. Leccisotti, 'Note in margine all'edizione dei
regesti di Clementi V', in *Mélanges E. Tisserant* V (Studi e Testi 235, Vatican City
1964), pp. 15-45.
[18] But it must be remembered that the *Repertorium Germanicum* is not a calendar,
and that, as its subtitle (*Regestum aus den päpstlichen Archiven zur Geschichte des Deutschen
Reichs und seiner Territorien im XIV. und XV. Jahrhundert*) clearly states, it confines its
use of ASV sources to entries relative to German areas. Sometimes it is cited as though
it were a continuation of the French School calendars. (The subtitle given above is
that of the original *Repertorium* in 1897; that of the revived *Repertorium*, 1916-, is
much the same).
[19] *Leonis X. (1513-1521) pontificis maximi regesta*, ed. J. Hergenröther, 2 vv. (Freiburg-im-Breisgau 1884-1891).

is A. Theiner's *Vetera monumenta Hibernorum et Scotorum historiam illustrantia* (Rome 1864), which covers the years 1216-1549. For the period 1216-1261 (RV 9-25) this is now largely superseded for Ireland by Maurice P. Sheehy, *Pontificia Hibernica* (2 vv., Dublin 1962, 1965), in which there is a critical edition of all papal letters concerning Ireland (almost 500) from the pontificate of John IV (640) to that of Alexander IV (1261).[20] Naturally, the Vatican Registers from 1198-1261 (RV 4-25) are the chief source of the work, but Dr Sheehy has also tracked down originals and copies, of both registered and unregistered letters, in various archives and libraries in Ireland and England, and on the continent.[21] For England and Wales, Christopher and Mary Cheney have done a similar volume for the pontificate of Innocent III (C.R. and Mary Cheney, *The Letters of Pope Innocent III, 1198-1216, concerning England and Wales*, Oxford 1967). Again the backbone of the Cheneys' work is provided by the registers of Innocent in the ASV (RV 4-7, 7A, 8), supplemented by Indice 254 (brief extracts from both surviving and now lost registers, compiled for cameral purposes about 1270) and by RV 8A (*rubricellae* of all of Innocent's registers made in the 14th century). The value of the volume, however, would not be very great if the editors had confined themselves simply to the ASV sources, most of which have already been calendared by Potthast and others (e.g. Theiner, who in his *Vetera monumenta Slavorum*, Rome 1863, printed the *rubricellae* from RV 8A to the lost registers of Innocent's pontifical years 3, 4, 18 and 19). But in fact the authors also have examined, calendared or edited every possible source outside the ASV in which letters from Innocent may be found or mentioned: deposits of original bulls in Great Britain (chiefly the Public Record Office and the British Museum); cartularies of religious houses, printed and in manuscript, both in England and in France; chronicles, episcopal registers, registers of later popes, decretal collections; and various loose deeds such as charters in the British Museum, the Bodleian Library, French departmental archives, and in other public and private records. As a result, the editors are able to present

---

[20] Here and there, however, Dr Sheehy has calendared rather than edited papal documents, so that for a full text of certain items one has to fall back on Theiner's *Monumenta* or some other collection. See *Speculum* 42 (1967) 554-556.

[21] There is also a calendar of letters of Innocent III in P. J. Dunning, 'The letters of Innocent III to Ireland', in *Traditio* 18 (1962) 229-253. See also Dunning's 'The Letters of Innocent III as a source for Irish history,' in *Irish Catholic Historical Committee Proceedings* (Dublin 1959), pp. 1-10; 'Pope Innocent III and the Irish Kings,' in *Journal of Ecclesiastical History* 8 (1957) 17-32.

some 258 new texts over and above the letters registered in the Vatican Registers.[22]

However, the greatest overall instrument for students of the ecclesiastical history of the British Isles will long remain the *Calendar of Papal Letters* (14 vv., 1893-1960), for this spans the years 1198-1492 for the Vatican Registers (RV 4-771), and the period 1389-1485 for the Lateran (RL 1-840). Although it was harshly treated when it first appeared,[23] and still continues to elicit odd rumbles of dissatisfaction, the *Calendar*, on the whole, has not missed too much of importance in the Vatican Registers. Its accuracy, and its sensitivity to the formal point of a papal letter, is quite another matter, for the editor(s) were not always aware of the ramifications of every papal letter, nor of the significance of seemingly negligible clauses. This drawback, of course, is not peculiar to the *Calendar*. It is also present in the French School calendars. In fact, if one is working seriously on a point which involves the use of papal letters, the only safe thing to do in the long run is to examine the various letters at first-hand in the ASV or on microfilm.[24] The present writer, when working on licences to study of the 14th century, found both the *Calendar* and the French School volumes to be wanting in precision: more often than not the all-important phrase "iuxta constitutionem Bonifatii octavi" is omitted by the calendars in letters concerning studies to the parochial clergy, with the result that the point of these letters is blunted, if not entirely destroyed.[25]

Nevertheless, the *Calendar of Papal Letters* is as indispensable as are

[See also the biblio-graphy under London: Public Record Office.]

[22] Original papal documents in general in various British deposits have been listed by H. I. Bell, 'A list of original papal bulls and briefs in the Department of Manuscripts, British Museum,' in *English Historical Review* 36 (1921) 393-419, 556-583; K. Major, 'Original papal documents in the Bodleian Library,' in *Bodleian Library Record* 3 (1950-1951) 242-256; J. Sayers, *Original Papal Documents in the Lambeth Palace Library: A Catalogue (Bulletin of the Institute of Historical Research*, Special Supplement, 6, London 1967). The foundations of a *Britannia Pontificia* were laid by W. Holtzmann, *Papsturkunden in England*, 3 vv. (Berlin 1930-1931, 1935-1936, 1952). See also W. Holtzmann and E. W. Kemp, *Papal decretals relating to the diocese of Lincoln in the Twelfth Century* (Lincoln, Publications of Lincoln Record Society, 47, 1954).

[23] See, for example, *Parliamentary Debates (Hansard)* 52 (2 August 1897), cols. 88-91.

[24] There is a good survey of microfilm deposits in the British Isles of ASV material in Ian B. Cowan, 'The Vatican Archives. A report on pre-reformation Scottish material,' in *Scottish Historical Review* 43 (1969) 227-242. Irish items in RV 4-320 (1198-1404), and British Isles entries in RV 775-990 (1492-1513), are on microfilm in the National Library of Ireland: see R. J. Hayes, ed., *Manuscript sources for the history of Irish civilization* (Boston 1965), II, pp. 584-608 (Roman material in general), 589-599 (papal registers, including transcripts in the British Museum).

[25] See L. E. Boyle, 'The Constitution *Cum ex eo* of Boniface VIII,' in *Mediaeval Studies* 24 (1962) 263-302.

the volumes of the French School, and it may be of use to students to present an outline here of the contents of the 14 volumes of entries in the papal registers of letters (the volume of Supplications will be noted later) that have appeared to date:[26]

Calendar of entries in the Papal Registers relating to Great Britain and Ireland: Calendar of Papal Letters, edd. W. H. Bliss, C. Johnson, J. A. Twemlow (H. M. Stationery Office, London, 1893-1960):

			Volume	Page
I: 1198-1304 (Bliss, 1893)				
Innocent III	(1198-1216)	RV	4-8	1
Honorius III	(1216-1227)		9-13	40
Gregory IX	(1227-1241)		14-20	117
Innocent IV	(1243-1254)		21-23	198
Alexander IV	(1254-1261)		24-25A	309
Urban IV	(1261-1264)		26-29	376
Clement IV	(1265-1268)		30-35	419
Gregory X	(1271-1276)		36-37	441
John XXI	(1276-1277)		38	451
Nicholas III	(1277-1280)		39	454
Martin IV	(1281-1285)		41-42	463
Honorius IV	(1285-1287)		43	479
Nicholas IV	(1288-1292)		44-46	491
Boniface VIII	(1294-1303)		47-50	558
Benedict XI	(1303-1304)		51	611
Urban IV-Honorius IV: *varia*			29A	619-621
II: 1305-1342 (Bliss, 1895)				
Clement V	(1305-1314)		52-61	1
John XXII	(1316-1334)		63-108 lc	123
			109-117 ls	414
(Nicholas V)	(1328-1330)		118	515
Benedict XII	(1334-1342)		119-129 lc	515
			130-136 ca	558-591
III: 1342-1362 (Bliss, Johnson, 1897)				
Clement VI	(1342-1352)		137-146 ls	1
			147-218 lc	51
Innocent VI	(1352-1362)		219-234 lc	475
			235-244K ls	609-635

Note. RV 214-218 are RA and were not calendared. Addenda to v. III are in v. XIII, p. XII.

[26] There are no extant registers for Innocent V (1276) and Celestine V (1294). — The editors of the *Calendar* have worked through the RV and RL volumes one by one for each pontificate. These volumes generally proceed consecutively through each year of a pontificate; sometimes, however, there are divisions of letters into *communes, de camera, de curia, secretae,* and each new division therefore begins with the first year of the pontificate. Hence within any pontificate a given year may occur many times, depending on the number of divisions. In the present schema of the *Calendar* the following abbreviations are used to show where these divisions occur: lc: *litterae communes;* dc: *litterae de curia;* ca: *litterae de camera;* ls: *litterae secretae.*

			Volume	Pages
IV: 1362-1404 (Bliss, Twemlow, 1902)				
Urban V	(1362-1370)	RV	245-250 ls	1
			252-260 lc	29
			261 dc	87
Gregory XI	(1370-1378)		263-271 ls	92
			274-281 ca	148
			282-287 lc	161
Clement VII	(1378-1394)		291-299	228
Urban VI	(1378-1389)		310-312 ls	257
Boniface XI	(1389-1404)		312-320 dc	274
	an. 1-12	RL	1	317
	an. 1-13		2-9	331
	an. 2-8		10-43	354-546

Note. RV 251, 262, 272, 273, 288-290, 300-309, 321-332, are mostly RA and hence were not calendared. Valuable *Addenda et Corrigenda* at pp. xvi-xxiv, and in v. VII, pp. xxi-xxix.

			Volume	Pages
V: 1396-1404 (Bliss, Twemlow, 1904)				
Boniface IX				
	an. 8-15	RL	44-118	1
	an. 1-2	RV	347	628

Note. Addenda to v. V are in v. XIII, pp. xii-xiii.

			Volume	Pages
VI: 1404-1415 (Twemlow, 1904)				
Innocent VII	(1404-1406)	RV	333-334 dc	1
		RL	119-127 lc	5
Gregory XII	(1406-1415)	RV	335-338 dc	94
		RL	128-135 lc	101
Alexander V	(1409-1410)	RV	339 dc	148
		RL	136-138 lc	149
John XXIII	(1410-1415)	RV	340-346 dc	167
		RL	139-185 lc	187
Council of Constance, 1415		RL	186	514-515

			Volume	Pages
VII: 1417-1431 (Twemlow, 1906)				
Martin V (1417-1431)				
	an. 1-14	RV	348-350	1
	1-13		352-356	5
	various years		357-359	19
	1-6	RL	187-236	39
	various years		237	305
	7-10		238-276	343-573

Note. Additions to v. VII are in v. XIII, p. xiii.

			Volume	Pages
VIII: 1427-1447 (Twemlow, 1909)				
Martin V				
	an. 11-14	RL	277-300	1
	10-14		301	206
Eugene IV	(1431-1447)			
	various years	RV	359-370	212
	an. 1-9		371-375	277
	various years		376-384	296
	an. 1-7	RL	302-358	321-678

	Volume	Pages

IX: 1431-1447 (Twemlow, 1912)
　Eugene IV

| an. 8-16 | RL   359-431 | 1-588 |

Note. Entries (all referring to Oxford) from a lost register of Eugene IV are printed from Fondo Santini in v. XIII, pp. xiv-xvi.

X: 1447-1455 (Twemlow, 1915)
　Nicholas V　　(1447-1455)

| | RV   380-435 dc | 1 |
| | RL   432-497 lc | 275-731 |

Note. Additions are printed at pp. xxv-xxvii.

XI: 1455-1465 (Twemlow, 1921)
　Calixtus III　　(1455-1458)

	RV 436-467	1
	502	195
	RL 498-534	196
Pius II　　(1458-1464)	RV 468-523	364-697

Note. Entries from Indici 319A, 325-327, are in the introduction. A list of lost bulls of Calixtus III is at pp. xxv-xxvi.

XII: 1458-1471 (Twemlow, 1933)
　Pius II
　Paul II　　(1464-1471)

	RL 535-599	1
	RV 519 dc	229
	524-545 ls	232
	RL 600-712	393-824

Note. Rubricellae of lost bulls of Pius and Paul are at pp. xx-xxxiv, followed by additions to vv. I, III, IV, VIII, XI, at pp. xlii-xliv.

XIII: 1471-1484 (Twemlow, 1955)
　Sixtus IV　　(1471-1484)

an. 1-5	RV 546-681	1
	RL 713-757	285
5-13	758-838	471
Indici 332-335		865-915

Note. Volume XIII is in two parts, but with continuous pagination. There are additions to vv. III, V-XII at pp. xii-xvi. The index of persons and places is by S. C. Ratcliff, that of subjects by U. G. Flanagan.

XIV: 1484-1492 (Twemlow, 1960)
　Innocent VIII (1484-1492)

| | RV   682-771 | 1 |
| an. 1 | RL   838-840 | 316-325 |

[For later volumes, see addenda on p. 102.]

II. THE AVIGNON REGISTERS

3.2.66

A. General description.

The greatest difference between the *Calendar of Papal Letters* noted above and the corresponding calendars of the French School in Rome is that the former uses the Vatican Registers only for "common letters" of the Avignon period (1305-1378) while the latter base themselves on the series of paper volumes known as the "Avignon Registers" (RA).

The difference is capital, since for the Avignon period the RV are not original chancery registers of common letters but are simply parchment copies of those letters as they were registered in the paper RA series. The Vatican Registers for the Avignon period are thus at least two removes from the original letters, and take a second place to the Avignon Registers in which the outgoing common letters were originally drafted or registered.[27] An RV volume, being a fair copy of the entries on paper in the RA series, is of course more legible and more pleasant to handle than a volume from the RA, but no one editing a papal letter from the Avignon period should rely solely on the RV series. As the late Msgr Mollat remarks, "Quoique les registres du Vatican, en parchemin, soient une transcription authentique de ceux d'Avignon, on les a toujours consultés de préférence à cause de leur meilleur état de conservation, et de leur meilleure ordonnance. Ils se sont pourtant exempts ni d'erreurs de dates, ni de fautes de lecture".[28] What is more, an RA volume often proves, for reasons we shall suggest presently, to contain many more letters than the corresponding fair copy in the RV series.

The RA series consists of 349 original paper volumes of registers of common letters, to which must be added a further four volumes of appendices put together from other ASV registers in

---

[27] The best general treatment of RA is F. Bock, *Einführung in das Registerwesen des Avignonesischen Papsttums* (= *Quellen und Forschungen aus italienischen Archiven und Bibliotheken*, 31, Rome 1941). An album of 39 plates accompanying this volume of the *Quellen und Forschungen* provides some excellent examples, both palaeographical and diplomatic, of the contents of RA. The conclusions of the present work are generally independent of those of Bock, though, of course, one could never have begun to form them without the patient work of the late Dr. Bock to guide one's steps.

[28] G. Mollat, *Les Papes d'Avignon*[10] (Paris 1965), p. 570.

1931.[29]   The volumes contain minutes, drafts and copies of letters sent out by the papal Chancery at Avignon between 1316
and 1378, and by the schismatic papacy between 1379 and 1418;
there is, besides, some cameral material (for which see section
V, below, p. 156).

Although the term "register" usually means a file-copy of an
incoming or outgoing letter, it is more elastic in the case of the
Avignon Registers. Basically the entries in the RA are drafts
rather than copies of letters, yet the Chancery clearly looked on
these drafts as registered copies: thus RA 51, f. 209r: "... est
registrata in sequenti caterno sub eodem numero...".   The volumes of these registers were formed from quaternions (generally
of a proper 16 pages) put together after the outgoing letters had
been completed (engrossed for expedition) and had been compared
with the drafts in the quaternions (or, if what was in the quaternion was a copy rather than a draft of a letter, after the copy had
been compared with the outgoing letter).[30]

The quaternions were numbered consecutively as they were
completed; possibly they were passed on one by one for copying
into the parchment (RV) registers, and were only bound together
into volumes after the RV officials had returned them.[31]   Certainly some RV copies seem to have been made very soon after
an RA quaternion was completed, if not, indeed, before the
final decision was taken by the Chancery on a letter already drafted in, or copied into, the RA quaternion in question.   Thus one
finds on occasion that an RA letter which later was cassated was
in fact copied into the RV before the cassation took place, e.g.
RA 66, ff. 22v-23v, n. 5: "Cassata est de mandato domini vicecancellarii, quia fuit correcta et alibi inferius registrata": yet,
although "inferius" is RA 66, f. 355v, n. 278 (and this also is
copied into RV 152, f. 402r, n. 278), the "cassated" letter occurs
without comment in RV 152, f. 259v, n. 5.   Again, although an

---

[29] To these 353 vv. there should also be added some RA volumes which are now
part of the RV series: RV 214-218, 242-244, 251, 262, 272-281, 288-290, 300-309,
321-332.   In the present book all RV volumes that are really RA in character are
cited as RVA to distinguish them from RV volumes proper.   In the table above
of the *Calendar of Papal Letters* it was noted that the editors have not calendared any
RVA volumes.

[30] The word "auscultatum" occurs regularly, as in RA 57, ff. 30v, 147v, 184v,
216v, probably to indicate that the letter or letters in question had been checked for
accuracy.

[31] Some RA volumes have been bound carelessly.   Thus in RA 159 (2 Urban V)
the quaternion "Litterae de provisione prelatorum," which bears an original foliation
562-585, now comes between ff. 49 and 62, occupying the place of quaternion 4 (ff.
50-61), now missing altogether.

entry in RA 68, f. 24v, was cassated "de mandato domini vice-cancellarii", the same letter is found in RV 153, f. 414r, but this time accompanied by a later note, "cassata est in papiro de mandato domini vicecancellarii". On another occasion, a letter in RA, 71, f. 532v, has a marginal note stating that the blank space in the letter is a "spacium pro executoribus"; when the RA letter was copied into RV 157, f. 436v, the executors were not yet known, for a space is left in RV at the very same point (but without any explanation).

This piecemeal process of handing over the paper (RA) quaternions one by one for copying on parchment was not always a great success, for in fact some quaternions seem not to have reached the RV scribes in time to be copied into the proper volume. This probably accounts for the failure of some RV volumes to agree exactly with the corresponding RA volume, and for the fact that there are at times quaternions in volumes of the RA that find no echo in the RV series: thus a quaternion of letters in RA 77, ff. 555r-569v, is not to be found anywhere in the corresponding RV 166. Notes in RA volumes lead one, indeed, to suspect that the liaison between the RA and RV departments sometimes broke down. Thus the first quaternion of letters of the second year of Clement VI (RA 76, ff. 403r-426v) arrived only "post redditionem litterarum", while the second quaternion (RA 76, ff. 427r-450v) did not reach the RV scribes until after the RV quaternions had been bound together in a volume: "post ligationem librorum". As a result, the letters in these two and in other similar RA quaternions are not to be found in RV — and this in spite of notes in the first quaternion (f. 412r, etc.) claiming that various letters in the quaternion were written "in pergameno". This type of "certification" usually occurs at the end of a quaternion (e.g. RA 58, f. 336v: q. 13; f. 362v: q. 14; f. 386v: q. 15; f. 416v: q. 16), but is often contradicted by the facts. Thus at the end of a quaternion in RA 62, f. 501v, there is a note, "scriptum est in pergameno", but in fact letter 71 of this quaternion (RA 62, f. 498r-v) is not in the corresponding RV 152. What happened was that the RV copyist skipped RA n. 71 and copied RA n. 72 in its place, but listing it as n. 71 in RV. Then, turning back to RA, he copied RA n. 73 into RV and gave it the same number (73), with the following result: RA 62, n. 70 = RV 152, n. 70 (f. 236r); RA 62, n. 71 is omitted; RA 62, n. 72 = RV 152, n. 71; RA 62, n. 73 = RV 152, n. 73. On the other hand, notes to the effect that "non est scriptum in pergameno" are equally untrustworthy. Thus a note of this kind in RA 58, f. 68r, is in fact contradicted by the presence of the letter in question at f. 112r in the corresponding RV 148.

In general it may be stated that the RA and RV series coincide for each pontificate. Thus, for John XXII (1316-1334), RA 2-47 are copied more or less faithfully in RV 63-108, although some further RA fragments or, indeed, whole quaternions, are to be found in other collections or in later RA volumes.[32] Likewise, RA 48-55 and RV 119-129 are in fundamental agreement on the common letters of Benedict XII (1334-1342); the *litterae secretae* of Benedict (RV130-136), being products not of the Chancery but of the Camera, are of course not to be found in RA. From Clement VI to Gregory XI (1342-1378) the cohesion between RA and RV is not quite so straightforward, as may be seen from a table (p. 118) of the relationship between the RA and RV volumes for half of the pontificate of Clement VI. The RV volumes in question are vv. 147-170 of the present series, but they do not correspond volume for volume with the RA volumes. On the other hand, the RA volumes (RA 56-83) of the regular RA series must be supplemented by some five paper or "Avignon" volumes which have strayed into the RV series (RV 214-218) and are here labelled RVA 214-218 to indicate that they properly belong to the RA series.

From this table it will be seen that there are many RA sections which find no counterpart in RV, and that, on the other hand, some quaternions of RA are no longer extant. What the table does not reveal, however, is that the number of entries copied from RA into RV can vary considerably from pontificate to pontificate, and indeed from year to year. Thus, while RA and RV are largely in agreement for the first year (1342-1343) of Clement VI, the position is otherwise for the first year (1352-1353) of Innocent VI, where some 85 letters in RVA 244 are not to be found in RV 219, or for the sixth year (1357-1358) of the same pope, where there are at least 116 letters more in RA 138-139 than in the corresponding RV 233.

The reason for these omissions is not always clear, but sometimes the omissions are quite deliberate: thus a letter in RA 87, ff. 392v-393v, is noted as "non scribatur" in the index to the volume, and in fact is not in the corresponding RV 174, f. 193r.

---

[32] For example, a section of 3 John XXII is in RA 160 (3 Urban V) at ff. 17-30. In RA 159, ff. 68r-69v (again 3 Urban V), there are "Rubrice litterarum curie tertii anni" of John XXII, numbered 1-201; while in RA 350 (RA Appendix I) there are letters of years 14, 15 and 17 of John XXII, numbered 2464-2730. In the latter case there are notes at ff. 50v, 94v, etc. stating, "Transcriptus in pergameno. Rubricatus est," and, in fact, some of the letters are in RV 95 and RV 97.

RA	ff.	range	= RV	ff.	range
56,	ff.	29-39	= RV 147,	ff.	1-6
		42-146			6-70
		154-514			70-303
57,		1-246			303-483
		247-382		148,	22-112
		397-523			—
58,		19-531			113-538
		532-589		149,	1-33
59,		14-562			34-394
		563-566			—
60,		19-560		150,	1-385
		563-577		151,	1-10
61,		34-57			129-144
		59-475			145-360
		490-541			—
62,		35-205			11-128
		206-530		152,	118-257
RVA 214,		1-128			1-117
		220-318		155,	405-444
		319-338			109-115
		339-344			383-385
		345-376			94-109
		385-402			120-129
		403-422			347-355
		424-474			379-404
		474-518			356-378
RA 63,		14-196			1-93
		201-488		153,	1-135
64,		14-503		154,	125-332
65,		15-162			332-418
		167-442			1-124
66,		19-378		152,	258-418
		379-603		154,	419-526
67,		29-401		155,	167-346
		410-491			130-166
		502-534			—
68,		5-105		156,	407-450
		110-581		153,	137-318
69,		1-244			318-406
		245-602		156,	1-133
70,		1-467			134-406
		473-518			—
		524-586			—
RA 71,	ff.	18-605	= RV 157,	ff.	71-480
72,		15-508		160,	1-390
73,		30-115		159,	67-110
		128-220			1-66
		224-378			111-196
		379-412			—
RVA 215,		1-256		161,	1-161
		—			162-458
RA 74,		28-466		162,	50-265
		467-554		157,	1-68
75,		18-564		158,	43-417
		569-611			1-42
76,		30-370		159,	197-465
		377-548			—
77,		30-526		166,	1-293
		555-569			—
RVA 216,		1-9		167,	—
		10-17			1-8
		18-426			8-338
		427-469		165,	276-307
RA 78,		33-122		166,	294-340
		129-150			373-378
		157-280		163,	144-231
		—			232-490
		285-409		164,	192-289
		410-540		165,	1-89
79,		40-266			90-270
		267-298			
		299-560		163,	1-143
80,		40-94		166,	341-372
		181-324		167,	338-444
		331-616		164,	1-183
81,		282-501			—
RVA 217,		1-6		169,	1-3
		7-10			15-16
		11-29			4-14
		30-481			17-301
RVA 218,		1-429		168,	214-474
RA 82,		25-545		170,	1-457
		—			457-462
83,		33-194		168,	112-213
		201-349		169,	302-397
		392-568		168,	1-111

Table comparing RA and RV

Some omissions are possibly due to oversight. Thus at the end of RV 164 there are 10 letters missing which are in RA 78 at ff. 409r-v, yet just before the 10 letters in RA there is the note, "perfectus est in pergameno per me Iohannem"; probably what happened was that the scribe who took over from John concluded from this note that the whole quaternion had been copied on parchment, and hence the 10 letters were passed over. Nevertheless, there probably was some general policy behind many of the omissions. For example, there is a note, "Non scribantur in pergameno nisi usque... hic", in the index to RA 84, f. 7v, and accordingly 14 letters of RA 84, ff. 306v-316v, are not copied into RV 171 at f. 162v. In fact this same RA 84 contains many examples of this procedure, but there is never any explanation given. Thus, various letters at ff. 26v (five entries), 30r, 31v, etc., are ordered not to be copied on parchment. Again at f. 50r (the middle of quaternion 8) there is the instruction,"non scribantur sequentes rubricae in pergameno", and as a result the parchment register RV 172, ff. 308v-310v, contains only 12 letters where RA 84, ff. 50r-53v, has 109 letters in all. Equally mysterious are notes in RA 79, 199r-v: "scriptus in pergameno exceptis duabus primis litteris"; in RA 80, f. 602r: "Quantum ad presens non scribatur nisi usque hic in pergameno" (hence RA 79 contains 7 letters more at this point — ff. 602r-607v — than RV 164, f. 184r); or in RVA 216, f. 468r: "Scriptum in pergameno excepta una littera" (but in fact two letters, not one, of RA are missing from the corresponding RV 165, f. 307v).

Some of the omissions in RV are of course for the very good reason that the RA letters in question had been cancelled (e.g. RA 58, ff. 116r, 119v, 162r, 188r) before they reached the RV department. A good example of cancellation (and hence of non-registration in RV — and of the importance of reading everything in RA) occurs in RA 67, ff. 533r-v, in the middle of a group of miscellaneous fragments which, as it happens, Bock (*Einführung*, p. 9) says are "impossible to identify". This is a letter of Clement VI of 25 October 1342 in which he provides Bricius, abbot of Clones in Ireland, to SS. Peter and Paul, Armagh, in spite of the fact that when the former abbot Oddo had died in the papal curia, and the abbacy of Armagh had thus become reserved to the Holy See, the monks of Armagh in ignorance of this reservation had illegally elected the same Bricius, who, in the absence of the archbishop, had been confirmed by the vicar-general of Armagh. For, the papal letter states, as soon as Bricius had heard of the papal reservation, he had journeyed to Avignon and had placed himself and the abbacy completely in the hands of the pope; whereupon the pope, being aware of the good name that Bricius had had as abbot of Clones, and being impressed by the fact that the monks of Armagh obviously wanted him as their abbot, duly provided Bricius to Armagh as though there had not been any irregularity. Although this letter of provision (which is followed by letters in the same strain to Bricius and the monks of Armagh) was cancelled and therefore does not appear in RV, it does provide some valuable information which might escape the student who examined only the RV series.

Another reason for some of the omissions of RA letters from RV is that groups of letters of one year of a pontificate have strayed into the RA volumes of another year, and, indeed, that letters from one pontificate sometimes turn up in volumes of another pontificate. Hence the RV copyist will ignore these ectopic letters, since he was supposed to confine himself to one pontificate at a time, and to keep the letters of each year together. Thus in RA 160 (3 Urban V, 1364-1365) there is a group of letters at ff. 17r-30v from 3 John XXII (1318-1319); these are not in RV, nor were they known to Mollat when he was calendaring the registers of John XXII. It is possible that this quaternion of letters (numbered, curiously, backwards, from 842-772) was on loan to some other department when the RA registers of John XXII were being bound, and was only recovered some 40 years later during Urban's pontificate. There is a nice case within the one pontificate in RA 159, ff. 575r-v (again 3 Urban V, 1364-1365), where the appointment of Gerald de Barry as bishop of Cork on 6 id. Nov. *anno primo* (8 November 1362) is registered and then cancelled with the note, "Attende de anno primo". There is not, of course, any record of this letter in the RV volumes for I Urban V (1362-1363), since, presumably, these volumes were already compiled by 1364-1365, when the letter to Gerald de Barry finally was registered out of place.[33] Now, since the editors of the *Handbook of British Chronology*[2] (London 1961, p. 326) state that there is "no date of provision" for Gerald de Barry as bishop of Cork, it may be useful to note here that the above provision of 8 November 1362 seems to have been

---

[33] But, on the other hand, letters of later years are sometimes found among those of the earlier years of a pontificate. Thus, three letters of 2 Clement VI (1353-1354) are in RA 61, ff. 40r-41v, among letters of 1 Clement VI. As notes in RA 61 at those points clearly state, these letters were not copied into the RV volume corresponding to RA 61. This suggests that there was quite a time-lag at the beginning of Clement's pontificate between the putting together of an RA volume and the making of the RV fair copy — and, indeed, that RA volumes themselves were undergoing some delays.

made by Urban V in ignorance of the fact that Gerald had already been provided to Cork sometime in the pontificate of Innocent VI (1352-1362). This we learn from a letter of Urban to Gerald on 1 February 1365 (RA 159, f. 225r), when Urban confirmed Gerald as bishop. As it happens, this confirmation was necessary because of the fact that, when Gerald had heard of the provision by Innocent VI, he had had himself consecrated immediately, without waiting for his letters of appointment to arrive, by Thomas, bishop of Leighlin, "ex mandato Radulphi archiepiscopi Cassellensis", and had then taken possession of Cork. Possibly Innocent's letters were never sent out; and it was only when Urban's provision of 8 November 1362 reached Cork, that Gerald found that his consecration was out of order, and that he had acted, as Urban put it nicely in the letter of 1365, "ex quadam simplicitate".

If bishops could nod, so too could the scribes of RA and RV: in RA 160, ff. 176v-177r, the name "Bitteren" was written as "Bittericen.", and had to be corrected; in RA 159, folio 537v-538r was written upside down, meriting a later comment, "istae duae paginae sunt scriptae ordine retrogrado per ignorantiam".

Sometimes the RV scribes were unable to read what was written in RA (and who is to blame them, since some RA hands are very untutored), as in RV 157, f. 154r, where there is a blank at a point where RA 71, f. 254r, has a slightly difficult "propterea". From the pontificate of Clement VI onwards there seems in fact to have been a falling off in the accuracy and in the control of RV transcriptions from RA. A good example is in RV 166, f. 136r, where a letter of Clement VI is dated as "Burdegalis VIII kal. iulii anno tertio". For when one turns to the letter in RA 77, ff. 260v-261r, which RV has copied, it will be found that Clement's letter is not dated as "Burdegalis VIII kal. iulii anno tertio" but as "Avinion. III kal. iulii anno tertio". Since Clement VI's letter of 29 June 1344 contains a rehearsal of a letter of Clement V of 24 September 1305, clearly what has happened is that the RV scriptor has coalesced the date of Clement V's letter ("*Datum Burdegalis VIII* kal. octobris pontificatus nostri anno primo") with that of Clement VI ("Datum Avinion. III *kal. iulii anno tertio*"), thus arriving at the spurious date and place of Clement VI's letter: "Datum Burdegalis VIII kal. iulii anno tertio."

The scribes of RA, in turn, seem very prone to duplication. This factor, however, should not deter one from examining both versions of a letter in RA. Thus, although a provision to a canonry in Dublin in RA 59, ff. 271v-272r (= RV 149, ff. 191v-192r = *Calendar of Papal Letters*, III, p. 59) appears to be duplicated at ff. 404r-404v (= RV 149, f. 277v = *Calendar*, III, p. 60), it will be found that the clause, "... seu quod in Lymericen. cancellariam et prebendam quorum fructus et redditus quattuordecim librarum sterlingarum valorem annuum secundum taxationem de iure, sicut asseritur, non excedunt..." (RA 59, f. 272r), has been changed on f. 404r to "... seu quod in Lymericen. cancellariam et prebendam *modici valoris*...".

Some of the duplication is, of course, simply an error of the scribes of RA, as in RVA 214, ff. 108r-108v, where there is a note, "vacat quia iteratus; est scriptus superius sub numero v"; but there is little excuse for the RV scribe whose job it was to copy RVA 214 on parchment, for he, too, copied the letter in question twice, and then had to repeat the above note of duplication (RV 152, f. 63r).[34]

One must allow, however, for the fact that some RV errors are due to the fact that on occasion the style of RA entries can be very abbreviated. Thus in RA 61, ff. 439v-440r, only the beginning of a letter is written out, and it was up to the RV scriptor (RV 151, ff. 385r-387v) to supply the remainder from common form. On the other hand, letters to executors, etc., are usually given in full in RA, but in RV are generally reduced to bare names, with a reference back to the main entry or to a previous letter for the full tenor of the letter. For example, letter 636 in RA 87, which occupies more than two pages (ff. 525r-526r), is given only five lines in RV 174, f. 243r, with a direction to seek the remainder "in superiore parte quae dirigitur Electen. et Tarvien. episcopis." This means that if one is using RV 174, one has to go back from f. 243r to ff. 239v-240v to put the letter together which RA has given in full. Hence, when ordering photographs or microfilms from RV references in the *Calendar of Papal Letters* or in the calendars of the French School, one has to be sure that the folio reference given in these publications really covers the complete letter.

Needless to say, where RA references exist they should be followed up in preference to the more legible RV entries. For apart from the fact that the RA are original registers of common

---

[34] RV scribes must have found it difficult on occasion to follow the order of letters in RA. Thus in RVA 214, ff. 22r-44r, there are 63 letters which were only sorted out chronologically after they had been written in. Hence the numbers 1-63 are not in sequence, and the scribe of RV 152, ff. 16r-26v, had to pick out the correct sequence from a veritable jumble of numbers in RVA.

letters, it is also important to remember that they often contain marginal notes which are not repeated in RV. In particular, indications in RA of the departmental origin of letters often are not copied into RV: thus at the end of RA 67 (ff. 398v-400r) there is a group of common letters not of the Chancery but "de camera", but these letters are not noted as such in RV 155; and similar notes in RA 67, ff. 33r, are again not repeated in RV 155, ff. 169r, 169v. Likewise, marks of taxation are usually, though not infallibly, in RA, but they are rarely, if ever, in RV. Cameral notes, too, of the exemption from tax of letters of provision to papal nephews ("Gratis pro nepote") or to officials of the curia (e.g., "Gratis pro abbreviatore") are not copied from RA into RV: thus, "Gratis pro auditore" in RA 66, ff. 132r-133r (the auditor in question being the Englishman Thomas Fastolf) is not in RV 152, ff. 298v-299r (= *Calendar of Papal Letters*, II, p. 76). Understandably, the departmental asides in RA find no place in RV. Hence, for example, one is deprived in RV 124, ff. 18r-18v (= *Calendar of Papal Letters*, III, p. 541) of a marginal note in RA 51, f. 26r (opposite a letter addressed to England) that throws some further light on the role of Andreas Sapiti, the great procurator at Avignon of English and Irish bishops from 1312-c.1338: "Non detur copia inconsulto magistro Andrea Sapiti".

From these scattered notes it will be seen at once that the *Calendar of Papal Letters* project was greatly mistaken when it decided to calendar the RV registers of the Avignon period in preference to, and, more astonishingly, without any cross-reference to the Avignon Registers. The French School calendars, on the other hand, rightly give the RA pride of place, and where possible give the corresponding RV reference. The result is that by the time the French School project is completed, students will have to hand an exceptional instrument for the study of the Avignon Papacy. This is not to say that the French School calendars are perfect in every respect. For one thing, the division of letters according to departmental origin into "clausae", "secretae" and "communes", does not reflect the normal layout of RA, and makes for very inconvenient consultation; in fact of all the volumes published thus far, the only volumes to follow the actual system of the registers is Mollat's *Lettres communes* for John XXII, but even here the letters are rearranged chronologically. For another thing, the calendaring of "Lettres relatives à la France" separately from "Lettres intéressant les pays autres que la France" surely has doubled the editorial work, and certainly can be misleading. For example, one often gets the impression from books on the Avignon Papacy or the Papal Chancery that all of RA and RV for John XXII are now calendared, whereas in fact the secret and the curial letters in RV have yet to be calendared for countries other than France. Again, an unwary student working on non-French areas might easily be persuaded that he could afford to skip the "French" volumes of the calendars. This would be a great mistake. A case in point is a letter of 2 Clement VI (21.10.1343) to the abbot of Grande-Sauve, Bordeaux (RA 73, ff. 180r-v; RV 159, ff. 32r-v). For in fact the letter has nothing to do with Grande-Sauve as such, but rather with the affairs of a certain William de Rath-drinath of Ireland, monk of St. James, Ratisbon, "in quo monasterio, ut asserit, non nisi veri hybernici in monachos admittuntur." In his letter the Pope instructs the abbot of Grande-Sauve to see that William is received by the monastery of Ste-Croix, Bordeaux, for in his petition he had stated that he had been badly treated by the monks of Ratisbon, being placed in prison there for 29 weeks, and had then been made to swear on the Gospels to depart the monastery for ever, and yet not to report the monks to the papal curia.

These drawbacks to the French School calendars are, to say the least, negligible; and it may seem, indeed, ungenerous to mention them. As the following list of these calendars from Gregory IX onwards should clearly suggest, students of all nations owe an incalculable debt to the generations of French scholars who have contributed to the *Deuxième série* (1884-1960) and *Troisième série* (1899-) of the *Bibliothèque* from the 1880's to the present day.[35] The list is arranged chronologically by Pope, but the serial number of the *Bibliothèque* (e.g. B 4) is given in brackets after each entry. All the volumes below are published by Éditions E. de Boccard, Paris; unless otherwise stated, each volume is complete.

---

[35] See R. Fawtier, 'Un grand achèvement de l'École Française de Rome: la publication des Registres des Papes du xiii⁰ siècle,' in *Mélanges d'archéologie et d'histoire* 72 (1960) I-XIII.

BIBLIOTHÈQUE DES ÉCOLES FRANÇAISES D'ATHÈNES ET DE ROME

Deuxième série: Registres et Lettres des Papes du XIIIe siècle

1. Gregory IX (1227-1241): *Les registres de Grégoire IX*, ed. L. Auvray, S. Vitte-Clémencet and L. Carolus-Barré: 4 vv. in 13 fascicules, 1890-1955. (B 4).
2. Innocent IV (1243-1254): *Les registres d'Innocent IV*, ed. É. Berger: 4 vv., 1884-1921. (B 5).
3. Alexander IV (1254-1261): *Les registres d'Alexandre IV*, ed. C. Bourel de la Roncière, J. de Loye, P. de Cénival and A. Coulon: 3 vv. in 8 fascicules, 1895-1959. (B 6).
4. Urban IV (1261-1264): *Les registres d'Urbain IV*, ed. J.Guiraud and S. Clémencet: 4 vv. in 11 fascicules, 1899-1958. (B 7).
5. Clement IV (1265-1268): *Les registres de Clément IV*, ed. E. Jordan: 1 v. in 6 fascicules, 1893-1945. (B 8).
6. Gregory X (1271-1276) and John XXI (1276-1277): *Les registres de Grégoire X et de Jean XXI*, ed. J. Guiraud, E. Cadier and G. Mollat: 1 v. in 6 fascicules, 1892-1960. (B 9).
7. Nicholas III (1277-1280): *Les registres de Nicolas III*, ed. J. Gay and S. Vitte-Clémencet: 1 v. in 5 fascicules, 1898-1938. (B 10).
8. Martin IV (1281-1285): *Les registres de Martin IV*, ed. F. Olivier-Martin: 1 v. in 3 fascicules, 1901-1935. (B 11).
9. Honorius IV (1285-1287): *Les registres d'Honorius IV*, ed. M. Prou: 1 v. in 4 fascicules, 1886-1888. (B 12).
10. Nicholas IV (1288-1292): *Les registres de Nicolas IV*, ed. E. Langlois: 2 vv. in 9 fascicules, 1887-1893. (B 13).
11. Boniface VIII (1294-1303): *Les registres de Boniface VIII*, ed. G. Digard, M. Faucon, A. Thomas, R. Fawtier: 4 vv. in 17 fascicules, 1884-1939. (B 14).
12. Benedict XI (1303-1304): *Les registres de Benoît XI*, ed. Ch. Grandjean: 1 v. in 5 fascicules, 1883-1905. (B 15).
13. Clement V (1305-1314): *Tables des registres de Clément V publiés par les Bénédictins*, ed. Y. Lanhers, C. Vogel, R. Fawtier and G. Mollat: 1 v. in 2 fascicules, 1948-1957, being an index to the *Regestum Clementis V*, ed. by Benedictines of Monte Cassino, 7 vv., Rome 1885-1888, followed by 1 v. of appendices (*Cameralia*), 1892. (B 25).

Troisième série: Registres et Lettres des Papes du XIVe siècle

14. John XXII (1316-1334):
   a. *Jean XXII. Lettres communes analysées d'après les registres dits d'Avignon et du Vatican*, ed. G. Mollat: 16 vv. in 31 fascicules, 1904-1947, being 13 vv. of text with 3 vv. (14, 15, 16) of indexes. (B 16).

Note. The numbering in v. 7, p. 130, jumps from 30999 to 40000, hence the final tally of letters (64421) is some 9000 more than in fact. In v. 9, pp. 201-206, the order of pages is wrong, and hence that of nn. 48441-48478. Mollat has not used a section of 3 John XXII which occurs in RA 160 (3 Urban V) at ff. 17r-30v, and RA references are therefore wanting in nn. 9050, 9165, 9194, 9492, 9497, 9541, 9549, 9566, 9567, etc. Likewise, RA Appendix I, containing letters (numbered 2464-2730, etc.) of 14-16 John XXII, has been used only fitfully by Mollat; accordingly the RA references corresponding to RV 95 are not present in the following British Isles entries (to note only those) in Mollat at nn. 49876, 49877, 49878, 49880, 49883, 49986, 50045, 50515, 53296, 53994, etc.

Besides RA and RV for the period 1316-1334, Mollat has also calendared the relevant *Instrumenta Miscellanea* and documents from the *Archivum Arcis, Schedario Garampi* and *Bullarium generale* at nn. 5465-5511, 8357-8388, 10245-20279, 12242-12296, 14330-14409, 16170-16224, 18137-18196, 20337-20605, 23137-23399, 26446-26492, 29686-29728, 42381-42497, 46222-46320, 50713-50815, 54806-54863, 58212-58252, 61261-61322, 63893-63933, 64228-64240. In v. 13, pp. 222-238 (nn. 64244-64421) there are *Addenda et Corrigenda* for all 13 volumes of text. The introduction to v. 8 contains Mollat's valuable essay, *La collation des bénéfices ecclésiastiques sous les papes d'Avignon, 1305-1378* (also published separately under the same title, Paris 1921).

b. *Lettres secrètes et curiales du pape Jean XXII relatives à la France,* ed. A. Coulon and S. Clémencet: incomplete: 2 vv. in 5 fascicules, 1900-1913; v. 3 has reached 1330-1332 (9th fascicule, 1967). There is nothing as yet for countries other than France. (B 26).

Note. For the register of the Antipope Nicholas V (1328-1330) see C. Eubel, 'Der Registerband des Gegenpapstes Nikolaus V.', in *Archivalische Zeitschrift* 4 (1893) 123-212; A. Mercati, 'Supplementi al registro dell'antipapa Niccolò V', in *Sussidi* III, pp. 59-76.

14. Benedict XII (1334-1342):
a. *Lettres communes et curiales analysées d'après les registres dits d'Avignon et du Vatican,* ed. J.-M. Vidal: 3 vv. in 6 fascicules, 1903-1911. (B 17).
b. *Lettres closes, patentes et curiales se rapportant à la France,* ed. G. Daumet: 1 v. in 3 fascicules, 1899-1920. (B 18).
c. *Lettres closes et patentes intéressant les pays autres que la France,* ed. J.-M. Vidal and G. Mollat: 2 vv. in 6 fascicules, 1913-1950. (B 19).

[for information as of 1996, see Blouin, p. 138]

15. Clement VI (1342-1352):
a. *Lettres closes, patentes et curiales se rapportant à la France,* ed. E. Déprez, J. Glenisson and G. Mollat: 3 vv. in 6 fascicules, 1910-1961. (B 20).
b. *Lettres closes, patentes et curiales intéressant les pays autres que la France,* ed. E. Déprez and G. Mollat: 1 v. in 3 fascicules, 1900-1961. (B 21).

16. Innocent VI (1352-1362):
a. *Lettres closes, patentes et curiales se rapportant à la France,* ed. E. Déprez: 1 fascicule (1909). All 281 letters of 1 Innocent VI in this fascicule have been calendared freshly in
b. *Lettres secrètes et curiales,* ed. P. Gasnault and M.-H. Laurent: 4 fascicules (1959-1968) to date. (B 27).

17. Urban V (1362-1370):
a. *Les registres d'Urbain V (1362-1363). Recueil des bulles de ce pape publiées ou analysées d'après les manuscrits originaux du Vatican,* ed. M. Dubrulle: 1 v., 1926. (B 25).
b. *Lettres secrètes et curiales se rapportant à la France,* ed. P. Lacacheux and G. Mollat: 1 v. in 4 fascicules, 1902-1955. (B 22).

c. *Lettres communes analysées d'après les registres dits d'Avignon et du Vatican,* ed. M.-H. Laurent, P. Gasnault, M. Hayez, etc.: v. 1 in 5 fascicules (1954-1958); v. 2 (1964-) has reached fascicule 3 (1967). (B 28).
18. Gregory XI (1370-1378):
a. *Lettres secrètes et curiales relatives à la France,* ed. L. Mirot, H. Jassemin, J. Vieillard, G. Mollat, E. R. Labande: 1 v. in 5 fascicules, 1935-1957. (B 23).
b. *Lettres secrètes et curiales intéressant les pays autres que la France,* ed. G. Mollat: 1 v. in 3 fascicules, 1962-1965. (B 24).

B. INDEXES TO THE AVIGNON REGISTERS.

a. *Contemporary indexes.* There are excellent contemporary indexes in the RA volumes. These should be consulted always, for in many volumes quaternions of letters are either incomplete or missing altogether. Thus quaternion 13 of RA 56 is wanting after f. 487v, but will be found indexed at f. 14r. Again, in the index to RA 57 (which in fact is in RA 56, since RA 56 and RA 57 were treated by the indexer as one volume) there are 37 items indexed at ff. 28r-28v of RA 56 which are in fact missing from RA 57 at f. 245v; as it happens, the section in question (all of the first quaternion "De dignitate" and part of the second) was not missing when RV 148 was being copied from RA 57, so the reliability of the index in RA 56 can be substantiated fully. Likewise, quaternion 11 and part of quaternion 12 are absent from RA 58, but are in the index to RA 58 at ff. 8v-9r, and in full in RV 148.

In many cases the RA indexes seem to have been ready before the volumes with which they go were copied into the RV parchment registers; and, indeed, the copying of the RA indexes on parchment seems to have been done without any dependence upon the copying of the RA letters into RV. Thus, although the index to RV 164 agrees perfectly with that to RA 78, there are in fact 10 letters in RA 78, ff. 409r-409v, which were not copied into RV 164. Moreover, there are not in RV the "certifications" that are in RA (e.g. RA 58, ff. 6v, 7r, 9v, 10r) of the faithfulness of the index to the contents of the volume. However, it should be noted that an index often covers more than the volume of RA which it prefaces. Thus RA 57 is indexed in RA 56, while the last of the 23 quaternions indexed in RA 58 is in fact to be found at the beginning of RA 59. Some indexes, of course, are even farther away from their proper volume; RVA 214, for example, is part of the RV series today, but its index is in RA 70.

b. *Later indexes*. As was noted above in Part One (p. 49), there are in the Vatican Archives two useful indexes to the RA series which were compiled at Avignon in the early 18th century. The first in order of time as well as of importance is what we may term here the *Martin Index* (Indici 642-669 in the ASV Index Room); the second we shall call the *Montroy Index* (Indici 557-641). The two differ in that the Martin Index, made at Avignon by Joseph de Martin in 1711, is a calendar of the Avignon Registers (excepting those of Gregory XI) volume by volume, item by item, while the Montroy Index, compiled at Avignon by Pierre de Montroy from 1718-1732, is rather an alphabetical index, diocese by diocese, of each volume of the RA series.

If we may conclude from the following summary comparison of Indice 664 (Tome VI at 2 Innocent VI) with the present RA 126 (2 Innocent VI), the Martin Index is indeed a very accurate and thorough calendar. The items noted in the comparative table all have reference to the British Isles, so for good measure I have included the RV volumes (RV 225-226) corresponding to RA 126 and to Indice 664, as well as the *Calendar of Papal Letters* (CPL). This should enable one to judge at a glance the relative fidelity of Indice 664 and the RV volumes to RA 126, and of the *Calendar* (here cited by page and item) to RV 225, 226. However, it must be pointed out that the closeness with which RV 225-226 follow RA 126 is not at all typical of the relationship of RV and RA during Innocent's pontificate as a whole. These volumes of RA and RV belong to the second year of Innocent VI; but in 1 Innocent VI (RA 121-125, RVA 244; RV 219-224), RVA 244 contains some 85 more entries in 415 folios than the corresponding RV 224 in 259 folios; while in 3 Innocent VI (RA 129-131; RV 230-231) there are 403 letters more in the RA volumes than in those of RV.

Indice 664 RA reference	Present RA 126	Present RV 225-226	CPL III
f. 1: *Quaternus primus de provisionibus Innocentii VI anno 2°*			
54	54v - 55r	225,42r	516.3
108	108v - 109r	79r	4
110	110r - 11r	80r	5
112	112v - 113r	82v	6
144	144r - 144v	104v	7
146: *De dignitatibus vacantibus anno secundo*			
154	154v - 155r	111v	517.1
165	165r - 166r	118r	2
186	186r - 186v	130r	3
206	206r	145r	4
215	215r - 215v	151v	5
240	240r - 240v	168r	6

Indice 664 RA reference	Present RA 126	Present RV 225-226	CPL III
244: *De praebendis vacantibus anno secundo*			
248	248v - 249v	174r	518.1
249	249v - 250r	174r	2
254	254r - 254v	177r	3
284: *De praebendis vacaturis anno secundo*			
293	293v - 294r	200v	4
314	314r - 314v	218v	5
317	317v - 318v	222r	6
332	332r - 332v	233v	7
348	348r - 348v	246r	519.1
349	349r - 350r	247r	2
353	353v - 354r	250v	3
358	358r - 358v	254v	4
361	361v - 362r	257r	5
375	375r - 375v	268r	6
382	382r - 282v	273v	7
383	383r - 384r	274v	8
389	388v - 389r	279v	520.1
397	397r - 397v	286v	3
398	397v - 398r	281r	2
401	401r - 401v	289r	4 *a*
408: *De litteris diversarum formarum anno secundo*			
409	409r	226,160v	521.5
413	413v - 414v	164v	6
423	423r - 423v	171v	7
423	423v	171v	522.1
425	425r - 425v	172v	2
452	452r	192v	3
471	471v	205r	4 *b*
475	475v	206v	− *c*
475	475v - 476v	207r	5
482	482r - 482v	211r	− *d*
484	484v	213r	6
486	486r - 486v	214r	7

Notes. From this comparative table it will be seen that Indice 664 and RV 225-226, respectively, miss only one British Isles letter in RA 126, but that the *Calendar of Papal Letters* fails to record four entries in RV 225-226. The following notes may help to document these and other points of interest in the table:

a. In RA 126, f. 401v, there is a note "Scriptum in pergameno usque hic." A number of letters follow now in RV 225 which are not in RA 126 (including four to the British Isles, as in CPL III, p. 520, 5-8). These letters, however, are to be found in RA 128, and are, in fact, calendared later on in Indice 664.

b. The month of this letter is not given in RA 126, and hence is also absent from RV 226 and the CPL.

c. The item not recorded by the CPL is a letter to Michael, bishop of London, in 19 May 1354 (RA 125, f. 475v; RV 226, ff. 206v-207r).

d. The letter in RV 226, ff. 211r-v (= RA 126, ff. 482r-v) which the CPL does not calendar, is a mandate to the Abbot of Mellifont and two others to reconcile to the Cistercian order the bearer of the letter, Stephen Trodan, priest, who is a professed monk of and fugitive from St. Mary's, Dublin. The letter is dated 31 May 1354, and is noted in RA as "Gratis pro Deo."

Indice 664 RA reference	Present RA 126	Present RV 225-226	CPL III
488	488v 489r	215v	8 *e*
503	503r	224v	9
503	503r	224v	523.1
504	504v - 505r	225v	2
509	509v - 510r	228v	3
—	510r - 510v	229r	4
510	510v	229r	5
535	535r	243v	6
535	535r - 535v	244r	— *f*
546	546r	250v	7
550	550r	252v	8
550	550r	253r	9
550	550v	253r	10 *g*
550	550v - 551r	253r	524.1
551	551r	253v	2
—	—	254r	3 *h*
557	557v	258r	4
559	559r - 559v	258v	5
569	569v	264v	6
573	573r	265v	7
576	576v	—	— *i*

e. This letter, calendared by the CPL III, 522.8, from RV 226, ff. 215v-216r (= RA 126, ff. 488v-489r), provides a good example of how inadequate the CPL can be on occasion. The CPL, by way of calendaring the letter, states: "Confirmation, with exemplification, at the request of Richard de Baskerville, knight, and Isabella, his wife, of the diocese of Hereford, of the letters issued by Clement VI, 2 Non. June, *anno* 3, ruling, in the case of John, earl of Warenne, and Joan de Barro, that dispensation for the marriage of persons related in the fourth degree of kindred shall hold good if they are related in the fourth and third degrees." What the CPL fails to record, however, is the important information (not, so far as I know, available elsewhere) that the letter of Clement VI (4 June 1344) rehearsed in full in this letter of Innocent VI, is a denial of the petition of John de Warenne to have his marriage of 33 years standing annulled on the ground that he and Joan de Barro were in fact related in the fourth and third degrees, and that the dispensation granted originally by Clement V from kinship in the fourth degree of consanguinity was therefore invalid.

f. The letter omitted by CPL III is an indulgence for all those who contribute to the fabric of St. Paul's, London.

g. The date of the Windsor letter in CPL III, 523.10, should be 19 Kal. Jan., not 2 Id. Dec., as both RA and RV attest.

h. A page is missing here in RA 126, and hence letters 4005-4007 are not in Indice 664.

i. The RA item not transcribed in RV concerns the diocese of Wells.

Unlike the Martin Index above, which calendars each RA volume in turn, the Montroy Index (Indici 557-641) proceeds alphabetically by diocese through all the RA volumes, one by one. Under "Littera A," for example, each volume of RA for each pontificate is taken in turn ("An. 1, pars 1, tom. 1," "An. 1, pars 1, tom. 2," etc.) and all letters addressed to dioceses beginning with A (*Achaden, Archaden, Armachan.*, etc.) are calendared briefly, with folio references. The Montroy Index certainly is more difficult to use than that of Martin, but its chief drawback is that, as a calendar, it is not as comprehensive or as informative. All the same, it does provide a ready conspectus of the content of each or of all of the RA volumes with respect to a given diocese. Thus, if we take the section of "Littera D" (Indice 578, ff. 19r-21r: "Innocentii VI... An. 2, pars 1, tom. 6") that covers the year of Innocent VI (2 Innocent VI: RA 126) already examined above in relation to the Martin Index, the results, so far as British Isles entries are concerned, are heartening: a letter to Dublin is noted as "fol. 186," and is indeed in RA 126, f. 186r, while letters to Durham are listed as "fol. 383" and "fol. 486", and are likewise in RA 126 at ff. 383r, 486r; however, the Dublin letter in RA 126, f. 482r, is not recorded. Again, if we take "Littera E" for the same year of Innocent VI, the following British Isles items are in Indice 578, ff. 153r-158v, and are again borne out by RA 126: *Exonien.*, fol. 215 (= RA 126, f. 215r); *Eboracen.*, fol. 332 (= RA 126, f. 332r); *Exonien.*, fol. 348 (= RA 126, f. 348r); *Eboracen.*, fol. 409 (= RA 126, f. 409r), ... fol. 423 (= RA 126, f. 423v).

In fine, it may be said of these two ASV indexes to the RA series that the Martin Index (Indici 642-699) is a good and reasonably complete guide, while the Montroy Index (Indici 557-641) is useful but not exhaustive.

III. THE LATERAN REGISTERS

A. General Description.

When the Great Schism began in 1378, the paper registers of common letters which we have examined above under the title "Avignon Registers" remained at Avignon to become the preserve of the Avignon Obedience; they come to an end in 1419, after the termination of the Schism. In the meantime, however, the popes of the Roman Obedience also carried on the practice of registering common letters. Their volumes of registers were simply a continuation at a distance of the old RA paper registers, and were likewise of paper. However, since the paper registers of Avignon were not fetched from there to Rome until 1783, these "Roman" registers of common letters never were united in fact with their predecessors but rather acquired a distinct identity over the years.

Like those in the Avignon Registers, the common letters registered in the "Roman" registers originated in the Chancery. But the registers as such, however, had the Datary as custodian from the middle of the 15th century, and were eventually housed in the *Archivum Bullarum* of the Datary in the Vatican Palace. They were taken from there to Paris by Napoleon, and on their return, much depleted in strength, to Rome in 1817, were placed by the Datary in the Lateran Palace, where they acquired the name by which they have been known since their transfer to the Vatican Archives in 1892: *Registra Lateranensia* (RL).

The long connection of these "Roman" or "Lateran" volumes of common letters with the Datary sometimes creates the impression that the RL are Datary in origin. With respect to their custodian from the 15th century onwards, they are, of course, Datary by provenance. But as registers of common letters sent through the Chancery, they are as surely Chancery in origin as the Avignon Registers. They are, however, original registers of the Chancery to a degree that the RA, for all their original quality, never quite achieved. Where the Avignon Registers always seem to be poor relations of the parchment RV (the hands are anything but calligraphic; the pages have an air of impermanence), the Lateran Registers probably were meant from the outset to eliminate the role played by RV in respect of RA, and to carry careful if not definitive copies of common letters. As it happens, the Vatican Registers cease during the Schism to contain copies of common letters or other Chancery material, becoming almost totally registers of letters of the Camera; and there is never the common ground between RV and RL that there was between RV and RA.

The Lateran Registers form, in effect, an original and independent series of Chancery registers, generally of common letters.[36] The series is as homogeneous and uniform as it is self-contained; and, in contrast to much of RA, the letters are nicely grouped under headings in each volume: benefices, pardons, dispensations, indulgences, etc. Since many of the outgoing letters of grace and of justice were occasioned by supplications, the text of the original supplication and papal reply that prompted a given letter may often be checked in the Registers of Supplications. Generally speaking, however, the letters in RL are registered not by the *Datum* of the grace, as in the Registers of Supplications, but by the date on which the letter in RL was sent out. Hence every letter in RL usually carries two dates: that of the *Datum* and that of expedition.[37]

The present strength of the series is 2467 volumes, but it is unknown how many more were lost when the papal archives were removed to Paris under Napoleon. For many pontificates only about one-third of the RL volumes has survived; altogether, perhaps as much as a half of the total series has perished. Some of the volumes disappeared during the journey to Paris in 1810, but in fact most of the damage to the series was done when, in order to cut down the costs of bringing the archives back from Paris in 1817, hundreds of RL volumes and masses of Holy Office material were sold by the papal commissioners as waste paper. Mario Marini, who was in charge of the return of the archives, later was able to track down and recover some 700 RL volumes;[38] but at least 13 eluded his search, finding their way

---

[36] The standard study of the RL is M. Giusti, 'Note sui registri Lateranensi', in *Mélanges E. Tisserant* V (Studi e Testi 234, Vatican City 1964), pp. 229-249, now reprinted in Giusti, *Studi*, pp. 98-119, where there is also a general survey of the RL by pontificate, pp. 152-159.

[37] For example, "Martinus etc. Dilecto filio archidiacono Armachan. Vite ac morum honestas... Datum Constancie sexto kal. martii anno primo." Then, in another hand, that of Franciscus de Agello, one of the *magistri registri*, there is written the date of expedition and the tax: "Franciscus xxiiii Octavo kal. Septembris anno primo de Agello" (RL 189, ff. 212r-213r).

[38] See his memoir, as printed in the introduction to *Regestum Clementis V*, I (Rome 1885), p. CCLXXII.

eventually, as we shall see later, to the library of Trinity College, Dublin.

The high point of the Lateran Registers was the 15th century. With the beginning of the 16th century, however, they gradually become of less importance, mainly because by then the common form of letters of grace, favour and justice was the Brief, and new registers of Briefs absorbed much that had previously been registered in RL (see *Brevia Lateranensia* above, pp. 52-53). Nevertheless, the RL are of very great value for the history of any century from 1400-1900. They were used widely by Garampi (who cites them as *AB*, because they were in the *Archivum Bullarum*) for his *Schedario* (1751-1772), but, unfortunately, it is often difficult to decipher his method of reference. A useful list of volumes by pontifical year is in *Sussidi* I, pp. 147-190. Of more value, however, is the typescript inventory in two volumes made by the late M.-H. Laurent, O. P., in 1939 (Index Room, Indice 1039, for vv. 1-1127; Indice 1040 for vv. 1128-2467). Laurent gives the present and the ancient numeration for each volume, as well as that used by Garampi; besides, he lists the number of folios, the pontifical year and the original subdivisions of each volume. In v. I at pp. 218 ff., and in v. II at pp. 248 ff., there is a chronological arrangement of the series.

Volumes of the RL have been used effectively by collections such as the *Repertorium Germanicum*, but the most extensive use of the series as a whole is that of the *Calendar of Papal Letters*. All the material in RL relative to the British Isles from 1389-1485 (RL 1-840) has been printed in summary in the CPL, vv. IV-V, by J. A. Bliss and J. W. Twemlow, and in vv. VI-XIV by Twemlow alone; while microfilms of RL 841-1127 (1486-1513) are deposited in the National Library, Dublin, in preparation for further volumes of the *Calendar*.[39] A list of the RL volumes used by the CPL was given above when treating of the Vatican Registers, but it may be of value to repeat it summarily here:

CPL		pp.				RL	
IV (1902)		317-546	Boniface IX	1389-1404	RL	1-43
V (1904)		1-627	Boniface IX	1396-1404		44-118
VI (1904)		5-93	Innocent VII	1404-1406		119-127
		101-147	Gregory XII	1406-1415		128-135
		149-165	Alexander V	1409-1410		136-138
		187-513	John XXIII	1410-1415		139-185
		514-515	Constance	1415		186
VII (1906)		39-573	Martin V	1417-1431		187-276

[39] These microfilms are the result of the researches of Fr Romuald Dodd, O. P., and Dr Peter Partner, between 1953 and 1956, and, for a time in 1955-1956, of the present writer. See n. 24 above, p. 110.

CPL VIII (1909)	pp.	1-211	Martin V	1427-1431	RL 277-301
		321-678	Eugene IV	1431-1437	302-358
IX (1912)		1-588	Eugene IV	1438-1447	359-431
X (1915)		275-731	Nicholas V	1447-1455	432-497
XI (1921)		196-363	Calixtus III	1455-1458	498-534
XII (1933)		1-228	Pius II	1458-1464	535-599
		393-824	Paul II	1464-1471	600-712
XIII (1955) 1.		285-470	Sixtus IV	1471-1476	713-757
2.		471-864	Sixtus IV	1476-1484	758-838
XIV (1960)		316-325	Innocent VIII	1484-1485	838-840

B. INDEXES TO THE LATERAN REGISTERS.

By the time the Archivio Segreto Vaticano was formed in 1611, the Lateran Registers were firmly in the custody of the Datary, and were located in the *Archivum Bullarum* in the Cortile di Sisto V. In spite of repeated efforts to obtain them, e.g., by Garampi in the middle of the ₁8th century, the RL remained in the possession of the Datary and outside the ASV until 1892.[40]

From the earliest days of the ASV, however, it was felt that there should at least be some record of the RL in the new Archives. Accordingly, work on reference calendars of RL was begun in 1618, and the volumes that resulted are now in the ASV Index Room as Indici 320-430 (there is a summary list of these Indici above in Part One, pp. 32-33).[41] Since so much of the RL series was irretrievably lost at the beginning of the 19th century, these Indici are now of great value. Some of them, of course, are no more than *rubricellae*, but many are calendars of such detail that they almost offset some of the RL losses. They have been used extensively by collections such as the *Repertorium Germanicum* and the *Calendar of Papal Letters* (e.g. Indici 319A, 325-327, in the introduction to v. XI; Indici 332-335 in v. XIII, pp. 865-895). Here I propose to examine only those Indici which the *Calendar* did not use, and in particular Indici 320, 323 and 324.

a. Indice 320. Indice 320 is a copy of a calendar of the RL of Boniface IX that is now in the Vatican Library as MS. Vat. lat. 6952, ff. 97r-362r. This manuscript as a whole, which Mercati used in 1950 for many Franciscan documents of the late 14th and early 15th centuries,[42] is an original draft by A. Ranaldi in 1618 of a calendar (*Summarium*) of Lateran Registers from Boniface IX to Martin V (1389-1431).

---

[40] A good list of the ASV "Lateran" Indici (Indici 320-430: 1389-1900) is in Giusti, *Studi*, pp. 109-110.

[41] H. Diener, 'Rubrizellen zu Kanzlei-registern Johanns XXIII. und Martins V.,' in *Quellen und Forschungen* 39 (1959) 117-172. Diener uses Indice 1, made in 1636 for Urban VIII, but, more specifically, MS. R. 32 of the Vallicelliana Library, Rome.

[42] See A. Mercati, 'Complementi al "Bullarium Franciscanum", in *Archivum Franciscanum Historicum* 43 (1950) 161-180, 335-359.

But although Vat. lat. 6952 is Ranaldi's autograph, it seems certain that Indice 320 is, in fact, a fair copy that Ranaldi himself commissioned for the ASV of the sections relative to Boniface IX in his autograph. It incorporates all of Ranaldi's revisions and corrections; and although it was written by a hand distinct from that of Ranaldi, it clearly had his approval, since he himself has added to it in his own hand an index that is also to be found in his autograph. For these reasons the text of Ranaldi's *Summarium* that is used in these pages is not that of the autograph in Vat. lat. 6952 but rather that of the fair copy in Indice 320. (Indice 321, written by F. Contelori, also contains a copy of the *Summarium*, but it is incomplete and, as well, appears to have been made from Indice 320 and not from Vat. lat. 6952).

Following Vat. lat. 6952, ff. 97r-362r, Indice 320 describes itself on the opening page as "Summarium quarundam Bullarum Pontificatus Bonifatii noni". It consists of 710 folios. The text of the *Summarium* of Boniface's letters runs from ff. 33-680, and is preceded and followed by detailed indexes, the second of which is in the hand of Ranaldi and provides a very useful set of references to cardinals, Roman churches, etc. The handwriting of the calendar itself, however, is not that of Ranaldi, and is in fact much more legible than that of his draft calendar in Vat. lat. 6952.

Indice 320 is, then, totally devoted to Ranaldi's summaries of the Lateran Registers of Boniface IX. Ranaldi's manner of distinguishing the volumes from each other is, of course, different from that of today, but in fact both the Indice volume and the original draft in Vat. lat. 6952 are very easy to handle, mainly because Msgr Mercati once collated them with the existing RL volumes and has pencilled in references to extant registers in both Indice 320 and Vat. lat. 6952. Hence it is always clear at a glance from Mercati's notes that, for example, the volume which Indice 320, ff. 33r-34r (= Vat. lat. 97r) lists as "Ex libro de beneficiis vacaturis et de diversis formis anno primo. Inscriptus liber decimus nonus", is no longer extant, and that, on the other hand, the section immediately following ("Ex libris de praebendis et dignitatibus vacaturis. Liber inscriptus decimus sextus... anno primo") is from the present RL 2.

By my calculation, 106 volumes in all of the RL volumes of Boniface IX are calendared in one form or another in Indice 320 (and its source); and of these 107 some 65 are to be found among the 117 extant RL registers, while 41 are RL registers that no longer exist in the ASV. And since 117 volumes are extant altogether, and we now know from Indice 320 that at least 41 more once existed, we can conclude that the Lateran Registers for

Boniface IX originally consisted of at least 158 volumes. As it happens, an invaluable note of Ranaldi (Vat. lat. 6952, f. 375r) shows that the total number of RL volumes which he examined in 1618 for the 15 years of Boniface IX's pontificate was 178, the volumes being distributed as follows: year 1: 12 vv.; year 2: 12; year 3: 10; year 4: 4; year 5: 11; year 6: 6; year 7: 7; year 8: 10; year 9: 14; year 10: 15; year 11: 18; year 12: 19; year 13: 10; year 14: 10; year 15: 7; and 13 volumes of various years. Thanks, therefore, to the 41 missing volumes covered by Ranaldi's *Summarium*, only 20 volumes of the RL for the pontificate of Boniface IX are now totally lost (or rather 19, if we include the RL volume in Trinity College, Dublin, which is described later in this chapter). This is not too heavy a loss, when one remembers that Mercati has calculated that altogether some 1458 volumes of RL are now lacking for the period 1389-1621.[43]

Before going on to give some samples (all, as usual, from entries relative to the British Isles) of the manner in which Ranaldi compiled his calendar of these missing volumes, it may be worthwhile here to give a brief table of the layout of the *Summarium* in both its autograph (Vat. lat. 6952) and fair copy (Indice 320) forms, noting as well whether the work has calendared extant or missing RL volumes, and what years of Boniface's pontificate the missing volumes cover.

Summarium		*Registra*	Years	Contents
Vat. lat. 6952	Indice 320			
1r - 96v	1r - 32v	Index		
97r	33r - 34r	—	1389-1390	De beneficiis vacaturis et de diversis formis.
98v	34r - 35r	RL 2		
98r - 101v	35v - 45r	—	1389-1390	De diversis formis.
102r - 102v	45r - 47r	RL 5		
102v - 104r	47r - 50r	—	1389-1390	De diversis, de exhibitis, de beneficiis vacantibus.
104r - 109r	50r - 62v	RL 12		
109r - 113v	62v - 73v	RL 17		
114r - 116v	73v - 80v	RL 14		
116v - 117v	80v - 82v	RL 10		
117v - 118v	82v - 85v	—	1390-1391	De diversis, de exhibitis, de regularibus, de curia.
119r	85v - 86r	RL 15		
119r - 119v	86r - 87v	—	1391-1392	De vacaturis, de fructibus, de officio tabell., de curia.

[43] Mercati, art. cit., p. 162. — In the Vatican Library, MS. Archivio di S. Pietro C. 116, there is an early 15th-century collection of mandates and other formulae, mostly undated, from the registers (both RV and RL) of Boniface IX. The volume (ff. 300), which I have examined cursorily, has some letters of Boniface which are not to be found in the present RV and RL volumes.

Summarium		*Registra*	Years	Contents
119v - 120r	87v - 89r	RL 21		
120r - 123r	89r - 95v	—	1391-1392	De exhibitis, de diversis, de curia.
123r - 123v	95v - 96v	—	1391-1392	De vac. et vacaturis, de exhibitis, de diversis.
123v - 126v	96v - 104v	RL 25		
126v - 131r	104v - 116r	RL 24		
131r - 133v	116r - 123r	—	1391-1392	De diversis, de exhibitis, de plenaria remissione.
134r	123r - 124r	RL 29		
134r - 135r	124r - 126v	RL 27		
135v - 137r	126v - 130v	RL 30		
137r - 140r	130v - 137v	—	1392-1393	De exhibitis.
140r - 142v	138r - 145r	—	1393-1394	De vacantibus, de exhibitis, de diversis, de fructibus...
143r	145r	RL 32		
143r - 143v	145r - 147r	—	1393-1394	De vac. et vacaturis, de diversis, de regularibus.
143v - 144r	147r - 148r	—	1393-1394	De vac. et vacaturis, de exhibitis...
144r - 144v	148r - 149r	—	1393-1394	De curia.
144v - 148v	149r - 159r	—	1393-1394	De diversis formis, de regularibus.
148v - 151r	159r - 165r	—	1393-1394	De exhibitis, de diversis formis.
151r - 152v	165r - 168v	—	1393-1394	De exhibitis.
152v - 153r	168v - 170v	RL 37		
153v - 159r	170v - 183v	RL 38		
159r - 162v	183v - 193r	RL 36		
162v - 168r	193r - 207r	—	1394-1395	De diversis formis.
168v - 170v	207r - 212r	RL 35		
170v	212v - 213v	RL 41		
171r - 172v	213v - 216r	RL 40		
172r - 174r	216r - 220v	RL 43		
174r	220v	RL 45		
174r - 178v	220v - 230v	RL 44		
178r - 183v	230v - 244v	—	1396-1397	De diversis formis.
183v - 188v	244v - 257r	RL 47		
188v - 194v	257v - 271v	RL 59		
194v - 196v	271v - 276v	—	1397-1398	De regularibus, de fructibus, de provisionibus.
196v - 200r	276v - 286r	—	1397-1398	De exhibitis, de diversis formis.
200r - 205r	286r - 299v	—	1397-1398	De diversis formis.
205r - 210r	299v - 312v	RL 61		
210v - 217r	312r - 329r	RL 52		
217r - 218v	329r - 333r	RL 64		
218v - 225v	333r - 350r	RL 66		
225v	350r - 350v	RL 65		
225v - 227r	350r - 354r	—	1398-1399	De exhibitis, de provisionibus, de regularibus.
227r - 228v	354v - 359r	—	1398-1399	De exhibitis, de diversis, de litteris cardinalium.
229r - 232r	359r - 367v	RL 69		
232v - 236v	368r - 379v	RL 71		
237r - 242v	379v - 394r	—	1398-1399	De diversis formis.
242v - 246v	394r - 404r	RL 67		
247r - 251r	404r - 415r	RL 80		

Summarium	*Registra*		Years	Contents
251v - 255r	415v - 424v	—	1399-1400	De diversis formis.
255r - 259r	425r - 435r	RL 73		
259r - 264r	435v - 447v	RL 79		
264r - 265r	447v - 450v	RL 74		
265r - 265v	450v - 451r	RL 77		
265v - 267r	451r - 454v	—	1399-1400	De vacantibus, de diversis, de regularibus, de confessionalibus.
267r - 268v	454v - 459r	—	1399-1400	De vacaturis, de diversis, de regularibus, de curia.
268v - 270r	459r - 463r	—	1399-1400	De regularibus, de fructibus, de litteris cardinalium...
270r - 275r	463r - 475v	RL 81		
275r - 281v	475v - 492r	RL 90		
281v - 289r	492r - 510r	RL 87		
289r - 294v	510r - 523v	—	1400-1401	De diversis formis.
294v - 299v	523v - 536r	—	1400-1401	De diversis formis.
300r - 305v	536r - 550r	RL 89		
305v - 308v	550r - 556v	—	1400-1401	De diversis, de vacantibus, de fructibus.
308v - 309r	556v - 558r	RL 94		
309r - 310v	558r - 562r	RL 91		
311r - 311v	562r - 563v	RL 97		
311v - 315v	563v - 574r	RL 85		
316r - 319v	574r - 583r	RL 93		
319v - 320r	583r - 584v	RL 103		
320r - 321r	584v - 586r	RL 99		
321r - 322v	586r - 590r	RL 102		
322v - 328r	590r - 603r	RL 104		
328r - 331r	603r - 610r	RL 100		
331r - 333v	610r - 615v	—	1401-1402	De diversis formis.
333v	615v - 616r	—	1401-1402	De vacantibus, de provisionibus, ... de regularibus.
333v - 336r	616r - 621r	RL 113		
336r - 337r	621r - 623r	—	1402-1403	De exhibitis, de diversis, de regularibus.
337r - 340r	623v - 630r	RL 109		
340r - 343v	630r - 638r	RL 108		
343v - 344r	638r - 639v	RL 107		
344r	639v	—	1403-1404	De vacantibus, de curia, ... de litteris cardinalium.
344r - 347r	640r - 646v	RL 115		
347r - 350r	646v - 653v	—	1403-1404	De diversis formis.
350v - 351v	653v - 657r	RL 116		
352r - 354r	657r - 662r	RL 8-9		
354r - 354v	662r - 663v	—	1389-1404	De diversis, etc.
354v - 355r	663v - 664r	—	various	De vacantibus, etc.
355r	664r - 664v	RL 26		
355r - 355v	665r - 665v	—	various	De vacantibus, etc.
355v - 357v	665v - 670v	RL 28		
357v - 358r	670v - 671r	RL 57		
358r - 359r	671r - 674r	—	1397-1400	De diversis, de regularibus.
359v - 360v	674r - 676v	RL 82		
360v - 361r	676v - 678v	RL 110		
361v	678v - 679v	—	1400-1404	De diversis formis
362r	680r	—	various	John XXIII
363r - 371v	687r - 710r	Index		

In all, then, 106 volumes of RL of Boniface IX are covered by Ranaldi, but it should be clearly understood that although the *Summarium* can be remarkably detailed on occasion, it is by no means a complete calendar of the volumes it surveys. Thus there is only one item each in the *Summarium* from the present RL 32, 65 and 77; while there are only 12 entries relative to the British Isles from RL 38 where the *Calendar of Papal Letters* (IV, pp. 516-529) has some 65. And when one comes to a section of the *Summarium* which calendars a missing RL volume, it is very frustrating to find on several occasions that Ranaldi, for his own good reasons, no doubt, has only calendared a few items altogether, as in Indice 320, ff. 86r-87v, where he notes only four entries "Ex libro inscripto liber secundus de beneficiis vacaturis et vacantibus. De fructibus percipiendis. De officio tabellionatus, De curia. De conservatoriis. Anno 3ᵒ"; or at ff. 82v-85v, where there are only 12 items from a lost volume of at least 200 folios. All the same, the *Summarium* more often than not proves to be quite adequate and accurate when compared with those extant RL volumes which it used. Sometimes, indeed, it is able to fill in a gap or two in existing volumes. For example, RL 52 is now missing two folios at the beginning which clearly were present when Ranaldi was compiling the *Summarium* in 1618. Hence an English privilege which the *Calendar of Papal Letters* (V, p. 86) was unable to identify because only the end of it appears in the present opening folio of RL 52, is now revealed by the *Summarium* (Indice 320, ff. 312v, 313r) to be in fact the second of two graces of 19 July 1398 to New College, Oxford, which were on the now-missing folios of RL 52 and were recorded by Ranaldi.

This is probably an isolated case of the possible value of Ranaldi's *Summarium* vis-à-vis the extant Lateran Registers. Its chief importance, of course, is that it calendars, however fitfully, some 41 RL volumes which are now missing. For the British Isles, for example, the *Summarium* yields some 150 items, all of which I hope to print elsewhere. This may not be a very impressive total for the 41 volumes in question, but it is surely better than nothing. The following handful of examples from Indice 320 may give an idea of Ranaldi's method, as well as suggest something of the quality and value of the *Summarium*:

1. Indice 320, f. 35v: "Archiepiscopo Cantuarien. et collegis mandat quatenus personaliter accedentes ad locum, ubi corpus Eduardi Regis Anglie requiescit, inquirant diligenter veritatem super eius vita, meritis, et miraculis, et transmittant ad Sedem apostolicam. Dat. Romae

apud S. Petrum 2 Non. Decembris an. primo. fo. 30." — This entry of 4 December 1389 is from a volume of Boniface IX's registers entitled "De diversis formis," and occurs there at f. 30.

2. Indice 320, f. 42r: "Joanni archiepiscopo Armachan. et collegis mandat ut diligenter inquirant veritatem super vita, sanctitate et miraculis bo. me. Riccardi Archiepiscopi Armachani, et destinent ad Sedem Apostolicam. Dat. Romae apud S. Petrum 3 id. Novembris anno primo fo. 241." — This mandate, here calendared from the same volume "De diversis formis" (f. 241), is of interest in that Boniface, as a cardinal, was one of the commission of inquiry set up by Urban VI (1378-1379) to report on the life and miracles of Richard Fitzralph, and that now, as pope, he takes the matter up again (11 November 1389), just two days after his consecration. Ten years later Boniface sent a similar mandate once more to the archbishop of Armagh (CPL, V, p. 245) in which he refers both to the original commission of Urban VI and to the results of the present mandate of 1389. See my note on Fitzralph in *Bibliotheca Sanctorum* XI (Rome 1968), pp. 221-222.

3. Indice 320, f. 91v: "Dublinen. Cassellen. ac Tuamen. archiepiscopis mandat quatenus universis fratribus ordinis Heremitarum S. Augustini in Hibernia consistentibus defensionis praesidio assistentes, non permittant eos contra tenorem privilegiorum suorum a quibuscumque molestari, nec gravamina vel iniurias irrogari super praedicationibus libere ab eisdem fratribus faciendis et audiendis confessionibus et aliis iuribus et libertatibus ipsis a sede apostolica concessis. Datum Romae apud S. Petrum X Cal. Martii anno 3º. fo. 129." (20 Feb. 1392. From a volume "De exhibitis. De diversis formis. De curia. Anno 3º", f. 129).

4. Indice 320, f. 117v: "Ad futuram rei memoriam. Revocat quasdam ordinationes seu regulas factas in Capitulis Provincialibus per fratres ordinis Praedicatorum in provincia Angliae contra Romanam Ecclesiam, et eorumdem Superiores, statuitque subesse in omnibus Generali Magistro, ipsiusque literis obedire et obtemperare, etc. Dat. Romae apud S. Petrum 12 Cal. Junii anno 3º. fo. 89." (21 May 1392. From a volume "De diversis formis. De exhibitis. De conservatoriis. De plenaria remissione. Anno tertio.")

5. Indice 320, f. 312v-313r: "Ad futuram rei memoriam. Declarat quod oblationes et obventiones, donata, legata, relicta et alia obvenientia emolumenta quaecumque per custodem et scolares Collegii in villa de Oxonia Linc. diocesis, per Willelmum episcopum Wint. institutum, post alias litteras ab eodemmet pontifice datas, infra Collegium supradictum facta et concessa, etc., spectare et pertinere debeant ad Collegium supradictum eiusque personas etc., quodque ipsi non teneantur ullas oblationes facere parochiali ecclesiae infra cuius limites dictum Collegium consistit etc. Non obstante. Datum Romae apud S. Petrum 14 (Cal.?) Augusti anno 9º. fo. 1." (19 July 1398. From the opening folio, now wanting, of the present RL 52. A further grace of the same date to New College, Oxford, is calendared by Ranaldi from

f. 2, now also missing, of the same RL 52. The end of the grace is all that appears in the present RL 52, f. 1r, whence it was calendared by Twemlow in CPL V, p. 86).

6. Indice 320, f. 534r-534v: "Ad futuram rei memoriam. Episcopo Meneven. eiusque successoribus plenam et liberam concedit facultatem compellendi omnes et singulos abbates, priores, archidiaconos, rectores et vicarios, et quoscumque alios beneficia quaecumque in ecclesiis, civitate et diocesi Meneven. obtinentes, ad faciendam personalem residentiam in huiusmodi monasteriis, prioratibus, dignitatibus, et ecclesiis, et aliis beneficiis huiusmodi secundum statuta et ordinationes fundationum et donationum ac voluntates fundatorum etc., et alias secundum ipsorum beneficiorum et ecclesiarum exigentias et naturas, necnon ad reparationem et constructionem domorum habitationes etc. Quibuscumque non obstantibus etc. Datum Rome 8° id. Maii an. 12. — fol. 236." (15 May 1401. "Ex libro quarto de diversis formis anno duodecimo)."

7. Indice 320, f. 623r: "Abbati monasterii de Pershore, Wigornien. diocesis mandat quatenus sub pena excommunicationis faciat observari consuetudinem ecclesiae maioris Wigornien. circa sonum campanae de sero et de mane, etc. Datum Romae apud S. Petrum 6° id. Junii an. 14. fol. 178)." (8 June 1403).

b. Indice 323. This calendar of the Lateran Registers of Alexander V (1409-1410) was made in 1618 (see ff. 37r, 87r) for the new ASV by G. B. Confalonieri, one of Paul V's secretaries. At present there are only three RL volumes for Alexander V (RL 136, 137, 138, being respectively the original books i, v and vii of the registers of common letters for his pontificate), but originally there were at least eight altogether, since five other volumes (described by Confalonieri as books ii, iii, iv, vi and viii) are calendared here at ff. 98r-119r, 121r-130v, 133r-150r, 165r-175v, 189r-200v (new foliation). It may also be noted in passing that four volumes of RL (128-131) are extant for Gregory XII (1406-1415), and that a fifth volume (1407-1408), now missing, was calendared by Confalonieri in Indice 322, ff. 151r-154r.

Confalonieri's method of calendaring in Indice 323 differs somewhat from that of Ranaldi in his *Summarium*. Like Ranaldi he is selective, but now and then he goes one better than Ranaldi by giving a general picture of blocks of papal provisions, indulgences, etc., that he has decided not to calendar, thus: "De plenaria remissione. Enumerantur 334 huiusmodi plenarie remissiones... pro archiepiscopo Eboracen... diocesibus Miden., Dublinen., ..." (Indice 323, f. 173v); "De provisionibus beneficiorum in forma pauperum sub expectatione anno primo et unico. Extant 710 provisiones beneficiales sub expectatione pro clericis pauperibus breviter registratae sub dat. Pisis, ... et quia dioceses tam provisorum quam beneficiorum sunt in magno numero, visum est eas hic praeterire, praesertim cum pleraque et fere omnes sint de numero eorum que supra notatae sunt in caeteris titulis sexti tomi, in partibus scilicet septentrionalibus, presertim in insulis Scotiae, Angliae, Hiberniae, ..." (Indice 323, f. 175v. Hence, a large section of the missing volume has not been calendared).

Indice 323 is not, therefore, an exhaustive calendar, though on occasion it can be surprisingly good. There are, for example, 49 items relative to the British Isles in the present RL 136, and all but nine prove to have been calendared by Confalonieri at ff. 37r-87r. Altogether there are about 100 British Isles' entries in the calendar of the five missing RL volumes. The following are some samples:

1. Indice 323, f. 89r: "Ad futuram rei memoriam. Confirmat auctoritate apostolica quascumque exemptiones, indulgentias, privilegia et gratias concessas a Bonifatio IX et Innocentio VII in favorem cappellae de novo erectae et dotatae a nobili viro Joanne de Colvyle milite (qui fuit orator Henrici Regis Angliae ad concilium Pisanum) in honorem Beatissimae Virginis Mariae prope villam de Neuton, Elien. diocesis, in loco ubi fuerat antiqua cappella in qua nonnulla miraculorum genera coruscationis luminum temporibus nocturnis antiquitus ƒplerumque facta fuerunt et eodem prope fiebant. Confirmat etiam exemptiones et privilegia concessa ab iisdem pontificibus in favorem presbyterorum et pauperum eiusdem cappellae. Datum Pisis octavo id. Julii anno primo. pagina 2." (8 July 1409. From "Liber secundus de diversis formis anno primo").

2. Indice 323, f. 91v: "Ricardus nobilis viri Geraldi fuzmoris comes Daren. et nobilis mulier Joanna Castelmantyn contraxerunt matrimonium vigore dispensationis Innocentii VII super tertio affinitatis gradu, nulla mentione facta secundi gradus. Tamen Alexander auctoritate apostolica declarat praedictam dispensationem, omissione mentionis dictae distantiae secundi gradus affinitatis non factae in illa nequaquam obstante, sufficientem et validam existere. Datum Pisis secundo idus Septembris (anno) primo. p. 19." (The dispensation of Innocent VII to Richard Fitzmorice was on 10 April 1405: see CPL VI, p. 23. Alexander's letter of 12 September 1409 comes again from "Liber secundus de diversis formis.")

3. Indice 323, f. 96r: "Archiepiscopo Eboracen. et episcopo Lincolnien. vel alteri eorum committit et mandat quatenus, si ita est, Abbatem et conventum monasterii de Thornton, ordinis sancti Augustini, Lincolnien. diocesis, quondam Thomam Gretam abbatem dicti monasterii, qui nondum viginti annis elapsis tunc ab hac vita migraverat et apud ipsum monasterium sepultus erat, non per sedem apostolicam canonizatum nec ut sanctum approbatum, ut questus et oblationes damna-

biliter extorquerent, propria temeritate sanctum populo praedicare presumere ac multis miraculis coruscantem, pro huiusmodi suis excessibus auctoritate apostolica debite puniant eosque ad desistendum deinceps a talibus per censuram ecclesiasticam et alia iuris remedia compellant iuxta canonicas sanctiones, invocato ad hoc si opus fuerit auxilio brachii secularis. Datum Bononiae xii Kal. Feb. anno primo. Pag. 59." (21 January 1410. From the same source as nn. 1 and 2 above).

4. Indice 323, f. 114r: "Philippo episcopo Cluanen. concedit facultatem monendi omnes illicitos et publicos occupatores seu detentores nonnullarum terrarum arabilium, domorum, possessionum et aliorum bonorum immobilium in sua ecclesia Cluanen. et alibi dictae diocesis consistentium, ut infra certum tempus ab huiusmodi occupatione desistent et terras et possessiones mensae episcopali libere dimittant, sub poena excommunicationis ipso facto necnon suspensionis et interdicti. Bononiae iiii Kal Martii anno primo. (Pag.) 227." (27 Feb. 1410. From the same volume).

c. **Indice 324.** This short volume of 57 ff. is entitled "Bullarum quarumdam Innocentii I, Joannis 23. De diversis formis." It is for the most part a copy of Ranaldi's *Summarium* in MS. Vat. lat. 6952, ff. 378-500. The RL for Innocent VII (1404-1406) are at ff. 4r-32v (= *Summarium*, ff. 378r-403v), and those of John XXIII (1410-1415) are at ff. 36r-57v.

According to the pencilled notes of Msgr Mercati (1928), only RL 119, 120, 122A, 123, 125, 127, of the present RL 119-127 of Innocent VII are covered by Indice 324, but three missing RL volumes are calendared at ff. 4r-8r, 15r-17v, 24v-32v of the Indice. Again, this part of Indice 324 (and its source, Ranaldi's *Summarium*) seems reasonably thorough. I have only examined entries for the British Isles — about 15 altogether for the three missing volumes — and the method of calendaring is not much different from that used by Ranaldi for Boniface IX's registers, thus:

1. Indice 324, f. 16r: "Ad futuram rei memoriam. Statuat et ordinat quod consuetudines et declarationes editas per Benedictum XII ad reformationem ordinis monachorum nigrorum in Cantuarien. et Eboracen. provinciis consistentium debeant in eodem rigore inviolabiliter perpetuo permanere in quo fuerant ante suspensionem et remissionem, et alia circa premissa per Clementem papam VI facta etc., necnon largitur licentiam abbatibus presidentibus in capitulis generalibus statuendi terminum futuri capituli generalis etc. Datum Romae apud S. Petrum X Cal. Feb. anno primo. fol. 228." (23 January 1405).
2. Indice 324, f. 26r-26v: "Ad futuram rei memoriam. Donationem iuris patronatus in rectoria parochialis ecclesiae S. Jacobi de Achboy Miden. dioc. per Riccardum regem Angliae factam Joanni archiepis-

copo Armachan. ad suum statum decentius tenendum, et a Bonifatio IX confirmatam et postea in sua generali revocatione revocatam, decernit perinde valere ac si nulla revocatio facta fuisset. Datum Viterbii VI Idus Februarii anno 2. fol. 60." (8 February 1406).

3. Indice 324, f. 30r: "Decano ecclesie Clonen. ad petitionem vicarii parochialis ecclesie de Kynsale Corkagen. diocesis. Provideat contra non solventes decimas ex piscatione maris etc. Datum Romae apud S. Petrum 3 nonas Julii anno 2°, fol. 217 — et vide declarationem istius in alio libro fol. 277." (5 July 1406. This item is taken by Ranaldi "Ex libro primo de diversis formis anno secundo," so the "other book, fol. 277" of which he speaks is probably a second book "De diversis." Such a volume is not in fact calendared by Ranaldi, nor is there any trace of a "declaratio" in the extant RL registers as calendared in the *Calendar of Papal Letters*, V.).

4. Indice 324, f. 31r: "Ad futuram rei memoriam. Joanni Colvyle militi, Elien. diocesis, confirmat cappellam a se extructam prope villam de Newiton eiusdem diocesis in quodam loco Marisco Salso vulgariter nuncupato sub vocabulo beatae Mariae Virginis etc., et ius patronatus reservatum, etc., necnon exemptionem obtentam a Bonifatio IX ab omni iure, dominio, visitatione, subiectione et potestate quorumcumque iudicum ecclesiasticorum etc., non obstantibus quibuscumque revocationibus super ea hucusque factis etc., et aliis etc. Datum Romae apud S. Petrum XIIII Cal. Aprilis anno secundo fol. 240." (19 March 1406. For a later confirmation — 8 July 1409 — of the same chapel, see Indici 323, f. 89r, above, p. 143).

The second part of Indice 324 (ff. 36r-57v) contains a summary of bulls of John XXIII's pontificate. Of the extant RL registers of John (RL 140-185), 21 are calendared very briefly here. There are, however, items from 7 vv. of registers now missing at ff. 37r-37v, 37v-38r, 44v-45v, 45v-46v, 47r-48r, 49r-49v, 55v. Although the entries (in Confalonieri's hand) appear to be based on Ranaldi's *Summarium* of the registers of John in Vat. lat. 6952, ff. 436r-500v, they are not as numerous or as complete. In Indice 324A (added to the Indici by Mercati in 1928) there are summaries by Confalonieri of two further RL volumes of John (ff. 85r-123v), but, unfortunately, the two volumes covered there are the present RL 141 and RL 146.

C. LATERAN REGISTERS IN TRINITY COLLEGE, DUBLIN. 3.2.6.3

It has been noted several times above that very many volumes of the Lateran Registers were lost or destroyed during and after the transfer of the papal archives to Paris in 1810. Thirteen of these volumes, together with volumes of Inquisition material, were bought in France from an unidentified source by the Duke of Manchester in 1841. From him they were purchased by C. N. Wall, Vice-Provost of Trinity College, Dublin, and were presented to the College Library in 1854.

These "Records of Roman Inquisition and Dataria," as they are called in T. K. Abbott's *Catalogue of Manuscripts in the Library of Trinity College, Dublin* (London 1900), fall into three groups:

   a. Cat. no. 1223: Thirteen registers of the Lateran series from Boniface IX (1389) to Pius VI (1787).

   b. Cat. nn. 1224-1242: Nineteen volumes of Holy Office material, 1564-1659.

   c. Cat. nn. 1243-1277: Thirty-five volumes of proceedings of Courts of the Inquisition in Italy, 1570-1660.

Since the Inquisition records have been noted briefly above in Part One (p. 85), we may turn our attention at once to the Lateran Registers (microfilms of which were presented to the ASV in 1953: see *L'Attività della Santa Sede nel 1953*, Vatican City 1954, p. 334). All thirteen volumes are listed in Abbott's *Catalogue* under n. 1223 and are ordered by that number (e.g. 1223.1, 1223.10), so I shall retain that numeration here:

   1. TCD 1223.1: Register of common letters of 1 Boniface IX (1389-1390). Ff. 291. Text begins at f. 5r, but the volume is incomplete. The following summary may be useful as an illustration of the layout of a typical Lateran register:

     6r - 23v: *De prebendis vacantibus anno primo.*
     24r - 43r: *De prebendis vacaturis de anno primo.*
     44r - 55r: *De prebendis vacaturis anno primo.*
     55r - 57v: Blank, save for the opening lines of a letter on f. 56r.
     58r - 81v: *De prebendis vacaturis anno primo.*
     82r - 267r: *De beneficiis vacaturis anno primo.*
     191v - 195v: Blank. Also 267v.
     268r - 291v: *De exhibitis, diversis formis et regularibus, anno primo.*

   The Library possesses a good typewritten "Calendar of Inquisition MS. I.1" compiled by H. J. Lawlor in 1932, with an alphabetical list of place-names at the end. I have not been able to identify this volume with any of the missing RL volumes calendared by Ranaldi in MS. Vat. Lat. 6952 (Indice 320, above). All the British Isles' entries concern England and Wales, e.g., provision of John Brugge, M.A., to a canonry at Wells, 12 November 1389 (ff. 51r-52r); provision of Reginald ap Jorwerth of diocese of St. Asaph to a benefice in the gift of the monastery of Worcester, O.S.B., 12 November 1389 (ff. 257v-258v).

   2. TCD 1223.2: "Liber secundus de beneficiis vacantibus Eugenii Pape IV." Ff. 309, and three blank folios at each end of volume. In this volume, which belongs to the 4th and 5th years of Eugene IV (Rome-Florence, 1424-1436), there is a large number of letters relative to the British Isles, e.g.,

   1. Ff. XVv-XVIr: mandate to provide Thomas Macaeda, diocese of Limerick, to the perpetual vicarage of Askeaton, vacant by the

resignation of Edward Macadam, notwithstanding that James O
Leam, on pretext of certain apostolic letters, has held it for six years.
Date of provision: 24 February 1435. Date of expedition of letters:
2 June 1435. (The time-lag between the provision and the expedition
of the letter of provision by the Datary is not so great in other letters
in this volume).

2. Ff. LXXXIIIr-LXXXIVr: mandate to the bishop of Amiens and
the Deans of Ardagh and Kilmore to habilitate Congall O Fergail
of the diocese of Kilfenora. In his petition O Fergail had stated that
he had been dispensed from illegitimacy, being the son of a priest
and an unmarried woman, and now asked for consideration of the
fact that when he had been collated to the perpetual vicarage of
Decluaingese, diocese of Ardagh, he had not proceeded to the priest-
hood within a year of his collation, and had now held the vicarage
without proper title for eight years. Provided at Rome, 30 October;
letter expedited, 26 November 1434.

3. TCD 1223.3: "Primus de regularibus et exhibitis anno VIIII°
Eugenii Pape IV." Ff. 313. Letters from Florence of 9 Eugene IV
(1439-1440). Many letters, sometimes in difficult hands, concern
the affairs of monasteries and churches in Rome and of the Dominican
Order. There are some letters in respect of England and Scotland
(ff. 20r, 85r, 95v, 97r, 140r, 265r, 286v), including one which possibly
illustrates the beginnings of penury in English friaries and monasteries: John Gerard, alias Sandwich, Carmelite, professor and lector
in theology, of the Carmelite house at Sandwich, is provided to a
cura animarum on 3 January 1440, because he claims that otherwise
he will be unable to support himself (f. 97r-97v).

The one Irish item in this volume is, perhaps, worth summarising,
since it refers to a register of Alexander V which, to my knowledge,
no longer exists: at the request of the vicar-general and the Irish
Dominican vicariate, Eugene IV rehearses "de verbo ad verbum"
from a register of Alexander V, and then confirms, a privilege given
at Pisa on 10 August 1409, whereby Alexander, at the petition of the
Dominican Order, and following in the footsteps of Nicholas IV and
Benedict XI, freed the whole Dominican Order (priests, brothers,
nuns, sisters, etc.) from subjection to any prelate, and "a solutione
cuiuscumque collectae, pedagii aut cuiuscumque alterius generis exac-
tionis, de apostolicae potestatis plenitudine et ex certa scientia prorsus
eximimus et totaliter liberamus, illasque in ius et proprietatem beati
Petri et sedis apostolice et sub eorumdem speciali et immediata pro-
tectione suscepimus atque nostra..." (ff. 82r-83r). Eugene's confirmation is dated from Florence, 21 November 1440.

4. TCD 1223.4: "Secundus de beneficiis vacantibus anno V° domini
nostri Pii pape II anno quinto." Ff. 335. Common letters of 5
Pius II (1462-1463).

5. TCD 1223. 5: "Secundus de vacantibus anno sexto domini Innocentii
Pape VIII." Ff. 327. Common letters of 6 Innocent VIII (1489-
1490).

6. TCD 1223.6: "Primus mixtus vacantium et diversorum annorum primi, et secundi, tertii et quarti Alexandri Pape VI." Ff. 317. Common letters of 1-4 Alexander VI (1492-1496). Many blanks. Folio 213 is misplaced.
7. TCD 1223.7: 7 Clement VII (1530).
8. TCD 1223.8: 1 Paul IV (1556).
9. TCD 1223.9: 2-3 Pius IV (1561-1562). Defective.
10. TCD 1223.10: 5-6 Benedict XIV (1745).
11. TCD 1223.11: 3 Pius VI (1777-1778).
12. TCD 1223.12: 10-13 Pius VI (1784-1787).
13. TCD 1223.13: Clement XIII, fragments, 1758-1769.

A supplication, as a diplomatic term, is a petition addressed to a sovereign to obtain a grace. So far as papal history is concerned, a supplication was the normal way of seeking a papal concession of any kind, even a nomination to the smallest benefice reserved to the papacy.

Supplications were originally drawn up by the suppliants themselves, but by the 12th century "scriveners" were to be found in the neighbourhood of the Lateran palace in Rome who would draw up papal petitions on request and couch them in a proper form. Collections of supplication formulae begin to make their appearance towards the end of the century, each formula opening with a conventional "Supplicat Sanctitati Vestrae devotus orator vester". In the 14th century, however, supplications take on an official character, and their text had to be drawn up "secundum stilum curiae".[44] Because of this, most bishops preferred to maintain their own procurators at the papal court for the proper expedition of their requests and of any other business. This, of course, was an expensive operation, and few bishops could really afford personal procurators. A simple solution was for bishops from one country or area to share a procurator, as bishops from the British Isles did at various periods. A classic case, perhaps, is that of Andreas Sapiti, who from about 1314 served the Kings of England and the English, Irish, Scottish and Welsh bishops for some thirty years at Avignon, and appears in many of their transactions with the curia.[45]

According to a procedure that developed at the end of the 13th century, and continued until the 19th, a properly-prepared

---

[44] See H. Bresslau, *Handbuch der Urkundenlehre* II[2] (Berlin-Leipzig 1931), pp. 104-115. For the beginnings of permanent procurators see R. von Heckel, 'Das Aufkommen der ständigen Prokuratoren an der päpstlichen Kurie im 13. Jahrhundert,' in *Miscellanea Francesco Ehrle* II (Studi e Testi 38, Rome 1924), pp. 311-343.

[45] A private note-book of Sapiti, with many petitions and formulae, is in MS. Barbarini lat. 2126 of the Vatican Library. See J. P. Kirsch, 'Andreas Sapiti, ein englischer Prokurator an der Kurie im 14. Jahrhundert,' in *Historisches Jahrbuch* 14 (1893) 582-603, 'Ein Formelbuch der päpstlichen Kanzlei aus der Mitte des XIV. Jahrhunderts,' *ibid.*, 814-820. Some letters from Sapiti's note-book are printed in J. A. Watt, 'Negotiations between Edward II and John XXII concerning Ireland,' in *Irish Historical Studies* 10 (1956) 1-20.

[A transcript is in the PRO in London [31/9/17A] (C.R. Cheney)]

supplication was presented by a procurator to a Referendary who examined it, and then, if satisfied, signed his name on it and "referred" it to the competent authority for a hearing. If the petition was successful, approval came either from the Pope (in which case the Pope wrote the autograph formula "Fiat ut petitur", followed by the initial of his baptismal name, on the supplication), or from the Vice-Chancellor (who appended "concessum ut petitur" and his signature), or from an authorized Referendary (who, however, had to write the formula "Concessum in praesentia domini nostri Papae" and his signature in the presence of the Pope). After approval, the supplication was handed over to the Datarius for the dating clause, and then a letter was prepared in the Chancery for expedition which embodied all or most of the original petition and the full tenor of the grace.

The outgoing letter (complete with two dates, that of the original grant and that of expedition) was entered into a register of common letters, as were the supplication and its outcome into a register of supplications. Hence for the period for which we possess registers of supplications (1342-), there is usually a double record of petitions: that in the *Registra Supplicationum* (RS) and that in the corresponding register of common letters (RA for the Avignon period; RL from the Schism onwards, but gradually giving ground to the *Brevia Lateranensia* from 1500, when the Brief came to be preferred to the letter for routine favours and graces). In certain cases, however, the Pope granted a supplication *sola signatura*, that is, the supplication itself as signed by the Pope became the definitive concession, and was returned to the petitioner, making unnecessary the expedition of a letter or a Brief. Apart from the survival of the original supplications, the only record of supplications of this type will be the entry in the RS.[46]

The *sola signatura* supplication was at once a less costly form of petition, since it by-passed the Chancery, and a very authoritative document, since it bore the Pope's signature. The only

---

[46] Not many original supplications survive: see E.-A. van Moé, 'Suppliques originales adressées à Jean XXII, Clément VI et Innocent VI,' in *Bibliothèque de l'École des Chartes* 92 (1931) 253-276, with some excellent plates. A useful general work is F. Bartoloni, 'Suppliche pontificie dei secoli XIII e XIV,' in *Bullettino dell'Istituto storico italiano per il medio evo e Archivio Muratoriano* 67 (1955) 1-187. Note that from time to time supplications will be found among the papers of apostolic nuncios, since these often had faculties to grant supplications: see C. Tihon, 'Suppliques originales adressées au Cardinal-légat C. Caraffa,' in *Miscellanea A. Mercati* (Vatican City 1952), pp. 1-10.

other form of Common grace which was of equal if not of higher standing was the *Motu proprio* supplication: a *fictio iuris* by which a petition was granted as though on the initiative of the Pope himself ("motu proprio") and not as a result of a supplication. One of the earliest examples, perhaps, of this form occurs in RA 56, f. 267v, where, in a grace of 12 December 1342, the words *motu proprio* are underlined. Unlike the *sola signatura* supplication, this type of *motu proprio* petition went through the ordinary Chancery process, and was registered in both RS and the registers of common letters.

Usually the petitions which procurators had to handle were single petitions, but it was a distinct advantage to a petitioner if his name was included in a roll of supplications sponsored by a magnate, a legate or some learned institution; universities, for example, sometimes submitted supplications for benefices for a number of selected graduates.[47] Group-petitions, too, often carried more weight than the single, isolated petition, particularly when the qualifications of the individuals who made up the group were not very persuasive on their own. A good case of this occurs in 1363, when a roll of petitions from Ireland was granted by Urban V on 12 November. The roll contained the petitions of some 16 Irish clerics from practically every diocese in Ireland, and it claimed to be the first that the Pope had ever received from them. Feeling that the Pope might be surprised to find that so few of the petitioners possessed university degrees, these clerics excused themselves on the ground that in the whole of Ireland there was no place of study, not to speak of a university. But since they were "from the ends of the earth" and, moreover, the churches of Ireland were not "burdened with papal provisions", they felt confident that the Pope would grant their petition, assuring him with a certain bravado that they were quite prepared to stand any examination he might care to stipulate.[48]

Supplications first began to be registered in the pontificate of Benedict XII (1334-1342), but there is not now any trace of his

---

[47] See E. F. Jacob, *Essays in the Conciliar Epoch*[2] (Manchester 1952), pp. 223-229; D. E. R. Watt, 'University clerks and rolls of petitions for benefices,' in *Speculum* 34 (1959) 213-229, 'University graduates in Scottish benefices before 1410', in *Records of Scottish Church History Society* 15 (1965) 77-88.

[48] RS 39, ff. 37r-39v: *Calendar of Papal petitions* I, pp. 467-469. For papal provisions in Ireland see U. G. Flanagan, 'Papal provisions in Ireland, 1307-1378,' in *Historical Studies* III (London 1961), pp. 92-103; R. D. Edwards, 'The Kings of England and Papal Provisions in fifteenth Century Ireland,' in *Medieval Studies presented to Aubrey Gwynn, S. J.*, ed. J. A. Watt, J. B. Morrall, F. X. Martin (Dublin 1961), pp. 265-280.

register of supplications.[49] The series of registers of supplications in the ASV today begins in fact with the pontificate of Clement VI (1342-1352) and continues to 1799, totalling in all 7365 volumes. An inventory of these, pontificate by pontificate, is in B. Katterbach, *Inventario dei registri delle Suppliche* (Vatican City 1932).[50] The first 99 volumes cover the Avignon Papacy and the Avignon Obedience (1342-1419), and did not reach the ASV from Avignon until 1783. The volumes from Martin V (1417-1431) onwards were housed in the Datary Archives until 1810, when they were taken to Paris. After their return from Paris in 1817 they were lodged with the RL and other material in the Lateran Palace until 1892, when they were moved with the Datary Archives to the ASV. Each volume consists of about 300 paper folios, and generally measures 16 × 13 inches.

The series is far from complete. For the 14th century there are no registers that survive for the pontificates of Gregory XI, Urban VI and Benedict IX; the losses for the 15th century may be as high as a third or a quarter. Nevertheless, the importance of the extant volumes of the RS for those two centuries is very great, for they are often the only surviving source for provisions, graces, etc., of the period. This is largely due to the fact that the registers of common letters (RA in the 14th century; RL in the 15th) contain only a percentage of the letters drawn up after the supplications had been granted; indeed the proportion in part of the 14th century is often as low as one in ten. But even where a corresponding common letter is extant, it will often be found that the RS entry gives a more detailed account of the petition than the outgoing letters as they are found registered.

As was noted in the introduction to this volume (above p. 11), the RS have been used or calendared in publications all over Europe with more or less success, notably by the *Analecta Vaticano-Belgica* (often printing full texts) and the *Repertorium Germanicum*.[51] So far only one volume of the *Calendar of Papal Registers* has been dedicated to supplications granted for the British Isles, although a beginning was made of a separate series

---

[49] See the detailed comments of Göller in *Repertorium Germanicum* I (Berlin 1916), pp. 66-67, etc.; Bresslau, *Handbuch* II, pp. 1-25, etc.

[50] A fine set of photographic samples of petitions is provided by B. Katterbach, *Specimina supplicationum ex registris Vaticanis* (Rome 1927).

[51] For these collections see the Bibliography under *Belgium* 1 and *Germany* 1; for others, see *Holland* 2; *Hungary* 3; *Italy* 3; *Pomerania*; *Scotland* 1.

of volumes for Scottish supplications of the 15th century.[52] The volume of the *Calendar* appeared as long ago as 1896 (*Petitions to the Pope*, I, A. D. 1342-1419, ed. W. H. Bliss), and covers all of the 99 registers of the Avignon Papacy and the Avignon Obedience:

RS	1-22	Clement VI	1342-1352	p.	1
	23-33	Innocent VI	1352-1362		237
	34-43	Urban V	1362-1366, only		384
	44-76	Clement VII	1378-1394		537
	77-99	Benedict XIII	1394-1419		579-640

[For the deficiencies of this volume see D.E.R. Watt, "Sources for Scottish History…" [cf. Bibliography below (p. 220)] (I.B. Cowan)]

---

[52] See E. R. Lindsay and A. I. Cameron, *Calendar of Scottish Supplications to Rome, 1418-1422* (Scottish Historical Society, Third Series, XXIII, Edinburgh 1934); A. I. (Cameron) Dunlop, *Calendar of Scottish Supplications to Rome, 1423-1428* (*ibid.*, XLVIII, 1956).

V. CAMERAL REGISTERS

Because of the central position that the *Reverenda Camera Apostolica* occupied in the papal curia, the study of its registers is of the greatest importance not only for financial aspects of the papacy but also for the economic life of countries, exchange rates, production, the movement of goods and money, the history of communications.[53] As Gottlob has put it, "Of all the authorities of the papal court, the Camera Apostolica was the greatest centre of ambition and of intrigue; and it was at the same time the most hated and feared. Its power extended over the whole world; towards the end of the Middle Ages it had outstripped in importance and significance all other institutions, financial organizations of the state included."[54]

The growth of the power of the Camera is intimately connected with, first, the emergence of laws that reserved to the Holy See the confirmation of all bishops and abbots in bishoprics and abbacies which were directly dependent upon it (4th Lateran Council, 1215, c. 26); second, with the development of papal provisions. Since provisions formed the largest single source of papal revenues in the Middle Ages, and in the 14th and 15th centuries in particular, it may be useful to dwell on them here for a moment.[55] The oldest known form of papal provision, that of Innocent II in 1137, was in fact nothing more than a simple request to a bishop to provide a certain cleric with a benefice. By the time of Adrian IV (1154-1159), this sort of papal request was turning into a formal mandate *de providendo*. A stabilized system of provisions begins to appear in the pontificate of Alexander III (1159-1181), and by 1240 was so well established as to

[53] Y. Renouard, 'Intérêt et importance des Archives Vaticanes pour l'histoire économique du Moyen Age spécialement du xive siècle,' in *Miscellanea A. Mercati* (Vatican City 1952), pp. 21-41.

[54] A. Gottlob, *Aus der Camera Apostolica des 15. Jahrhunderts* (Innsbruck 1889), p. 177.

[55] See G. Mollat, *La collation des bénéfices ecclésiastiques sous les papes d'Avignon, 1305-1378* (Paris 1921; also printed in the introduction to vol. VIII of Mollat's calendar, *Jean XXII, Lettres communes*); G. Barraclough, *Papal Provisions. Aspects of Church History, Constitutional, Legal and Administrative, in the Later Middle Ages* (Oxford 1935). See also C. Samaran and G. Mollat, *La fiscalité pontificale en France au XIVe siècle. Période d'Avignon et Grand Schisme d'Occident* (Paris 1905).

be almost notorious. It was only in 1265, however, that the papacy formulated in theory what it had practiced and achieved in the course of the preceding century: in the decretal *Licet ecclesiarum* of 27 August 1265, Pope Clement IV set out for the first time ever the papal right to dispose of all ecclesiastical benefices. After further legislation by Boniface VIII, Clement V and John XXII, the system had grown into an efficient and highly profitable business by 1350, and began to occasion stiff opposition in several countries, notably in England (Statutes of Provisors, 1351, 1353, 1365, 1389). The high point of the system was reached in the pontificate of Urban V, when on 4 August 1363 all appointments to abbacies and bishoprics were reserved to the Holy See, "quotiescumque sibi uti placuerit reservatione huiusmodi sive providendo vel mandando provideri de ecclesiis et monasteriis ipsis."[56]

These and other similar measures ensured a steady intake of revenue for the maintenance of the papacy, its buildings and officials. By the 14th century, when most of the cameral registers of the ASV begin, the revenues of the papacy fell into two broad classes:

a. Taxes paid directly to the papacy: common and minute services; chancery taxes for the writing, sealing, expedition and registration of all letters of grace and justice; *ad limina* visits; *pallium* taxes; the census from nations "subject to" the papacy: Naples, Sicily, Corsica, Sardinia, England.
b. Taxes paid to local agents: tithes; annates; procurations; *spolia*; charitable subsidies; taxes in return for the protection of the Holy See (census); Peter's Pence; fruits of vacant benefices, provision to which was reserved to the papacy.[57]

Accounts of these taxes, and of papal income and expenditure in general, were entered into special registers, most of which have been summarily listed above in Part One (pp. 41-48), under the title "Cameral Holdings". Here I propose to discuss in general only the three main series of cameral registers — *Obligationes et Solutiones, Collectoriae, Introitus et Exitus* — and their contents,

---

[56] C. Lux, *Constitutionum apostolicarum de generali beneficiorum reservatione, collectio et interpretatio* (Bresslau 1904), pp. 4-8, 21-46, 51-54, etc.; E. von Ottenthal, *Die päpstlichen Kanzleiregeln von Johannes XXII. bis Nikolaus V.* (Innsbruck 1888).

[57] An excellent introduction to these forms of revenues is in W. E. Lunt, *Papal Revenues in the Middle Ages* (New York 1934), esp. I, pp. 81-91 ; and in E. Göller, *Die Einnahmen der apostolischen Kammer unter Johann XXII.*, (Paderborn 1910), pp. 3*-134*.

but before doing so it may be useful to note here that over and above the cameral holdings of the ASV and the Archivio di Stato, there is also much cameral material in the Avignon Registers, as may be seen from the following list taken from Indice 1036 of the ASV:[58]

RA	34,	ff. 400-548:	IE 1328-1329
	36,	524-670:	1329-1330
	46,	174-309:	1318-1319
		630-729:	1334-1335
	47,	378-488:	1320-1321
		489-571:	1321-1322
		572-650:	1322-1323
		652-725:	1326-1327
	54,	471-488:	*Exitus*, 1326-1327
	73,	414-522:	Quittances of minute services, 1331-1334
	83,	352-357:	Monies collected in England by Legate, 1316
	84,	486-519:	*Solutiones*, 1321-1322
	122,	345-488:	*Solutiones et prorogationes*, 1353-1357
	133,	401-444:	Cameral formulary
		457-489:	Chancery formulary
	149,	57-164:	IE 1362
	172,	455-465:	Debts to Camera, 1370
	173,	51-102:	List of curial officials, 1371
	182,	201-248:	Debts to Camera, 1371
	198,	475-485:	Letters of Quittance, 1362-1369
	259,	1-115:	*Rationes Collectorum*, 1341-1366
	270,	15-78 :	*Litterae de curia*, 1392-1394
	272,	66-147:	*Litterae Camerales*, 1392-1393
	274,	1-40 :	*Litterae Camerales*, 1393-1394
	275,	1-129:	*Litterae de curia*, 1388-1389
	277,	1-281:	*Litterae de curia*, 1387-1390
	279,	13-229:	OS 1376-1378
	299,	42-47 :	*Solutiones*, 1394
	308,	80-159:	Letters of common services, 1404-1405
	321,	6-313:	IE 1404-1405
	328,	115-329:	IE 1406-1407
	332,	206-515:	IE 1409
	339,	171-430:	IE 1411-1412
	340,	185-380:	OS, Annates, etc., 1408-1413
	344,	2-290:	IE 1412
		291-540:	IE 1413
	346,	13-104:	*Condemnationes*, 1414-1417
		251-298:	Annates, 1414-1417
	347,	11-269:	IE 1414
	348,	352-385:	IE 1415
		532-763:	*Introitus*, 1415
	349,	621-769:	IE 1416
		778-835:	*Litterae Camerales*, 1417

[58] A general survey of the Cameral Holdings of the ASV and the Archivio de Stato di Roma is to be found above, pp. 41-48, but it should be noted that there is also much cameral material in other ASV holdings, such as the *Instrumenta Miscellanea* (e.g., nn. 7156, 7172, 7274, 7190, 7195, 7203).

A. Obligationes et Solutiones (OS).

3.2.3.44
3.2.3.55

This series of cameral registers, 91 volumes (1295-1555) of which are in the ASV, is mainly a record of financial obligations incurred by bishops and abbots on their nomination to a see or an abbacy. These obligations were of two kinds: *servitia communia* and *servitia minuta.*[59]

The *servitia communia* were so called because the tax imposed on abbots and bishops was in the "common interest" of the College of Cardinals and the Apostolic Camera, each of which had a right to a half of the tax levied on all bishops and abbots whom the Holy See nominated to or confirmed in bishoprics or abbacies of an annual income of 100 florins or more. This tax was normally reckoned as one-third of the income of any one year (usually the first after nomination); it was expressed in gold florins of Florence at first, but from the middle of the 14th century in those of the Camera, since these were now of equal value with those of Florence. The system of common service taxation dates from the beginning of the 14th century, but it is clear that at least a hundred years earlier some payment was involved in the collation of bishops and abbots by the pope.[60] The first instance of payments to the College of Cardinals occurs in the pontificate of Alexander IV (1254-1261), when also the word *servitium* is encountered for the first time. The custom of giving half of each tax to the cardinals dates at least from 1289, but those cardinals only qualified for a share who had been present at the consistory in which the provision in question was made (see OS 1A, f. 1r: "Nomina cardinalium inter quos est facta dicta divisio)".

Servitia minuta, on the other hand, were the payments made by nominees to members of the papal family and officials of the curia. Although the term "minuta" does not occur before the 15th century, these services were in existence as early as 1263. By 1295 they were being called "servitia consueta familiarium domini papae et cardinalium". In 1303 it was decided that these familiars and officials should be divided into five classes (four cameral, one cardinalitial), and that the total of the *servitia consueta* or *quinque servitia* would be calculated as five times that of the share of each of the cardinals who were present at the moment of provision. Hence, if the income of a given diocese for one year

3.2.3.54

[59] A. Clergeac, *La curie et les bénéfices consistoriaux. Étude sur les communes et menus services, 1300-1600* (Paris 1911).
[60] A. Gottlob, *Die Servitientaxe im 13. Jahrhundert* (Stuttgart 1903).

was reckoned as 600 florins, then a newly-appointed bishop had to promise (*se obligare*) to pay 200 florins (one-third of a year's revenue) by way of common service to the Camera, half of which went to the Camera and half to the cardinals who were present at the provision. And supposing that the number of cardinals present was 25, then the new bishop was obliged to another 20 florins by way of *quinque servitia*, since each of the 25 cardinals received 4 florins from their half of the common service of 200 florins, and the *quinque servitia* therefore came to five times four. A good example of the sharing of the four cameral services between the various cameral officials (Vice-Chancellor, Camerarius, clerks, familiars, cursors) from monies received druing the period 3 February-30 June 1351 is in IE 262, ff. 1r-5v. The total for the four services came to 5584 florins, 23 scudi, 55 pounds sterling (or 5660 florins, 11 scudi, at an exchange rate of 50 florins for 23 scudi, and 46 florins, 11 scudi, for the 55 pounds sterling), to which, for example, the archbishop of Dublin had contributed 146 pounds (f. 1r). Since Dublin's normal common service obligation was 2600 florins from 1317 onwards, this means that the archbishop of Dublin, when appointed on 17 November 1349, had promised in all, between common and minute services, some 2750 florins.

By the time of John XXII (1316-1334) this calculation of the common service tax as one-third of one year's revenue was regarded as an "old custom". The actual calculation of the year's revenue was determined by the local collectors of papal revenues or their deputies.[61] Thus when Nicholas O hEadhra, O. Cist., was provided to the see of Achonry on 22 October 1348, and was consecrated at Avignon on the same day, he was unable to say precisely what the revenue of his diocese was. However, he obliged himself to pay the minimum 33 1/3 florins for common service on 31 January 1349, and swore an oath that he would take back to Ireland and present to the archbishop of Tuam a letter commissioning the archbishop to inquire into and to report to the Camera on the real value of Achonry (Collectoriae 456, f. 128v). Again, when Roger Cradock, O.F.M., was appointed to Waterford, there was some doubt about the relation of his common obligation to the actual revenue of his diocese, so his letters of provision were sent on 21 May 1350 to the collector in England

---

[61] E. Göller, 'Der *Liber Taxarum* der päpstlichen Kammer', in *Quellen und Forschungen* 8 (1905) 113-173, 305-343, esp. pp. 125-127.

with a request for information on the revenue of Waterford (Collectoriae 456, f. 154v). The information seems to have been sent back to Avignon within a month, for on 25 June of the same year Cradock obliged himself to 40 florins (Hoberg, *Taxae*, p. 129).[62] Generally speaking, once a tax was established it was rarely changed, although on occasion it might be waived or temporarily reduced if an abbey or diocese was in financial difficulties. Thus, although the common service of 120 florins was waived "propter paupertatem" when John, bishop of Emly, made his obligation on 27 August 1353, the entry in OS 27, f. 85r, adds, "et fuit facta protestatio quod si dicta ecclesia deveniret ad pinguiorem futuram, quod praesens obligatio non praeiudicaret quin posset ad plus taxari."

As a rule the common service was not paid immediately on the collation of a bishopric or abbacy, but rather a promise was made personally or by proxy to pay the common service within the appointed time; whether at the curia itself or "in partibus extra romanam curiam," this promise was made before a commissary deputed by the Camera and the College of Cardinals. If a prelate died before he had completed his obligation, his successor had to enter into recognizance for his predecessor's debt when making his own *obligatio*;[63] if, however, a benefice fell vacant twice within the one year, the common service had to be paid only once. Failure to pay within the specified time was punished by excommunication, suspension or interdict. In this respect prelates from the British Isles (and particularly those from Ireland) are as prominent in the registers as any others, as in Collectoriae 469, where the archbishops of Armagh and Dublin and the bishop of Clonfert are among those who "fuerunt denuntiati et in audientia publica litterarum excommunicationis, suspensionis et interdicti sententias reatum periurii incurrisse pro eo quod sua communia et quinque servitia sicut se obligaverunt non solverunt, die quinta Iulii anno domini MCCCXXVIII" (ff. 48r-49v).

Obligations for *servitia communia* between 1295-1455 are listed by Msgr Hermann Hoberg in his *Taxae pro servitiis communibus ex libris obligationum ab anno 1295 usque ad annum 1455 confectis* (Studi e Testi 144, Vatican City 1949). The corresponding payment

---

[62] Both these cases are also noted by Göller, art. cit., at pp. 79, 86.
[63] The Council of Constance abolished this condition: see A. Mercati, *Raccolta di Concordati*[2] (Rome 1954), pp. 144-168, esp. pp. 148, 155, 161.

(*solutio*) of the common and minute services between 1316-1378[64] is to be found in the *Einnahmen* volumes of the great series *Vatikanische Quellen zur Geschichte der päpstlichen Hof- und Finanzverwaltung 1316-1378* (Paderborn, 1910-) of the Görresgesellschaft:

I. *Die Einnahmen der apostolischen Kammer unter Johann XXII.*, ed. E. Göller, 1910.

IV. *Die Einnahmen der apostolischen Kammer unter Benedikt XII.*, ed. E. Göller, 1920.

V. *Die Einnahmen der apostolischen Kammer unter Klemens VI.*, ed. L. Mohler, 1931.

VII. *Die Einnahmen der apostolischen Kammer unter Innocenz VI.*, I: *Die Einnahmenregister des päpstlichen Thesaurars*, ed. H. Hoberg, 1955.

Without detracting in any way from these publications, it must be admitted that they have their limitations. For Hoberg's *Taxae* no more covers all common obligations undertaken by bishops and abbots between 1295 and 1455 than the *Einnahmen* volumes of the *Vatikanische Quellen* exhaust all the information about *Introitus* and *Solutiones* for the period 1316-1378. If, for example, one relies on the *Taxae* alone, one will not always end up with an adequate picture of the range of obligations for common service. Thus, to take Ireland again, there is no record in the *Taxae* (p. 4) of an obligation by a bishop of Achonry before 1401; yet in fact, as we have already seen above from Coll. 456, f. 128v, a bishop of Achonry named Nicholas O hEadhra obliged himself to the minimum 33 1/3 florins on 31 January 1349. Again, although the list of obligations for Killala in the *Taxae* (p. 6) suggests that there is no record of an obligation between 1346 and 1451, it can be shown from Coll. 456, f. 166v, that there was at least one between those dates, on 9 August 1351. Further, there is no obligation for Cashel in the *Taxae* (p. 31) between 1322 and 1362, yet in fact one occurred on 27 January 1346 (OS 14, f. 105r; OS 22, f. 5v); nor is the obligation of Elphin on 19 February 1383 (OS 43, f. 88v) noted at p. 50, thus leaving a gap of some 40 years between Elphin obligations.

Some of the lacunae in the *Taxae* are due, no doubt, to the fact that the editor discarded some OS volumes as duplicates of the ones he chose for the *Taxae*.[65] However, the whole question

---

[64] For Benedict XII (1334-1342) see J. M. Vidal, *Benoît XII, Lettres communes* II (Paris 1906), pp. 425-435 (drawing on OS 6 only for *obligationes communes*). The Monte Cassino edition of the registers of Clement V contains all obligations from 1305-1314: *Regesti Clementis papae V, Appendices* I (Rome 1892), pp. 199-257.

[65] "Extant insuper nonnulli codices, qui ex originalibus supra enumeratis sunt exscripti quibusque proinde non usi sumus": p. xv.

of the relationship between original OS volumes and alleged copies is not all that clear. Thus the *Taxae* uses only part of OS 14 (ff. 1-35) and ignores the remainder of it; yet in fact the second part of OS 14 contains obligations for 1345-1347 (e.g. that for Cashel cited above) that are not to be found in the sources preferred by the editor of the *Taxae*. Again, there are obligations in OS 16 (e.g. 116v: San Vitale, Ravenna) which are not in OS 22, the sole source of the *Taxae* at this point; so also there are obligations in OS 2 (e.g. f. 17v: Durham on 9 June 1310) which are not in the *Taxae*.

There are several other drawbacks to the *Taxae*, chiefly because of the nature of the work. For one thing, only the sum of money promised for common service is noted; that pledged for minute services is not given. Hence the sum actually promised by bishops and abbots is always higher than that noted in the *Taxae* for common service, depending, of course, on the number of cardinals present at the moment of provision. For example, if for some reason or other one were interested in the finances of the diocese of Killaloe, Ireland, in the 14th century, all that one would learn from the *Taxae* (pp. 65-66) is that the usual common service obligation was 100 florins, and that this obligation was taken in 1326 and 1355, as well as in 1400, 1409, 1423, 1430, 1443. Yet on each of these occasions the sum promised by the newly-provided bishop was somewhat higher, since it also included the obligation to the minute services. Thus when Thomas, bishop-elect of Killaloe, undertook the usual obligation of 100 florins on 30 May 1355, there were 21 cardinals present who therefore were entitled as a body to half of that sum (OS 22, f. 173v); this means that the total personal obligation of Thomas came roughly to 112 florins, since he had to pay some 12 florins for the minute services (the share of each cardinal from half the common obligation, multiplied by five).

For another thing, the *Taxae*, of necessity, omits all kinds of useful information which is to be found in the OS volumes, for example, names of bishops and procurators; whether the obligation was made in person or by proxy; whether the new bishop or abbot also took over an unpaid obligation of his predecessor. A good example of the importance of consulting OS volumes directly instead of taking the excellent but ascetic entries in the *Taxae* as the last word, is provided by the list of obligations for Emly in the *Taxae* (p. 63): "1353. 27. 8: 120 fl. *OS 22 fol. 147*'. 1356. 15. 3: 120 fl. *OS 22 fol. 184*." As this entry stands it implies that two bishops undertook obligations, one in 1353 and another in 1356. Yet the *Handbook of British Chronology*[2] (London 1961), p. 327, gives only one bishop, John Esmond (11 January 1353-4 April 1362), in these years, noting that his temporalities were restored on 27 April 1356. And if one turns to OS 22 itself, it will be found that the obligation of 27 August 1353 (f. 147r; *Taxae*, p. 63) was in fact ineffective, since, as the obligation taken on 15 March 1356 (*Taxae*, p. 63) informs us (OS 22, f. 184r), the see of Emly was not at all vacant when Esmond took the obligation in 1353. Hence the first entry in the *Taxae* should be disregarded, and, as well, the entry in the *Handbook* should not read "11 Jan. 1353" for Esmond's provision to Emly but "*ante* 15 March 1356" (the date on which Esmond's second — and definitive — obligation was incurred, and one which is somewhat nearer to the date of the restoration of his temporalities — 4 April 1356 — than 1353). Further, the latest date of Esmond's predecessor at Emly (Richard le Walleys) in the *Handbook* (p. 327: "*a.* 11 Jan. 1353") must be revised to "*a.* 15 Mar. 1356." (Note, however, that although the obligation taken in 1353 by Esmond was premature, the *protestatio* made by Esmond on that occasion — see above, p. 159 — still held good in 1356, and was not repeated).

The *Taxae*, too, never lists anything more than personal common service, with the result that one is deprived of the important information, e.g. that the bishop of Meath, when taking his own obligation on 22 February 1327 (OS 6, f. 60v), also undertook the debts of his predecessor, or that the archbishop of Cashel shouldered those of his predecessor on 9 July 1327 (*ibid.*, f. 64v).

Much OS information will, of course, be found, after some poking about, in the *Einnahmen* volumes of the *Vatikanische Quellen*, but it is not always as complete as one would wish. For example, the bleak statement in the *Taxae*, p. 14, "Armachan, 1323. 11. 5: 1000 fl. *Göller 662*," might suggest to the unwary that this is all that the source (OS 6) used by Göller, *Einnahmen unter Johann XXII.*, contains. Yet Göller further notes that the archbishop of Armagh not only promised 1000 florins for himself but also obliged himself to another 1500 for his two predecessors. But the information in OS 8, f. 5v, is rather more meaty. For on 11 May 1323, Stephen Segrave, who had been appointed archbishop of Armagh on 16 March 1323, "recognovit servitium integrum unius sui predecessoris immediati non solutum, et servitia familiaria et medietatem alterius predecessoris servitii, quod est in universo 1500 fl.

aurei, et decem servitia familiaria. Et promisit pro communi servitio 1000 fl., et quinque servitia familiaria persolvere in terminis infrascriptis et tribus annis proxime futuris, videlicet, in primo anno inchoando ab hodie completo 500 fl., et pro rata servitiorum; in secundo anno 1000 fl., et pro rata servitiorum; et in tertio et ultimo anno alios 1000 fl., et residua servitia famulorum predictorum, alioquin... Et iuravit ut in forma." So in fact Stephen had to shoulder 15 minute services (5 for himself, 10 for his two predecessors) as well as 2500 florins for himself and his predecessors.

As it happens, Stephen never paid off all these monies, nor did his successor, David O Hiraghty, so when Richard Fitzralph was provided to the see of Armagh in 1347, he had to commit himself not only to the payment of his own common service (*Taxae*, p. 14: 8 March 1347) and minute services, but also for the services of four predecessors, Walter Jorz, Roland Jorz, Stephen and David. Some small sums were paid by him in 1347 and 1349 (OS 22, f. 52r; OS 24, f. 31v), and a series of extensions were granted him after the three statutory years were up in 1350 (OS 25, ff. 56v, 78v). The situation was complicated by the discovery that the diocese was also in arrears with respect to visitations *ad limina*, and a commission set up on 5 October 1350 reported that the accountants "had searched the registers of the Camera" but were unable to find any record of payment of *ad limina* taxes since 1301 (OS 25, ff. 97r-97v; OS 26, f. 90r-90v; not in Mohler, *Einnahmen unter Klemens VI*). Partial payments followed through procurators of Fitzralph such as his nephew M. Richard Fitzralph, or M. John Brackley, or M. William Napton; but there had to be numerous extensions (OS 25, f. 175v, and in Mohler; f. 112v, not in Mohler; OS 26, f. 164r, and in Mohler; etc.) before an absolute quittance of all Armagh's debts to the Camera was finally effected on 10 May 1356 (OS 26, ff. 448r-448v; see OS 24, f. 109r).[66]

Finally, the most important aspect of the OS volumes is the information they can yield on the appointment of bishops and abbots. Hoberg's *Taxae* volume, unfortunately, is of no help whatever at this juncture, for it never gives the names of those who promised common service. Since the date of provision of an abbot or bishop often is not known, the date of obligation in the OS volumes often provides a useful *terminus ante quem* for

---

[66] Generally speaking, Mohler's *Einnahmen unter Klemens VI.* contains most of the Armagh references, but the names of the procurators are not always included.

provisions, as the following examples (all Irish again) show fairly clearly:

1. *The Handbook of British Chronology*, p. 337, says of Thomas Dene, bishop of Ferns, that there is "no date of provision," but gives the date of his consecration as 18 June 1363. Yet OS 36, f. 53r (cf. *Taxae*, p. 54) records his obligation on 15 April 1363, so his provision is at least *ante* that date.

2. The same *Handbook*, p. 340, notes the provision of John Young to Leighlin as "*ante* Sept. 1363," but from OS 36, f. 59r (cf. *Taxae*, p. 67) it is clear that he must have been provided before 12 May 1363, when he undertook his obligation of common service.

3. A "Guillelmus electus Leighlinensis" promised services on 3 November 1348 (OS 22, f. 58r; cf. *Taxae*, p. 67), yet in the *Handbook*, p. 340, there is no mention of a bishop between Ralph Kelly (ineffective provision, 1344) and Thomas of Brakenberg (provided 20 March 1349). Hence the date of the death of the previous bishop, Miler le Poer (1320-), should probably be *ante* 3 November 1348 rather than the *Handbook's* "*ante* April 1349."

4. Thomas Barrett of Elphin is given in the *Handbook*, p. 348, as "prov. 1372," whereas according to OS 35, f. 165v (cf. *Taxae*, p. 50), his obligation was on 16 July 1372.

5. The *Handbook* says that the same Thomas Barrett of Elphin died in 1404 and that John (O Grada) was provided *ante* 12 October 1407 (p. 348). Yet OS 43, f. 88v (not in *Taxae*) notes that John, bishop of Elphin, promised for himself and his predecessor, Thomas, on 19 February 1383.

6. William (O Dubhda) was provided to Killala on 24 June 1347, according to the *Handbook*, p. 349, yet in fact he promised services as "Willelmus electus" on 16 November 1346 (OS 14, f. 113v; cf. *Taxae*, p. 6).

7. The *Handbook* goes on to state that O Dubhda's successor, Robert Elyot, was bishop of Killala from 8 June 1351 until *ante* January 1390, the *ante* depending on the fact that Thomas Horwell was provided on 31 January of that year. Elyot's episcopate, however, must have ended somewhat earlier, since a certain Cornelius took on service obligations on 19 February 1383 (OS 43, f. 88r; cf. *Taxae*, p. 6).

8. According to the *Handbook*, p. 332, Thomas le Reve of Lismore was provided *ante* 6 June 1358, but OS 22, f. 220r (cf. *Taxae*, p. 70) shows that his obligation was taken on 18 May 1358.

9. Maurice of Clonfert is listed in the *Handbook*, p. 347, as "cons.1378," but he must have been provided quite early in that year, since his obligation was on 6 March 1378 (OS 43, f. 55v; cf. *Taxae*, p. 38).

B. COLLECTORIAE (Coll.).

3.2.3.22

In general the volumes of the *Collectoriae* series (504 vv. 1274-1447) are a very important source for understanding papal finances and the social economy of the middle ages. They contain an accounting of all the business of the *Collectores*, that is, of the officials appointed directly by the pope for the collection of certain monies due to the Apostolic Camera. They were not, however, concerned with monies paid directly to the Camera (services, pallium taxes, various taxes of the Chancery and Camera, *ad limina* visitations, etc.), but rather with:

a. The *census*, or annual tribute from exempt monasteries.
b. Tithes levied for Crusades or other needs of the papacy.
c. "Subsidia caritativa", or voluntary contributions of the clergy.
d. Peter's Pence, or *Obolus S. Petri*.
e. Revenues of benefices which the pope had reserved to himself for one year after provision. After Clement VI (1342-1352), however, it became the custom not to hand over the bull of provision to a cleric until he had obliged himself formally to pay his "annates", in much the same way that bishops and abbots obliged themselves in respect of the *servitia*. Hence the Collectors rarely had anything to do with these revenues from then onwards.

One of the chief merits of the *Collectoriae* volumes, at least until the time of Clement VI, is that entries concerning provisions contain not only a record of monies collected for the year after the provision, but also a full statement of the provision itself, its terms, its success or failure (and in the case of failure it gives the precise reasons, as in the section "Provisiones inutiles" in Coll. 12, ff. 50r-57r). In as much as there is often no other record of a given supplication or letter of provision, these details can be very enlightening (see, for example, the use made of the *Collectoriae* by Helena Chew in her edition of a Salisbury Chapter Act Book, 1329-1347, which she published under the title *Hemingby's Register*, Devizes 1963). And even where a provision is otherwise unknown, an entry in a *Collectoriae* volume often allows one to see a provision from a Collector's point of view. Thus Coll. 291, f. 146r, nicely illustrates part of the process by which the provision of William Bull to the Deanery of Cork on 9 June 1363 (*Calendar of Papal Petitions*, I, p. 425) became effective.

Moreover, the *Collectoriae* series has a fascination all its own in that it affords now and then a glimpse of the day-to-day business of the Camera. From this point of view Coll. 350 is noteworthy. For, among other things, there are lists of letters sent for distribution to legates and collectors in areas all over Europe, from Sweden to Spain. Thus on f. 67r eight letters are noted, with incipits and dates, which the new Collector for England, Rigaud d'Asserio took with him to England on 18 June 1317 on his "Legatio Anglie et Scocie Regnis, Wallie et Ibernie partibus": two letters to the archbishops and bishops, one "cum filo cerico", on Rigaud's appointment, the other, "cum filo canapis", on the collection of Peter's Pence; four to Rigaud himself, "cum filo canapis"; one to the legates Gaucelinus and Luke; one closed letter to King Edward II. These are followed on f. 67v by a group of letters — one "bullata cum filo canapis"; one "aperta bullata"; one "littera grossata"; two "litterae clausae"; eight "clausae bullatae" — sent on 8 November 1317 to the papal legates in England, with a note of their contents; and on f. 68r by a number of letters of the same date to Rigaud, who is also noted as having been sent in July 1318 "unam (litteram) bullatam et registratam continentem constitucionem novam *Suscepti regiminis*". Two years later, when Rigaud was appointed bishop of Winchester, a formidable batch of letters was sent to him for distribution on 17 August 1320 (f. 54r):

Anno domini millesimo CCC°XX° die XVII^a mensis Augusti fuerunt misse XXVIII littere bullate ad partes Anglie.

Item alie due, videlicet reverendo patri domino Rigaldo Wintonien. electo, per magistrum Raymundum de Solomniaco, quarum litterarum una est aperta et dirigitur episcopo Londonen. et dicto electo.

Alie sunt clause, quarum quinque diriguntur domino Eduardo regi Anglie illustri.

Item alie due diriguntur nobili viro domino Thome comiti Lancastrie.

Item alie due littere diriguntur domino Ademario comiti de Pembroc.

Item alie due diriguntur domino Johanni comiti Richemundie.

Item alia littera dirigitur domino Thome comiti Marescallo.

Item alie due littere diriguntur domino Hugoni Dispensatori, domini Eduardi regis Angliae illustris Cambellano.

Item alia littera dirigitur domino Aymoni, nato clare memorie domini Eduardi regis Anglie.

Item alia littera dirigitur domino Bartholomeo de Radehner Senescallo domini Eduardi regis Anglie illustris.

Item alie due littere clause diriguntur dicto electo Wintonien.

Item alie due littere diriguntur episcopo Londonen.

Item alie due littere diriguntur episcopo Exonien.

Item alie due littere diriguntur archiepiscopo Cantuarien.

Item alie due littere diriguntur episcopo Norwicen.

Item alia littera dirigitur episcopo Erforden.

Item alia littera dirigitur episcopo Elien.

Item alia que dirigitur regi Anglie clausa, qua signatur processus Scotie.

Item alia eidem quod abstineat ab exactione decime Wintonien.

It goes without saying that the *Collectoriae* volumes have been the object of much study in various countries. They have been used extensively by J. P. Kirsch, *Die päpstlichen Kollectorien in Deutschland während des XIV. Jahrhunderts* (Paderborn 1914), by U. Berlière, *Les collectories pontificales dans l'anciens diocèses de Cambrai, Thérouanne et Tournai au XIVe siècle* (Analecta Vaticano-Belgica 10, Rome 1929), and, among others, by the editors of the *Vatikanische Quellen* and of the *Rationes decimarum Italiae*. For the British Isles, the late W. E. Lunt has used them to great effect in his *Financial Relations of the Papacy with England*, I: *To 1327*, II: *1327-1534* (Cambridge, Mass., 1939, 1962), and particularly in his posthumous *Accounts rendered by Papal Collectors in England, 1317-1378*, ed. E. B. Graves (Philadelphia 1968).

Stray letters and items relative to the British Isles turn up sometimes in unlikely volumes (e.g. as part of the cover of Coll. 70 — a volume of accounts of the collector of Toulouse — there is a letter of Benedict XII to Alexander de Bicknor, archbishop of Dublin, with respect to a quarrel between the prioress and convent of Graney, co. Kildare, and a sub-Collector, Hugo de Calce), but generally speaking British and Irish material is to be found in the volumes of the Collectors of England. Although Lunt in his *Accounts* has splendidly edited the main volumes for 1317-1378, it may be useful for the sake of reference to list those and some others here:

1. Coll. 11: "Collectio fructuum beneficiorum, denariorum beati Petri, censuum, legatorum, etc. in Anglia et Hibernia... Iste sunt rationes Iohannis de Cabrespino doctoris decretorum, canonici Narbon., in partibus Anglie et Ybernie apostolice sedis nuncii..." The accounts range from 1363-1366, and are now edited in Lunt, *Accounts*, pp. 172-236.
2. Coll. 12: ff. 1-139: accounts of J. de Cabrespino, 1363-1371, now in Lunt, *Accounts*, pp. 236-362; ff. 143-367: accounts of Arnald Garnerii, 1371-1379, now in Lunt, pp. 484-541.
3. Coll. 13: ff. 1-200: accounts of Garnerii, 1371-1379, now in Lunt, pp. 363-483.
4. Coll. 14: ff. 1-22: "Registrum societatum mercatorum habentium pecuniam decime sexennalis collecte in Anglia, 1283," published by Lunt, *Financial relations of the Papacy with England to 1327*, Cambridge, Mass., 1939; ff. 23-157: accounts of Hugh Pelegrini, 1349-1363, now in Lunt, *Accounts*, pp. 78-171; ff. 158-193: Scottish benefices and accounts of William de Grenlaw for Scotland, 1352-1362 — *not* in Lunt, *Accounts*.
5. Coll. 227: ff. 34-45: accounts of Itier de Concoreto, 1328-1335, now in Lunt, *Accounts*, pp. 29-34; ff. 103-115: accounts, including a "Collectio arreragiorum" at ff. 146-155, of Bernard de Sistre, 1335-1343,

now in Lunt, *Accounts*, pp. 35-77 (who also edits at pp. 1-28 the accounts of Rigaud d'Asserio, 1317-1323, from IE 15, ff. 1-46).

6. Coll. 144: Census, 1340-1360 (with a few British Isles' notes).
7. Coll. 280: "Registrum collationum beneficiorum in universa ecclesia": ff. 1-114: 1329-1332; 115-137: 1334; 138-163: 1335. The volume is useful on occasion for details not available in the *Collectoriae* volumes (11, 12, 13, 14, 227) edited by Lunt.
8. Coll. 289: ff. 1-26: "Registrum resignationum et permutationum beneficiorum," 1346.
9. Coll. 291: ff. 1-183: "Provisiones in universa ecclesia," 1362-1363.
10. Coll. 497: ff. 1-17: "Varia cameralia," 1345; ff. 18-134: a notebook, 1338-1358 (e.g. f. 31v: Ossory; f. 75r: Dublin).

3.2.3.31   **C. INTROITUS ET EXITUS (IE).**

This series of ledgers of the income and expenditure of the papal exchequer comprises some 565 volumes running from 1270 to 1524, to which must be added the IE material which is now part of the series of Avignon Registers as RA 34, 36, 46, 47, 54, 149, 321, 328, 332, etc. (see the list given above at p. 156). All the ledgers are of paper, and are generally of quarto size.

Receipts from any and every source are registered in the IE volumes, e.g., "Recepta pro passagio terre sancte" (IE 42, f. 22r), as well as payments for the smallest work done by *bullatores* and others, e.g., IE 565, f. 116v: "Clonen. pro littera, 2 fl."; 117v: "Dunen. pro littera, 3 ;., ... Armachan. pro littera, 2 fl.". All this income for 1316-1378 is faithfully recorded now in print in the *Einnahmen* volumes of the *Vatikanische Quellen zur Geschichte der päpstlichen Hof- und Finanzverwaltung* (Paderborn 1910-) which were listed above when treating of the OS series.

All sorts of entries, too, will be found in the expenditure columns: the running expenses of the Duchy of Spoleto, 1332-1334, in IE 60; the personal expenses of Urban VI in Burgundy, 1382-1386, in IE 357; payments to special envoys such as that of 80 gold florins on 30 December 1320 "pro expensis necessariis fratris Guilelmi de Lauduno, magistri in theologia, qui per dominum nostrum papam missus fuit ad partes Anglie pro certis negociis sibi commissis et secum duxit vi. equitaturas" (RA 4, f. 440v). There are disbursements also for food and clothing (RA 47, f. 481r, 23 June 1321: "pro duobus palmis de saya de Irlanda et de Catalonia, precio lxxiiii l. xviii x. xi d."), for building and repairs, for horses and stables, for art and books (e.g. RA 47, f. 539r, 27 April 1322: a sum of money to Fr Gregory, O.S.A., master in theology, for his work *Super moralitaïes Job*), and for various pittances, e.g. 20 gold florins to the

Dominicans of Avignon on the day that Thomas Aquinas was canonized in their church at Avignon, 18 July 1323. Again, the *Vatikanische Quellen* series has admirably printed these *Exitus* parts of IE and related sources for the Avignon period in the *Ausgaben* volumes:[67]

> II: *Die Ausgaben der apostolischen Kammer unter Johann XXII., nebst den Jahresbilanzen von 1316-1375*, ed. K. H. Schäfer, 1911.
>
> III: *Die Ausgaben der apostolischen Kammer unter Benedikt XII., Klemens VI. und Innocenz VI., (1335-1362)*, ed. K. H. Schäfer, 1914.
>
> VI: *Die Ausgaben der apostolischen Kammer unter den Päpsten Urban V. und Gregor XI., (1362-1378)*, nebst Nachträgen und einem Glossar für alle drei Ausgabenbände, ed. K. H. Schäfer, 1937.

The IE series is, of course, a rich source for the economic or the social historian.[68] To a local historian, however, the value of the IE ledgers often lies in the fact that they confirm if they do not add to information which he has already extracted from the OS or *Collectoriae* series. From this point of view the *Introitus* sections of IE volumes are of more importance than the *Exitus* parts. For it is precisely here that the IE volumes overlap the "obligationum solutiones" of the OS series, although there are, as I shall note, some differences, chiefly because the IE accountants were more interested in the amount of money paid in respect of common and minor services than in the actual manner in which a given obligation was honoured. Only the "obligatio" aspect of these services was considered above when discussing the OS series; "solutiones" or quittances, on the other hand, are best seen in relation to the *Introitus* parts of IE, if only because the cameral accountants depended heavily on them. Hence the following remarks bear as much on OS volumes as on those of IE.

As I have noted above, most of the IE volumes for the Avignon period have been used by the great *Vatikanische Quellen* series. This does not mean, however, that any and every detail from those IE volumes is now available in print, and that further research is superfluous. For if, as Yves Renouard has pointed out, the financial figures in the *Quellen* are not always complete,[69] it is, on the other hand, precisely the editors' preoccupation with

---

[67] For later periods see, for example, A. I. Dunlop, *The Apostolic Camera and Scottish benefices, 1418-1488* (Edinburgh 1934), calendaring Scottish material in the IE and OS series.

[68] See Y. Renouard, *Les relations des Papes d'Avignon et des Compagnies commerciales et bancaires de 1316 à 1378* (Paris 1941); B. Guillemain, *La cour pontificale d'Avignon (1309-1376). Étude d'une société* (Paris 1962), *passim*.

[69] Y. Renouard, art. cit., n. 53 above.

financial details that prompts them to overlook certain areas of IE volumes or to rely too exclusively on IE where an OS volume provides information of more general interest.

Some examples may help to make this point a little clearer. In *Einnahmen unter Johann XXII.*, pp. 105-116, Göller uses IE 16 and IE 563 for the revenues of 1316-1317, but if one compares the quittances of common and minute services in those IE volumes with the corresponding "solutiones" in OS 3, it will be found that the procurators' and cardinals' names are often omitted by IE (and hence are not in Göller). Thus OS 3, f. 21v, when recording the payment of 225 florins on 17 March 1317 for the common services of the bishop of Dunkeld, also notes the name of his proctor (M. John de Pilmor) and, as well, the names of those cardinals who were present at the taking of the obligation on 1 June 1312; whereas the corresponding IE entry (IE 16, f. 10r; Göller, p. 105) states simply that on 17 March 1317 the Camera received "a procuratore domini Guillelmi Dunkelden. episcopi in Scotia 225 flor. aur.". Again, Göller, p. 154, using IE 54 and RA 47, lists Andreas Sapiti as procurator of the archbishop of Tuam on September 1322, but the corresponding OS 3, f. 99v, notes a second procurator in M. John Ynoudhan, canon of Tuam. As for Sapiti himself, this is one of the few occasions on which he is noted in Göller as procurator of an Irish bishop. Yet in fact Sapiti was procurator time and again for Irish bishops in the pontificate of John XXII, e.g. for Cashel (OS 3, f. 119v: 27.1.1324), Dublin (OS 3, f. 125r: 3.5.1324), Cloyne (OS 6, f. 31r: 24.5.1322), Cashel again (OS 6, f. 92v: 28.5.1330), Meath (OS 8, f. 31r: 3.1.1325), Armagh (OS 8, f. 126v: 9.8.1329; RA 47, v. 664r: 23.11.1326), Cork (OS 8, f. 100v: 24.10.1328). Likewise, Sapiti is not very prominent in Göller as procurator for English bishops, yet there is a formidable number of references to him in OS volumes, especially in vv. 3, 6, 8, 12, and in RA 47.

Of course the IE volumes take on a special quality when, for one reason or another, there is no corresponding OS volume. But where they overlap, it is unwise to prefer IE to OS. Often, indeed, the IE accountants do not get names right when copying from an original OS register: thus Göller, p. 121, following IE, gives William Fit as procurator of Cashel on 20 January 1319, where OS 3, f. 52v, reads William Losit. Above all else, the fuller entries in OS volumes often reveal the presence at Avignon of an abbot or bishop. Thus, OS 13 (which Göller does not use) notes that the quittance of John Brid, bishop of Cloyne, was "per manus proprias" on 2 May 1334, and OS 15, f. 24v, states that he paid his minor services personally ("manualiter excoluit") on the same day.

One last point — and again it is made not in order to minimize the value of the *Vatikanische Quellen* but rather to correct further an impression that the *Quellen* have exhausted the possibilities of the OS and IE volumes for the Avignon Papacy; to be fair, one should not expect more from the *Quellen* than the series set out to accomplish: to document the finances of the Avignon Papacy. It is a fact, however, that although the *Quellen* have used the OS volumes extensively for prorogations of taxes, dispensations and absolutions, there are documents which, for reasons that are not always clear, are not recorded. The two examples I give here reflect, need it be said, my own interests; they properly belong to Göller's *Einnahmen unter Johann XXII.*, and possibly do not have parallels in other volumes of the *Quellen*.

The first example (OS 8, ff. 110v-111r) concerns the absolution of John O Grada, archbishop of Cashel, on 4 March 1329. He had paid 300 florins for his services on the day before (OS 8, f. 111r; a fact which Göller, p. 218, does note), but finding himself burdened by cameral debts incurred, because of the poverty of Cashel, by his predecessors Stephen, William and Maurice (1290-1326), who in turn had been excommunicated, John petitioned the pope for a reduction of the debts; whereupon the pope, "ecclesie et persone compaciens, et de valore dicte Cassellensis ecclesie volens cercius informari, per suas certi tenoris litteras (marginal note: Nota quod ista littera non fuit sigillata per dominum camerarium nec processit) de universo valore ipsius Cassellensis ecclesie inquiri mandavit et mandat". The actual mandate of inquisition, addressed to the papal legate in England, is to be found further on in OS 8, f. 114r-114v, but likewise is not in Göller, although in fact he prints selections from OS 8 at pp. 688-690.

The second example concerns Armagh, and is a shade more interesting; again it is from OS 8, at ff. 69v-70v. In a letter of 21 February 1322, cardinal Peter of S. Susanna and Gasbert, archbishop of Arles, "dicti domini camerarii commissarii seu delegati," inform Hugh of Angoulême, archdeacon of Canterbury, that they have received from one Tellutrius of Camerino, a papal *cursor*, the following supplication ("quamdam commissionis seu supplicationis cedulam in hec verba") in the name of Stephen, archbishop of Armagh, "tocius Hiberniae primas." In this petition, the text of which the officials now give, Stephen states that in order to pay off cameral debts he had commissioned masters John Popard, rector of Bedford in the diocese of Coventry, and Richard of Chaddesden, rector of Charwelton in the diocese of Lincoln, to collect "redditus suos et proventus et certum subsidium" from the clergy of Armagh. These collectors, however, had later refused to hand over to the archbishop the 360 marks sterling that they had collected, so he now begs the Camera for redress against them. Having thus rehearsed Armagh's petition, the two officials now commission Hugh of Angoulême to invite the two rectors to release the Armagh money to the archbishop within forty days of the receipt of his invitation, failing which they must appear before the Camera to explain themselves.

Apart from the light it throws on the methods as well as the hazards of "tithing" in Northern Ireland in the early 14th century, this document in OS 8 provides an interesting example of the manner in which cameral supplications were heard and expedited in this period. What the cameral commissioners received from the papal *cursor* was Armagh's own, original supplication, on which there was written, in another hand, the grant of the petition. But since, apparently, the Referendary had forgotten to initial the grant, the commissioners had to treat the grant with some circumspection. Hence when issuing a mandate to Hugh of Angoulême along the lines indicated by the note, the commissioners carefully document their action and protect themselves against a charge of proceeding too hastily, with the words: "In fine vero cedule (i.e. Armagh's supplication) scripta erat de alterius manus litera, et a litera superiori dissimili et diversa, videlicet hec verba: *Committit dominus quod per viam iustitie compellant eosdem, et quod possint citari in curia et extra curiam ad partes.*"

GENERAL BIBLIOGRAPHY

a. Full texts or calendars of letters of individual popes are listed under the pope in question, but national or local collections of papal letters are given under the country or locality in question. Thus Mollat's *Lettres communes* of John XXII are noted under *John XXII*, but Coulon's *Lettres secrètes et curiales du pape Jean XXII relatives à la France* are to be found under *France*.

b. Inventories or lists of papal letters or records in various local archives are listed under the compiler's name and not under the locality or country. Thus Largiadèr's *censimento* of papal letters extant in Swiss collections is given under *Largiadèr*, but Bernouilli's *Acta Pontificum Helvetica* is to be found under *Switzerland*.

c. General collections of papal letters and records are listed under the title of the series, e.g., *Regesta Pontificum Romanorum; Vatikanische Quellen zur Geschichte der päpstlichen Hof- und Finanzverwaltung*.

d. Multiple entries are numbered so as to facilitate cross-references from the General Index to the Bibliography.

e. By and large the Bibliography limits itself to publications carrying texts of or commentaries on the medieval holdings of the ASV. For this reason no attempt is made to cover the wide range of Nunciature publications, for which one can now turn readily to Halkin's *Les archives des Nunciatures* (1968).

f. The Bibliography is quite selective. Its main purpose is to introduce a beginner to some of the more important authors in the field of papal diplomatics, and to the names and writings of many of those who have laboured over the past eighty or ninety years to make the medieval holdings of the ASV better known.

For items marked *, see the addenda to the bibliography following p. 221.

See also the bibliography in Blouin, pp. 459-503.

ABBREVIATIONS

Unlike Parts One and Two of this *Survey*, the Bibliography employs sigla for periodical literature, but even here only the more common 'diplomatic' periodicals are given sigla, as follows :

AHP   *Archivum historiae pontificiae*, Rome, 1963 —

BAPI   *Bollettino dell'Archivio paleografico italiano*, Rome, 1908 —

BEFAR   *Bibliothèque des Écoles Françaises d'Athènes et de Rome: Deuxième série*: Registres et Lettres des Papes du XIIIe siècle; *Troisième série*: Registres et Lettres des Papes du XIVe siècle. Paris, 1884 —

BIHRB   *Bulletin de l'Institut historique Belge de Rome*, Rome-Brussels, 1919 —
BISIAM   *Bullettino dell'Istituto Storico Italiano per il medio evo e Archivio Muratoriano*, Rome, 1886 —
MAH   *Mélanges d'archéologie et d'histoire* [École Française de Rome], Rome-Paris, 1881 —
MIöG   *Mitteilungen des Instituts für österreichische Geschichtsforschung*, Graz-Vienna, 1880 —
QFIAB   *Quellen und Forschungen aus italienischen Archiven und Bibliotheken* [Deutsche Historische Institut], Rome-Tübingen, 1898 —
RHE   *Revue d'histoire ecclésiastique*, Louvain, 1900 —
RHM   *Römische historische Mitteilungen*, [Oesterreichische Institut], Rome-Vienna, 1956 —
RQ   *Römische Quartalschrift für christliche Altertumskunde und für Kirchengeschichte* [Görresgesellschaft], Freiburg-im-Breisgau, 1887 —
ZSSRGKA   *Zeitschrift der Savigny-Stiftung für Rechtsgeschichte, kanonistische Abteilung*, Weimar, 1911 —

Abate, P., 'Lettere "secretae" d'Innocenzo IV e altri documenti in una raccolta inedita del secolo XIII', in *Miscellanea Francescana* 55 (1955), 317-373.
Acht, P., 1. 'Der Recipe-Vermerk auf den Urkunden Papst Bonifaz' VIII', in *Zeitschrift für bayerische Landesgeschichte*, 18 (1955), 243-255.
          2. 'Drei Fälschungen von Papsturkunden des 13. Jahrhunderts', in BAPI, 3rd series, 2-3 (1956-1957), 33-57.
Acta Pontificum Romanorum inedita, ed. J. von Pflugk-Harttung: I: *Urkunden der Päpste vom Jahre 748 bis zum Jahre 1198*, Tübingen, 1881; II: *Urkunden der Päpste vom Jahre c. 97 bis zum Jahre 1197*, Stuttgart, 1884; III: *Urkunden der Päpste vom Jahre c. 590 bis zum Jahre 1197*, Stuttgart, 1888.
Alexander III (1159-1181), fragments of registers of, in *Epistolae Pontificum Romanorum ineditae*, ed. S. Löwenfeld, Leipzig, 1885, pp. 149-209. See also Holtzmann 2, below.
Alexander IV (1254-1261): C. Bourel de la Roncière, J. de Loye, P. de Cénival, A. Coulon, *Les registres d'Alexandre IV. Recueil des bulles de ce Pape, publiées ou analysées d'après les manuscrits originaux des Archives du Vatican*, 3 vv., Paris, 1895-1899 (BEFAR. B. 6). Selections in MGH [5].
Alessandri, L. and F. Pennacchi, 'Bullarium Pontificium quod exstat in archivo sacri conventus S. Francisci Assisiensis (nunc apud publicam Bibliothecam Assisii), 1220-1832', in *Archivum Franciscanum Historicum*, 8 (1915), 592-617; 10 (1917), 185-219; 11 (1918), 206-250, 442-490; 12 (1919), 132-186, 471-543; 13 (1920), 136-180, 508-585.
Ambrosini, M. L., *The Secret Archives of the Vatican*, Boston, 1969.

Analectus II (1130-1138): P. Ewald, 'Registrum Anacleti II antipapae', in *Neues Archiv*, 3 (1878), 164-168.

Audard, E., 'L'histoire religieuse de la Révolution française aux Archives Vaticanes', in *Revue d'histoire de l'Église de France*, 4 (1913), 516-535, 625-639.

Austria (and Germany): *Mitteilungen aus dem Vatikanischen Archive*, herausgegeben von der kaiserlichen Akademie der Wissenschaften: I: *Aktenstücke zur Geschichte des Deutschen Reiches unter den Königen Rudolf I. und Albrecht I*, ed. A. Fanta, F. Kaltenbrunner and E. von Ottenthal, Vienna, 1889.

II: *Eine Wiener Briefsammlung zur Geschichte des Deutschen Reiches und der österreichischen Länder in der zweiten Hälfte des 13. Jahrhunderts*, ed. A. Starzer and O. Redlich, Vienna 1894.

Auvergne: *Monumenta Pontificia Arverniae decurrentibus IX°, X°, XI°, XII° saeculis: Correspondance diplomatique des papes concernant l'Auvergne depuis le pontificat de Nicolas I*er *jusqu'à celui d'Innocent III*, ed. A.-C. Chaix de Lavarène, Clermont-Ferrand, 1880.

Bååth, F. M., 'L'inventaire de la Chambre Apostolique de 1440', in *Miscellanea Archivistica A. Mercati* (Studi e Testi 165), Vatican City, 1952, pp. 135-157.

Baethgen, F., 'Quellen und Untersuchungen zur Geschichte der päpstlichen Hof- und Finanzverwaltung unter Bonifaz VIII', in QFIAB, 20 (1928-1929), 114-237.

Baix, F., 'De la valeur historique des actes pontificaux de collation des bénéfices', in *Hommage à Dom Ursmer Berlière*, Brussels, 1931, pp. 57-66. See also Belgium, 1, XI.

Baluze, É., *Vitae Paparum Avenionensium*, ed. G. Mollat, 4 vv., Paris, 1916-1927.

* Barbiche, B., 'Les "scriptores" de la chancellerie apostolique sous le pontificat de Boniface VIII (1295-1305)', in *Bibliothèque de l'École des Chartes*, 128 (1970), 114-187.

Barraclough, G. 1. 'The Chancery Ordinance of Nicholas III', in QFIAB, 25 (1933-1934), 192-250.

2. *Public Notaries and the Papal Curia. A Calendar and a Study of a Formularium Notariorum Curie from the early years of the Fourteenth Century*, London, 1934.

3. *Papal Provisions. Aspects of Church History, Constitutional, Legal and Administrative, in the later Middle Ages*, Oxford, 1935.

4. 'Formulare für Suppliken aus der ersten Hälfte des 13. Jahrhunderts', in *Archiv für katholisches Kirchenrecht*, 115 (1935), 435-456.

5. 'Audientia litterarum contradictarum', in *Dictionnaire de droit canonique*, I (1935), cols. 1387-1399.

6. 'Ordo judiciarius qui in romana curia consuevit communiter observari', in *Jus Pontificium*, 17 (1937), 111-130, 209-217.

7. 'Minutes of Papal Letters', in *Miscellanea Archivistica A. Mercati*, Vatican City, 1952, pp. 109-127.

8. 'The English Royal Chancery and the Papal Chancery in the reign of Henry III', in MIöG, 62 (1954), 365-378.

9. 'The making of a bishop in the Middle Ages: the part of the pope in law and in fact', in *Catholic Historical Review*, 19 (1933), 275-319.

10. 'The Executors of Papal Provisions in the Canonical Theory of the 13th and 14th centuries', in *Acta Congressus iuridici Internationalis Romae* 1934, III (Rome, 1936), pp. 109-150.

Bartoloni, F., 1. 'Per un censimento dei documenti pontifici da Innocenzo III a Martino V (escluso)', in *Atti del Convegno di studi delle fonti del medio evo europeo in occasione del settantesimo della fondazione dell'Istituto storico italiano, Roma, 14-18 aprile 1953*, II: *Comunicazioni*, Rome, 1957, pp. 3-22. This is also to be found in *Relazioni, Comunicazioni ed Atti...*, Rome, 1953, II, pp. 7-40; and separately as *Per un censimento dei documenti pontifici da Innocenzo III a Martino V (escluso). Relazione, discussione e voto finale al Convegno internazionale di studi per le fonti del medio evo europeo*, Rome, 1955.

2. 'Additiones Kehrianae', in QFIAB, 34 (1954), 31-64.

3. 'Suppliche pontificie dei secoli XIII e XIV', in BISIAM, 67 (1955), 1-187.

Battelli, G., 1. 'Una supplica originale per fiat di Urbano V. Contributo alla storia della Cancellaria pontificia nel secolo XIV', in *Scritti di Paleografia e Diplomatica in onore di Vincenzo Federici*, Florence, 1944, pp. 275-292.

2. 'Archivi ecclesiastici — Speciali provvidenze della Santa Sede per la conservazione degli archivi ecclesiastici' in *Enciclopedia Cattolica* I (Rome, 1948), col. 1832.

3. 'Epistula circa il prestito del materiale conservato negli archivi ecclesiastici in Italia', in *Monitor ecclesiasticus*, 78 (1953), 205-208.

4. 'Registri Pontifici', in *Enciclopedia Cattolica*, X (1953), cc. 656-660.

5. 'La scuola di Archivistica presso l'Archivio Segreto Vaticano', in *Archivum*, 3 (1953), 45-49.

6. *Adnotationes ad "Statuto della Scuola Vaticana di Paleografia e Diplomatica eretta presso l'Archivio Vaticano"*, Rome, 1954.

7. 'Archivio Vaticano', in *Enciclopedia Cattolica*, XII (1955), cols. 1131-1135.

8. 'Le ricerche storiche nell'Archivio Vaticano' in *Relazioni del X Congresso internazionale di Scienze Storiche, Roma, 1955*, I (Florence, 1955), pp. 448-477.

9. 'Due frammenti dei registri membranacei di Clemente VI', in BAPI, new series, 2-3 (1956-1957), I, 69-76.

10. 'La Bibliografia dell'Archivio Vaticano', in *Rivista di Storia della Chiesa in Italia*, 14 (1960), 135-137.

11. 'Il censimento dei documenti pontifici dal 1198 al 1417', *ibid.*, 138-140.

12. 'Aspetti giuridici ed esigenze scientifiche nella fotografia dei fondi archivistici', in *Archiva Ecclesiae*, 3-4 (1960-1961), 58-81.

13. 'Mezzi bibliografici d'informazione e di studio presso l'Archivio Vaticano', in *Rassegna degli Archivi di Stato*, 22 (1962), 25-32.

14. 'Archivi, Biblioteche e Musei: Compiti comuni e zone d'interferenza', in *Archiva Ecclesiae*, 5-6 (1962-1963), 20-40.

15. '*Membra disiecta* di registri pontifici dei secoli XIII e XIV', in *Mélanges Tisserant*, IV, Vatican City, 1964, pp. 1-34.

16. *Acta Pontificum* (*Exempla Scripturarum* III), Vatican City, 1965².

17. See also *Bibliografia dell'Archivio Vaticano* (1962 —) and Baumgarten 8, *Schedario Baumgarten*.

Batzer, E., *Zur Kenntnis der Formularsammlung des Richards von Pofi*, Heidelberg, 1910.

Baumgarten, P. M., **1.** *Untersuchungen und Urkunden über die Camera Collegii Cardinalium für die Zeit von 1295 bis 1437*, Leipzig, 1898.
2. *Aus Kanzlei und Kammer. Erörterungen zur kurialen Hof- und Verwaltungsgeschichte im XIII. XIV. und XV. Jahrhundert: Bullatores, Taxatores domorum, Cursores*, Freiburg-im-Breisgau, 1907.
3. *Von der apostolischen Kanzlei. Untersuchungen über die päpstliche Tabellionen und die Vizekanzler der heiligen Römischen Kirche im XIII. XIV. und XV. Jahrhundert*, Cologne, 1908.
4. 'Institutes, Roman Historical', in *The Catholic Encyclopedia*, III (Washington, 1910), pp. 61-65.
5. 'Vatican Archives', *ibid.*, XV (1912), 286-290.
6. 'Ueber einige päpstliche Kanzleibeamte des XIII. und XIV. Jahrhunderts', in *Kirchengeschichtliche Festgabe Anton de Waal* (= *Römische Quartalschrift*, Supplementheft XX), Freiburg-im-Breisgau, 1913, pp. 37-102.
7. 'Die transsumierende Tätigkeit der apostolischen Kanzlei', in RQ, 28 (1914), 215-219.
8. *Schedario Baumgarten*. *Descrizione diplomatica di Bolle e Brevi originali da Innocenzo III a Pio IX*, ed. G. Battelli: I: *Innocenzo III - Innocenzo IV*, an. *1198-1245*, Vatican City, 1965; II: *Alessandro IV - Benedetto XI, 1254-1304*, *ibid.*, 1966.

Bavaria: *Bavarica aus dem Vatikan, 1461-1491*, ed. J. Schlecht and Th. J. Scherg (= *Archivalische Zeitschrift*, Beiheft 4), Munich, 1932.

Belgium: **1.** *Analecta Vaticano-Belgica*, First Series. Recueil des documents concernants les anciens diocèses de Cambrai, Liège, Thérouanne et Tournai, publiés par l'Institut Historique Belge de Rome, Rome-Paris-Bruges-Brussels, 1906 —:

I: *Suppliques de Clément VI (1342-1352)*, ed. U. Berlière, 1906.

II: *Lettres de Jean XXII (1316-1334), I (1316-1324)*, ed. A. Fayen, 1908.

III: *Lettres de Jean XXII (1316-1334)*, II, 1 (1325-1330), ed. A. Fayen, 1909; II, 2 (1330-1334), ed. A. Fayen, 1912.

IV: *Lettres de Benoît XII (1334-1342)*, ed. A. Fierens, 1910.

V: *Suppliques d'Innocent VI (1352-1362)*, ed. U. Berlière, 1911.

VI: *Lettres de Clément VI (1342-1352), I (1342-1346)*, ed. Ph. Van Isacker and U. Berlière, 1924.

VII: *Suppliques d'Urbain V (1362-1370)*, ed. A. Fierens, 1924.

VIII: *Documents relatifs au Grand Schisme, I, Suppliques de Clément VII (1378-1379)*, ed. K. Hanquet, 1924.

IX: *Lettres d'Urbain V (1362-1370), I (1362-1366)*, ed. A. Fierens and C. Tihon, 1928.

X: *Les collectories pontificales dans les anciens diocèses de Cambrai, Thérouanne et Tournai au XIVᵉ siècle*, ed. U. Berlière, 1929.

XI: *Lettres de Grégoire XI (1371-1378)*, I, ed. C. Tihon, 1958.

XII: *Documents relatifs au Grand Schisme, II, Lettres de Clément VII (1378-1379)*, ed. K. Hanquet and U. Berlière, 1930.

XIII: *Documents relatifs au Grand Schisme, III, Suppliques et Lettres de Clément VII (1379-1394)*, ed. H. Nélis, 1934.

XIV: *La Chambre apostolique et les "Libri annatarum" de Martin V (1417-1431)*, I: *Introduction et Textes*, ed. P. Baix, 1947; II: *Tables*, ed. F. Baix and A. Uyttebrouck, 1960.

XV: *Lettres d'Urbain V*, II *(1366-1370)*, ed. C. Tihon, 1932.

XVI: Not yet published.

XVII: *Lettres d'Innocent VI (1352-1362), I (1352-1355)*, ed. G. Despy, 1953.

XVIII: Not yet published.

XIX: *Documents relatifs au Grand Schisme, V: Lettres de Benoît XIII (1394-1422)*, II (1395-1422), ed. M.-J. Tits-Dieuaide, 1960.

XX: *Lettres de Grégoire XI (1371-1378)*, II, ed. C. Tihon, 1961.

XXI: This volume, and vv. XXII, XXIII, not yet published.

XXIV: *Les "Libri annatarum" pour les pontificats d'Eugène IV à Alexander VI*, IV: *Pontificats d'Innocent VIII et d'Alexander VI, 1484-1503*, ed. E. Brouette, 1963.

XXV: *Lettres de Grégoire XI (1371-1378)*, III, ed. C. Tihon, 1964.

2. U. Berlière, *Inventaire analytique des Libri obligationum et solutionum des Archives Vaticanes au point de vue des anciens diocèses de Cambrai, Liège, Thérouanne et Tournai*, Bruges, 1904.

3. U. Berlière, *Inventaire analytique des Diversa Cameralia des Archives Vaticanes (1389-1500) au point de vue des anciens diocèses de Cambrai, Liège, Thérouanne et Tournai*, Rome-Namur-Paris, 1906.

4. U. Berlière, 'Inventaire des Instrumenta Miscellanea des Archives Vaticanes au point de vue de nos anciens diocèses', in BIHBR, 4 (1924), 5-162 ; 7 (1927), 117-138 (supplement; with further supplement by P. Lefèvre in the same *Bulletin*, 9 (1929), 323-340).

Bell, H. I., 'A list of original papal bulls and briefs in the Department of Manuscripts of the British Museum', in *English Historical Review*, 36 (1921), 393-419, 556-583.

Benedict XI (1303-1304): Ch. Grandjean, *Les Registres de Benoît XI. Recueil des bulles de ce pape publiées ou analysées d'après le manuscrit original des Archives du Vatican*, 1 v., Paris, 1883-1905 (BEFAR B. 15).

Benedict XII (1334-1342): 1. J.-M. Vidal, *Benoît XII (1334-1342). Lettres communes et curiales analysées d'après les registres dits d'Avignon et du Vatican*, 3 vv., Paris, 1903-1911 (BEFAR, B. 17).

2. G. Daumet, *Benoît XII (1334-1342). Lettres closes, patentes et curiales se rapportant à la France*, 1 v., Paris, 1899-1920 (BEFAR, B. 18).

3. J.-M. Vidal and G. Mollat, *Benoît XII (1334-1342). Lettres closes et patentes intéressant les pays autres que la France*, 2 vv., Paris, 1913-1950 (BEFAR, B. 19).

Benoît, F., 'Les archives de la Sacrée Congregation d'Avignon au Vatican', in *Mélanges de l'Académie de Vaucluse*, 23 (1923), 1-28.

Berlière, U., 1. 'Aux Archives Vaticanes', in *Revue Bénédictine*, 20 (1903), 132-173 (= *Aux Archives Vaticanes*, Bruges, 1903).

2. 'Épaves d'archives pontificales du XIVᵉ siècle', in *Revue Bénédictine*, 24 (1907), 456-476 (= *Épaves d'archives pontificales du XIVᵉ siècle (MS. Rheims)*, Bruges, 1908). See also Belgium, *passim*.

Berthold, O., *Kaiser, Volk und Avignon. Ausgewählte Quellen zur antikurialen Bewegung in Deutschland in der ersten Hälfte des 14. Jahrhunderts*, Berlin, 1960.

Biaudet, H., *Les nonciatures apostoliques permanentes jusqu'en 1648*, Helsinki, 1910. See also Karttunen, De Marchi.

Bibliografia dell'Archivio Vaticano [ed. G. Battelli], 4 vv., Vatican City, 1962-1966.

Bock, F., 1. 'Die Geheimschrift in der Kanzlei Johanns XXII. Eine diplomatische Studie', in RQ, 42 (1934), 279-303.

2. 'Studien zum politischen Inquisitionsprozess Johanns XXII.', in QFIAB, 26 (1935-1936), 20-112; 27 (1936-1937), 108-134.

3. 'Mittelalterliche Kaiserurkunden im alten Urbinater Archiv', in QFIAB, 27 (1936-1937), 252-263.

4. *Einführung in das Registerwesen des Avignonesischen Papsttums*, Rome, 1941 (= QFIAB, 31).

5. 'Annotationes zum Register Gregors VII.', in *Studi Gregoriani*, 1 (Rome, 1947), 281-306.

6. 'Die erste urkundlich greifbare Ordnung des päpstlichen Archivs', in MIöG, 62 (1954), 317-335.

7. 'Osservazioni sulle lettere executorie della seconda metà del secolo XIII', in *Rivista di Storia della Chiesa in Italia*, 8 (1954), 185-206.

8. 'Studien zu den Originalregistern Innocenz' III. (Reg. Vat. 4-7A)', in *Archivalische Zeitschrift*, 50-51 (1955), 329-364. See Kempf, 3.

        9. 'Studien zu den Registern Innocenz, IV.', *ibid.*, 52 (1956), 11-48.
        10. 'Originale und Registereinträge zur Zeit Honorius III.', in BAPI, 3rd series, 2-3 (1956-1957), pt 1, 101-116.
        11. 'Kodifizierung und Registrierung in der spätmittelalterlichen kurialen Verwaltung', in *Archivalische Zeitschrift*, 56 (1960), 11-75.
        12. 'Päpstliche Sekretregister und Kammerregister. Ueberblick und Ergänzung früherer Studien zum Registerwesen des Spätmittelalters', *ibid.*, 59 (1963), 30-58.

* Boix

Bonenfant, P., 'Rapport au Comité Directeur de l'Institut historique Belge de Rome sur les publications à faire pour le xvᵉ siècle', in BIHBR, 28 (1953), 357-366.

Boniface VIII (1294-1303): G. Digard, M. Faucon, A. Thomas, R. Fawtier, *Les Registres de Boniface VIII (1294-1303)*. *Recueil des bulles de ce pape publiées ou analysées d'après les manuscrits originaux des Archives du Vatican*, 4 vv., Paris, 1884-1939 (BEFAR, B. 14). See also Acht; Baethgen; Barbiche; Fawtier; Waley.

Boyce, G. K., 'Documents of Pope Leo X in the Morgan Library', in *Catholic Historical Review*, 35 (1949-1950), 163-175.

Boyle, L. E., 1. 'The Constitution *Cum ex eo* of Boniface VIII. Education of Parochial Clergy', in *Mediaeval Studies*, 24 (1962), 263-302.
        2. Review of O. Hageneder and A. Haidacher, edd., *Die Register Innocenz' III.*, I, Band 1, *Pontifikatsjahr 1198-1199: Texte*, Graz-Cologne, 1964, in *Speculum*, 42 (1967), 153-162. See Innocent III, 7.

Brackmann, A., 1. 'Papsturkunden des östlichen Deutschlands (Berlin, Stettin, Magdeburg, Zerbst, Dresden, Meissen, Leipzig, Zeitz), in *Nachrichten der Gesellschaft der Wissenschaften zu Göttingen, Philol.-hist. Klasse*, 1902, pp. 193-223.
        2. 'Papsturkunden des Nordens, Nord- und Mittel-Deutschlands (Stockholm, Uppsala, Copenhagen, Hanover, Hildesheim, ... Meiningen)', *ibid.*, 1904, pp. 1-45.
        3. 'Papsturkunden der Schweiz (Basel, ... Aarau)', *ibid.*, 1904, pp. 417-517. See *Regesta Pontificum Romanorum*, 3 B.
        4. *Papsturkunden* (= *Urkunden und Siegel in Nachbildungen*, ed. G. Seeliger, v. 2), Leipzig-Berlin, 1914.

Brady, W. M., *The Episcopal Succession in England, Scotland and Ireland, A.D. 1400-1875*, 3 vv., Rome, 1875.

Bresslau, H., *Handbuch der Urkundenlehre für Deutschland und Italien*, Berlin, 1889 (2nd ed.: v. I, Leipzig, 1912; v. II, ed. H. W. Klewitz, Leipzig, 1931; index by H. Schulze, Berlin, 1960).

Brom, G., *Guide aux Archives du Vatican*, Rome, 1911².

Bulgaria: I. Dujčev, *Innocentii PP. III epistolae ad Bulgariae historiam spectantes: Prepiskata na Papa Inokentija III s Búlgarité*, Sofia, 1942.

Burchi, P., *Catalogus Processuum Beatificationis et Canonizationis qui in tabulariis et bibliothecis Urbis asservantur*, Rome, 1965.

Burger, H., 'Beiträge zur Geschichte der äusseren Merkmale der Papst-urkunden im späteren Mittelalter', in *Archiv für Urkundenforschung*, 12 (1931-1932), 206-243.

Calabria: D. Taccone-Galucci, *Regesti dei Romani Pontifici per le chiese della Calabria, 416-1581*, Rome, 1902.   * Burns

Calixtus II (1119-1124): U. Robert, *Bullaire du Pape Calixte II (1119-1124). Essai de Restitution*, 2 vv., Paris, 1891.

Calixtus III (1455-1458): M. Sciambra, G. Valentini and I. Parrino, *Il Liber Brevium di Callisto III: La Crociata, l'Albania e Skanderbeg*, Palermo, 1968.

Cambrai: H. Dubrulle, *Suppliques du pontificat de Martin V (1417-1431)* (= Société d'études de la province de Cambrai. Recueil 6), Dunkirk, 1922.

Cameron, A. I., 'Vatican Archives, 1073-1560', in *An Introductory Survey to the Sources and Literature of Scots Law*, Edinburgh, 1936, pp. 274-281. See also Scotland.

Capasso, R., 'Contributo allo studio delle suppliche pontificie', in BAPI, 3rd series, 2-3 (1956-1957), I, 169-173.

Carusi, E., *Dispacci e lettere di Giacomo Gherardi, nunzio pontificio a Firenze e Milano (11 settembre 1487 - 10 ottobre 1490)* (= Studi e Testi 21), Rome, 1909.

Caspar, E., 'Studien zum Register Gregors VII', in *Neues Archiv*, 38 (1913), 145-226.

Cau, A., 'Tre lettere pontificie inedite del sec. XIII. Contributo alla diplomatica pontificia', in *Ricerche Medievali* (Pavia), 3 (1968), 33-45. (Gregory X, Innocent IV, Urban IV).

Cauchie, A., 'De la création d'une école belge à Rome', in *Congrès de la Fédération archéologique et historique de Belgique. Compte rendu des travaux du dixième congrès tenu à Tournai du 5 au 8 août 1895*, Tournai, 1896, pp. 739-802.

Célier, L., *Les dataires du XVe siècle et les origines de la Daterie apostolique*, Paris, 1910.

Cenci, P., 'L'archivio della cancellaria della Nunziatura Veneta', in *Miscellanea Ehrle V* (= Studi e Testi 41), Rome, 1924, pp. 273-330.

Cerchiari, E., *Capellani Papae et Apostolicae Sedis Auditores causarum sacri palatii apostolici seu Sacra Romana Rota, ab origine ad diem usque 20 Septembris 1870. Relatio historica-iuridica*, 4 vv., Rome, 1919-1921.

Cheney, C. R., *The Study of the Mediaeval Papal Chancery*, Glasgow, 1966. See also England.

Clement IV (1265-1268): E. Jordan, *Les registres de Clément IV. Recueil des bulles de ce Pape publiées ou analysées d'après les manuscrits originaux des Archives du Vatican*, 1 v., Paris, 1893-1945. (BEFAR, B. 8). Selections in MGH [5].

Clement V (1305-1314): 1. [Benedictines of Monte Cassino] *Regestum Clementis Papae V ex Vaticanis archetypis S. D. N. Leonis XIII P. M. iussu et munificentia, cura et studio monachorum ordinis S. Benedicti editum*, 8 vv., Rome, 1885-1892. See also Leccisotti.

2. Y. Lanhers, C. Vogel, R. Fawtier, and G. Mollat, *Tables des registres de Clément V publiés par les Bénédictins*, 1 v., Paris, 1948-1957 (BEFAR, B. 25).

Clement VI (1342-1352): 1. É. Déprez and G. Mollat, *Clément VI. Lettres closes, patentes et curiales intéressant les pays autres que la France*, 1 v., Paris, 1900-1961. (BEFAR, B. 21).

2. É. Déprez, J. Glenisson and G. Mollat, *Clément VI. Lettres closes, patentes et curiales se rapportant à la France*, 3 vv., Paris, 1910-1961. (BEFAR, B. 20).

Clergeac, A., *La curie et les bénéfices consistoriaux. Étude sur les communes et menus services, 1300-1600*, Paris, 1911.

Cluny: *Bullarium Sacri Ordinis Cluniacensis, complectens plurima privilegia per summos Pontifices tum ipsi Cluniacensi Abbatiae tum ei subditis Monasteriis hactenus concessa, nunc primum collecta per unum ex religiosis strictioris observantiae ejusdem Ordinis*, Lyons, 1680.

Cobban, A. B., 'Edward II, John XXII and the University of Cambridge' in *Bulletin of the John Rylands Library* (Manchester), 47 (1964), 49-78.

Combaluzier, F., 'Sacres épiscopaux à Rome de 1565 à 1662. Analyse intégrale du Ms. "Miscellanea XIII, 33" des Archives Vaticanes', in *Sacris Erudiri*, 18 (1967-1968), 120-305.

Constance: K. Rieder, *Römische Quellen zur Konstanzer Bistumsgeschichte zur Zeit der Päpste in Avignon, 1305-1378*, Innsbruck, 1908 (= Monumenta Vaticana historiam episcopatus Constantiensis in Germania illustrantia, I).

Conway, D., 'Guide to Documents of Irish and British interest in the Fondo Borghese', in *Archivium Hibernicum*, 23 (1960), 1-147, 24 (1961), 31-102.

Corbo, A. M., 'Martino V, Eugenio IV e la ricostituzione dell'archivio papale dopo Costanza', in *Rassegna degli Archivi di Stato*, 28 (1968), 36-66.

Corvisieri, C., 'Compendio dei processi del Santo Uffizio di Roma (da Paolo III a Paolo IV)', in *Archivio della Società Romana di Storia Patria*, 3 (1879), 261-290, 449-471.

* Cowan, I. B., 'The Vatican Archives. A report on pre-reformation Scottish material', in *Scottish Historical Review*, 48 (1969), 227-242.

Crump, C. G., 'The arrest of Roger Mortimer and Queen Isabel', in *English Historical Review*, 26 (1911), 331-332 (on secret correspondence between Edward III of England and John XXII).

Czechoslovakia: *Monumenta Vaticana res gestas Bohemicas illustrantia*, Prague, 1903: 1. L. Klieman, *Acta Clementis VI, 1342-1352*, 1903.

2. J. F. Novák, *Acta Innocentii VI, 1352-1362*, 1907.

3. F. Jenšovský, *Acta Urbani V, 1362-1370*, 2 vv., 1944, 1954.

4. C. Stloukal, *Acta Gregorii XI, I: 1370-1372*, 1949.

5. C. Krofta, *Acta Urbani VI et Bonifatii IX*, 2 vv., 1903, 1905.

Daly, L. W., 'Early alphabetical indices in the Vatican Archives', in *Traditio*, 19 (1963), 483-485.

de Bertier, G., 'L'histoire religieuse de la Restauration (1814-1830) aux Archives du Vatican', in *Revue d'histoire de l'Église de France*, 38 (1952), 77-89.

de Boüard, A., *Manuel de diplomatique française et pontificale*, 2 vv., Paris, 1928, 1948; with 2 vv. of plates, 1949, 1954.

Deeley, A., 'Papal provisions and rights of royal patronage in the early 14th century', in *English Historical Review*, 43 (1928), 497-527.

Deeters, W., 'Ueber das *Repertorium Germanicum* als Geschichtsquelle. Versuch einer methodischen Anleitung', in *Blätter für Deutsche Landesgeschichte* (Wiesbaden), 105 (1969), 27-43.

Delehaye, H., 'Les lettres d'indulgence collectives', in *Analecta Bollandiana*, 44 (1926), 341-379, 45 (1927), 97-123, 323-343, 46 (1928), 149-157, 287-343.

Delisle, L., 1. 'Mémoire sur les actes d'Innocent III', in *Bibliothèque de l'École des Chartes*, 19 (1858), 1-73.

    2. 'Lettres inédites d'Innocent III', *ibid.*, 34 (1873), 397-419.

    3. 'Les registres d'Innocent III', *ibid.*, 46 (1885), 84-94.

    4. 'Les "litterae tonsae" à la chancellerie romaine au XIIIe siècle', *ibid.*, 62 (1901), 256-263.

de Loye, J., *Les archives de la chambre apostolique au XIVe siècle*, Paris, 1899.

del Re, N., *La curia romana: lineamenti storico-giuridici*, Rome, 1952².

de Marchi, G., *Le nunziature apostoliche dal 1800 al 1956*, Rome, 1956. See also Biaudet; Karttunen.

Denifle, H.-S., 1. 'Die päpstlichen Registerbände des 13. Jahrhunderts und das Inventar derselben vom J. 1339', in *Archiv für Literatur- und Kirchengeschichte*, 2 (1886), 1-105.

    2. *La désolation des églises, monastères et hôpitaux en France pendant la guerre de cent ans*, 2 vv., Paris, 1897, 1899.

Denmark: 1. *Acta pontificum Danica. Pavelige aktstykker vedrørende Danmark, 1316-1536*, ed. J. L. Moltesen, A. Krarup and J. Lindback, 7 vv., Copenhagen, 1904-1943.

    2. *Bullarium Danicum II. Pavelige aktstykker vedrørende Danmark, 1198-1316*, ed. A. Krarup, Copenhagen, 1932.

    3. *Diplomatarium Danicum*, second series [1250-1334], edd. S. F. Blatt, G. Hermansen and C. A. Christensen, 12 vv., *ibid.*, 1938-1960; third series [1340-1412], edd. C. A. Christensen, H. Nielsen and P. Jørgensen, 6 vv. to date, *ibid.*, 1958 —.

de Vargas-Zuñiga, A., M. de Espinosa, and B. Cuartero y Huerta, *Indice de la colección de don Luis de Salazar y Castro, I: Bulas y documentos pontificios (590-1670); Cartas y documentos del reino de Aragón (1213-1516)*, Madrid, 1949.

de Witte, Ch.-M., 'Notes sur les plus anciens registres de brefs', in BIHBR, 31 (1958), 153-168.

Di Capua, F., 1. *Il ritmo prosaico nelle lettere dei papi e nei documenti della cancellaria romana dal IV al XIV secolo*, 3 vv., Rome, 1937, 1939, 1946.

2. *Fonti ed esempi per lo studio dello "Stilus Curiae Romanae" medioevale*, Rome, 1941.

Diekamp, W., 1. 'Zum päpstlichen Urkundenwesen des XI., XII. und der ersten Hälfte des XIII. Jahrhunderts', in MIöG, 3 (1882), 565-627.

2. 'Zum päpstlichen Urkundenwesen von Alexander IV. bis Johann XXII. (1254-1334)', *ibid.*, 4 (1883), 497-540.

* Diener, H., 1. 'Rubrizellen zu Kanzleiregistern Johanns XXIII. und Martins V.', in QFIAB, 39 (1959), 117-172.

2. 'Ein Formularbuch aus der Kanzlei der Päpste Eugen IV. und Nicolaus V.', *ibid.*, 42-43 (1963), 370-411.

3. 'Zum Persönlichkeit des Johannes de Segovia. Ein Beitrag zur Methode des Auswertung päpstlicher Register des späten Mittelalters', *ibid.*, 44 (1964), 289-365.

Donkin, E. M., 'A collective letter of Indulgence for an English beneficiary', in *Scriptorium*, 17 (1963), 316-323.

Donnelly, A., 'The *Per obitum* volumes in the Archivio Vaticano', in *Archivium Hibernicum*, 1 (1912), 28-38.

Dudík, B., *Iter Romanum*, 1 v. in two parts (2: *Das päpstliche Regestenwesen*), Vienna, 1855.

Dunning, P. J., 1. 'Pope Innocent III and the Irish Kings', in *Journal of Ecclesiastical History*, 8 (1957), 17-32.

2. 'The letters of Innocent III as a source for Irish history', in *Irish Catholic Historical Committee Proceedings* (Dublin, 1959), 1-10.

3. 'The letters of Innocent III to Ireland', in *Traditio*, 18 (1962), 229-253.

Edwards, R. D., 'The Kings of England and Papal Provisions in Fifteenth-Century Ireland', in *Medieval Studies presented to Aubrey Gwynn S.J.*, ed. J. A. Watt, J. B. Morrall and F. X. Martin, Dublin, 1961, pp. 265-280.

Ehrle, F., 1. 'Zur Geschichte des Schatzes, der Bibliothek und des Archivs der Päpste im vierzehnten Jahrhundert', in *Archiv für Literatur- und Kirchengeschichte des Mittelalters*, 1 (1885), 1-48, 228-364.

2. 'Die Uebertragung des letzten Restes des päpstlichen Archivs von Avignon nach Rom', in *Historisches Jahrbuch*, 11 (1890), 727-729.

3. *Miscellanea Francesco Ehrle* II (*Storia di Roma*), IV (*Paleografia e Diplomatica*), V (*Biblioteca e Archivio Vaticano*), (= Studi e Testi, 38, 40, 41), Rome, 1924.

Ehses, S., 1. 'Clemens VII. und Karl V. zu Bologna 1533', in RQ, 5 (1891), 301-307.

2. 'Die Carte Farnesiane des Vatikanischen Archivs', *ibid.*, 28 (1914), 41-47.

Elze, R., 1. 'Die päpstliche Kapelle im 12. und 13. Jahrhundert', in ZSSRGKA, 36 (1950), 145-204.

2. 'Das Sacrum Palatium Lateranense', in *Studi Gregoriani* IV, ed. G. B. Borino, Rome, 1952, pp. 33-40.

3. 'Der Liber Censuum des Cencius (Cod. Vat. Lat. 8486) von 1192 bis 1228. Zur Ueberlieferung des Kaiserkrönungsordo Cencius III.', in BAPI, 2-3 (1956-1957), I, 251-270.

Enchiridion Archivorum ecclesiasticorum. Documenta potiora Sanctae Sedis de Archivis ecclesiasticis a Concilio Tridentino usque ad nostras dies, edd. S. Duca and P. Simeon a S. Familia, O.C.D. (Pubblicazioni della Pontificia Commissione per gli archivi ecclesiastici d'Italia, II), Vatican City, 1966.

England: 1. C. R. Cheney and W. H. Semple, *Selected Letters of Pope Innocent III concerning England (1198-1216)*, London, 1953.

2. C. R. and Mary Cheney, *The Letters of Pope Innocent III, 1198-1216, concerning England and Wales. A Calendar with an Appendix of Texts*, Oxford, 1967.

3. W. E. Lunt, *Accounts rendered by Papal Collectors in England, 1317-1378*, ed. E. B. Graves, Philadelphia, 1968.

Erben, W., 'Bemalte Bittschriften und Ablassurkunden', in *Archiv für Urkundenwesen*, 8 (1923), 160-188.

Erdmann, C., *Papsturkunden in Portugal* (Abhandlungen der Gesellschaft der Wissenschaften zu Göttingen, Neue Folge, 20, n. 3), Berlin, 1927.

Erler, G., *Der Liber Cancellariae Apostolicae vom Jahre 1380*, Leipzig, 1888.

Estonia: H. Hildebrandt, *Livonica, vornehmlich aus dem 13. Jahrhundert im vatikanischen Archiv*, Riga, 1887.

Eubel, C., 1. 'Der Registerband des Cardinal Grosspönitentiars Bentevenga', in *Archiv für katholisches Kirchenrecht*, 64 (1890), 3-69.

2. 'Der Registerband des Gegenpapstes Nikolaus V.', in *Archivalische Zeitschrift*, 4 (1893), 123-212.

3. 'Elenchus Romanorum pontificum epistolarum quae in archivo sacri conventus Assisiensis O. Min. Conv. exstant', in *Archivum Franciscanum Historicum*, 1 (1908), 601-616, 2 (1909), 108-122.

Exempla Scripturarum: I. B. Katterbach, A. Pelzer and C. Silva-Tarouca, *Codices latini saeculi XIII*, Rome, 1929.

II. B. Katterbach, C. Silva-Tarouca, *Epistolae et Instrumenta Saeculi XIII*, Vatican City, 1930.

III. G. Battelli, *Acta pontificum*, ibid., 1965[2].

Fabian, P., *Prunkbittschriften an der Papst*, Graz, 1931.

Favier, J., 1. 'Introitus et Exitus sous Clément VII et Benoît XIII', in BAPI, 3rd series, 2-3 (1956-1957), I, 285-294.

2. *Les finances pontificales à l'époque du Grand Schisme d'Occident 1378-1409* (= Bibliothèque des Écoles françaises d'Athènes et de Rome, 211), Paris, 1966.

Fawtier, R., 1. 'Documents négligés sur l'activité de la chancellerie apostolique à la fin du XIIIe siècle: le registre 46A et les comptes de la chambre sous Boniface VIII', in MAH, 52 (1935), 244-272.

2. 'Un grand achèvement de l'École française de Rome: La publication des Registres des Papes du xiiie siècle', *ibid.*, 71 (1960), I-XIII.

Fedele, P., 'La Commission internationale pour la bibliographie des Archives du Vatican', in *Bulletin of the International Committee of Historical Sciences*, II (1939), 224-235.

Feigl, H., 1. 'Die Ueberlieferung der Register Papst Innocenz' III.', in MIöG, 65 (1957), 242-295.

2. 'Die Registrierung der Privilegien unter Papst Innocenz III.', *ibid.*, 68 (1960), 114-127.

Felici, G., *La Reverenda Camera Apostolica*, Rome, 1940.

Fenicchia, V., 'Documenti trasferiti dall'Archivio di Anagni all'Archivio di Castel S. Angelo nel 1578', in *Mélanges Tisserant*, IV, Vatican City, 1964, pp. 189-204.

Fichtenau, H., *Arenga. Spätantike und Mittelalter im Spiegel von Urkunden-formeln*, Graz, 1957.

Fink, K. A., 1. 'Die ältesten Breven und Brevenregister', in QFIAB, 25 (1933-1934), 292-307.

2. 'Zur Geschichte des päpstlichen Referendariats', in *Analecta Sacra Tarraconensia*, 10 (1934), 75-100.

3. 'Untersuchungen über die päpstlichen Breven des 15. Jahrhunderts', in RQ, 43 (1935), 55-86.

4. 'Die politische Korrespondenz Martins V. nach den Brevenregistern', in QFIAB, 26 (1935-1936), 172-244.

5. 'Zu den Brevia Lateranensia des Vatikanischen Archivs', *ibid.*, 32 (1942), 260-266.

6. *Das Vatikanische Archiv. Einführung in die Bestände und ihre Erforschung* (Bibliothek des Deutschen Historischen Instituts in Rom, XX), Rome, 1951².

7. 'Neue Wege zur Erschliessung des Vatikanischen Archivs', in *Vitae et Veritati: Festgabe für Karl Adam*, Düsseldorf, 1956, pp. 187-203.

8. 'Urkundenwesen, päpstlicher', in *Lexikon für Theologie und Kirche²*, 10 (1965), pp. 560-563.

9. 'Vatican Archives', in *New Catholic Encyclopedia*, 14 (1967), pp. 551-555.

Finke, H., *Aus den Tagen Bonifaz' VIII.*, Berlin, 1902.

Fish, C. R., *Guide to the Materials for American History in Roman and other Italian Archives*, Washington, D.C., 1911.

Flanagan, U. G., 1. 'Papal letters of the 15th century as a source for Irish history', in *Irish Catholic Historical Committee Proceedings*, Dublin, 1959, pp. 11-15.

2. 'Papal Provisions in Ireland, 1307-1378', in *Historical Studies III: Papers read before the Fourth Irish Conference of Historians*, London-Cork, 1961, pp. 92-103.

Fliniaux, A., 'Contribution à l'histoire des sources de droit canonique. Les anciennes collections des *Decisiones Rotae*', in *Revue historique de droit français et étranger*, 4th series, 4 (1925), 61-93, 382-410.

Förstemann, J., *Novae constitutiones audientiae litterarum contradictarum in Curia Romana promulgatae A.D. 1375*, Leipzig, 1897.

Foerster, H., *Urkundenlesebuch für den akademischen Gebrauch*, Bern, 1947. See also *Liber Diurnus*.

Fournier, E., 'Abréviateurs', in *Dictionnaire de droit canonique*, I (1935), cols. 98-106.

France: *Bibliothèque des Écoles Françaises d'Athènes et de Rome*, 3rd series: *Registres et Lettres des Papes du XIVe siècle:*

[a] B. 26: *Lettres secrètes et curiales du pape Jean XXII [1316-1334] relatives à la France*, ed. A. Coulon and S. Clémencet, Paris, 1900: 2 vv., 1900-1913, 3rd in progress. See also above, pp. 125-126.

[b] B. 18: *Lettres closes, patentes et curiales du pape Benoît XII [1334-1342] se rapportant à la France*, ed. G. Daumet, 1 v., Paris, 1899-1920. See p. 126 above.

[c] B. 20: *Lettres closes, patentes et curiales du pape Clément VI [1342-1352] se rapportant à la France*, ed. É. Déprez, J. Glenisson and G. Mollat, 3 vv., Paris, 1910-1961. See p. 126 above.

[d] B. 27: *Lettres closes, patentes et curiales du pape Innocent VI [1352-1362] se rapportant à la France*, ed. G. Daumet, 1 fasc. only, Paris, 1909 (but all the 281 letters of 1 Innocent VI here calendared by Daumet have been calendared anew in *Lettres secrètes et curiales du pape Innocent VI*, ed. P. Gasnault and M.-H. Laurent, Paris, 1959). See p. 126 above.

[e] B. 22: *Lettres secrètes et curiales du pape Urbain V [1362-1370] se rapportant à la France*, ed. P. Lacacheux and G. Mollat, 1 v., Paris, 1902-1955. See p. 126 above.

[f] B. 23: *Lettres secrètes et curiales du pape Grégoire XI [1370-1378] relatives à la France*, ed. L. Mirot, H. Jassemin, J. Vieillard, G. Mollat and E. R. Labande, 1 v., Paris, 1935-1957. See p. 127.

François, M., 'Les sources de l'histoire religieuse de la France au Vatican', in *Revue d'histoire de l'Église de France*, 19 (1933), 305-346 (reprinted in V. Carrière, *Introduction aux études d'histoire ecclésiastique locale*, I, Paris, 1940, pp. 377-434).

Friedländer, I., *Die päpstlichen Legaten in Deutschland und Italien am Ende des 12. Jahrhunderts (1181-1198)*, Berlin, 1928.

Friesland: H. Reimers, *Friesische Papsturkunden aus den vatikanischen Archiven zu Rom*, Leeuwaarden, 1908.

Fürst, C. G., *Cardinalis. Prolegomena zu einer Rechtsgeschichte des römischen Kardinalskollegiums*, Munich, 1967.

Fuhrmann, H., 'Die Fälschungen im Mittelalter. Ueberlegungen zum mittelalterlichen Wahrheitsbegriff', in *Historische Zeitschrift*, 197 (1963), 529-554, 555-579 (discussion), 580-601 (reply).

Gachard, M., *Les Archives du Vatican*, Brussels, 1874.

Galicia (Spain): A. V. Martínez, *Documentos pontificios de Galicia (1088-1341)*: I: *Relación de bulas, breves, epistolas*, Coruña, 1941.

Ganzer, K., *Papsttum und Bistumsbesetzungen in der Zeit von Gregor IX. bis Bonifaz VIII: Ein Beitrag zur Geschichte der päpstlichen Reservationen*

(Forschungen zur kirchlichen Rechtsgeschichte und zum Kirchenrecht, 9), Cologne-Graz, 1968.

Gascony: L. Guérard, *Documents pontificaux sur la Gascogne, d'après les archives du Vatican. Pontificat de Jean XXII (1316-1334)*, 2 vv., Paris, 1896, 1903.

Gasnault, P., 1. 'Quatre suppliques inéditées adressées à Jean XXII', in BAPI, 2-3 (1956-1957), I, 317-323.

2. 'Suppliques en matière de justice au XIVᵉ siècle', in *Bibliothèque de l'École des Chartes*, 115 (1957), 43-57.

Gasparolo, G., 'Costituzione dell'Archivio Vaticano e suo primo indice, sotto il pontificato di Paolo V. Manoscritto inedito di Michele Lonigo', in *Studi e Documenti di Storia e Diritto*, 8 (1887), 3-64.

* Germany: 1. *Repertorium Germanicum: Regesten aus den päpstlichen Archiven zur Geschichte des Deutschen Reichs und seiner Territorien im XIV. und XV. Jahrhundert*, herausgegeben durch das Königlich Preussische Historische Institut in Rom: *Pontifikat Eugens IV. (1431-1447)*, v. 1, ed. J. Haller, J. Kaufmann, J. Lulvès and R. Arnold, Berlin, 1897.

2. *Repertorium Germanicum. Neue Folge: Verzeichnis der in den päpstlichen Registern und Kameralakten vorkommenden Personen, Kirchen und Orte des Deutschen Reiches, seiner Diözesen und Territorien, vom Beginn des Schismas bis zur Reformation*, herausgegeben vom Preussischen [Deutschen] Historischen Institut in Rom, Berlin, 1916—:

I: *Clemens VII. von Avignon, 1378-1394*, ed. E. Göller, 1916.

II: *Urban VI., Bonifaz IX., Innozenz VII. und Gregor XII.*, 1378-1415, ed. G. Tellenbach, 1933-1961.

III: *Alexander V., Johann XXIII., Konstanzer Konzil, 1409-1417*, ed. U. Kühne, 1935.

IV: *Martin V., 1417-1431*, ed. K. A. Fink, 1943-1979.

3. *Germania pontificia*: see *Regesta Pontificum Romanorum*, 3 B.

Giblin, C., 1. 'Miscellaneous Papers', in *Archivium Hibernicum*, 16 (1951), 66-73.

2. 'Vatican Library: MSS. Barberini Latini', *ibid.*, 18 (1955), 67-144.

3. '*The Processus Datariae* and the appointment of Irish bishops in the 17th century', in *Father Luke Wadding Commemorative Volume*, Killiney-Dublin, 1957, pp. 508-616.

4. 'Material relative to Ireland in the Albani collection of MSS in the Vatican Archives', in *Irish Ecclesiastical Record*, 5th series, 102 (1964), 389-396.

Gieysztor, A., 'Une bulle de Pascal II retrouvée', in BAPI, 3rd series, 2-3 (1956-1957), I, 361-365.

Girgensohn, D., 'Territoriale Sammlungen', in L. Santifaller, *Neuere Editionen mittelalterlicher Königs- und Papsturkunden*, Vienna, 1958, pp. 43-56. See also Kehr, 3j.

Giusti, M., 1. 'I registri Vaticani e le loro provenienze', in *Miscellanea Archivistica A. Mercati*, Vatican City, 1952, pp. 383-459 (now in *Studi*, pp. 1-79).

2. 'I registri Vaticani e la loro continuazione', in *La Bibliofilia*, 60 (1958), 130-140 (now in *Studi*, pp. 83-96).

3. 'Note sui registri Lateranensi', in *Mélanges Tisserant*, V, Vatican City, 1964, pp. 229-249 (now in *Studi*, pp. 98-122).

4. *Studi sui registri di bolle papali* (Collectanea Archivi Vaticani 1), Vatican City, 1968.

Göller, E., 1. 'Der *Liber Taxarum* der päpstlichen Kammer. Eine Studie über seine Entstehung und Anlage', in QFIAB, 8 (1905), 113-173, 305-343.

2. 'Die Kommentatoren der päpstlichen Kanzleiregeln vom Ende des 15. bis zum Beginn des 17. Jahrhunderts', in *Archiv für katholisches Kirchenrecht*, 85 (1905), 441-460, 86 (1906), 20-34, 259-265.

3. *Die päpstliche Pönitentiarie von ihren Ursprung bis zu ihrer Umgestaltung unter Pius V.* (Bibliothek des königlichen Preussischen Historischen Instituts in Rom, III-IV, VII-VIII), Rome, 1907, 1911.

4. 'Das alte Archiv der päpstlichen Pönitentiarie', in *Kirchengeschichtliche Festgabe Anton de Waal* (= *Römische Quartalschrift*, Supplementheft XX), Freiburg-im-Breisgau, 1913, pp. 1-19.

5. 'Inventarium instrumentorum Camerae apostolicae aus der Zeit Urbans V.', in RQ, 23 (1909), 65-109.

6. 'Die Grundlagen des päpstlichen Benefizialwesens und die Praxis der Stellenbesetzung zur Zeit des grossen Schismas', in *Repertorium Germanicum, neue Folge*, I, Berlin, 1916, pp. 43-98.

7. 'Die neuen Bestände der *Camera Apostolica* im päpstlichen Geheimarchiv', in RQ, 30 (1922), 38-53.

8. 'Aus der *Camera apostolica* der Schismapäpste', *ibid.*, 32 (1924), 82-147.

9. 'Die Kubikulare im Dienste der päpstlichen Hofverwaltung vom 12. bis 15. Jahrhundert', in *Papsttum und Kaisertum. Forschungen... Paul Kehr zum 65. Geburtstag dargebracht*, ed. A. Brackmann, Munich, 1926, pp. 621-647.

10. See also *Vatikanische Quellen*, I, IV.

Goldinger, W., 'Oesterreich und die Eröffnung des Vatikanischen Archivs', in *Archivalische Zeitschrift*, 47 (1951), 23-52.

Goñi Gaztambide, J., 1. 'Juan XXII y la provision de los obispados españoles', in AHP, 4 (1966), 25-58.

2. 'El fiscalismo pontificio en España en tiempo di Juan XXII', in *Anthologica Annua*, 14 (1966), 65-99.

Gottlob, A., 1. *Aus der Camera apostolica des 15. Jahrhunderts*, Innsbruck, 1889.

2. *Die päpstlichen Kreuzzugssteuern im XIII. Jahrhundert*, Heiligenstadt, 1892.

3. *Die Servitientaxe im 13. Jahrhundert*, Stuttgart, 1903.

Grat, F., *Étude sur le Motu proprio, des origines au début du XVIe siècle*, Melun, 1945.

Great Britain and Ireland: **1.** *Calendar of entries in the Papal Registers relating to Great Britain and Ireland*, London, 1893:
[A]   *Calendar of Petitions to the Pope*, I, *1342-1419*, ed. W. H. Bliss, 1896. See above, p. 153.
[B]   *Calendar of Papal Letters*, edd. W. H. Bliss, C. Johnson, J. A. Twemlow: 14 vv. to date (1893-1960), as listed above, pp. 111-113.
    2. *Calendar of State Papers relating to English Affairs, preserved principally at Rome in the Vatican Archives and Library*, ed. J. M. Rigg, I: *Elizabeth*, 1558-1571; II: *Elizabeth*, 1572-1578, London, 1916, 1926.

Gregory I (590-604): *Gregorii I papae Registrum epistolarum*, edd. P. Ewald and L. M. Hartmann, 2 vv. (Monumenta Germaniae Historica, Epistolae, I and II), Berlin, 1887, 1889. See also Norberg; Peitz; Posner.

Gregory VII (1073-1085): *Gregorii VII Registrum. Das Register Gregors VII.*, ed. E. Caspar, 2 vv. (Monumenta Germaniae Historica, Epistolae Selectae, I and II), Berlin, 1920, 1923. See also Bock 5; Murray; Posner; Santifaller 7.

Gregory IX (1227-1241): L. Auvray, S. Vitte-Clémencet and L. Carolus-Barré, *Les Registres de Grégoire IX. Recueil des bulles de ce pape publiées ou analysées d'après les manuscrits originaux au Vatican*, 4 vv., Paris, 1890-1955. (BEFAR, B. 4). Selections in MGH [5].

Gregory X (1271-1276): J. Guiraud, *Les Registres de Grégoire X et de Jean XXI: Les Registres de Grégoire X (1271-1276). Recueil des bulles de ce pape publiées ou analysées d'après les manuscrits originaux des Archives du Vatican*, 1 v., Paris, 1892-1906. (BEFAR, B. 9, with John XXI).

Gregory XI (1370-1378): G. Mollat, *Grégoire XI. Lettres secrètes et curiales intéressant les pays autres que la France*, 1 v., Paris, 1962-1965. (BEFAR, B. 24). See also p. 127; Belgium 1; France[f];

Grisar, G., 'Le biblioteche e gli archivi dei dicasteri della curia romana', in *Il Libro e le Biblioteche: Atti del primo Congresso Bibliografico Francescano internazionale*, II, Rome, 1950, pp. 33-60.

Gualdo, G., **1.** 'Il "Liber brevium de curia anni septimi". Contributo allo studio del Breve pontificio', in *Mélanges Tisserant*, IV, Vatican City, 1964, pp. 301-345.
    2. 'Lo "Schedario Baumgarten" e gli studi di diplomatica pontificia', in *Rivista di Storia della Chiesa in Italia*, 20 (1966), 71-81.

Guérard, L., *Petite introduction aux Inventaires des Archives du Vatican*, Rome-Paris, 1901.

Guerello, F., *Lettere di Innocenzo IV dai cartolari notarili genovesi* (Miscellanea Historiae Pontificiae XXIII), Rome, 1961.

Guidi, P., *Inventari di libri nelle serie dell'Archivio Vaticano, 1287-1459* (= Studi e Testi 135), Vatican City, 1948.

Guillemain, B., **1.** *La politique bénéficiale du pape Benoît XII (1334-1342)*, Paris, 1952.
    2. *La cour pontificale d'Avignon, 1309-1376. Étude d'une société*, Paris, 1962. See Perrin.

Hagan, J., 1. 'Some papers relative to the Nine Years War', in *Archivium Hibernicum*, 2 (1913), 274-300.
    2. 'Miscellanea Vaticano-Hibernica, 1580-1631', *ibid.*, 3 (1914), 227-565.
    3. 'Miscellanea Vaticano-Hibernica, 1420-1631', *ibid.*, 4 (1915), 215-318.
    4. 'Miscellanea Vaticano-Hibernica', *ibid.*, 6 (1917), 94-115.
    5. 'Miscellanea Vaticano-Hibernica, 1572-1585', *ibid.*, 7 (1918-1922), 66-356.

Hageneder, O., 1. 'Die äusseren Merkmale der Originalregister Innozenz' III.', in MIöG, 65 (1957), 296-339.
    2. 'Das Sonne-Mond-Gleichnis bei Innozenz III.', *ibid.*, 340-368.
    3. 'Quellenkritisches zu den Originalregistern Innozenz' III.', *ibid.*, 68 (1960), 128-139.

Haidacher, A., 'Beiträge zur Kenntnis der verlorenen Registerbände Innozenz' III.', in RHM 4 (1960-1961), 36-62.

Halkin, L.-E., 1. (with D. van Derveeghde), *Les sources de l'histoire de la Belgique aux Archives et à la Bibliothèque Vaticanes. État des collections et répertoire bibliographique* (Bibliothèque de l'Institut historique Belge de Rome, III), Brussels-Rome, 1951.
    2. 'Les Archives des Nunciatures. Rapport au Comité Directeur de l'Institut historique Belge de Rome', in BIHBR, 33 (1961), 649-700, now available in a revised form as:
    3. *Les Archives des Nunciatures* (Bibliothèque de l'Institut historique Belge de Rome, XIV), Brussels-Rome, 1968.

Haller, J., 1. 'Zwei Aufzeichnungen über die Beamten der Curie im 13. und 14. Jahrhundert', in QFIAB, 1 (1897), 1-38.
    2. 'Die Verteilung der Servitia Minuta und die Obligation der Prälaten im 13. und 14. Jahrhundert', *ibid.*, 281-295.
    3. 'Die Ausfertigung der Provisionen. Ein Beitrag zur Diplomatik der Papsturkunden des 14. und 15. Jahrhunderts', *ibid.*, 2 (1899), 1-40.
    4. *Piero da Monte, ein Gelehrter und päpstlicher Beamter des 15. Jahrhunderts. Seine Briefsammlung* (Bibliothek des Deutschen Historischen Instituts in Rom, XIX), Rome, 1941.

Halphen, L., *Études sur l'administration de Rome au moyen-âge, 751-1252* (Bibliothèque de l'École des Hautes Études, 166), Paris, 1907.

Hamburg: F. Curschmann, *Die älteren Papsturkunden des Erzbistums Hamburg. Eine diplomatische Untersuchung*, Hamburg-Leipzig, 1909.

Hammermayer, L., 'Grundlinien der Entwicklung des päpstlichen Staatssekretariats von Paul V. bis Innocenz X., 1605-1655', in RQ, 55 (1960), 157-202.

Hartmann, H., 'Beiträge zum Urkundenwesen des Reformpapsttums, I: Ueber die Entwicklung der Rota', in *Archiv für Urkundenforschung*, 16 (1939), 385-412.

Haskins, C. H., 1. 'The Vatican Archives', in *American Historical Review*, 2 (1896-1897), 40-58.

2. 'Two Roman Formularies in Philadelphia', in *Miscellanea Ehrle* IV (Rome, 1924), 275-286.

Heller, E., *Die Ars Dictandi des Thomas von Capua*, Heidelberg, 1929.

Henggeler, R., 'Die mittelalterlichen Papsturkunden im Stiftsarchiv Einsiedeln', in *Miscellanea Archivistica A. Mercati*, Vatican City, 1952, pp. 201-225.

Herde, P., 1. *Beiträge zum päpstlichen Kanzlei- und Urkundenwesen im 13. Jahrhundert*, Kallmünz, 1967².

2. 'Der Zeugenzwang in den päpstlichen Delegationsreskripten des Mittelalters', in *Traditio*, 18 (1962), 255-288.

3. 'Papal formularies for letters of justice (13th-16th centuries). Their development and significance for medieval canon law', in *Proceedings of the Second International Congress of Medieval Canon Law*, edd. S. Kuttner and J. J. Ryan (= Monumenta Iuris Canonici, Series C, Subsidia I), Rome-New Haven, 1965, pp. 321-346.

4. 'Ein Formelbuch Gerhards von Parma mit Urkunden des Auditor Litterarum Contradictarum aus dem Jahre 1277', in *Archiv für Diplomatik*, 13 (1967), 225-312.

5. *Marinus von Eboli Super revocatoriis et De confirmationibus*, Tübingen, 1964.

6. *Audientia litterarum contradictarum. Untersuchungen über die päpstlichen Justizbriefe und die päpstliche Delegationsgerichtsbarkeit vom 13. bis zum Beginn des 16. Jahrhunderts*, 2 vv., (= Bibliothek des Deutschen Historischen Instituts in Rom, XXXI, XXXII), Tübingen, 1970.

Hierarchia Catholica medii et recentioris aevi [1198-1903], ed. C. Eubel, G. Van Gulik, L. Schmitz-Kallenberg, P. Gauchat, R. Ritzler and P. Sefrin: vv. I-IV [1198-1667], Münster-in-W., 1913², 1914², 1923², 1935; vv. V-VI [1667-1799], Pavia, 1952, 1958. See Ritzler 1.

Hilling, N., 'Die römische Rota und das Bistum Hildesheim am Ausgang des Mittelalters (1464-1513)', in *Reformationsgeschichtliche Studien und Texte*, 6 (1908), 6-27.

Hoberg, H., 1. *Die Inventare des päpstlichen Schatzes in Avignon, 1314-1376* (= Studi e Testi, 111), Vatican City, 1944.

2. *Taxae pro servitiis communibus ex libris obligationum ab anno 1295 usque ad annum 1455 confectis* (= Studi e Testi, 144), Vatican City, 1949.

3. 'Die Protokollbücher der Rotanotare von 1464-1517', in ZSSRGKA, 39 (1953), 177-277.

4. 'Die "Admissiones" des Archivs der Rota', in *Archivalische Zeitschrift*, 50-51 (1955), 391-408.

5. 'Register von Rota in 14. Jahrhundert im vatikanischen Archiv', in RQ, 51 (1956), 54-69.

6. 'Vatikanische Archiv', in *Lexikon für Theologie und Kirche*², XII (1964), cols. 635-636.

7. 'Der Fonds Missioni des Vatikanisches Archivs', in *Euntes Docete,* 21 (1968), 91-107.

Hoffmann, H. L., *De Archivo Secreto Vaticano qua centrali,* Rome, 1962.

Holland: **1.** G. Brom, *Archivalia in Italië belangrijk voor de geschiedenis van Nederland,* I, *Vatikaansch archief,* The Hague, 1908-1909 (vv. II and III, *ibid.,* 1911 and 1914, concern the Vatican Library and other libraries in Rome).

2. R. R. Post, *Supplieken gericht aan de pausen Clemens VI, Innocentius VI en Urbanus V, 1342-1366* (= Studien van het Nederlandsch historisch Instituut te Rome, 2), The Hague, 1937.

Holtzmann, W., **1.** *Papsturkunden in England,* 3 vv. (Abhandlungen der Gesellschaft der Wissenschaften zu Göttingen, Philol.-hist. Klasse, Neue Folge, 25, 1-2, Dritte Folge, 14, Dritte Folge, 33), Berlin, 1930-1931, 1935, 1952.

2. 'Die Register Papst Alexanders III. in die Händen der Kanonisten', in QFIAB, 30 (1940), 13-87.

3. 'Ueber eine Ausgabe der päpstlichen Dekretalen des 12. Jahrhunderts', in *Nachrichten der Akademie der Wissenschaften zu Göttingen,* Philol.-hist. Klasse, 1945, pp. 15-36.

4. 'Paolo Kehr e le ricerche archivistiche per l'*Italia Pontificia*', in *Miscellanea Archivistica A. Mercati,* Vatican City, 1952, pp. 43-49.

5. (with E. W. Kemp), *Papal decretals relating to the diocese of Lincoln in the Twelfth Century,* Lincoln, 1954.

6. 'Das Deutsche historische Institut in Rom', in *Arbeitsgemeinschaft für Forschung des Landes Nordrhein-Westfalen,* 46 (1955), 7-43.

7. *Beiträge zur Reichs- und Papstgeschichte des hohen Mittelalters,* Bonn, 1957.

8. 'Kanonistische Ergänzungen zur *Italia Pontificia*', in QFIAB, 37 (1957), 55-102, 38 (1958), 67-175 (also published separately, Tübingen, 1959).

9. (with D. Girgensohn), 'Nachträge zu den Papsturkunden Italiens, X', in *Nachrichten der Gesellschaft der Wissenschaften zu Göttingen,* Philol.-hist. Klasse, 1962, pp. 205-247.

10. See also *Regesta Pontificum Romanorum,* 3, A: *Italia Pontificia* IX, X.

Honorius III (1216-1227): *Regesta Honorii Papae III iussu et munificentia Leonis XIII p. m. ex vaticanis archetypis aliisque fontibus,* ed. P. Pressutti, 2 vv., Rome, 1885, 1895. See also Bock 10; selections in MGH [5].

Honorius IV (1285-1287): M. Prou, *Les registres d'Honorius IV publiées d'après le manuscrit des Archives du Vatican,* 1 v., Paris, 1886-1888. (BEFAR, B. 14).

Hungary: **1.** A. Theiner, *Vetera monumenta historica Hungariam sacram illustrantia, maximam partem nondum edita ex tabulariis vaticanis,* 2 vv. [1216-1526], Rome-Paris-Vienna, 1859, 1860.

2. *Monumenta Vaticana historiam regni Hungarici illustrantia*, series 1, Budapest, 1885-1891:

1. *Rationes collectorum pontificiorum in Hungaria, 1281-1375,* 1887.
2. *Acta legationis cardinalis Gentilis, 1307-1311,* 1885.
3. *Bullae Bonifatii IX, I, 1389-1396,* 1888.
4. *Bullae Bonifatii IX, II, 1396-1404,* 1889.
5. *Liber confraternitatis Sancti Spiritus de Urbe, 1446-1523,* 1889.
6. *Mathiae Corvini Hungariae regis Epistolae ad romanos pontifices datae et ab eis acceptae, 1458-1490,* 1891.

3. B. Árpád, *Regesta supplicationum. Avignoni korszak,* 2 vv. [1342-1394], Budapest, 1916, 1918.

Hussites: J. Prokeš, *Husitika vatikanské knihovny v Římě,* Prague, 1928.

Ilardi, V., 'Fifteenth-century Diplomatic Documents in Western European Archives and Libraries (1450-1494)', in *Studies in the Renaissance,* 9 (1962), 64-112 (= V. Ilardi, 'I documenti diplomatici del secolo XV negli archivi e biblioteche dell'Europa occidentale', in *Rassegna degli Archivi di Stato,* 28 (1968), 349-403.

Illyria: C. Silva-Tarouca, *Epistularum Romanorum Pontificum ad vicarios per Illyricum aliosque episcopos collectio Thessalonicensis, ad fidem codicis Vat. lat. 5751,* Rome, 1937.

Inguanez, M., 'Le bolle pontificie di S. Spirito del Morrone conservate nell'archivio di Montecassino (1157-1698)', in *Gli Archivi Italiani,* 5 (1918), 111-132, 158-176 (and separately: Siena, 1918).

Innocent III (1198-1216): 1. E. Baluze, *Epistolarum Innocentii III romani pontificis libris undecim,* 2 vv., Paris, 1682.

2. L. G. O. F. de Bréquigny, *Diplomata, chartae, epistolae et alia documenta ad res Francicas spectantia: Pars altera, tomus primus Innocentii III epistolas... exhibens,* ed. F. I. G. La Porte du Theil, 2 vv., Paris, 1791.

3. J. P. Migne, *Patrologiae latinae cursus completus,* vv. 214-217 (Paris, 1855): *Innocentii papae III Opera omnia*: vv. 214-215: *Regesta*; v. 216, cols. 995-1174: *Regestum super negotio Romani imperii* ; cols. 1175-1272: *Prima collectio decretalium*; v. 217: *Supplementum ad Regesta.*

4. *Regesta Pontificum Romanorum,* ed. A. Potthast, I, Berlin, 1874, pp. 1-467.

5. *Regestum Domini Innocentii tertii PP. super negotio Romani Imperii (Reg. Vat. 6),* riprodotto in fototipia... con introduzione di W. M. Peitz (= Codici Vaticani riprodotti fototipicamente, Series maior, XV), Rome, 1927.

6. *Regestum super negotio Romani Imperii Innocentii III,* ed. E. Kempf, Rome, 1947.

7. *Die Register Innocenz' III., I, 1 Pontifikatsjahr, 1198/9: Texte,* ed. O. Hageneder and A. Haidacher, with H. Eberstaller, F. Eheim, H. Feigl, F. Grill-Hillbrand, G. Möser-

Mersky, H. Paulhart, K. Peball, E. Popp, C. Thomas and G. Trenkler (= Publikationen der Abteilung für historische Studien des Österreichischen Kulturinstituts in Rom, II. Abteilung: Quellen, I. Reihe), Graz-Cologne, 1964; with indices by A. A. Strnad, *Die Register Innocenz' III.*, *I Band, 1 Pontifikatsjahr: Indices*, Graz-Vienna-Cologne, 1968.

Innocent IV (1243-1254): É. Berger, *Les registres d'Innocent IV publiées ou analysés d'après les manuscrits originaux du Vatican et de la Bibliothèque nationale*, 4 vv., Paris, 1884-1921 (= BEFAR, B. 5). See also Abate; Guerello; Mooney; Sambin 2; and selections in MGH [5].

Innocent VI (1352-1362): P. Gasnault and M.-H. Laurent, *Innocent VI. Lettres secrètes et curiales*, Paris, 1959 (= BEFAR, B. 27). See also France d.; Renouard 1.

Ireland: 1. A. Theiner, *Vetera monumenta Hibernorum et Scotorum historiam illustrantia, quae ex Vaticani, Neapolis ac Florentiae tabulariis deprompsit et ordine chronologico disposuit Augustinus Theiner. Ab Honorio PP. III usque ad Paulum PP. III, 1216-1547*, Rome, 1864.

2. M. A. Costello, *De Annatis Hiberniae, I: Ulster*, ed. A. Coleman, Dundalk, 1909; later continued in *Archivium Hibernicum* (AH) by various editors from Costello's notes, as follows:

1. 'Obligationes pro Annatis diocesis Dublinensis,1421-1520', AH 2 (1913), app., pp. 1-72;

2. '... diocesis Laoniensis, 1421-1535', ed. D. F. Gleeson, AH 10 (1943), 1-103;

3. '... diocesis Limiricensis, 1421-1519', ed. M. Moloney, AH 10 (1943), 104-162;

4. '... diocesis Waterfordensis, 1421-1507', ed. P. Power, AH 12 (1946), 1-14;

5. '... diocesis Lismorensis, 1426-1529', ed. P. Power, AH 12 (1946), 15-61;

6. '... diocesis Fernensis, 1413-1524', ed. J. Ranson, AH 18 (1955), 1-15;

7. '... diocesis Ossoriensis, 1413-1531', ed. T. J. Clohosey, AH 20 (1957), 1-37;

8. '... diocesis Ardfertensis, 1421-1517', ed. J. O'Connell, AH 21 (1958), 1-51;

9. '... diocesis Clonfertensis, 1420-1531', ed. P. K. Egan, AH 21 (1958), 52-74;

10. '... diocesis Elphinensis, 1426-1548', ed. G. Mac Niocaill, AH 22 (1959), 1-27;

11. '... diocesis Cloynensis, 1413-1526', ed. D. Buckley, AH 24 (1961), 1-30;

12. '... provinciae Tuamensis, 1413-1548', ed. J. F. O'Doherty, AH 26 (1963), 56-117;

13. '... diocesis Cassellensis, 1433-1534', ed. L. Ryan and W. Skehan, AH 28 (1966), 1-32;

14. '... diocesis Imelacensis, 1429-1444', ed. L. Ryan and W. Skehan, AH 28 (1966), 33-44.

3. R. J. Dodd, 'Vatican Archives: Instrumenta Miscellanea: Documents of Irish interest', in *Archivium Hibernicum*, 14 (1956), 229-253.

4. M. P. Sheehy, *Pontificia Hibernica. Medieval Papal Chancery Documents, 640-1262*, 2 vv., Dublin, 1962, 1965.

Italy: **1.** *Rationes decimarum Italiae nei secoli XIII e XIV*, ed. P. Guidi, P. Sella and others, 12 vv. (Studi e Testi — ST — series), Vatican City, 1932-1952:

> I: *Tuscia I: La decima degli anni 1274-1280*, ed. P. Guidi (ST 58), 1932.
>
> II: *Aemilia: Le decime dei secoli XIII-XIV*, ed. A. Mercati, E. Nasalli-Rocca, P. Sella (ST 60), 1933.
>
> III: *Aprutium, Molisium: Le decime dei secoli XIII-XIV*, ed. P. Sella (ST 69), 1936.
>
> IV: *Apulia-Lucania-Calabria*, ed. D. Vendola (ST 84), 1939.
>
> V: *Venetiae-Histria-Dalmatia*, ed. P. Sella, G. Vale (ST 96), 1941.
>
> VI: *Campania*, ed. M. Inguanez, L. Mattei-Cerasoli, P. Sella (ST 97), 1942.
>
> VII: *Tuscia II: Le decime degli anni 1295-1304*, ed. M. Giusti, P. Guidi (ST 98), 1942.
>
> VIII: *Sicilia*, ed. P. Sella (ST 112), 1944.
>
> IX: *Sardinia*, ed. P. Sella (ST 113), 1945.
>
> X: *Latium*, ed. G. Battelli (ST 128), 1946.
>
> XI: *Marchia*, ed. P. Sella (ST 148), 1950.
>
> XII: *Umbria*, 2 vv., ed. P. Sella (ST 161, 162), 1952.

2. J. Fraikin, *Bulles inédites relatives à diverses églises d'Italie*, Rome, 1900.

3. T. Gasparrini Leporace, *Le suppliche di Clemente VI: 1 (19 maggio 1342 - 28 maggio|1343)* (= Regesta Chartarum Italiae, 32), Rome, 1948.

4. *Italia Pontificia*: see *Regesta Pontificum Romanorum*, 3 A.

5. *Papsturkunden Italiens*: see Kaltenbrunner, 1; Kehr, 3.

Ivrea: F. Gabotto, *Le carte dell'Archivio vescovile d'Ivrea fino al 1313, II: Le bolle pontificie dei registri Vaticani relative ad Ivrea*, Pinerolo, 1900.

Jadin, L., 'Procès d'information pour la nomination des évêques et abbés des Pays-Bas, de Liège et de Franche-Comté d'après les archives de la Daterie, 1631-1775', in BIHBR, 11 (1931), 347-389.

Janssen, W., *Die päpstlichen Legaten in Frankreich vom Schisma Anaklets II. bis zum Tode Coelestins III., 1130-1198*, Cologne-Graz, 1961.

Jensen, O., 'The *Denarius Sancti Petri* in England', in *Transactions of the Royal Historical Society*, new series, 15 (1901), 204-241.

John VIII (872-882): E. Caspar, *Registrum Iohannis VIII papae*, in *Monumenta Germaniae Historica, Epistolae VII (Epistolae Karolini Aevi V)*, Berlin, 1928, pp. 1-272; *Fragmenta registri Iohannis VIII papae*, *ibid.*, 273-312. See further *Monumenta Germaniae Historica* [4], below; Lohrmann 2; Steinacker.

John XXI (1276-1277): E. Cadier, *Les registres de Grégoire X et de Jean*

XXI: Le registre de Jean XXI (1276-1277). Recueil des bulles de ce pape publiées ou analysées d'après le manuscrit des Archives du Vatican, 1 v., Paris, 1892-1906, with an index to the volume (= BEFAR, B. 9) in 1960 by G. Mollat.

John XXII (1316-1334): G. Mollat, *Jean XXII (1316-1334)*. Lettres communes analysées d'après les registres dits d'Avignon et du Vatican, 13 vv., Paris, 1904-1933, with 3 vv. of indices, 1935-1947 (= BE-FAR, B. 16). See also pp. 125-126, above; and *France* in Bibl.

Jordan, K., 1. 'Die päpstliche Verwaltung in Zeitalter Gregors VII.', in *Studi Gregoriani*, ed. G. B. Borino, I, Rome, 1947, pp. 111-135.

2. *Die Entstehung der römische Kurie*, Darmstadt, 1962.

Kaltenbrunner, F., 1. 'Papsturkunden in Italien', in *Sitzungsberichte der kaiserlichen Akademie der Wissenschaften zu Wien*, Phil.-hist. Klasse, 94 (1879), 627-705. See Löwenfeld 1.

2. 'Römische Studien. Die päpstlichen Register des 13. Jahrhunderts', in MIöG, 5 (1884), 213-294.

Karttunen, L., *Les nonciatures apostoliques permanentes de 1650 à 1800*, Geneva, 1912. See also Biaudet; de Marchi.

Katterbach, B., 1. 'Päpstliche Suppliken mit der Klausel der *sola signatura*', in RQ, 31 (1924), 185-196.

2. (with W. M. Peitz), 'Die Unterschriften der Päpste und Kardinäle in den "Bullae maiores" vom 11. bis 14. Jahrhundert', in *Miscellanea F. Ehrle*, IV (= Studi e Testi, 40), Rome, 1924, pp. 177-274.

3. *Specimina Supplicationum ex registris Vaticanis*, Rome, 1927.

4. 'Archivio e Archivistica', in *Enciclopedia Italiana*, IV, Rome, 1929, pp. 83-88.

5. 'Archivio Vaticano', ibid., 88-90.

6. (with C. Silva-Tarouca), *Epistolae et Instrumenta saeculi XIII* (= Exempla Scripturarum II), Vatican City, 1930.

7. *Referendarii utriusque Signaturae a Martino V ad Clementem XI, et Praelati Signaturae supplicationum a Martino V ad Leonem XIII* (Sussidi per la consultazione dell'Archivio Vaticano II = Studi e Testi, 55), Vatican City, 1931.

8. *Inventario dei Registri delle Suppliche* (= Inventari dell'Archivio Segreto Vaticano I), Vatican City, 1932.

Kehr, P. F., 1. 'Bemerkungen zu den päpstlichen Supplikenregistern des 14. Jahrhunderts', in MIöG, 8 (1887), 84-102.

2. 'Ueber den Plan einer kritischen Ausgabe der Papsturkunden bis Innocenz III.', in *Nachrichten der kgl. Gesellschaft der Wissenschaften zu Göttingen*, Philol.-hist. Klasse, Geschäftliche Mitteilungen, 1896, 72-86.

3. Presentations by Kehr from 1896-1924 in the *Nachrichten der (kgl.) Gesellschaft der Wissenschaften zu Göttingen*, Philol.-hist. Klasse, of researches done by himself, M. Klinkenborg, L. Schiaparelli, and W. Wiederhold, on 'Papsturkunden Italiens':

a. 1896: 'Papsturkunden in Venedig', 277-308.

b. 1897: '... Pisa, Lucca und Ravenna', 175-216; '... Reggio nell'Emilia', 223-233; '... Nonantola, Modena und Verona', 234-262 (= Klinkenborg); '... Brescia und Bergamo', 263-282 (= Klinkenborg); '... Padova, Ferrara und Bologna, nebst einem Nachtrag über die Papsturkunden in Venedig', 349-389.

c. 1898: '... in der Romagna und den Marken', 6-44 (= Klinkenborg and Schiaparelli); '... in Benevent und der Capitanata', 45-97 (= Schiaparelli); '... in Apulien', 237-289 (= Schiaparelli); '... in den Abruzzen und am Monte Gargano', 290-334 (= Klinkenborg and Schiaparelli); '... im Principato, in der Basilicata und in Calabrien', 335-348 (= Klinkenborg); '... in Umbrien', 349-396.

d. 1899: '... in Venetien', 197-249 (= Schiaparelli); '... in Friaul', 251-282 (= Schiaparelli); '... in Sizilien', 283-334; '... in Malta', 369-409 (= Schiaparelli).

e. 1900: '... in Parma und Piacenza', 1-75 (= Schiaparelli); '... in Rom. Erster Bericht', 111-197 (Vatican Archives: 112-125); '... in Salerno, La Cava und Neapel', 198-269; '... in Campanien', 286-344; '... in Rom. Zweiter Bericht', 360-434 (Vatican Archives: 361-399).

f. 1901: '... in Turin', 57-115 (= Schiaparelli); '... in Piemont', 117-170 (= Schiaparelli); '... im ehemaligen Patrimonium und südlichen Toscana', 196-228; '... in Rom. Dritte Bericht', 239-271; '... in Florenz', 306-325 (= W. Wiederhold).

g. 1902: 'in Mailand', 67-129; '... in der Lombardei', 130-167 (= Schiaparelli); '... in Ligurien', 169-192 (= Schiaparelli); 'Ältere Papsturkunden in den päpstlichen Registern von Innocenz III. bis Paul III.', 393-558.

h. 1903: 'Papsturkunden in Rom [4]. Die römischen Bibliotheken', 1-161; 'Nachträge zu den römischen Berichten', 505-591 (Vatican Archives: 507-532); 'Papsturkunden im westlichen Toscana', 592-641.

i. 1904: 'Papsturkunden im östlichen Toscana', 139-203.

j. 'Nachträge zu den Papsturkunden Italiens' in same *Nachrichten*: I: 1905, 321-380; II: 1908, 223-304; III: 1909, 435-517; IV: 1910, 229-288; V: 1911, 267-335; VI: 1912, 321-383; VII: 1912, 414-480; VIII: 1914, 52-92; IX: 1924, 156-193; [X: W. Holtzmann and D. Girgensohn, *ibid.*, 1962, 205-247]. See also Bartoloni, 'Additiones Kehrianae'; Volpini, 'Additiones Kehrianae'; *Regesta Pontificum Romanorum*, 3A: *Italia Pontificia*.

4. 'Ueber die Papsturkunden für S. Maria de Valle Josaphat', in *Nachrichten*, 1899, 338-368.

5. 'Le bolle pontificie anteriori al 1198 che si conservano nell'archivio di Montecassino', in *Miscellanea Cassinense*, 2 (1899), 1-90.

6. 'Le bolle pontificie che si conservano negli archivi Senesi', in *Bullettino Senese di storia patria*, 6 (1899), 51-102.

7. 'Scrinium und Palatium', in MIöG, *Erganzungsband*, 6 (1901), 70-112.

8. 'Diplomatische Miszellen', in *Nachrichten*, 1901, 1-27.

9. 'Le bolle pontificie che si conservano nell'archivio

diplomatico di Firenze', in *Archivio storico italiano*, 5th series, 32 (1903), 1-18.

    10. 'Anzeige von Regesta Pontificum Romanorum, Germania Pontificia II, 1', in *Deutsche Literaturzeitung*, 45 (1924), 1128-1134.

    11. 'Die ältesten Papsturkunden Spaniens', in *Abhandlungen der Preussischen Akademie der Wissenschaften*, Phil.-hist. Klasse, 2 (1926) 1-61. And see below, *Papsturkunden*, NF 18, 2 (1926), etc.

    12. 'Ueber die Sammlung und Herausgabe der älteren Papsturkunden bis Innozenz III. (1198)', in *Sitzungsberichte der Preussischen Akademie der Wissenschaften*, Phil.-hist. Klasse, 10 (1934), 83-92.

Kempf, F., **1.** *Die Register Innocenz' III. Eine paläographisch-diplomatische Untersuchung* (= Miscellanea Historiae Pontificiae, IX), Rome, 1945. See also Innocent III 6.

    2. *Papsttum und Kaisertum bei Innocenz III.* (= Miscellanea Historiae Pontificiae, XIX), Rome, 1954.

    3. 'Zu den Originalregistern Innocenz' III.', in QFIAB, 36 (1956), 86-137. See Bock 8.

Kirsch, J. P., **1.** 'Andreas Sapiti, ein englischer Prokurator an der Kurie im 14. Jahrhundert', in *Historisches Jahrbuch*, 14 (1893), 582-603.

    2. 'Ein Formelbuch der päpstlichen Kanzlei aus der Mitte des 14. Jahrhunderts', *ibid.*, 814-820.

    3. *Die päpstlichen Kollectorien in Deutschland während des XIV. Jahrhunderts*, Paderborn, 1894.

    4. *Die päpstlichen Annaten in Deutschland während des XIV. Jahrhunderts*, Paderborn, 1903.

Klewitz, H.-W., **1.** 'Die Entstehung des Kardinalskollegiums', in ZSSRGKA, 25 (1936), 115-221.

    2. (with H. Hartmann), 'Beiträge zum Urkundenwesen des Reformpapsttums', in *Archiv für Urkundenwesen*, 16 (1939), 385-424.

Knöpfler, J., 'Papsturkunden des 12., 13. und 14. Jahrhunderts aus dem germanischen Nationalmuseum in Nürnberg, mit einer historischen Skizze des venetianischen Klosters Brondolo', in *Historisches Jahrbuch*, 24 (1903), 307-318, 763-785.

Kopczynski, M., *Die Arengen der Papsturkunden nach ihrer Bedeutung und Verwendung bis zu Gregor VII.*, Berlin, 1936.

Korzeniowski, J., *Excerpta ex libris manuscriptis archivi consistorialis Romani, 1409-1590*, Cracow, 1890.

Kowalsky, N., *Inventario dell'Archivio storico della S. Congregazione de Propaganda Fide* (= Les Cahiers de la Nouvelle Revue de science missionaire, 17), Schöneck-Beckenried (Switzerland), 1961.

Kraus, A., **1.** 'Die Sekretäre Pius' II.', in RQ, 53 (1968), 28-50.

    2. '*Secretarius und Sekretariat.* Der Ursprung der Institution des Staatssekretariats und ihr Einfluss auf die Entwicklung moderner Regierungsformen in Europa', *ibid.*, 55 (1960), 43-84.

3. *Das päpstliche Staatssekretariat unter Urban VIII.*, *1623-1644*, Rome-Freiburg-Vienna, 1964.

Künzle, P., 'Del cosidetto "Titulus Archivorum" di Papa Damaso', in *Rivista di Storia della Chiesa in Italia*, 7 (1953), 1-26.

Kuttner, S., '*Cardinalis.* The History of a Canonical Concept', in *Traditio*, 3 (1945), 129-214.

Laemmer, H., *Monumenta Vaticana historiam ecclesiasticam saeculi XVI illustrantia*, Freiburg-im-Breisgau, 1861.

Lang, G., *Studien zu Brevenregistern und Brevenkonzepten des XV. Jahrhunderts*, Rome, 1938.

Largiadèr, A., **1.** 'Zum Problem der Papsturkunden des Spätmittelalters', in BAPI, 3rd series, 2-3 (1956-1957), II, 13-25.

          2. *Die Papsturkunden des Staatsarchivs Zürich von Innozenz III. bis Martin V. Ein Beitrag zum Censimentum Helveticum*, Zürich, 1963.

          3. *Die Papsturkunden der Schweiz von Innozenz III. bis Martin V., ohne Zürich: Ein Beitrag zum Censimentum Helveticum*, I: *von Innozenz III. bis Benedikt XI, 1198 bis 1304*, Zürich, 1968; II: 1305-1418: *Die Urkunden-empfänger und ihre Archive. Ein Beitrag zum Censimentum Helveticum*, Zürich, 1970.

Laurent, M.-H., **1.** 'Guillaume des Rosières et la bibliothèque pontificale à l'époque de Clément VI', in *Mélanges Auguste Pelzer*, Louvain, 1947, pp. 579-604.

          2. 'Trois nouveaux rôles de suppliques "per fiat" présentés à des papes du xive siècle (Vat. lat. 14400)', in MAH, 66 (1954), 219-239.

          3. 'Une supplique de Pierre de Gambacorta présentée par Ludovico Barbo à Eugène IV', in BAPI, 3rd series, 2-3 (1956-1957), II, 27-32. See also Sella 2.

Lea, H. C., *A Formulary of the Papal Penitentiary in the Thirteenth Century*, Philadelphia, 1892.

Leccisotti, T., 'Note in margine all'edizione dei regesti di Clemente V', in *Mélanges Tisserant*, V (Studi e Testi, 235), Vatican City, 1964, pp. 15-45. See also Montecassino.

Lefebvre, Ch., **1.** 'Rote romaine', in *Dictionnaire de droit canonique*, VII (1960-1961), cols. 742-771.

          2. 'Les origines et la rôle du Cardinalat au moyen âge', in *Apollinaris*, 4 (1968), 59-70.

Leflon, J., and A. Latreille, 'Répertoire des fonds napoléoniens aux Archives Vaticanes', in *Revue historique*, 203 (1950), 59-63.

Legros, H. M., and E. Kerchner, 'Lettres d'indulgences de la cour de Rome au xve siècle, in *Revue des études historiques*, 92 (1933), 543-556.

Leo X (1513-1521): *Leonis X pontificis maximi regesta*, ed. J. Hergenröther, 2 vv., Freiburg-im-Breisgau, 1884, 1891.

Lesellier, J., 'Notaires et archives de la curie romaine', in MAH, 50 (1933), 250-275.

Liber Censuum: P. Fabre and L. D. Duchesne, *Le Liber censuum de l'Église romaine*, 3 vv., Paris, 1889-1910 (v. 3 has been re-edited by G. Mollat, Paris, 1952). See also Elze; Pfaff.

Liber Diurnus: Liber Diurnus Romanorum Pontificum, ed. Th. von Sickel, Vienna, 1889; ed. H. Foerster, Bern, 1958. See also Peitz; Santifaller, 1.

Liber Pontificalis: L. D. Duchesne, *Le Liber Pontificalis: Texte, introduction et commentaire*, 2 vv., Paris, 1886, 1892; v. 3 (with corrections and additions by C. Vogel), 1957.

Liège: J. Paquay, *Documents pontificaux concernant le diocèse de Liège* (= Analecta ecclesiastica Leodiensia, 5), Liège, 1936.

Lincoln: W. Holtzmann and E. W. Kemp, *Papal decretals relating to the diocese of Lincoln in the Twelfth Century*, Lincoln, 1954.

Llorca, B., *Bulario Pontificio de la Inquisición Española en su periodo constitucional, 1478-1525* (= Miscellanea Historiae Pontificiae, XV), Rome, 1949.

Lodolini, A., 1. *L'archivio di Stato di Roma e l'archivio del Regno d'Italia*, Rome, 1932.

    2. *L'archivio di Stato di Roma. Epitome d'una guida degli archivi dell'amministrazione dello Stato Pontificio*, Rome, 1960.

Löwenfeld, S., 1. 'Papsturkunden in Italien. Ein Nachtrag', in *Sitzungsberichte der kaiserlichen Akademie der Wissenschaften zu Wien*, Phil.-hist. Klasse, 97 (1880), 55-68. See Kaltenbrunner 1.

    2. *Epistolae pontificum Romanorum ineditae*, Leipzig, 1885. See also *Regesta Pontificum Romanorum* 1.

* Lohrmann, D., 1. 'Berard von Neapel, ein päpstlicher Notar und Vertrauter Karls von Anjou', in *Adel und Kirche: Gerd Tellenbach zum 65. Geburtstag*, Freiburg-im-Breisgau, 1968, pp. 477-498.

    2. *Das Register Papst Johannes' VIII. (872-883). Neue Studien zur Abschrift Reg. Vat. 1, zum verlorenen Originalregister und zum Diktat der Briefe* (= Bibliothek des Deutschen Historischen Instituts im Rom, 30), Tübingen, 1968.

London: Public Record Office: *Lists of diplomatic documents, Scottish documents and papal bulls preserved in the Public Record Office*, London (Public Record Office, Lists and Indexes, 19), 1923 (reprinted with corrections, New York, 1963).

Lorraine: H. V. Sauerland, *Vatikanische Urkunden und Regesten zur Geschichte Lothringens [1294-1370]*, 2 vv., Metz, 1901, 1905.

Lunt, W. E., 1. *Papal Revenues in the Middle Ages*, 2 vv., New York, 1934.

    2. *Financial relations of the Papacy with England to 1327*, Cambridge, Mass., 1939; *Financial relations of the Papacy with England, 1327-1534*, ibid., 1962.

Lux, C., *Constitutionum apostolicarum de generali beneficiorum reservatione, collectio et interpretatio*, Bresslau, 1904.

Lyons: J.-B. Martin, *Conciles et bullaire du diocèse de Lyon, des origines à la réunion du Lyonnais à la France en 1312*, Lyons, 1905.

Macfarlane, L., 1. 'The Vatican Archives: with special reference to sources for British medieval history', in *Archives* (Journal of the British Records Association), 4 (1959), n. 21, 29-44; n. 22, 84-101. 2. 'The Vatican Library and Archives. Opportunities for English-speaking students', in *Wiseman* (formerly *Dublin*) *Review*, 488 (1961), 128-141.

MacFhinn, E., 'Scríbhinní i gCartlainn an Vatican: Tuarascbháil', in *Analecta Hibernica*, 16 (1946), 1-280.

Maguelone: J.-B. Rouquette, A. Villemagne and F. Fabrège, *Bullaire de l'église de Maguelone*, 2 vv., Montpellier, 1911, 1914.

Maier, A., 'Der Handschriftentransport von Avignon nach Rom im Jahr 1566', in *Mélanges Tisserant*, VII, Vatican City, 1964, pp. 9-27.

Majic, T., 'Die apostolische Pönitentiarie im 14. Jahrhundert', in RQ, 50 (1955), 129-177.

Major, K., 'Original papal documents in the Bodleian Library', in *Bodleian Library Record*, 3 (1950-1951), 242-256.

*   Mansilla, D., 'La documentación pontificia del archivo de la catedral de Burgos', in *Hispania Sacra*, 1 (1948), 141-162, 427-438. See also Spain, 3, 4.

Marini, G., *Memorie istoriche degli Archivi della Santa Sede*, ed. A. Mai, Rome, 1823.

Marini, M., 'Memorie storiche dell'occupazione e restituzione degli Archivi della Santa Sede', printed in *Regestum Clementis Papae V*, I, Rome, 1885, pp. CCXXVIII-CCCXXV.

Maronites: T. Anaissi, *Bullarium Maronitarum complectens bullas, brevia, epistolas, constitutiones aliaque documenta a Romanis pontificibus ad patriarchas Antiochenos Syro-Maronitarum missa, ex tabulario secreto S. Sedis, bibliotheca Vaticana, bullariis variis excerpta et juxta temporis seriem disposita*, Rome, 1911.

Martin IV (1281-1285): F. Olivier-Martin, *Les registres de Martin IV. Recueil des bulles de ce pape publiées ou analysées d'après les manuscrits originaux des Archives du Vatican*, 1 v., Paris, 1901-1935 (BEFAR, B. 11).

McNulty, J., *Thomas Sotheron v. Cockersand Abbey. A suit as to the advowson of Mitton Church, 1369-70* [= Coll. 417 A], Manchester, (Chetham Society), 1939.

Meinert, H., *Papsturkunden in Frankreich. Neue Folge* I, 2 vv. (Abhandlungen der Gesellschaft der Wissenschaften zu Göttingen, Philol.-hist. Klasse, Dritte Folge 3-4), Berlin, 1932. See Wiederhold 2, for the original series, and Ramackers for the continuation of this "Neue Folge". See also *Papsturkunden*.

Meister, A., *Die Geheimschrift im Dienste der päpstlichen Kurie von ihren Anfängen bis zum Ende des XVI. Jahrhundert*, Paderborn, 1906.

Melampo, G., and Ranuzzi, V., *Saggio bibliografico dei lavori eseguiti nell'Archivio Vaticano*, Rome, 1909.

Mercati, A., 1. 'Schema della disposizione dei fondi nell'Archivio

Vaticano', in *Bulletin of the International Committee of Historical Sciences*, 5 (1933), 909-912.

2. 'Cité du Vatican', in *Guide international des Archives, Europe* (= Bibliothèque des *Annales Institutorum*, IV), Paris-Rome, 1934, pp. 326-341.

3. 'Dagli Instrumenta Miscellanea dell'Archivio Vaticano', in QF, 27 (1936-1937), 135-177.

4. *Il sommario del processo di Giordano Bruno, con appendice sull'eresia e l'Inquisizione a Modena nel secolo XVI* (= Studi e Testi, 101), Vatican City, 1942.

5. 'La Biblioteca Apostolica e l'Archivio Segreto Vaticano', in *Vaticano*, edd. G. Fallani and M. Escobar, Florence, 1946, pp. 489-493.

6. 'Le pergamene di Melfi all'Archivio Segreto Vaticano', in *Miscellanea G. Mercati*, V, Rome, 1946, pp. 263-323.

7. *Il "Bullarium generale" dell'Archivio Vaticano e supplemento al registro dell'antipapa Niccolò V. — Dall'Archivio dei SS. Gregorio e Siro di Bologna all'Archivio Vaticano* (= Studi e Testi, 134: *Sussidi per la consultazione dell'Archivio Vaticano*, III), Vatican City, 1947.

8. 'Complementi al "Bullarium Franciscanum", in *Archivum Franciscanum Historicum*, 43 (1950), 161-180, 335-359.

9. 'Documenti dall'Archivio Segreto Vaticano', in *Miscellanea Pio Paschini*, II, Rome, 1950, pp. 1-37.

10. *Dall'Archivio Vaticano: I. Una corrispondenza fra curiali della prima metà del Quattrocento. II. Diari di Concistori del Pontificato di Adriano VI* (= Studi e Testi, 157), Vatican City, 1951.

11. *Raccolta di concordati su materie ecclesiastiche tra la Santa Sede e le autorità civili*, 2 vv., Rome, 1954².

12. *Miscellanea archivistica Angelo Mercati* (= Studi e Testi, 165), Vatican City, 1952.

Mercati, G.,: *Miscellanea Giovanni Mercati*, V (*Storia ecclesiastica. Diritto* = Studi e Testi, 125), Vatican City, 1946.

Metzler, G., 'Indici dell'Archivio storico della S. C. De Propaganda Fide', in *Euntes Docete*, 21 (1968), 109-130.

Michaud, M., 'Chambre apostolique', in *Dictionnaire de droit canonique*, III (1942), cols. 388-431.

Migne, J.-P., *Patrologiae Latinae Cursus Completus... Series secunda in qua prodeunt Patres, doctores scriptoresque Ecclesiae Latinae a Tertulliano ad Innocentium III*, vv. 221, Paris, 1844-1864. For a conspectus, volume by volume, of papal letters and other papal material in the *Patrologia Latina*, see L. Santifaller, *Neuere Editionen mittelalterlicher Königs- und Papsturkunden: eine Uebersicht*, Vienna, 1958, pp. 57-62.

Millares Carlo, A., *Documentos pontificios en papiro de archivos catalanos*, Madrid, 1918.

Miller, M., 'Das römische Tagebuch des Ulmer Stadtammans Konrad Locher aus der Zeit des Papstes Innocenz' VIII.', *Historisches Jahrbuch*, 60 (1940), 270-300.

Millett, B., 'The Archives of the Congregation *de Propaganda Fide*', in *Proceedings of the Irish Catholic Historical Committee, 1956*, Dublin, 1956, pp. 20-27.

Miquel Rosell, F. J., *Regesta de Letras Pontificias del Archivo de la Corona de Aragón, Sección Cancellaria Real (Pergamenos)*, Madrid, 1948.

Mollat, G., 1. *La collation des bénéfices ecclésiastiques sous les Papes d'Avignon, 1305-1378*, Paris, 1921 (also printed in the introduction to v. 8 of Mollat's calendar of the common letters of John XXII: see John XXII, above).

    2. 'Contribution à l'histoire de l'administration judiciaire de l'Église romaine au xive siècle', in RHE, 32 (1936), 877-928.

    3. 'Bénéfices ecclésiastiques en Occident', in *Dictionnaire de droit canonique*, II (1937), cols. 406-449.

    4. 'Contribution à l'histoire de la Chambre apostolique au xive siècle', in RHE, 45 (1950), 82-94.

    5. 'Contribution à l'histoire du Sacré Collège de Clément V à Eugène IV', *ibid.*, 46 (1951), 22-112, 566-594.

    6. 'Correspondance de Clément VI par cédules', in BAPI, 3rd series, 2-3 (1956-1957), II, 176.

    7. 'Le St.-Siège et la France sous le pontificat de Clément VI (1342-1352)', in RHE, 55 (1960), 5-24.

    8. 'Registres pontificaux', in *Dictionnaire de droit canonique*, VII (1965), cols. 536-538.

    9. *Les Papes d'Avignon*, Paris, 1965[10]. (This 10th edition, completed shortly before Mollat's death in 1970, differs from the 9th edition of 1949 chiefly in that the bibliographies have been brought up to date for each section. An English version of the 9th edition — *The Popes at Avignon, 1307-1378*, trans. J. Love, London, 1963 — omits most of the excellent bibliographies).

    10. See also Samaran and Mollat; and many of the volumes of the *Troisième série* of BEFAR calendars listed above, pp. 125-127.

Monaco, M., 1. *La situazione della reverenda Camera Apostolica nell'anno 1525. Ricerche d'archivio. Contributo alla storia delle finanze pontificie*, Rome, 1960.

    2. 'The *De officio Collectoris in Regno Angliae* by Pietro Griffi of Pisa (1469-1516)', in *Miscellanea Historiae Ecclesiasticae III, Colloque de Cambridge, 1968*, Louvain, 1970, pp. 175-183.

Montecassino: 1. C. Margarini, *Bullarium Casinense seu Constitutiones summorum pontificum, imperatorum, regum, principum et decreta sacrarum congregationum pro congregatione Casinensi*, 2 vv., Venice, 1750, Todi, 1770.

    2. T. Leccisotti, *Documenti Vaticani per la storia di Montecassino. Pontificato di Urbano V*, Montecassino, 1932.

Monumenta Germaniae Historica: volumes containing letters of popes or matters bearing on the papal chancery:

    [1] *Epistolae* III (= *Epistolae Merovingici et Karolini Aevi* I), Berlin, 1892: items edited by W. Gundlach: I (pp. 1-83): *Epistolae Arelatenses genuinae*;

II (pp. 84-109): *Epistolae Viennenses spuriae*; VII (pp. 434-468): *Epistolae aevi Merovingici collectae*; VIII (pp. 469-657): *Codex Carolinus*; X (pp. 691-715): *Epistolae Langobardicae collectae.*

[2] *Epistolae* V (= *Epistolae Karolini Aevi* III), Berlin, 1899: I (pp. 1-44): K. Hampe, *Epistolae selectae pontificum Romanorum Carolo Magno et Ludowico Pio regnantibus scriptae*; II (pp. 85-104): K. Hampe, *Leonis III papae [795-816] Epistolae selectae*; XI (pp. 581-614): A. de Hirsch-Gereuth, *Epistolae selectae Sergii II, Leonis IV, Benedicti III [844-858].*

[3] *Epistolae* VI (= *Epistolae Karolini Aevi* IV), Berlin, 1925: items edited by E. Perels: III (pp. 207-240): *Epistolae variorum [860-868] ad divortium Lotharii II regis pertinentes* (inc. Nicholas I and Hadrian II); V (pp. 267-690): *Nicholai I papae [858-867] Epistolae*; VI (pp. 691-765): *Hadriani II papae [867-872] Epistolae.*

[4] *Epistolae* VII (= *Epistolae Karolini Aevi* V), Berlin, 1928: I (pp. 1-272): E. Caspar, *Registrum Iohannis VIII papae [872-882]*; II (pp. 273-312): E. Caspar, *Fragmenta registri Iohannis VIII papae*; III (pp. 313-329): E. Caspar and G. Laehr, *Johannis VIII papae Epistolae passim collectae*; IV (pp. 330-333): E. Caspar, *Johannis VIII papae Epistolae dubiae*; V (pp. 334-353): E. Caspar, *Fragmenta registri Stephani V papae [885-891]*; VI (pp. 354-365): G. Laehr, *Stephani V Epistolae passim collectae quotquot ad res Germanicas spectant*; VII (pp. 366-370): G. Laehr, *Formosi papae [891-896] Epistolae quotquot ad res Germanicas spectant*; VIII (pp. 371-384): E. Caspar and G. Laehr, *Epistolae ad res Orientales spectantes* [= Stephan V and John IX, 885-891, 898-900].

[5] G. H. Pertz and C. Rodenburg, *Epistolae saeculi XIII e regestis Pontificum Romanorum selectae*, 3 vv., Berlin, 1883-1894: I (1883), pp. 1-260: *Ex Honorii III registro* [1216-1227]; pp. 261-728: *Ex Gregorii IX registro* [1227-1241]. II (1887): *Ex Innocentii IV registro, 1* [1243-1249]. III (1894), pp. 1-313: *Ex Innocentii IV registro, 2* [1250-1254]; pp. 314-473: *Ex Alexandri IV registro* [1254-1261]; pp. 474-626: *Ex Urbani IV registro* [1261-1264]; pp. 627-726: *Ex Clementis IV registro* [1265-1268].

For other volumes of the *Monumenta*, see Gregory I; Gregory VII.

Mooney, C., 'Letters of Pope Innocent IV concerning Ireland', in *Collectanea Hibernica*, 2 (1959), 7-12.

Moran, C., 'Les archives du Saint-Siège, importantes sources de l'histoire politico-religieuse du Canada', in *Culture* (Ottawa), 7 (1946), 151-176.

Moravia: B. Dudík, *Auszüge für Mährens allgemeine Geschichte aus den Registern der Päpste Benedikt XII. und Clemens VI.*, Brno, 1885.

Moroni, G., 'Archivi della Santa Sede', in G. Moroni, *Dizionario di erudizione storico-ecclesiastica*, II (Venice, 1840), pp. 277-288.

Müller, G., *Die römische Kurie und die Reformation, 1523-1524: Kirche und Politik während des Pontifikats Clemens' VII.*, Gütersloh, 1969.

Murray, A., 'Pope Gregory VII and his letters', in *Traditio*, 22 (1966), 149-202.

Nélis, H., 'L'application en Belgique de la règle de chancellerie apostolique "De idiomate beneficiatorum" aux xive et xve siècles', in BIHBR, 2 (1922), 129-141.

Nicholas III (1277-1280): J. Gay and S. Vitte-Clémencet, *Les registres de Nicolas III (1277-1280).* Recueil des bulles de ce pape publiées ou analysées d'après les manuscrits originaux du Vatican, 1 v., Paris, 1898-1938 (= BEFAR, B. 10).

Nicholas IV (1288-1292): E. Langlois, *Les registres de Nicolas IV (1288-1292).* Recueil des bulles de ce pape publiées ou analysées d'après le manuscrit original des Archives du Vatican, 2 vv., Paris, 1887-1893 (= BEFAR, B. 13).

Nicholas V (antipope: 1328-1330): C. Eubel, 'Der Registerband des Gegenpapstes Nikolaus V.', in *Archivalische Zeitschrift,* 4 (1893), 123-212; and A. Mercati, 'Supplementi al registro dell'antipapa Niccolò V', in *Sussidi per la consultazione dell'Archivio Vaticano,* III, Vatican City, 1947, pp. 59-76.

Nîmes, etc.: H. Grange, *Sommaires des lettres des papes concernant le Gard (anciens diocèses de Nîmes, d'Uzès et parties d'Avignon et d'Arles), émanant des Papes d'Avignon, XIVe siècle,* 2 vv., Nîmes, 1911, 1922.

Norberg, D., *In Registrum Gregorii Magni Studia Critica,* 2 vv., Uppsala, 1937, 1939.

Norway: 1. G. Storm, *Afgifter fra den Norske Kirkeprovins til det Apostoliske Kammer of Kardinalkollegiet, 1311-1523,* Christiania, 1897.

2. G. Storm, *Regesta Norwegica. Kronologisk fortegnelse over dokumenter vedkommende norge, nordmaend og den norske kirkeprovins, I, 991-1263,* Christiania, 1898.

Oldenburg (Lower Saxony): H. Reimers, *Oldenburgische Papsturkunden (1246-1500),* Oldenburg, 1907.

Opitz, G., 1. 'Ueber Registrierung von Sekretbriefen. Studien zu den Sekretregistern Clemens VI.', in QFIAB, 29 (1938-1939), 89-134.

2. 'Die Sekretäre Franciscus de Sancto Maximo und Johannes de Sancto Martino', *ibid.,* 30 (1940), 189-206.

3. 'Die Sekretärexpedition unter Urban VI. und Gregor XI.', *ibid.,* 33 (1944), 158-198.

Oriental Church: Pontificia Commissio ad redigendum Codicem Iuris Canonici Orientalis: *Fontes, Series III, Vaticani,* ed. A. L. Tăutu (unless otherwise noted), Vatican City, 1943—:

1: *Acta Romanorum pontificum a S. Clemente I (an.c. 90) ad Coelestinum III (1198),* 2vv., 1943.

2: *Acta Innocentii III (1198-1216) e registris Vaticanis aliisque fontibus,* ed. T. Haluščynskyj, 1944.

3: *Acta Honorii III (1216-1227) et Gregorii IX (1227-1241) e registris Vaticanis aliisque fontibus,* 1941.

5, 1: *Acta Urbani IV, Clementis IV, Gregorii X (1261-1276) e registris Vaticanis aliisque fontibus, 1953.*

5, 2: *Acta Romanorum pontificum ab Innocentio V ad Benedictum XI (1276-1304)...,* ed. F. M. Delorme and A. L. Tăutu, 1954.

7, 1: *Acta Clementis V (1305-1314)...,* edd. iidem, 1955.

7, 2: *Acta Ioannis XXII (1317-1334)*..., 1952.
   8:    *Acta Benedicti XII (1334-1342)*..., 1958.
   9:    *Acta Clementis VI (1342-1352)*..., 1960.
  10:    *Acta Innocentii VI (1352-1362)*..., 1961.
  11:    *Acta Urbani V (1362-1370)*..., 1964.
  12:    *Acta Gregorii XI (1370-1378)*..., 1966.
  13, 1: *Acta Urbani VI (1378-1379)*, *Bonifatii IX (1389-1404)*, *Innocentii VII (1404-1406)*, *et Gregorii XII (1406-1415)*, 1970.

O'Sullivan, M. D., 'Italian Merchant Bankers and the collection of papal revenue in Ireland in the 13th century', in *Galway Archeological Association Journal*, 22 (1946-1947), 132-163.

Papal States: A. Theiner, *Codex diplomaticus dominii temporalis S. Sedis. Recueil de documents pour servir à l'histoire du gouvernement temporal des états du Saint-Siège, extraits des archives du Vatican*, 3 vv. [756-1793], Rome, 1861-1862. See also Partner, 2.
Papsturkunden volumes published among the *Abhandlungen der Gesellschaft* (now *Akademie*) *der Wissenschaften zu* (now *in*) *Göttingen, Philologisch-historische Klasse: Neue Folge* (= NF), *Dritte Folge* (= DF), Berlin 1926 — :

NF 18, 2: P. Kehr, *Papsturkunden in Spanien. Vorarbeiten zur Hispania Pontificia*, I, 1926.
   20, 3: C. Erdmann, *Papsturkunden in Portugal* (= *Lusitania Pontificia*), 1928.
   22, 1: P. Kehr, *Papsturkunden in Spanien*, II, 1928.
   25, 1: W. Holtzmann, *Papsturkunden in England* (= *Britannia Pontificia*), I, 1, 1930.
   25, 2: Idem, *Papsturkunden in England*, I, 2, 1931.
DF 3: H. Meinert, *Papsturkunden in Frankreich, Neue Folge*, I, 1, 1932. [See Wiederhold 2 for original series].
     4: Idem, *Papsturkunden in Frankreich*, 1, 2, 1932.
     8: J. Ramackers, *Papsturkunden in den Niederlanden, Belgien, Luxemburg, Holland und Französisch-Flandern*, I, 1, 1933.
     9: Idem, *Papsturkunden in den Niederlanden...*, I, 2, 1934.
    14: W. Holtzmann, *Papsturkunden in England*, II, 1, 1935.
    15: Idem, *Papsturkunden in England*, II, 2, 1936.
    21: J. Ramackers, *Papsturkunden in Frankreich*, II, 1937.
    23: Idem, *Papsturkunden in Frankreich*, III, 1940.
    27: Idem, *Papsturkunden in Frankreich*, IV, 1942.
    33: W. Holtzmann, *Papsturkunden in England*, III, 1952.
    35: J. Ramackers, *Papsturkunden in Frankreich*, V, 1956.
    41: Idem, *Papsturkunden in Frankreich*, VI, 1958.

Partner, P., 1. '*Camera Papae*. Problems of Papal Finance in the late Middle Ages', in *Journal of Ecclesiastical History*, 4 (1953), 55-68.
   2. *The Papal State under Martin V. The Administration and Government of the Temporal Power in the early 15th Century*, London, 1958.

Pasture, A., 'Archives du Vatican. Inventaire du fonds Borghèse au point de vue de l'histoire des Pays-Bas', in *Bulletin de la Commission Royale d'histoire* (Brussels), 79 (1910), 1-217.

Pásztor, E., 1. 'Una raccolta di sermoni di Giovanni XXII', in BAPI, 3rd series, 2-3 (1956-1957), II, 265-289.

2. 'Au sujet d'une source des "Vitae Paparum Avenionensium" de Baluze provenant des Archives Vaticanes', in RHE, 54 (1959), 507-512.

3. 'Contributo alla storia dei registri pontifici del secolo XIII', in BAPI, 3rd series, 1 (1962), 37-83.

4. 'Studi e problemi relativi ai registri di Innocenzo III', in *Annali della Scuola speciale per Archivisti e Bibliotecari dell'Università di Roma*, 2 (1962), 289-304.

5. 'Riconstruzione parziale di un registro pontificio deperdito del sec. XIII', in *Mélanges Tisserant*, V, Vatican City, 1964, pp. 199-207.

6. 'Per la storia dei registri pontifici nel duecento', in *Archivum Historiae Pontificiae*, 6 (1968), 71-112.

Pásztor, L., 1. 'Per la storia della Segretaria di Stato nell'Ottocento. La riforma del 1816', in *Mélanges Tisserant*, V, Vatican City, 1964, pp. 200-250.

2. 'Contributo di un fondo miscellaneo all'archivistica e alla storia: L'Arm. LII dell'Archivio Segreto Vaticano', in *Annali della Scuola speciale per Archivisti e Bibliotecari dell'Università di Roma*, 6 (1966), 1-31.

3. 'La Segretaria di Stato di Pio IX durante il triennio 1848-1850', in *Annali della Fondazione italiana per la storia amministrativa*, 3 (1966), 308-365.

4. 'Il Sostituto del Concistoro e il suo archivio', in *Archivum Historiae Pontificiae*, 5 (1967), 355-372.

5. 'La Congregazione degli Affari Ecclesiastici Straordinari tra il 1814 e il 1850', *ibid.*, 6 (1968), 191-318.

6. 'Per la storia dell'Archivio Segreto Vaticano nei secoli XVII-XVIII (Eredità Passionei, Carte Favoriti-Casoni, Archivio dei Cardinali Bernardino e Fabrizio Spada', in *Archivio della Società Romana di Storia Patria*, 91 (1968), 157-249.

7. 'L'histoire de la curie romaine, problème d'histoire de l'Église', in RHE, 64 (1969), 353-366.

8. *Guida delle fonti per la storia dell'America Latina negli archivi della Santa Sede e negli archivi ecclesiastici d'Italia* (= Collectanea Archivi Vaticani, 2), Vatican City, 1970.

Paulhart, H., 'Papsturkunden in Oberösterreich. Originale spätmittelalterlicher Papsturkunden in Oberösterreichischen Archiven aus der Zeit 1198-1417', in *Mitteilungen des Oberösterreichischen Landesarchivs*, 8 (1964), 160-172.

Peball, K., 'Zu den kanonistischen Randzeichnen im Register Papst Innozenz' III. (Reg. Vat. 4-7A)', in RHM, 1 (1958), 77-105.

Peitz, W. M., 1. *Liber Diurnus. Beiträge zur Kenntnis der ältesten päpstlichen*

Kanzlei vor Gregor dem Grossen, I: *Ueberlieferung des Kanzleibuches und sein vorgregorianischer Ursprung*, Vienna, 1918.
    2. *Liber Diurnus*: *Methodisches zur Diurnusforschung* (= *Miscellanea Historiae Pontificiae* II-III), Rome, 1940.

Pelagius I (556-561): P. M. Gassó and C. M. Batllè, *Pelagii I epistolae quae supersunt*, Montserrat, 1956.

Pellicia, G., *La preparazione ed ammissione dei chierici ai santi ordini nella Roma del sec. XVI*, Rome, 1946.

Perrin, Ch.-E., 'La cour pontificale d'Avignon (1309-1376)', in *Revue historique*, 232 (1964), 361-378 (reviewing Guillemain, 2, above).

Petrucci, A., 'Note di diplomatica pontificia: I. Un privilegio solenne di Innocenzo III; II. I capitoli di Innocenzo VIII per Perugia; III. L'origine dei brevi pontifici e gli antichi eruditi', in *Archivio della Società Romana di Storia Patria*, 89 (1966), 47-85.

Pfaff, V., **1.** 'Die Einnahmen der römischen Kurie am Ende des 12. Jahrhunderts', in *Vierteljahrschrift für Sozial- und Wirtschaftsgeschichte*, 40 (1953), 97-118.
    2. 'Der *Liber Censuum* von 1192. (Die im Jahre 1192/93 der Kurie Zinspflichtigen)', *ibid.*, 44 (1957), 78-96 (= LC nn. 1-194), 105-120 (= nn. 195-361), 220-242 (= nn. 362-537), 325-351 (= nn. 538-682).

Pisa: C. Fedeli, *I documenti pontifici riguardanti l'Università di Pisa*, Pisa, 1903.

Pitra, J. P., *Analecta Novissima. Spicilegii Solesmensis altera continuatio*, I, Rome, 1885.

Poland: **1.** W. Meysztowicz, *Repertorium bibliographicum pro rebus Polonicis Archivi Secreti Vaticani*, Vatican City, 1943.
    2. A. Theiner, *Vetera monumenta Poloniae et Lithuaniae gentiumque finitimarum historiam illustrantia, maximam partem nondum edita ex tabulariis vaticanis*, 2 vv., Rome, 1860, 1861.
    3. *Monumenta Poloniae Vaticana*, Cracow, 1913—: nn. 1 and 2: J. Ptasnik, *Acta Camerae Apostolicae, 1207-1344*; *Acta Camerae Apostolicae, 1344-1374*, 1913; n. 3: Idem, *Analecta Vaticana 1202-1366*, 1914; n. 8: *Acta Pontificum Romanorum, I: Acta Bonifatii Papae IX, 1389-1391*, ed. E. Dlugopolski, 1939-1946.

Pomerania: A. Motzki, *Urkunden zur Caminer Bistumsgeschichte auf Grund der Avignonesischen Supplikenregister*, Stettin, 1913.

Pontificum Romanorum diplomata papyracea quae supersunt in tabulariis Hispaniae, Italiae, Germaniae phototypice expressa iussu Pii PP. XI consilio et opera procuratorum Bibliothecae Apostolicae Vaticanae [= E. Carusi, K. Silva-Tarouca and C. Erdmann], Rome, 1928. See also Millares Carlo.

Poole, R. L., **1.** *Lectures on the Papal Chancery down to the time of Innocent III*, Cambridge, 1915.
    2. *Studies in Chronology and History*, Oxford, 1934.

Portugal: **1.** V. de Santarem, L. A. Rebello da Silva and J. da Silva Mendes Leal, *Quadro elementar das relações politicas e diplomaticas de Portugal com as diversas potencias do mundo*, XVII: *Relações politicas e* *diplomaticas entre Portugal e la Curia de Roma*, 5 vv. [1137-1580], Lisbon, 1864-1876.

2. L. M. Jordão, *Bullarium patronatus Portugalliae regum in ecclesiis Africae, Asiae atque Oceaniae bullas, brevia, epistolas, decreta actaque Sanctae Sedis ab Alexandro III ad hoc usque tempus amplectens*, I [1171-1600], Lisbon, 1868.

3. J. dos Santos Abranches, *Fontes do Direito ecclesiastico Portuguez*, I: *Summa do Bullario Portuguez*, Coimbra, 1895.

4. *Monumenta Portugaliae Vaticana*, I: A. D. de Sousa Costa, *Súplicas dos pontificados de Clemente VI, Inocêncio VI e Urbano V*, Braga, 1970.

Posner, E., 'Das Register Gregors I.', in *Neues Archiv*, 41 (1922), 243-315.

Pou y Marti, J. M., *Archivo de la embajada de España cerca de la Santa Sede*, Rome, 1925.

Prussia, East: H. Ehrenberg, *Italienische Beiträge zur Geschichte der Provinz Ostpreussen. Im Auftrage des Provinzial-Ausschusses der Provinz Ostpreussen in italienischen Handschriften-Sammlungen, vornehmlich dem vatikanischen Archive gesammelt*, Königsberg (Kaliningrad), 1895.

Puglia: D. Vendola, *Documenti tratti dai registri vaticani (da Innocenzo III a Nicola IV)*, Trani, 1940.

Quilon (India): A. Mercati, *Monumenta Vaticana veterem diocesim Columbensem (Quilon) et eiusdem episcopum Jordanum Catalani ord. praed. respicientia*, Rome, 1923.

Rabikauskas, P., 1. *Die römische Kuriale in der päpstlichen Kanzlei* (= Miscellanea Historiae Pontificiae, XX), Rome, 1958.

2. 'Zur fehlenden und unvollständigen Skriptumzeile in den Papstprivilegien des 10. und 11. Jahrhunderts', in *Saggi storici intorno al Papato* (= Miscellanea Historiae Pontificiae, XXI), Rome, 1959, pp. 91-116.

3. '"Annus Incarnationis" et "Annus Pontificatus" nei privilegi di Innocenzo III', in *Archivio della Società Romana di Storia patria*, 91 (1968), 45-55.

4. *Diplomatica pontificia*, Rome, 1968².

Ramacciotti, A., *Gli archivi della Reverenda Camera Apostolica, con inventario analitico-descrittivo dei registri camerali conservati nell'Archivio di Stato di Roma nel Fondo Camerale Primo*, Rome (Reverenda Camera Apostolica), 1961.

Ramackers, J., 1. *Papsturkunden in Niederlanden, Belgien, Luxemburg, Holland und Französisch-Flandern* (= Abhandlungen der Gesellschaft der Wissenschaft zu Göttingen, Philol.-hist. Klasse, Dritte Folge, 8, 9), 2 vv., Berlin, 1933, 1934. See also *Papsturkunden*.

2. *Papsturkunden in Frankreich, Neue Folge*, vv. II-VI, Berlin, 1937-1958. See also *Papsturkunden*.

3. 'Zwei unbekannte Briefe Urbans II. Zugleich ein Beitrag zum Problem der Register dieses Papstes', in QFIAB, 26 (1935-1936), 268-276.

Raponi, N., 'Recenti edizioni di Nunziature pontificie e le "Nunziature d'Italia"', *Rassegna degli Archivi di Stato*, 25 (1965), 245-266.

Regesta Imperii: J. F. Böhmer, *Regesta Imperii V, Die Regesten des Kaiserreichs, 1198-1272*, part 3: *Päpste und Reichssachsen*, Innsbruck, 1892-1894, pp. 1055-1579 (= nn. 5621b-10624), for papal letters between 1198 and 1268. [For an earlier period see now J. F. Böhmer, *Regesta Imperii, II, Sächsische Zeit*, part 5: *Papstregesten, 911-1024*, ed. H. Zimmermann, Vienna-Cologne-Graz, 1969].

Regesta Pontificum Romanorum: [1] P. Jaffé, *Regesta Pontificum Romanorum ab condita ecclesia ad annum post Christum natum MCXCVIII*, second edition by S. Löwenfeld, P. Ewald and F. Kaltenbrunner [with G. Wattenbach], 2 vv., Leipzig, 1885, 1888.

[2] A. Potthast, *Regesta Pontificum Romanorum inde ab A. post Christum natum MCXCVIII ad A. MCCCIV*, 2 vv., Berlin, 1874, 1875.

[3] *Regesta Pontificum Romanorum* iubente Regia Societate Gottingensi congessit P. F. Kehr:

[A] *Italia Pontificia* sive *Repertorium privilegiorum et litterarum a Romanis pontificibus ante annum 1198 Italiae ecclesiis, monasteriis, civitatibus singulisque personis concessorum*, 10 vv., Berlin, 1906-1966: vv. 1-8 ed. P. F. Kehr; vv. 9-10 ed. P. F. Kehr and W. Holtzmann: I: *Roma*, 1906; II: *Latium*, 1907; III: *Etruria*, 1908; IV: *Umbria, Picenum, Marsia*, 1909; V: *Aemilia sive provincia Ravennas*, 1911; VI: *Liguria sive provincia Mediolanensis*, 1: *Lombardia*, 1913; 2: *Pedemontium, Liguria maritima*, 1914; VII: *Venetiae et Histria*, 1: 1923, 2: 1925; VIII: *Regnum Normannorum: Campania*, 1935; IX: *Regnum Normannorum: Samnium, Apulia, Lucania*, 1961; X: *Sicilia, Sardinia, Corsica*, 1966. See also Kehr 3 ("Papsturkunden Italiens").

[B] *Germania Pontificia* sive *Repertorium privilegiorum et litterarum a Romanis pontificibus ante annum MCLXXXXVIII Germaniae ecclesiis, monasteriis, civitatibus singulisque personis concessorum*, ed. A. Brackmann, Berlin, 1910-1935: I: *Provincia Salisburgensis et episcopatus Tridentinus*, 1910-1911; II: *Provincia Maguntinensis*, 1, 1923; 2 (*Helvetia pontificia*), 1927; III: *Provincia Maguntinensis*, 3, 1935. See Brackmann 1-3; Kehr 10.

Regolamento dell'Archivio Vaticano, Rome, 1927.

Reims: H. H. Dubrulle, *Bullaire de la province de Reims sous le pontificat de Pie II*, Lille, 1905.

Renouard, Y., 1. 'Les minutes d'Innocent VI aux archives du Vatican' [= RV 244 A-N], in *Archivi d'Italia e Rassegna internazionale degli archivi*, 2 (1935), 14-27 (now in *Études*, below, pp. 833-845).

2. 'Comment les papes d'Avignon expédiaient leur courriers', in *Revue historique*, 180 (1937), 1-29 (now in *Études*, pp. 740-764).

3. *Les relations des Papes d'Avignon et des compagnies commerciales et bancaires de 1316 à 1378*, Paris, 1941.

4. 'Intérêt et importance des Archives Vaticanes pour l'histoire économique du Moyen Age, spécialement du XIVe

siècle', in *Miscellanea Archivistica A. Mercati*, Vatican City, 1952, pp. 21-41 (now in *Études*, pp. 193-210).
    5. *La Papauté à Avignon* (= Que sais-je ? n. 630), Paris, 1954, now translated into English by D. Bethell as *The Avignon Papacy, 1305-1403*, London, 1970.
    6. 'Edouard II et Clément V d'après les rôles gascons', in *Annales du Midi*, 67 (1955), 119-141.
    7. *Études d'histoire médiévale*, 2 vv. (with continuous pagination), Paris, 1968.

Rest, I., 'Illuminierte Ablassurkunden aus Rom und Avignon aus der Zeit von 1282-1364', in *Festgabe H. Finke*, Münster-in-W., 1925, pp. 147-168.

Rhineland: H. V. Sauerland, *Urkunden und Regesten zur Geschichte der Rheinlande aus dem Vatikanischen Archiv*, 7 vv., [= 1294-1415], Bonn, 1902-1913.

Richard, P., 1. 'Origines des nonciatures permanentes: la représentation pontificale au xve siècle (1450-1513)', in RHE, 7 (1906), 52-70, 317-338.
    2. 'Origine et développement de la Secrétairerie de l'État apostolique, 1417-1823', *ibid.*, 11 (1910), 56-72, 505-529, 728-754.

Riezler, S., *Vatikanische Akten zur deutschen Geschichte in der Zeit Kaiser Ludwigs des Bayern*, Innsbruck, 1891.

Ritzler, R., 1. 'Die archivalischen Quellen der Hierarchia Catholica', in *Miscellanea Archivistica A. Mercati*, Vatican City, 1952, pp. 61-64.
    2. 'Bischöfliche Informativprozesse im Archiv der Datarie', in RQ, 50 (1955), 95-101.
    3. 'Procesos informativos de los obispos de España y sus dominios en el Archivo Vaticano', in *Anthologica Annua*, 4 (1956), 465-498.
    4. 'Die bischöflichen Informativprozesse in den "Processus Consistoriales" im Archiv des Kardinalskollegs bis 1907', in *Römische historische Mitteilungen*, 2 (1957-1958), 204-220.
    5. 'Per la storia dell'Archivio del Sacro Collegio', in *Mélanges Tisserant* V, Vatican City, 1964, pp. 300-338.
    6. 'Die Verschleppung der päpstlichen Archiv nach Paris unter Napoleon I. und deren Rückführung nach Rom in den Jahren 1815 bis 1817', in *Römische historische Mitteilungen*, 6-7 (1964), 144-190.

L. Rockinger, ed., *Briefsteller und Formelbücher des elften bis vierzehnten Jahrhunderts*, Munich, 1863.

* Roegiers

Rogers, J. F., 'Les bénéfices en Angleterre', in *Dictionnaire de droit canonique*, II (Paris, 1937), cols. 658-670.

Sägmüller, J.-B., *Die Thätigkeit und Stellung der Cardinäle bis Papst Bonifaz VIII.*, Freiburg-im-Breisgau, 1896.

Salamanca: P. U. González de la Calle and A. Huarte y Echenique, *Constituciones y bulas complementarias dadas a la universidad de Salamanca por el pontifice Benedicto XIII, Pedro de Luna. Edición paleográfica con prólogo y notas*, Saragossa, 1931.

Salzburg: A. Lang, *Die Urkunden über die Beziehungen der päpstlichen Kurie zur Provinz und Diözese Salzburg in der Avignonischen Zeit, 1316-1378* (= Acta Salzburgo-Aquilejensia: Quellen zur Geschichte der ehemaligen Kirchenprovinzen Salzburg und Aquileja, I), 1 v., in two parts, Graz, 1903-1906.

Samaran, Ch., and Mollat, G., *La fiscalité pontificale en France au XIVe siècle. Période d'Avignon et du Grand Schisme d'Occident*, Paris, 1905.

Sambin, P., 1. *Un formulario di lettere vescovili del secolo XIV*, Padua, 1961.

2. *Lettere inedite di Innocenzo IV*, ibid., 1961.

Sandri, L., 'Note sui registri delle "Rationes decimarum" dell'Archivio di Stato di Roma', in *Mélanges Tisserant*, V, Vatican City, 1964, pp. 339-359.

Santifaller, L., 1. 'Die Verwendung des Liber Diurnus in den Privilegien der Päpste von den Anfängen bis zum Ende des 11. Jahrhunderts', in MIöG, 49 (1935), 225-366.

2. 'Beiträge zur Geschichte der Kontextschlussformeln der Papsturkunde', in *Historisches Jahrbuch*, 57 (1937), 233-257.

3. *Die Abkürzungen in den ältesten Papsturkunden*, Weimar, 1939.

4. 'Saggio di un elenco dei funzionari, impiegati e scrittori della cancellaria pontificia dall'inizio all'anno 1099', in BISIAM, 56-57 (1940), 1-165.

5. *Beiträge zur Geschichte der Beschreibstoffe im Mittelalter, mit besonderer Berücksichtigung der päpstlichen Kanzlei*, Graz, 1953.

6. Editor, *Studien und Vorarbeiten zur Edition der Register Papst Innozenz' III.*, in MIöG, from v. 65 (1957) and in RHM, from v. 1 (1958): see Santifaller, 'Vorbemerkung', in MIöG, 65 (1957), 237-241; and Feigl, 1, 2; Hageneder, 1, 2, 3; Haidacher; Peball.

7. (with H. Feigl, H. Schmidinger, W. Szaivert, H. Zimmermann), *Quellen und Forschungen zum Urkunden- und Kanzleiwesen Papst Gregors VII.*, I, *Quellen: Urkunden, Regesten, Facsimilia* (= Studi e Testi, 190), Vatican City, 1957.

8. (with D. Girgensohn), *Neuere Editionen mittelalterlichen Königs- und Papsturkunden: eine Uebersicht*, Vienna, 1958.

9. 'Der "Censimento" der spätmittelalterlichen Papsturkunden', in MIöG, 72 (1964), 122-134.

10. 'Uebersicht über die Verleihung päpstlicher Privilegien für deutsche Klöster bis zum Jahre 1099', in *Zur Geschichte des ottonisch-salischen Reichskirchensystems*, Vienna, 1964, pp. 68-77.

Santini, P., *De referendariorum ac signaturae historico-iuridica evolutione*, Rome, 1951.

Sardinia: D. Scano, *Codice diplomatico delle relazioni fra la S. Sede e la Sardegna*, 2 vv., Cagliari, 1940, 1941.

Savoy: F. Cerasoli and C. Cipolla, *Innocenzo VI e casa Savoia: documenti dell'archivio vaticano*, Turin, 1900.

Saxony: G. Schmidt, *Päbstliche Urkunden und Regesten die Gebiete der heutigen Provinz Sachsen betreffend*, 2 vv. [1295-1378], Halle, 1886; 1889 (with P. Kehr).

Sayers, J., 1. 'Canterbury proctors at the court of the Audientia Litterarum Contradictarum', in *Traditio*, 22 (1966), 311-345.

    2. *Original Papal Documents in the Lambeth Palace Library. A Catalogue* (= Bulletin of the Institute of Historical Research, Special Supplement 6), London, 1967.

Schillmann, F., 1. 'Ein päpstliche Formelbuch des XIV. Jahrhunderts', in *Zeitschrift für Kirchengeschichte*, 21 (1910), 283-300.

    2. *Die Formularsammlung des Marinus von Eboli*, I (= Bibliothek des Deutschen Historischen Instituts in Rome, XVI), Rome, 1929.

Schmitz, L., 'Die Libri Formatarum Camerae Apostolicae', in RQ, 8 (1894), 451-472.

Schmitz-Kallenberg, L., 1. *Practica cancellariae apostolicae saeculi XV exeuntis*, Münster-in-W., 1904.

    2. 'Papsturkunden', in A. Meister, *Grundriss der Geschichtswissenschaft*, I. 2, Leipzig-Berlin, 1913, pp. 56-116.

Schneider, F. E., 1. 'Zur Entstehungsgeschichte der römischen Rota als Kollegialgericht', in *Kirchengeschichtliche Festgabe Anton de Waal* (= Römische Quartalschrift, Supplementheft XX), Freiburg-im-Breisgau 1913, pp. 20-36.

    2. *Die römische Rota*, I, Paderborn, 1914.

    3. 'Ueber den Ursprung und die Bedeutung des Namens Rota als Bezeichnung für den obersten päpstlichen Gerichtshof', in RQ, 41 (1933), 29-43.

Schreiber, G., 'Das päpstliche Staatssekretariat', in *Historisches Jahrbuch*, 79 (1960), 175-198.

Schütte, L., *Vatikanische Aktenstücke zur italienischen Legation des Duranti und Pilifort der Jahre 1305-1306*, Leobschütz (= Glubczyce), 1909.

Schwalm, J., *Das Formelbuch des Heinrich Bucglant an die päpstliche Kurie in Avignon*, Hamburg, 1910.

Scotland: 1. *Calendar of Scottish Supplications to Rome*: [1] *Calendar of Scottish Supplications to Rome, 1418-1422*, ed. E. R. Lindsay and A. I. Cameron, Edinburgh, 1934; [2] *Calendar of Scottish Supplications to Rome, 1423-1428*, ed. A. I. [Cameron] Dunlop, *ibid.*, 1956 (= Scottish Historical Society, Third Series, vv. 23, 48).

    2. A. I. Cameron, *The Apostolic Camera and Scottish Benefices, 1418-1488*, Edinburgh-London, 1934. See also Ireland 1 (Theiner); Brady; Cowan; Watt, D.

Seidlmayer, M., *Die spanischen Libri de Schismate des vatikanischen Archivs*, Münster-in-W., 1940.

Sella, P., 1. *Le bolle d'oro dell'Archivio Vaticano* (= Inventari dell'Archivio Segreto Vaticano, 2), Vatican City, 1934.

    2. *I sigilli dell'Archivio Vaticano*, 3 vv. (v. 1 with M.-H. Laurent), *ibid.*, 1937, 1946, 1964 (= Inventari dell'Archivio Segreto Vaticano, 3-5).

Semmler, J., *Das päpstliche Staatssekretariat in den Pontifikaten Pauls V. und Gregors XV.*, *1605-1623* (= Römische Quartalschrift Supplementheft, 32), Freiburg-im-Breisgau, 1968.

Serafini, A., 'Le origini della pontificia Segretaria di Stato e la "Sapienti consilio" del Pio X', in *Apollinaris*, 25 (1952), 165-239.

Sicily: J. Glénisson, 'Documenti dell'Archivio Vaticano relativi alla collettoria di Sicilia, 1372-1375', in *Rivista di Storia della Chiesa in Italia*, 2 (1948), 225-262.

Silva-Tarouca, K., 1. 'Die Quellen der Briefsammlungen Papst Leos des Grossen', in *Papsttum und Kaisertum... Paul Kehr zum 65. Geburtstag*, Munich, 1926, pp. 23-47.

      2. 'Nuovi studi sulle antiche lettere dei papi', in *Gregorianum*, 12 (1931), 3-56, 349-425, 547-598. See also *Exempla Scripturarum*, 1 and 2.

Spain: 1. R. de Hinojosa, *Los despachos de la diplomacia pontificia en España. Memoria de una missión oficial en el Archivo Secreto de la Santa Sede*, Madrid, 1896.

    2. *Rationes decimarum Hispaniae*, ed. J. Rius Serra, 2 vv., Madrid, 1949.

    3. *Monumenta Hispaniae Vaticana*, *Sección Registros*: I: D. Mansilla, *La documentación pontificia hasta Innozencio III, 965-1216*, Rome, 1955; II: Idem, *La documentación pontificia de Honorio III, 1216-27*, Rome, 1965 (see P. Linehan, 'La documentación pontificia de Honorio III: unas adicónes a la Regesta de D. Demetrio Mansilla', in *Anthologica Annua*, 16 (1968), 385-408).

    4. D. Mansilla, *La documentación española del archivo del Castel S. Angelo, 395-1498*, Rome, 1959.

    5. M. Milian Boix, *El fondo "Instrumenta Miscellanea" del Archivo Vaticano. Documentos referentes a España* (= Publicaciones del Instituto Español de Historia Eclesiástica, Subsidia, 10), Rome, 1969.

See also Goñi Gaztambide; *Papsturkunden*, NF 18, 2.

Specimina palaeographica ex Vaticani tabularii Romanorum Pontificum registris selecta ab Innocentio III ad Urbanum V [edd. H.-S. Denifle and G. Palmieri], Rome, 1888.

Steiermark: A. Lang, *Beiträge zur Kirchengeschichte der Steiermark und ihrer Nachbarländer aus römischen Archiven*, Graz, 1903.

Steinacker, H., 'Das Register Papst Johanns VIII.', in *Homenatge a Antonio Rubió i Lluch: Miscellanea d'Estudis literaris, històrics i lingüistics*, Barcelona, 1936, I, pp. 479-505.

Stelzer, W., 'Beiträge zur Geschichte der Kurienprokuratoren im 13. Jahrhundert', in *Archivum Historiae Pontificiae*, 8 (1970), 113-138.

Stephen V (885-891): *Fragmenta registri Stephani V papae*, ed. E. Caspar in *Monumenta Germaniae Historica*, *Epistolae* VII, Berlin, 1928, pp. 334-353; *Stephani V Epistolae passim collectae quotquot ad res Germanicas spectant*, ed. G. Laehr, *ibid.*, pp. 354-365.

Stickler, A. M., *Historia iuris canonici latini. Institutiones academicae I, Historia fontium*, Turin, 1950.

Strasbourg: E. Hauviller, *Analecta Argentinensia. Vatikanische Akten und Regesten zur Geschichte des Bistums Strassburg im 14. Jahrhundert* [*Johann XXII.*, *1316-1334*], *und Beiträge zur Reichs- und Bistumsgeschichte*, I, Strasbourg, 1900.

Strong, E., 'Istituti stranieri a Roma. Cenni storici', in *Annales Institutorum*, 1 (1929), 15-60.

Summers, N., 'Vatican City', in *Guide to the Diplomatic Archives of Western Europe*, edd. D. H. Thomas and L. M. Case, Philadelphia, 1959, pp. 290-300.

Sussidi per la consultazione dell'Archivio Vaticano:
  I. *Schedario Garampi. Registri Vaticani. Registri Lateranensi. Rationes Camerae. Inventario del Fondo Concistoriale* (= Studi e Testi, 45), Rome, 1926.
  II. B. Katterbach, *Referendarii utriusque Signaturae a Martino V usque ad Clementem IX, et Praelati Signaturarum supplicationum a Martino V ad Leonem XIII* (= Studi e Testi, 55), Vatican City, 1931.
  III. A. Mercati, *Il 'Bullarium generale' dell'Archivio Segreto Vaticano, e Supplementi al registro dell'antipapa Niccolò V. — Dall'Archivio dei SS. Gregorio e Siro di Bologna* (= Studi e Testi, 134), Vatican City, 1947.

Sweden: 1. *Apparatus ad historiam Sueo-Gothicam, quo monumentorum et scriptorum, praesertim antiquorum, hanc illustrantium cognitio datur.* Sectio prima: Magnus a Celse (= Celsius), *Bullarii Romano-Sueo-Gothici recensio*, Stockholm, 1782. See also H. G. Porthan, *Ad recensionem Bullarii Romano-Sueogothici a nobil. a Celse editam accessio*, Åbo [Turku], p. 1796; H. G. Lindhult and C. J. Ljungstedt, *Ad bullarium Romano-Suegothicum a Magno von Celse et Porthan editum accessio nova*, Uppsala, 1854.
  2. *Acta Pontificum Svecia* (= Diplomatarium Svecanum, Appendix): I: *Acta cameralia*, ed. L. M. Bååth, 2 vv. [1062-1492], Stockholm, 1936-1942, 1957.

Switzerland: 1. *Acta pontificum Helvetica. Quellen schweizerischer Geschichte aus dem päpstlichen Archiv in Rom*, I: *1198-1268*, ed. J. Bernouilli, Basel, 1891.
  2. *Akten über die diplomatischen Beziehungen der römische Curie zu der Schweiz, 1512-1552*, Basel, 1895.
  3. C. Wirz, *Bullen und Breven aus italienischen Archiven, 1116-1623*, Basel, 1902.
  4. C. Wirz, *Regesten zur Schweizergeschichte aus den päpstlichen Archiven, 1447-1513*, 6 vv., Bern, 1911-1915.
  See also Brackmann, 3; Largiadèr.

Sydow, J., See also 'Untersuchungen zur kurialen Verwaltungsgeschichte im Zeitalter des Reformpapsttums', in *Deutsches Archiv*, 11 (1954), 18-73.

Tallone, A., *Le bolle pontificie degli archivi Piemontesi*, Pinerolo [Turin], 1900.

Tamburini, F., 'Il primo registro di suppliche dell'Archivio della Sacra

Penitenzieria Apostolica (1410-1411)', in *Rivista di Storia della Chiesa in Italia*, 23 (1969), 384-427.

Tangl, M., 1. 'Das Taxwesen der päpstlichen Kanzlei vom 13. bis zur Mitte des 15. Jahrhunderts', in MIöG, 13 (1892), 1-106 (reprinted in *Das Mittelalter*, II, pp. 734-838).

    2. *Die päpstlichen Kanzleiordnungen von 1200-1500*, Innsbruck, 1894.

    3. *Das Mittelalter in Quellenkunde und Diplomatik: Ausgewählte Schriften*, 2 vv. (with continuous pagination), Berlin-Graz, 1966.

Teige, J., 1. 'Beiträge zum päpstlichen Kanzleiwesen des 13. und 14. Jahrhunderts', in MIöG, 17 (1896), 408-440 (supplementing von Ottenthal, 3).

    2. *Beiträge zur Geschichte der Audientia litterarum contradictarum*, Prague, 1897.

Tellenbach, G., 'Beiträge zur kuriale Verwaltungsgeschichte im 14. Jahrhundert', in QFIAB, 24 (1932-1933), 155-161. See also Germany 2 : *Repertorium Germanicum* II.

Tessier, G., 1. *La diplomatique* (= Que sais-je ? n. 536), Paris, 1952.

    2. 'Diplomatique' in *L'Histoire et ses méthodes*, ed. Ch. Samaran (= *Encyclopédie de la Pléiade*, XI), Paris, 1961, pp. 633-676.

    3. 'Note sur un manuel à l'usage d'un officier de la Cour pontificale (xiiie siècle)', in *Études d'histoire du droit canonique dédiées à Gabriel Le Bras*, Paris, 1965, I, pp. 357-371.

Teutonic Knights: A. Motzki, *Avignonesische Quellen zur Geschichte des Ordenlandes (1342-1366)*, Braunsberg, 1914.

Theiner, A., 1. *Annales ecclesiastici, 1572-1585*, 3 vv., Rome, 1856, continuing the *Annales* of Baronius.

    2. *Documents inédits relatifs aux affaires religieuses de la France (1790-1800)*, 2 vv., Paris, 1858.

    3. *Vetera monumenta historica Hungariam sacram illustrantia, maximam partem nondum edita ex tabulariis vaticanis*, 2 vv., Rome, 1859, 1860.

    4. *Vetera monumenta Poloniae et Lithuaniae gentiumque finitimarum historiam illustrantia, maximam partem nondum edita ex tabulariis vaticanis*, 2 vv., Rome, 1860, 1861.

    5. *Codex Diplomaticus Dominii Temporalis S. Sedis. Recueil de documents pour servir à l'histoire du gouvernement temporel des États du Saint-Siège, extraits des Archives du Vatican*, 3 vv., [756-1793], Rome, 1861-1862.

    6. *Vetera monumenta Slavorum meridionalium historiam illustrantia, maximam partem nondum edita ex tabulariis vaticanis*, Rome, 1863.

    7. *Vetera monumenta Hibernorum et Scotorum historiam illustrantia, ... ex Vaticani, Neapolis et Florentiae tabulariis...*, Rome, 1864.

    8. *Monumenta spectantia ad unionem ecclesiae Graecae et Romanae*, Rome, 1871.

    9. *Acta genuina Concilii Tridentini*, 2 vv., Agram [Zagreb], 1871.

Thiel, A., *Epistolae Romanorum pontificum genuinae*, Braunsberg, 1868.

Thompson, J. W., 'The Papal Registers', in *Church Quarterly Review*, 127 (1938), 37-75.

Tihon, A., 1. 'Les expectatives *in forma pauperum*, particulièrement au xive siècle', in BIHBR, 5 (1925), 51-118.

    2. 'Grâces et faveurs accordées par le cardinal Carlo Caraffa pendant sa légation à Bruxelles (1557-1558)', *ibid.*, 27 (1952), 269-291.

    3. 'Suppliques originales adressées au Cardinal-légat C. Caraffa, 1557-1558,' in *Miscellanea Archivistica A. Mercati*, Vatican City, 1952, pp. 1-10.

    4. See also Belgium 1: *Analecta* IX, XI, etc.

Tisserant, E.: *Mélanges Eugène Tisserant*, IV-V (*Archives Vaticanes. Histoire ecclésiastique*), VI-VII (*Bibliothèque Vaticane*) (= Studi e Testi 234-235, 236-237), Vatican City, 1964.

Tjäder, J.-O., 'Le origini della scrittura curiale romana', in BAPI, 3rd series, 2-3 (1963-1964), 7-54.

Tours: E.-R. Vaucelle, *Catalogue des lettres de Nicolas V concernant la province ecclésiastique de Tours d'après les registres des Archives Vaticanes (1447-1455)*, Paris, 1908.

Ugolino, M., *La nuova Biblioteca Leonina nel Vaticano*, Rome, 1893.

Ukraine: 1. A. G. Welykyj, *Documenta Pontificum Romanorum historiam Ucrainae illustrantia (1075-1953)*, 2 vv., Rome, 1953.

    2. *Monumenta Ucrainae historica*, I (1075-1623), ed. A. Septyckyj, Rome, 1964.

Ullmann, W., 1. 'On the heuristic value of medieval chancery products, with special reference to papal documents', in *Annali della Fondazione italiana per la storia amministrativa*, 1 (1963), 117-134.

    2. 'A decision of the Rota Romana on the benefit of clergy in England', in *Studia Gratiana* XIII (= *Collectanea Stephan Kuttner*, III), Bologna, 1967, pp. 457-489.

Urban IV (1261-1264): J. Guiraud and S. Clémencet, *Les registres d'Urbain IV. Recueil des bulles de ce pape publiées ou analysées d'après les manuscrits originaux du Vatican*, 4 vv., Paris, 1899-1958 (= BEFAR, B. 6).

Urban V (1362-1370): 1. M. Dubrulle, *Les registres d'Urbain V. Recueil des bulles de ce pape publiées ou analysées d'après les manuscrits originaux du Vatican*, 1 v., Paris, 1926 (= BEFAR, B. 25).

    2. P. Lacacheux and G. Mollat, *Urbain V. Lettres secrètes et curiales se rapportant à la France*, 1 v., Paris, 1902-1955 (= BEFAR, B. 22).

    3. M.-H. Laurent, P. Gasnault, M. Hayez, etc., *Urbain V. Lettres communes analysées d'après les registres dits d'Avignon et du Vatican*, Paris, 1954 (= BEFAR, B. 28).

Utrecht: G. Brom, *Bullarium Trajectense. Romanorum Pontificum diplomata quotquot olim usque ad Urbanum papam VI (1378) in veterem episcopatum Traiectensem destinata reperiuntur*, 2 vv., The Hague, 1891, 1896.

Van Caenegem, R. C., and F. L. Ganshof, *Kurze Quellenkunde des west-europäischen Mittelalters. Eine typologische, historische und bibliographische Einführung*, Göttingen, 1964 (being a translation of a revised version of *Encyclopedie van de Geschiedenis der Middeleeuwen*, Ghent, 1962).

Van Moè, E.-A., 'Suppliques originales, adressées à Jean XXII, Clément VI et Innocent VI', in *Bibliothèque de l'École des Chartes*, 92 (1931), 253-276.

Vanyo, T., 'Das Archiv der Konsistorialkongregation', in *Festschrift Leo Santifaller*, I (= *Mitteilungen des österreichischen Staatsarchiv*), Vienna, 1950, pp. 151-179.

* *Vatikanische Quellen zur Geschichte des päpstlichen Hof- und Finanzverwaltung 1316-1378, in Verbindung mit ihrem historischen Institut in Rom herausgegeben von der Görresgesellschaft*, Paderborn, 1910— :

    I: *Die Einnahmen der apostolischen Kammer unter Johann XXII.*, ed. E. Göller, 1910.

    II: *Die Ausgaben der apostolischen Kammer unter Johann XXII., nebst den Jahresbilanzen von 1316-1375*, ed. K. H. Schäfer, 1912.

    III: *Die Ausgaben der apostolischen Kammer unter Benedikt XII., Klemens VI. und Innocenz VI. (1335-1362)*, ed. Schäfer, 1914.

    IV: *Die Einnahmen der apostolischen Kammer unter Benedikt XII.*, ed. E. Göller, 1920.

    V: *Die Einnahmen der apostolischen Kammer unter Klemens VI.*, ed. L. Mohler, 1931.

    VI: *Die Ausgaben der apostolischen Kammer unter den Päpsten Urban V. und Gregor XI., (1362-1378)*, nebst Nachträgen und einem Glossar für alle drei Ausgabenbände, ed. K. H. Schäfer, 1937.

    VII: *Die Einnahmen der apostolischen Kammer unter Innocenz VI.*, I: *Die Einnahmenregister des päpstlichen Thesaurars*, ed. H. Hoberg, 1955.

Vehse, O., *Die älteren Papsturkunden der grossen Karthause zu Farneta* [Lucca], in *Festschrift A. Brackmann*, ed. L. Santifaller, Weimar, 1931, pp. 422-433.

Veszprém: *Monumenta Romana episcopatus Vesprimiensis* [1110-1492], ed. Collegium historicorum Hungarorum Romanum, 3 vv., Budapest, 1896-1902.

Vidal, J.-M., *Bullaire de l'inquisition française au XIVe siècle et jusqu'à la fin du grand schisme*, Paris, 1913.

Volpini, R., 'Additiones Kehrianae', in *Rivista di Storia della Chiesa in Italia*, 22 (1968), 313-424, 23 (1969), 313-361. See also Bartoloni, 2; Kehr, 3 j.

von Heckel, R., 1. 'Das päpstliche und sizilische Registerwesen in vergleichender Darstellung mit besonder Berücksichtigung der Ursprünge', in *Archiv für Urkundenforschung*, 1 (1908), 371-501. 2. 'Das Aufkommen der ständigen Prokuratoren an der päpstlichen Kurie im 13. Jahrhundert', in *Miscellanea Fr. Ehrle* II (= *Studi e Testi*, 38), Rome, 1924, pp. 311-343.

3. 'Beiträge zur Kenntnis des Geschäftsgangs in der päpstlichen Kanzlei im 13. Jahrhundert', in *Festschrift A. Brackmann*, ed. L. Santifaller, Weimar, 1931, pp. 434-460.

4. 'Die Verordnung Innocenz' III. über die absolute Ordination und die Forma "Cum secundum apostolum"', in *Historisches Jahrbuch*, 55 (1935), 277-304.

5. 'Studien über die Kanzleiordnung Innocenz' III.', *ibid.*, 57 (1937), 258-289.

von Hofmann, W., *Forschungen zur Geschichte der kurialen Behörden vom Schisma bis zur Reformation*, 2 vv. (= Bibliothek des kgl. Preussischen Historischen Instituts in Rom, XII-XIII), Rome, 1914.

von Ottenthal, E., 1. 'Die Bullenregister Martin V. und Eugen IV.', in MIöG, *Erganzungsband* 1 (1885), 401-589.

2. 'Römische Berichte IV: Bemerkungen über päpstliche Cameralregister des 15. Jahrhunderts', in MIöG, 6 (1885), 615-626.

3. *Regulae cancellariae apostolicae. Die päpstlichen Kanzleiregeln von Johannes XXII. bis Nikolaus V.*, Innsbruck, 1888 (see Tcige 1, for supplement).

von Pflugk-Harttung, J., 'Das Komma auf päpstlichen Urkunden', in MIöG, 5 (1884), 434-440. See also *Acta Pontificum*.

Wahrmund, L., *Quellen zur Geschichte des römisch-kanonischen Prozesses im Mittelalter*, 5 vv., Innsbruck, 1905-1931.

Waley, D. P., 'A Register of Boniface VIII's Chamberlain', in *Journal of Ecclesiastical History*, 8 (1957), 141-152.

Watt, D. E. R., 1. 'Sources for Scottish history of the fourteenth century in the archives of the Vatican', in *Scottish Historical Review*, 32 (1953), 101-122.

2. 'University clerks and rolls of petitions for benefices', in *Speculum*, 34 (1959), 213-229.

3. 'University graduates in Scottish benefices before 1410', in *Records of the Scottish Church History Society*, 15 (1965), 77-88.

Watt, J. A., 1. 'Negotiations between Edward II and John XXII concerning Ireland', in *Irish Historical Studies*, 10 (1956), 1-20.

2. 'The Papacy and Episcopal Appointments in 13th century Ireland', in *Proceedings of the Irish Catholic Historical Committee*, Dublin, 1959, pp. 1-9.

Weakland, J. E., 'Administration and Fiscal Centralization under Pope John XXII, 1316-1334', in *Catholic Historical Review*, 54 (1968), 39-54, 285-310.

Weber, F. J., 'The Secret Vatican Archives', in *American Archivist*, 27 (1964), 63-66.

Werunsky, E., 1. *Excerpta ex registris Clementis VI. et Innocentii VI historiam S. R. Imperii sub regimine Karoli IV illustrantia*, Innsbruck, 1885.

2. 'Bemerkung über die im Vatikanischen Archiv befindlichen Register Clemens VI. und Innozenz VI.', in MIöG, 6 (1885), 140-155.

Westphalia: *Die Papsturkunden Westfalens bis zum Jahre 1378, I: Bis zum Jahre 1304,* ed. H. Finke, Münster, 1888.

Wiederhold, W., 1. 'Papsturkunden in Florenz', in *Nachrichten der kgl. Gesellschaft der Wissenschaften zu Göttingen,* Philol.-hist. Klasse, 1901, pp. 306-325.

2. 'Papsturkunden in Frankreich', *ibid., Beiheft,* 1905, pp. 1-145; 1906, pp. 1-98; 1907, pp. 1-172; 1910, pp. 1-179; 1911, pp. 1-112; 1913, pp. 1-202.

Würzburg: W. Engel, *Vatikanische Quellen zur Geschichte des Bistums Würzburg im XIV. und XV. Jahrhundert,* Würzburg, 1948.

Zacour, N., *Talleyrand: the Cardinal of Périgord, 1301-1364,* Philadelphia, 1960.

Zöllner, W., *Die Papsturkunden des Staatsarchivs Magdeburg von Innozenz III. bis zu Martin V., I: Erzstift Magdeburg,* Halle, 1966.

* Zutshi

Addenda

An extensive bibliography of materials relating to the Vatican Archives, including material published after 1972, is found in Blouin, pp. 459-503.

The following items are those noted by L.E.B., or by his reviewers, as being especially relevant to the Middle Ages and to his book. It is in no way complete; much more information can be found under the relevant entries in Blouin.   [–R.B.T.]

Barbiche, Bernard. *Les Actes pontificaux originaux des Archives nationales de Paris.* 3 vols. Vatican: BAV, 1970-1982.
> [Description and précis of the contents of 3,695 original papal letters (1198-1415) in the National Archives in Paris. *Source: D. Williman*]

Boix, Manuel. "El fondo 'Instrumenta Miscellanea' del Archivo Vaticano." *Anthologica Annua* 15 (Rome 1967), 489-1014.
> [Docuemnts from the Instrumenta Miscellanea relevant to Spanish history. *Source: I.B. Cowen*]

Burns, Ch. "Sources of British and Irish History in the Instumenta Miscellanea of the Vatican Archives." AHP 9 (1971), 7-141.
> [for 1191 to 1831; calendars at pp. 16 ff.. *Source: W. Ullmann*.]

Cowan, I.B. "British Research in the Vatican Archives." In *L'Archivio Segreto Vaticano e le ricerche storiche,* ed. Paolo Vian, pp. 141-158. Rome, 1983.
> [Includes an extensive bibliography. *L.E.B.*]

Diener, H. "Die grossen Registerserien im Vatikanischen Archiv (1378-1523). Hinweise und Hilfsmittel zu ihrer Benutzung und Auswertung." QFIAB 51 (1971) 305-368.

Also published separately–Tübingen: Niemeyer, 1972.
> [for the Avignon Registers; with facsimiles and many useful tables. *Source: W. Ullmann*]

Diener, H. "Rubrizellen zu Supplikenregistern Papst Clemens' VII (1378/79)," QFIAB 51 (1971) 591-605.

Germany: 2. *Repertorium Germanicum. Neue Folge: Verzeichnis der in den päpstlichen Registern und Kameralakten* ...:
> [V: *Eugene V, 1431-1447*: see p. 188–Germany: 1. *Repertorium Germanicum: Regesten aus den päpstlichen Archiven* ....]
>
> VI: *Nikolaus V., 1447-1455,* ed. J.F. Abert and W. Deeters, 1985-1989.
>
> VII: *Calixts III., 1455-1458,* ed. E. Pitz, 1989.
>
> VIII: *Pius II., 1458-1464,* ed. D. Brosius and U. Scheschkewitz, 1993.

Lohrmann, D. "Zwei Miszellen zur Geschichte der Päpstlichen Register im Mittelalters." AHP 9 (1971), 401-410.
> [For John VIII's Register; also (at 409ff.) some interesting remarks supplementary to A. Maier, "Der Katalog der päpstlichen Bibliothek in Avignon vom Jahr 1411," AHP 1 (1963), 97-177 about the return of the Vatican Registers from the anti-pope Benedict XIII's (Peter de Luna) residence in Catalonia to Rome (1429-30). *Source: W. Ullmann*]

Mansilla, D. "Fondos españoles de archivos romanos." Anthologica Annua 2 (1954) 393-455; 3 (1955) 553-602.

[*Arm*. XXXII, vols. 3-5; the first part covers the years 1184-1447 and the second part the years 1447-1560]

Roegiers, J. "Quelques pièces égarées des archives de la Nonciature de Flandres." *Bulletin de l'Institut historique belge de Rome* 43 (1973) 561-573.

[Considerably augments the publications of L.-E. Halkin, already cited in the Bibliography. *Source: D. Van den Auweele*]

Vatikanische Quellen zur Geschichte des päpstlichen Hof- und Finanzverwaltung 1316-1378.... VIII: *Die Einnahmen der apostolischen Kammer unter Innocenz VI., II: Die Servitienquittungen des päpstlichen Kamerars,* ed. H. Hoberg, 1972.

Zutshi, P.N.R. "The Bibliography of the Vatican Archives." *Archives* 20 (1992), 40-44.

GENERAL INDEX

See also the addenda to the index, p. 250.

1. The Index covers persons, places and subjects which are to be found both in the *Survey* itself and in the Bibliography.

2. Page-references are to the *Survey* as such. An asterisk * denotes the Bibliography.

3. Editors, co-editors and joint-authors who do not have a main entry in the Bibliography are indexed by a cross-reference to the author or collection under whom or which they occur in the Bibliography.

4. The Holdings of the Vatican Archives are listed under as many forms as possible and are printed in bold type, thus: **Acta Datariae.** Citations in the *Survey* from individual Holdings are listed together under *Holdings.*

munitatis ecclesiae: 72 (*Misc. Arm.* IX), 89; **Lauretana**: 89; negotiis et consultationibus Episcoporum et Regularium praeposita: 88; *pro consultationibus regularium*: 88; pro disciplina Sacramentorum: 88; pro negotiis ecclesiasticis extraordinariis: 88; pro sacris Ritibus et Caeremoniis: 87; *Signaturae gratiae*: 93; Status (de Statu) Regularium: 72 (*Misc. Arm.* VIII), 88: super Consultatione (= *S. Consulta*): 89; *super consultationibus Episcoporum et aliorum Praelatorum*: 88; *super Disciplina Regulari*: 88; super negotiis Avenionis: 89; Visitationis Apostolicae: 89.

Congregationes Consistoriales: 87.

Congregations: Archives of: 84-89 (K); Extant: 85-88 (K.I); Extinct: 88-89 (K.II).

Consecration of bishops at Rome, 1565-1622: *Combaluzier.

Consensi = *Resignationes et Consensus*: 47.

Consistoria = *Archivio del Sostituto*: 82-83.

Consistorial benefices: 86-87, *Clergeac, *Vanyo.

Consistorialis, Congregatio: 86-87.

Consistorium: 80; archives of: 80-83, *Jadin, *Korzeniowski, *Pásztor, L.4; diaries of: *Mercati 9; relation of to Consistorial Congregation: 86.

Consolato di Venezia = *Archivio della Nunziatura di Venezia*: 78.

*Constance: papal archives after Council of: *Corbo; letters from RL volume of Council of: 112 (CPL VI).

Consulta = *Congregatio super Consultatione*: 89.

Contelori, G. B.: 21, 32 (*Ind.* 321), 45 (*Arm.* XXVII), 136.

Context in papal letters: *Santifaller 2.

Conti annuali of Camera in Archivio di Stato: 48 (C.IV).

Contradicted Letters, Court of: see *Audientia litterarum*.

*Conway, D., on *Fondo Borghese*.

Copenhagen, *Papsturkunden* in: *Brackmann 2.

Copies of papal registers: *Arm.* XXXI, XXXII, XXXV: 38.

*Corbo, A. M., on papal archives in Conciliar Epoch.

Corsica, Nunziatura di: 76.

Corsini Library, Rome, consistorial acts in: 82.

Cortile del Belvedere: 13.

Corvinus (Mathias I of Hungary), letters of, to popes: *Hungary 2.6.

*Corvisieri, C., on processes of Holy Office: 85.

Costello, M. A., *De Annatis Hiberniae*: 42, 46, 48, *Ireland 2.

Coulon, A., ed.; *France a.

*Cowan, I. B., report on ASV and Scotland.

CPL = *Calendar of Papal Letters*: *Great Britain and Ireland 1B.

CPP = *Calendar of Papal Petitions*: *Great Britain and Ireland 1A.

Cradock, R., bp of Waterford, Ireland: 158-159.

Crocifisso in S. Marcello, Arciconfraternità del SS.: 95 (M.1).

Cruciatae = RV 519.

*Crump, C. G., on secret correspondence of John XXII and Edward III of England.

Crusade taxes and costs: 48, *Gottlob 2.

Cryptography in papal curia, etc.: *Bock 1, *Crump, *Meister.

Cuartero y Huerta, B., joint ed.: *de Vargas-Zuñiga.

' *Cum secundum Apostolum*' formula: *von Heckel 4.

Curia, Abbreviatori di = *Abbreviatores de Curia*.

Curia, Roman: archives of departments of: *Grisar; history of: *del Re, *Jordan 2, *Pásztor, L. 7; officials of: *Haller 1, *Lesellier, *Santifaller 4; tenants of, 1192-1193: *Pfaff 2.

Curschmann, F., ed.: *Hamburg.

Cursores papales: *Baumgarten 2, Renouard 2.

Cursus in papal letters: *Di Capua.

Cybo, Fondo: 97 (M.42).

*Czechoslovakia: Academy of, in Rome: 16; see also *Hussites.

da Gambacorta, Pietro: *Laurent 3.

Dalmatia: collectors' accounts for: 48 n.; letters to: *Illyria; tithes in: *Italy 1.V.

*Daly, L. W., on ASV indexes.

Damasus I (366-384), ' *Tibulus Archivorum*' of: *Künzle.

Damiani, Sergio: 19.

da Monte, Piero: letter-collection of: *Haller.

da Silva, L. A. R., ed.: *Portugal 1.

da Silva Mendes Leal, J., ed.: *Portugal 1.

Datarius, office of: 50, *Célier.

Datary, archives of: 50-56, *Célier,

ADDENDA